INSTRUCTOR'S ANNOTATED EDITION

Contexts

Writing and Reading

INSTRUCTOR'S ANNOTATED EDITION

Contexts
Writing and Reading

THIRD EDITION

Jeanette Harris
UNIVERSITY OF SOUTHERN MISSISSIPPI

Ann Moseley
EAST TEXAS STATE UNIVERSITY

Houghton Mifflin Company   BOSTON   TORONTO

Dallas   Geneva, Illinois   Palo Alto   Princeton, New Jersey

For our children—

Elaine	Christie
Rachel	Davy
Paul	
J.H.	A.M.

Senior Sponsoring Editor: Mary Jo Southern
Senior Development Editor: Lynn Walterick
Editorial Assistant: Nicole Ng
Senior Production/Design Coordinator: Pat Mahtani
Production/Design Coordinator: Jill Haber
Senior Manufacturing Coordinator: Priscilla Bailey
Marketing Manager: George Kane

ACKNOWLEDGMENTS

The authors are grateful to the following for granting permission to reprint excerpts from their works:

From "Safer Sex" by Jerry Adler from *Newsweek*, December 12, 1991. Copyright © 1991, Newsweek, Inc. All rights reserved. Reprinted by permission.

Mortimer J. Adler, "How to Mark a Book," *Saturday Review of Literature*, July 6, 1940. Copyright © 1940 by Mortimer J. Adler; copyright © renewed 1967 by Mortimer J. Adler. Reprinted by permission of the author.

From "A Celebration of Grandfathers" by Rudolpho A. Anaya. Copyright © RUDOLPHO ANAYA. Reprinted by permission of the author.

Mary Arguelles, "Money for Morality," from the "My Turn" column of *Newsweek*, October 28, 1991. Reprinted by permission of the author.

From *Iron John: The New American Man* by Robert Bly. Copyright © 1990 by Robert Bly. Reprinted with permission of Addison-Wesley Publishing Company.

From "That Lean and Hungry Look" by Suzanne Britt. Reprinted by permission of the author.

From *Changing Channels: Living (Sensibly) with Television* by Peggy Charren and Martin Sandler. Copyright © 1983, Reprinted by permission of the author.

Athlone G. Clarke, "Crossing a Boundary," from the "My Turn" column of *Newsweek*, May 13, 1991. Reprinted by permission of the author.

Eric V. Copage, "Prime-Time Heroes." Copyright © 1992 by The New York Times Company. Reprinted by permission.

Thomas J. Cottle, "Overcoming an Invisible Handicap." REPRINTED WITH PERMISSION FROM PSYCHOLOGY TODAY MAGAZINE. Copyright © 1980 (Sussex Publishers, Inc.)

From "The Wedding Dress: What Do Women Want?," *Real Property* by Sara Davidson. Copyright © 1980 by Sara Davidson. Used by permission of Doubleday, a division of Bantam Doubleday Dell Publishing Group, Inc.

Acknowledgments are continued on page 394.

Student Edition ISBN: 0-395-63837-2

Instructor's Annotated Edition ISBN: 0-395-63843-7

123456789-B-96 95 94 93

Contents

Preface

Contexts, Third Edition, like the first and second editions, reflects our conviction that writing and reading are most effectively taught together so that they provide a learning context for each other. *Contexts* teaches writing and reading as an integrated process and provides numerous examples and exercises to help students learn the concepts and develop the skills that are essential to both.

NEW TO THIS EDITION

We have made a number of changes that make the integration of reading and writing instruction more effective in this Third Edition.

■ *New organization.* We have rearranged the sequence of instruction in Part One so that students are introduced to the essay earlier. Although the first four chapters still focus on paragraph instruction, paragraphs are viewed primarily as units of discourse that most often occur in the context of a longer composition. Essay instruction now begins with Chapter 5.

■ *New thematic focus in "Reading and Writing About" sections.* Each assignment includes at least two reading selections that focus on a single theme (memories, television, social problems, heroes, etc.). These reading selections, over 90 percent of which are new to this edition, are accompanied by suggestions for prereading and prewriting activities, review and reaction questions, vocabulary instruction, and writing assignments.

■ *Increased variety in the writing assignments.* Rather than a single writing assignment, three to five different assignments are provided at the end of the "Reading and Writing About" sections in each chapter. The assignments offer detailed suggestions for responding in writing to the theme of the reading selections. They are accompanied by questions and instructions for revising papers in peer groups. This increased number of writing assignments allows both students and instructors greater variety and flexibility.

- *Additional editing-in-context exercises.* Each chapter in Part Two now includes an exercise that requires students to edit a paragraph for a certain type of error. These exercises reinforce the concepts emphasized in each of these chapters.

- *Expanded instruction in study skills.* Sections on taking essay exams and reading charts and graphs have been added to Chapter 8.

- *New exercises in appendices.* We have added exercises to reinforce the concepts presented in the four appendices: capitalization, spelling, irregular verb forms, and punctuation.

ORGANIZATION

As before, Part One begins with reading and writing paragraphs and moves to essays, Part Two covers sentence structure, usage, and punctuation. This organization reflects our belief that students need a language context in which to develop reading and writing skills and that the paragraph is initially the most effective context for learning these skills. All of the concepts that the students learn in studying the paragraph can be applied later to the essay. We encourage teachers to intersperse instruction on the sentence with instruction on the paragraph and essay, but we believe that instruction on the sentence, and the corresponding emphasis on editing skills, can also be covered in the latter half of the course.

Part One leads students step by step through the process of reading and writing essays. Chapter One provides students with an overview of the reading and writing processes. Chapter Two introduces students to the important concept of general and specific and to simple outlining. In Chapter Three, "Main Ideas," we emphasize the importance of main ideas in both reading and writing. Chapter Four, "Supporting Main Ideas," distinguishes between factual and sensory details, provides students with three ways of expanding main ideas (using coordinate details, expanding coordinate details, and using increasingly specific details), and introduces them to planning outlines. With Chapter Five, "Reading and Writing Essays," students begin to read and write essays as well as paragraphs. Chapter Six, "Arranging and Connecting Ideas," focuses on the familiar methods of development—narration, description, illustration, comparison/contrast, classification, cause and effect, and definition. Chapter Seven, "Developing Ideas," discusses the most common patterns of organization—chronological order, space order, and order of importance—and the use of transitions. Chapter Eight, "Studying and Reacting to Ideas," concludes the first part with instruction on study outlines, summarizing, drawing conclusions, critical reading and writing, taking essay exams, and reading charts and graphs.

Part Two emphasizes the sentence but also continues instruction on reading and writing paragraphs and essays in the "Reading and Writing

About" sections at the end of each chapter. Chapter Nine, "The Simple Sentence," focuses on the essential elements and the basic patterns of the sentence. Chapter Ten illustrates how the simple sentence can be expanded through modification. Chapter Eleven, "Coordination: The Compound Sentence," and Chapter Twelve, "Subordination: The Complex Sentence," continue the instruction on coordination and subordination, this time at the sentence level. The editing sections included at the end of each chapter focus on writing correct sentences, with particular attention to punctuation, misplaced and dangling modifiers, fragments, and common run-on sentence errors.

The *exercises* in the text focus consistently on the important role of *context* in both reading and writing. Sentence composition, sentence combining, and cloze passages promote reading comprehension as well as writing fluency. Various exercises allow students to develop their abilities to use effective transitions, establish paragraph coherence and unity, and write different types of sentences. Most exercises emphasize correctness rather than errors, providing models but also pointing out options; however, practice in editing and proofreading for specific types of errors is also included.

The four *appendices*, "Capitalization," "Spelling," "Forms of Irregular Verbs," and "Punctuation," offer additional instruction that can be used by individual students or by the class as a whole.

ANCILLARIES AVAILABLE

Contexts is supported by an *Instructor's Annotated Edition*, which provides suggestions for teaching as well as answers for all exercises, and an *Instructor's Resource Guide*, which includes supplementary instructional materials and suggestions for using computers to teach composition.

ACKNOWLEDGMENTS

We would like to thank the following reviewers for their commentaries on the previous edition and manuscript for this Third Edition: Charley Boyd, Genessee Community College (NY); Sumitra Chaudhery, Schoolcraft College (MI); Holly Cordova, Contra Costa College (CA); Dorothy Ergun, College of San Mateo (CA); Sherry Kam, Portland Community College (OR); Irma Luna, San Antonio College (TX); Christine Miller, Davenport College (MI); and Doris Snyder, Northeastern Oklahoma A&M (OK).

We would also like to thank the students who contributed paragraphs and essays and our colleagues who have made helpful suggestions to this edition. Finally, we would like to thank our families and friends, whose support was as essential to this edition as it was to the first two.

J. H.
A. M.

To the Instructor

INTRODUCTION

Contexts is predicated on the assumption that beginning college students, especially those whose verbal skills are inadequate for college-level work, need instruction in both reading and writing and that the most effective and efficient approach integrates instruction in these two skills and emphasizes concepts basic to both.

Recognition of the relationship between reading and writing is not new. For years we have known that students who read widely are usually competent writers and that those who write well are usually proficient readers. In fact, we are beginning to realize that reading and writing are essentially one process, more accurately viewed as a continuum than as separate functions. The two skills require the same cognitive functions and are limited by and dependent on the same prior knowledge and experiences.

Current reading research, strongly influenced by psycholinguistic theories, has discredited the view of reading as a sequential, linear process. Reading theorists now emphasize the recursive nature of reading, observing that readers move not in a progressive, linear motion but both backward and forward—sampling from the text, predicting meaning, going forward to confirm guesses, and if the guesses are not confirmed, going backward to sample once more and make new predictions based on additional clues from the text.

Similarly, composition researchers have concluded that writing does not progress in an uninterrupted linear fashion. Like readers, writers constantly move forward and backward, rereading, reflecting, and revising as they create a text. Writers sample not only from what they have already written but also from the semantic and syntactic options available to them, basing their choices on what they think will best communicate with their audience. Like readers, writers frequently recheck or confirm their predictions by pausing, rereading, checking, anticipating, and revising. Hence, there is no neat division of stages, but rather a constant shifting from what is in a writer's mind to what the writer predicts the reader will understand and back to what has been written.

This recursive pattern involves not only the written text but also the background experience of the reader or writer. A reader brings previous experiences and knowledge to the process, and this knowledge interacts with the information on the page to produce questions, comprehension, and even new ideas. The writer similarly uses background information and experiences to compose.

Thus, both reading and writing are meaning-making processes. Our awareness of the integral relationship between reading and writing caused us to reevaluate our methods of teaching reading and writing and provided the impetus for *Contexts*. In short, we believe that we cannot effectively teach one without also teaching the other.

Process

Contexts stresses the importance of perceiving both reading and writing as process. In addition to providing an overview of process in the first chapter, we have incorporated instruction in process into each lesson. Students need to learn to write and read by engaging in those activities. Thus, we have structured the reading/writing assignments that conclude each lesson to lead students through the process. Rather than merely *tell* them how to prewrite or how to revise, we lead them through the entire process.

Students should begin with a well-defined, even simplified version of the process, one they can readily grasp and effectively use. As part of such a structured approach, we not only stress the usual tripartite model of writing—prewriting, writing, and rewriting—but also encourage students to think of rewriting as a process within a process by dividing rewriting into three stages: revising, editing, and proofreading.

Students often confuse revising with editing and proofreading, collapsing the entire process into a cursory reading or recopying of a paper. These students need a clear, simple view of the process to understand the different purposes and functions involved. Thus, we break down rewriting in the following manner:

■ Revising refers specifically to substantive textual alterations—modifications that involve significant changes in content, focus, organization, and meaning.

Editing is a more discrete modification at the syntactic and semantic levels of discourse. Refinements in diction and sentence structure render a text not only more readable but also more correct and more stylistically interesting and appropriate.

Proofreading is then the last effort to eliminate distracting minor errors, such as spelling mistakes, from the final copy of the text.

Sequencing of Instruction

Given the importance of context in both reading and writing, students will learn to read and write most effectively if they begin with paragraphs and essays and move to sentences later. Therefore, even Part Two, the unit on sentence, includes reading/writing assignments to give students the opportunity to apply what they are learning to larger pieces of discourse.

Because inexperienced writers and readers usually find it easiest to write and read narratives and personal experience essays, the reading/writing assignments start with these and only later move to expository and persuasive discourse. As students progress through the text, they will read and write increasingly challenging assignments that require them to deal with progressively more objective, informative discourse.

Vocabulary Instruction

It is important that vocabulary, like sentences, be taught in context; memorizing lists of vocabulary words has little value. Emphasizing several approaches to vocabulary development (structural analysis, context clues, personal vocabularies, dictionary use, etc.), each Reading and Writing About assignment includes vocabulary instruction, illustrated with words from the reading selections.

Although students can be asked to work through the vocabulary sections on their own, much more can be accomplished if you discuss the vocabulary instruction as you discuss the reading selection, allowing students to mention other words with which they are unfamiliar or expanding the lesson to include other words that lend themselves to discussion or analysis.

We introduce various strategies for improving vocabulary and provide students with different ways of looking at vocabulary. These lessons are brief and should be supplemented by your own ideas and experiences and by those the students can suggest. Vocabulary study should never be routine and predictable but rather should provide students with new and interesting ways to think about words.

Readability

We have as much as possible avoided using difficult words that students cannot define by context or that we do not define for them. We have also consciously structured our sentences so they will be easy for students to comprehend. We have not, however, attempted to write so simply that students will not occasionally be challenged. Since the students who use this text will at the same time be taking college-level courses such as history and biology, we believe this text should give them strategies to use with more difficult reading assignments. Thus, we have tried to make the level of difficulty of *Contexts* midway between the students' reading abilities at the beginning of the term and the level of reading they are expected to handle in other courses.

Rhetorical Considerations

Writing and reading at any level cannot be divorced from rhetoric; the principles of audience and purpose, for example, are central to any reading or writing assignment. Therefore, our text includes instruction in those rhetorical considerations that are integral to reading and writing. We stress from the beginning the importance of writing for an audience and of reading with an awareness of the writer's purposes.

Use of Models

Included *throughout the text* are specific models for students to use in structuring what they write and in comprehending what they read. They provide a framework within which students can work until they are ready to experiment. These models are meant to help students arrive at structures that work when they write and give them guidelines in analyzing other writers' organizational patterns when they read. Each time we present a model, we point out that it is not the only possible pattern. Once students have internalized that basic structure, they can and should go beyond it to more original, less restrictive types of expression.

Reading and Writing About Assignments

Each lesson concludes with a Reading and Writing About assignment in which students are introduced to a topic, engaged in prereading/writing activities appropriate to that topic, given reading selections related to the topic, guided (by questions and comments) through a review of the reading selection, asked to write a paragraph or essay on some aspect of the topic, and finally led through a series of rewriting activities. Students are prepared for and guided through the process; they are encouraged to review and react to what they read and rewrite what they write. These lessons thus emphasize the importance of process and the interrelatedness of reading and writing.

Exercises

In addition to the major reading/writing assignments that conclude each lesson, numerous exercises are included to reinforce instruction. These exercises are predicated on the following pedagogical principles:

1. *Exercises should be presented in context.* Our exercises are always in the context of complete sentences, and when possible, these sentences are placed in the context of paragraphs or larger pieces of discourse.

2. *Exercises should not be error based.* Research in error analysis suggests that inexperienced writers and readers need to work on only one error at a time and to practice writing correct forms rather than simply identifying incorrect forms. Therefore, we present our instruction in usage, sentence structure, and punctuation in a positive way, emphasizing the need for such knowledge in editing and asking students to write correct sentences. Only in a few proofreading exercises do we ask students to identify errors, and then we concentrate on one particular error and ask students to supply the correct form.

3. *Exercises should reinforce both reading and writing skills and should develop those concepts that are basic to both.* Designed

to reflect our premise that instruction in reading and writing should be integrated, the exercises in *Contexts* are of three general types: (1) sentence or paragraph composition or comprehension, (2) sentence combination, and (3) cloze procedure. The first type is self-explanatory; students learn to read and write by reading and writing. The second type, sentence combination, not only increases students' awareness of syntactic options and encourages them to incorporate those options into their own writing, but also provides instructors with an ideal opportunity to present incidental instruction in punctuation, usage, and sentence structure. Reading researchers maintain that sentence-combining practice also improves reading comprehension. This text uses sentence combining to reinforce such basic concepts as modification, coordination, and subordination in the hope that instructors will also use these exercises creatively to teach other skills and concepts.

The third type of exercise, the cloze procedure, emphasizes and reinforces the role of prediction in the reading process. Most of the cloze exercises in this text use a random deletion pattern in which words are deleted on the basis of their syntactic category or function. In *Contexts* the cloze procedure is used to reinforce skills, to teach basic concepts, and to increase students' awareness of their own language processes. By focusing their attention closely on a written text, cloze passages help students learn about the interaction of vocabulary and syntax, the subtle influence of diction on style, and the grammatical relationships among words in a sentence.

In cloze exercises students may supply words that are different from the author's choices but nevertheless appropriate. As long as students do not violate either the semantic or the syntactic integrity of the passage, their responses should be considered acceptable; as in sentence combining, no one answer is "right." Inappropriate responses should be analyzed to determine, if possible, why the student responded as he or she did.

CHAPTER NOTES

CHAPTER ONE   ## The Reading/Writing Process

Although students learn about reading and writing processes primarily by engaging in them rather than discussing them, this overview of the reading and writing processes provides a context for subsequent lessons and chapters.

You might assign Chapter One as an initial reading assignment on the first day of class and devote the following class period to a discussion of the ideas about reading and writing the students have encountered in the chapter. We suggest that you focus on the student's own experiences with reading and writing rather than merely repeating the information we have included. Let them talk about their own processes, and emphasize that each person has his or her own individual process, which is similar to but not exactly like anybody else's. Ideally, this discussion should be an exploration of the subject based on the students' own ideas and experiences.

The idea of prereading and prewriting may be new to your students, so you may want to spend some time discussing and illustrating this preparation stage. Point out to your students the value of using these prereading strategies with reading assignments in other courses. We have essentially adapted SQ3R (Survey, Question, Read, Recite, Review), modifying it slightly and making it more flexible. You may want to present this method in detail or talk about other study/reading methods with which you are familiar.

Emphasize throughout the discussion the similarities between reading and writing. If students understand the advantages of studying reading and writing at the same time, the instruction they receive will be more meaningful.

READING AND WRITING ABOUT *READING AND WRITING*

This first Reading and Writing About assignment provides students with two effective strategies: annotating and freewriting. It is best not only to discuss but also to demonstrate these strategies. You can use one of the chapters in *Contexts* as well as the reading selection by Adler included in this assignment to show students how to annotate a reading passage. You will find that students are often reluctant to write in their books, even a book such as *Contexts,* which is specifically designed for this purpose. Divide the students into groups so they can compare their markings and written responses to the readings. Encourage them to develop individual methods of "marking a book," which will help them become active readers and will later facilitate review.

The reading selection by Elbow tells students *how* to freewrite, but they need to practice freewriting also. Emphasize to students that, when freewriting, they need not be concerned about correctness or even coherence. It is important that students realize that freewriting is not the same as a rough draft. They cannot freewrite for ten minutes and then later make a few corrections and assume they have produced a legitimate draft. Emphasize that the purpose of freewriting is to generate ideas—to initiate the process, not to complete it. Although occasionally a piece of freewriting can become the basis for a draft with only slight modifications, most often the writer is fortunate if a single idea or sentence from the freewriting emerges as the basis for a paper.

Following each reading selection, you will find two types of questions. First, in the "Reviewing the Reading" section are questions designed to help students (1) understand the basic content, (2) appreciate the rhetorical features, and (3) respond personally to the reading selection. Then, in the sections entitled "Reacting Critically" are questions that encourage students to think critically about the ideas presented in the readings. Both types of questions are important if students are to become better readers and writers. Although both types of questions are primarily intended to promote discussion, students could also be asked to respond in writing. However, we suggest that you include an oral discussion of the questions even if you have asked students to write their responses. Most of the questions do not have a single correct answer, but students will learn from comparing their responses to those of their classmates.

In the first vocabulary section we suggest that students keep some kind of record of the words they want to learn. If you decide to pursue this suggestion, you should emphasize that each student's record will be different. There is very little, if any, value in having students keep general vocabulary lists, since each student's vocabulary is unique. Students should also realize that everyone has at least four different vocabularies—reading, writing, listening, and speaking—and that "improving our vocabulary" often means moving words from one vocabulary to another. In other words, a student may recognize a word in reading that he or she doesn't use in speaking or writing—or, more likely in our oral society, the student recognizes a word when he or she hears it or even uses it in speaking but is not able to use or recognize it in writing. Thus, vocabulary study will expand students' existing vocabularies to different levels as well as add totally new words.

Using the word *freewriting* as an example, the vocabulary section that follows the Elbow selection introduces students to an important vocabulary strategy: structural analysis. Use this discussion to help students understand that words often provide readers with "internal clues" as to their meaning and to familiarize them with the terms *prefix, root,* and *suffix* so that you can discuss word parts with them in future lessons.

This reading/writing assignment does not include a specific writing assignment, but we do suggest that students freewrite about their own writing process. This assignment not only introduces students to freewriting but also encourages them to explore their own writing process.

The suggested group exercise gives you an opportunity to emphasize that peer editing should focus primarily on content rather than form. Since freewritings are obviously not intended as final drafts, students will be forced to discuss one another's ideas rather than the form these ideas will eventually assume.

CHAPTER TWO
General and Specific

Until students can distinguish between general and specific, they will not understand the relationship between main ideas and supporting details. Therefore, you need to spend as much time as necessary to ensure that your students have a good grasp of this essential concept. The first exercise asks only that students identify the most general word in a list of four words. The examples and exercises that follow become gradually more challenging; in the second exercise students are asked to supply a general word, and in the third exercise they are asked to arrange words according to level of specificity.

All of these exercises can be done by students individually, but they work even better as class or group activities. Discussing the exercises orally, you can suggest other examples, compare options, and elicit further examples from the students until you are reasonably certain that each student has an adequate command of the concept. The diagrams in the text should be helpful, especially in a discussion of levels of specificity. You might use similar diagrams on the chalkboard as you and the students come up with additional examples. You might also want each student to write on the board an example of a general word and several words of increasing specificity. At this point, you could mention the obvious similarity between what the students are doing in these exercises and what is done in outlining.

After the students can distinguish between general and specific *words*, they are ready to progress to general and specific *statements*. These exercises are especially important in that they foreshadow paragraph structure. At this point they should begin to understand how general statements need support in the form of specific details and how specific statements need to be organized under more general statements. Again, do not rush through this seemingly simple material. Ask students to suggest other examples and discuss their suggestions, emphasizing the relationship between the general statements and the more specific supporting statements. You should include in your discussion an acknowledgment that generality and specificity are relative—that is, a statement may be more general than a second statement and more specific than a third. Do not overemphasize this idea, however; it may be confusing to students who are just beginning to grasp the concept of general and specific.

Having just worked with the concept of general and specific, students should be ready to begin outlining. This first lesson on outlining is very simple, extending the concept of general and specific only slightly to demonstrate how basic outlines are constructed. Simple as this lesson may seem to you, however, students may have difficulty with it. Many students have encountered only formal outlines and are therefore more concerned with whether they have used the "right" sequence of numbers and letters than with what an outline can accomplish. Stress the informality and flexibility of outlining, encouraging students to recognize the difference between formal outlines (intended for an audience other than the writer) and informal outlines (intended for the writer's own purposes) and to see how they may use outlines and maps to organize their ideas and summarize the ideas of others.

READING AND WRITING ABOUT *MEMORIES*

The reading/writing assignment in Chapter Two introduces students to journal writing, especially as a prewriting strategy. You may want to ask your students to keep journals, writing in them daily or at regular specified times, or you may prefer to ask your students to write a journal entry only occasionally as a prewriting exercise. However you use journals in your course, we suggest that you introduce students to the idea that when they write in their journals they are writing primarily for themselves. The purposes here are to introduce the concept of audience and to stress that prewriting is an essential part of the writing process.

The reading selection by Tobi Gillian Sanders is a series of journal entries, written by a black student who was attending college in New York when Martin Luther King was killed. Thus, it provides students with a model for journal writing.

The vocabulary lessons focus primarily on structural analysis, especially on prefixes. The words chosen from the reading selections for the vocabulary lessons illustrate how analysis of the structure of a word can be an effective strategy to improve vocabulary. After discussing the words given in the text, you might want to suggest other words that lend themselves to this type of analysis. You might introduce an expanded list of common prefixes for the students to study, and you might explain the difference between prefixes, which affect meaning, and suffixes, which usually affect function. (See the Instructor's Resource Guide for additional vocabulary lessons.)

Since students have not yet been introduced to paragraphs, we suggest that you ask them to begin a journal by writing about a memory and its significance for them.

Asking students to write a personal narrative in the form of an unstructured journal entry serves several purposes in addition to providing experience in prewriting and journal writing. You can discuss Amy Tan's account of an experience from her past and introduce narration as a way of organizing and comprehending material. Students should begin to see how narration provides a familiar framework, making readers feel secure and helping them understand the particular sequence of events that makes up a story. They should also recognize that the simple chronological order used in most stories is an effective way of organizing material. You might suggest other ways in which narration can be useful—as an anecdote within a larger context, as a description of a process, and so on. It is important that students begin to see narration not as a single mode of discourse but as a strategy for organizing and developing various kinds of discourse. Since most students, even those who have very weak verbal skills, are comfortable with narration, it is appropriate to begin with it, but from the start students can begin to understand its broader applications.

CHAPTER THREE   **Main Ideas**

Using the concept of general and specific as a point of departure, Chapter Three introduces students to the paragraph. The chapter begins by asking students to work inductively toward their own definitions of a paragraph by reading the sample paragraph and answering the questions about it. Students can work on their own initially, but their definitions should then be read and compared in a class discussion. Ideally, the class should agree on a definition.

In discussing paragraph structure, be sure the students understand that a topic sentence is a general statement that expresses the main idea of a paragraph; it should be clear that the terms *general statement*, *main idea*, and *topic sentence* are synonymous and may be used interchangeably.

Like most models, the paragraph model introduced in this chapter is fairly rigid. Although other models are certainly possible and in many cases even desirable, at this point students should concentrate on writing paragraphs that are similar to the model—a clearly stated topic sentence developed by specific supporting details. However, because students will encounter paragraphs in their reading that follow other patterns, this chapter also includes paragraphs in which the topic sentence is not the first sentence of the paragraph. Examples of paragraphs with implied topic sentences are included as well.

Although students need to be aware that not all paragraphs are alike, the main purpose of this chapter is to give them a thorough understanding of the traditional paragraph as a separate unit of disclosure—a minor composition with an internal structure of its own. Later we will present instruction on paragraphs in essays and discuss how a paragraph does and does not change as it becomes part of a larger unit of discourse.

In this chapter, as throughout the text, the exercises may be done on an individual basis. However, we strongly recommend that you discuss the exercises in class either before or after the students work them. No textbook is complete in and of itself; it can always be improved by the comments and insights of the instructor. It is especially important to discuss assignments in a group. Not only do these students need the additional instruction provided by a teacher, but they also benefit from discussions of their work in relation to that of their classmates. Furthermore, it is never safe to assume that students really understand; you should check their individual work carefully and listen to their explanations of what they have done.

In this chapter in particular, we suggest that you discuss several points extensively. First, you should be sure that students understand why a fact cannot be a topic sentence. Second, you should emphasize the difference between topics and topic sentences. You could effectively begin instruction on the sentence at this point, explaining briefly that a topic is a fragment whereas a topic sentence is a complete statement that says something about the topic.

The third point you should discuss is the narrowing of topic sentences. Probably the most common cause of a poorly written paragraph is a topic sentence that is too broad. You may have to spend some time explaining how a topic sentence, which is supposed to be general, can be *too* general. The exercises in the text provide a basis for such a discussion, which you might supplement with additional examples and practice.

The exercises that ask students to identify the topic sentences in a series of paragraphs progress from rather simple, obvious examples taken from student writings to more challenging paragraphs taken from textbooks. Again, these exercises work well as a class activity, providing you with an opportunity not only to discuss paragraph organization and to evaluate topic sentences but also to introduce other features of reading and writing, such as vocabulary, inference, tone, purpose, audience, sentence structure, and content.

READING AND WRITING ABOUT *PEOPLE*

This reading/writing assignment introduces mapping, an invention strategy that reinforces the concept of general and specific. Mapping is especially effective for students who need visual representation of the process of narrowing a topic and focusing on a particular subject. You should point out to your students that this strategy involves moving from a very general concept to increasingly specific details. Be sure to give students practice with mapping as well as discussing it with them.

We suggest that students prepare for this reading/writing assignment not only by going through a mapping exercise but also by freewriting on the specific idea from their mapping that interests them most. It is important that students learn a variety of prewriting strategies and how to use them in combination. Ideally, by the end of the course, students should be able to select and use the strategies that work best for them. They should also recognize that different writing tasks require different prewriting strategies. For example, freewriting seems to work best for assignments that demand recall, whereas brainstorming or outlining may be more appropriate for assignments that require the generation of new information or the organization of existing information.

The three reading selections in this assignment describe three very different people—an Athabaskan Indian woman with the wonderful name of Bessie Wholecheese, a forceful English teacher also named Bessie (Miss Bessie to her students), and a much loved *abuelo* (grandfather). Each of these readings provides students with an interesting topic for discussion and an effective model for writing about people. Use all three, if possible. Students may find the Bessie Wholecheese selection the most difficult because the author's attitude toward her subject is less obvious in this reading. Therefore, you may need to point out the subtle clues that suggest that the author not only admires this woman but also identifies with her even though their lives are very different.

Since students have been working with the concept of main ideas in this chapter, be sure to emphasize the main idea in each of these readings. The review questions should help students arrive at the main idea of each reading, but they may have difficulty articulating the main idea of the Fejes piece. Because the controlling idea of this reading is implied and is not at all obvious, encourage your students to discuss possibilities and arrive at a collaborative decision about the point the author is making.

The vocabulary lessons in this chapter assist students in understanding words with which they may not be familiar. In particular, the vocabulary sections accompanying the Fejes and Anaya readings focus on the French and Spanish words included in the readings. These lessons emphasize how English accommodates words from other languages. If you have students who speak French or Spanish, you might ask them to suggest other words from these languages that have been absorbed into the English language.

This writing assignment is the first one that requires students to write either a paragraph or essay. Depending upon the course you are teaching, you may choose which one you want your students to write. Even though we do not introduce the essay until Chapter Five, you can certainly ask your students to write essays, and you may want to proceed to Chapter Five after Chapter Two. Although this is not the sequence we had in mind, we think you can make it work if it suits your purposes.

Each of the two writing assignments for this chapter asks students to write about a person. In the first assignment they are asked to write about any interesting person they know, although we suggest they write about the person they used for their mapping exercise. You may want to give your students some guidance in their selection of a person about whom to write. For example, you may want to stipulate that this person must be someone they have known since they were a child. Or you may want to exclude roommates and boy/girl friends as topics since, in our experience at least, these subjects often evoke subjective, emotional, superficial responses. You could also stipulate that they write about someone who is very different from them (as Bessie Wholecheese was different from Claire Fejes). Finally, you may want to require that they interview the person whom they write about and include the information derived from the interview in their paragraph or essay.

The second writing assignment is more structured, requiring that students write about a specific person (a teacher whom they admire) for a specific purpose (to nominate the teacher for an award) and audience (the judges of the contest). If you choose this assignment, you may want to return to Chapter One to review the concepts of subject, audience, and purpose.

Encourage students to revise, edit, and proofread their paragraphs or essays. It is essential to establish from the beginning the importance of rewriting as part of the writing process. You might collect the students' papers and then return them the next period, asking them to revise and rewrite after they have gained some psychological as well as chronological distance from their writing.

CHAPTER FOUR   ## Supporting Main Ideas

Chapter Four reinforces the importance of paragraph structure begun in Chapter Three; specifically, Chapter Four focuses on development of the main idea. The exercises that ask students to supply both factual and sensory details to support a general statement can be done individually and the students' responses can then be compared in a class discussion. Although some students will have difficulty with the distinction between factual and sensory details, it is important to help them understand that good writing requires a *variety* of supporting details.

In discussing sensory details, emphasize that visual details are not always the only or even the best ones to use. Encourage students to stretch their imaginations to think of a variety of nonvisual sensory details—details sensed by taste, touch, hearing, and smell. You might even bring to class some food that has a distinct odor and taste and ask your students to write a description of it using nonvisual sensory details.

Once students are comfortable with the idea that supporting details are essential in developing their main ideas, you can introduce them to the concepts of coordination and subordination. In previous editions we used the terms *coordination* and *subordination*, but in this edition we have simplified the language we use to discuss these concepts. Although we continue to use the terms *coordinate* and *coordination*, we have eliminated the terms *subordinate* and *subordination*, which students seemed to have difficulty understanding. Instead we teach the concepts of coordination and subordination by identifying three patterns:

1. Coordinate Details
2. Expanded Coordinate Details
3. Increasingly Specific Details

We discuss each of these patterns, giving students both examples and diagrams to help them understand how one pattern differs from the others. Then we ask students to replicate these patterns in paragraphs that they write themselves. If you prefer to use the term *subordination*, you can use the patterns we provide to explain this term to your students.

The diagrams used to introduce these patterns provide students with a framework to use in composing their own paragraphs. Students need to be able to organize the details they use to support their own topic sentences; they also need to be able to perceive these familar patterns in the paragraphs they read. Recognition of patterns of organization greatly facilitates reading comprehension. This chapter provides extensive practice in using coordination and subordination when writing as well as in recognizing these patterns when reading. The reading selections progress from quite simple student paragraphs to more complex textbook paragraphs. The writing exercises can be group activities in which several students (or the entire class) work together to compose an appropriate paragraph.

This chapter also continues the instruction on outlining begun in Chapter Two. Now that they have a grasp of coordination and subordination as well as of general and specific, your students should be ready to begin using informal outlines to plan their own writing assignments. They need to realize that a formal outline is essentially a table of contents, to be compiled after the paper it outlines has already been written. A formal outline is most useful to an audience other than the writer. They also need to understand that there are other types of outlines that can be useful to them in reading and writing. Thus, in addition to giving the form for a formal outline, the text illustrates several alternative forms for informal planning outlines, and students are given a chance to practice with both (study outlines are discussed in Chapter Eight). The emphasis here is on the usefulness of the informal outline or map, which is a planning tool.

READING AND WRITING ABOUT *PLACES*

The introduction to this reading/writing assignment focuses on the strategies of observing, listing, and clustering—all of which are useful when students are writing about places but which can also be used when they are writing on other topics. We encourage students to **observe** a particular place, **list** the specific details they observe, and then **cluster** those details that are related in some way. This prewriting activity should produce not only an abundance of detailed information for students to use when they write but also a main idea to control their content. Encourage your students to include both sensory and factual details in their observation list. Remind them also not to rely solely on their sense of sight but to include other types of sensory details.

The readings in this assignment, Eudora Welty's "The Little Store" and Anna Quindlen's "City Kid," offer interesting contrasts. Welty's piece is written from the perspective of a child and is an idealized description of a place she obviously remembers fondly. Quindlen's essay, in contrast, is much more objective, realistic, and analytical, and is written from an adult perspective. However, both essays are notable for their use of abundant specific details. Spend some time discussing the details that are included and what they contribute to the effectiveness of both descriptions.

For "Revising Your Writing," we suggest a peer review session. Most students will be reluctant to evaluate a peer's writing and may want to focus on correctness rather than content. To prepare your students for this activity, provide them with questions to help them evaluate a classmate's writing. You might also first give them a paragraph or essay to evaluate as a class, directing them to notice features such as focus, unity, development, organization, and content.

If possible, provide enough copies of each essay so that each group member has a copy of each essay to be discussed. Then instruct groups to focus on one essay at a time, perhaps reading it aloud before applying the revision questions. Remind students not only to encourage their classmates by identifying strong points but also to help them improve by identifying weak points.

The writing assignment asks students to use their initial observing, listing, clustering exercise as the basis for a paragraph or essay about a place that holds a special interest or significance for them. They may write about a place to which they have a strong reaction, a place they visited as a child, or a place they consider home. We suggest that you allow each student to choose which specific topic he or she prefers since students may not be equally comfortable with all of these topics.

Encourage students to begin with a main idea (even if they do not state it) and to use lots of specific details to develop their main idea. You may also want to encourage them to use one or more of the patterns of coordination and subordination that we introduce in this chapter (coordinate details, expanded coordinate details, and increasingly specific details) to develop their paragraph(s).

CHAPTER FIVE   ## Reading and Writing Essays

Chapter Five is intended to help students make the transition from the paragraph to the essay. Because students often have trouble seeing the basic similarities between the two, our approach to this topic is fairly structured.

However, inexperienced writers, at least initially, need the specific guidelines and structure provided by such a framework. As your students gain experience and confidence writing essays, we hope you will encourage them to vary the pattern we have presented.

The examples and diagrams in this chapter demonstrate that an essay is structured and developed in the same way as a paragraph. Be sure that the students understand these essential relationships and are able to see, for example, that a thesis serves the same purpose as a topic sentence, that both paragraphs and essays have introductions, bodies, and conclusions, and that the development of an essay is the same as that of a paragraph. At the same time, encourage students to continue to think of individual paragraphs in an essay as separate units of discourse that must have an internal structure of their own.

Students also need help seeing that what they have learned about reading paragraphs also applies to reading essays and larger units of discourse. They should be encouraged to make the same distinctions between main ideas and supporting details in essays that they have been making in paragraphs. Again, however, they should also continue to see paragraphs as individual units and to identify the main idea of each.

READING AND WRITING ABOUT *WORK*

The reading/writing assignment in this chapter focuses on work experiences. Most of your students will have had some type of work experience, and those who have not will at least have career plans for the future. We begin this assignment by introducing students to the familiar reporter's questions—*who, why, where, when, what,* and *how.* Be sure your students understand that these questions are useful not only for this assignment but for most writing tasks.

The readings by Toth and Sherrill should provoke lively discussions as students explore such issues as these:

1. Is there intrinsic value in work or is it merely a source of income?
2. Have jobs for teenagers changed in the last fifty years and, if so, how?
3. Have jobs for females changed in the last fifty years and, if so, how?
4. How much compensation should the government provide those who are out of work?
5. What is it like to be unemployed in an affluent society such as ours?
6. How do work experiences and employment patterns today differ from those of the last fifty years?

The vocabulary instruction in this assignment offers you the opportunity to discuss with students how words come into existence and change over the course of time.

The writing suggestions for this reading/writing assignment are fairly challenging. You may want to suggest that students begin by writing a paragraph and then expand it into an essay, following the instruction on moving from paragraph to essay in this chapter.

CHAPTER SIX   ## Arranging and Connecting Ideas

This chapter is designed to give students explicit instructions in how to achieve coherence in their writing and to recognize it in their reading. One type of exercise we use to do this is the cloze passage, which asks students to supply appropriate transition words. Students need not supply exactly the same transition words that were deleted from the original passage; rather, they should suggest transitions that indicate the right relationships among the ideas expressed in the passage. You might ask students to work on this exercise individually and then compare their responses, discussing why some are appropriate while others are not. Emphasize that there are no right or wrong answers, only appropriate ones.

Another challenging exercise is the "scrambled" paragraph, in which students are given a list of sentences and asked to arrange them into a logically organized, coherent paragraph. We suggest that the first one or two of these be tackled as a class activity; thereafter students might work individually on them. You might ask your students to rewrite the entire paragraph rather than merely numbering the sentences in the appropriate sequence. Although students may find recopying the sentences tedious, it is valuable insofar as it shows them exactly how the "revised" paragraph looks and reads.

The three patterns of logical arrangements discussed in this section—time order, space order, and order of importance—should be presented as a means of organizing writing and of recognizing patterns in reading. Students should be encouraged to use the pattern that best fits their ideas, not to force their ideas into certain patterns. In fact, they should begin to see that these patterns correspond to the way we think; they are natural to our way of processing information.

READING AND WRITING ABOUT *HEROES*

The readings in this assignment were selected to help your students understand the complex role heroes play in their lives. The selection by Sudo encourages them to explore the meaning of the term *hero* and to resolve such conflicts as how both Nelson Mandela and Saddam Hussein can both be considered heroes. The essay about Christa McAuliffe reminds them that females can also be heroes. In your discussion of this reading, you may want to focus on why there are so few female heroes in our society and what this means to young girls as they grow up. Finally, the essay by Copage on television heroes not only points out the dearth of black heroes in our society (and especially on television) but also argues that young people do not need famous heroes because the real adults in their lives are more important hero figures.

Since the six writing suggestions that are included are varied in level of difficulty, some students may need more help in formulating and supporting a thesis. Weaker students will probably want to write about a specific hero (suggestions 1, 4, 5, or 6 allow this approach) while more capable students may choose to define what a hero is (2) or argue whether celebrities should or should not be considered heroes (3).

CHAPTER SEVEN   Developing Your Ideas

We suggest that this instruction in methods of development be presented not as an end in itself but as a means to an end—another tool or strategy to enable readers to discern familiar patterns in what they read and writers to develop material that will be accessible to readers. We also suggest that students learn to use these traditional patterns as prewriting strategies—different ways of looking at a subject and of generating new ideas. Rhetorical methods of development can be used productively in a variety of ways other than in writing assignments in which students are instructed to follow patterns.

READING AND WRITING ABOUT *TELEVISION*

This reading/writing assignment begins by introducing students to cubing, another useful invention strategy. Cubing is especially useful when writers need to view a topic or issue from multiple perspectives. The terms that are used in this strategy—describe, compare, associate, analyze, apply, and argue—are terms that students need to know when they take essay exams, so be sure they understand each one and can do what is indicated.

You should have no difficulty getting students to talk about television, but the readings in this assignment should give students some new issues to consider. Help them see that these authors are not just being negative about television but are encouraging people to control television rather than being controlled by it.

The vocabulary lessons in this assignment not only focus on words from the readings that students may not know but also review two strategies for figuring out the meanings of unfamiliar words—context clues and structural analysis. Students need lots of practice in these strategies if they are going to learn to use them on their own, so spend some time on these vocabulary lessons in class.

The suggestions for writing are varied enough that students should have no difficulty finding one they like. However, some students may be inclined merely to tell about a television show. Discourage this approach as it rarely results in an effective essay. At the same time, encourage students to use specific examples from television to support their thesis. Thus, they may very well summarize briefly several different programs if they are arguing, for example, that daytime television programming is intellectually inferior to that found during the evening hours.

The rewriting activity for this chapter also involves peer review. You might want to emphasize audience in this assignment, pointing out that each group provides a "real" audience for each essay discussed. Students might even role play specific audiences, such as parents (assignment 2) or a director of programming (option for assignment 1).

| CHAPTER EIGHT | **Studying and Reacting to Ideas** |

Chapter Eight introduces the difficult tasks of critical reading and writing. If students are to survive in college, they must be able to read a text both literally and critically as well as to summarize and evaluate what they read.

This chapter first introduces outlining as a study aid. You should compare the purpose of study outlines with that of planning outlines, pointing out that both are informal insofar as the sole intended audience is the writer. The next topic is summarizing, which can also be a valuable study skill. Emphasize that summarizing is frequently used by writers, who either summarize another piece of discourse to support their own ideas (here a word of warning about plagiarism might be in order) or summarize their own ideas to produce a conclusion. Even adequately prepared college students often have difficulty summarizing, so expect your students to need extensive practice. The guided practice provided in the chapter should help. You may also want to give your students additional paragraphs or brief essays to summarize. Keep the selections simple, brief, and straightforward so students can summarize them successfully.

As your students work with summarizing, emphasize repeatedly that it is both a reading and a writing skill. Most students fail to spend enough time and effort on the reading part; insist that they carefully read and reread the selection to be summarized before attempting to write. You may want to work with them as a class on several summaries before asking them to work on their own. Since summarizing requires an understanding of organization, an ability to distinguish between general and specific, an attention to transition signals, and, ideally, skill in outlining, it presents you with an excellent opportunity to review much of the material covered in earlier chapters.

Following the sections on outlining and summarizing, we have added a new section on graphics. In addition to the graphics included in this section—bar and line graphs and a table—you can use other graphics used throughout this book—most notably, a variety of diagrams (see especially Chapter One) and a pie chart (see p. 184)—to help students learn how to interpret different types of graphics and to understand how they support and reinforce written text.

The study skills part of this chapter culminates with a section on essay exams. Help students understand that writing an essay exam answer requires them to use most of the skills discussed earlier in the chapter—outlining, summarizing, even reading charts or graphs. Encourage students to learn the exam terms and to practice predicting and writing practice answers for courses they are actually taking.

The next topic in this chapter is drawing conclusions, or making inferences, an important reading skill that should be reinforced at every opportunity. Finally, the chapter introduces critical reading and writing, which require all of the other reading and writing skills combined. The suggestions provided are rather prescriptive, since we feel that students initially work best with a definite guide. Encourage your students to work through the guided practice and the assignment very deliberately, step by step. They will, of course, not be able to master critical reading and writing completely at this point, but they should begin to understand what is involved.

READING AND WRITING ABOUT *MANHOOD AND WOMANHOOD*

This topic should be one that most students are eager to explore, but they may find the readings by Davidson and Bly rather difficult although both are largely narratives. You may want to devote some class time initially (i.e., before students read the selections) to a discussion of the quest motif and how it has been used in literature. You could even read your students an Arthurian legend or Greek myth that illustrates a quest.

You may also want to discuss the vocabulary lesson for the Davidson piece *before* the students read it, since it is important to their understanding of the story that they know the meaning of the word *sovereignty*. The vocabulary lesson for "Iron John" offers you an opportunity to discuss the difference between the vocabulary Bly uses for his essay and the Iron John story he includes. Students need to realize that using "big" words is not as important as using appropriate words.

The first suggestion for writing ("write an essay about manhood or womanhood") should be narrowed drastically before students begin to write. Help them understand how their own thesis can narrow these broad, abstract topics effectively.

From start to finish, this assignment allows students to employ their oral-aural skills. In the "Preparing" assignment, they are asked to tell a story to their classmates; you may also choose to read or tell the students a story, or ask them to read their essays orally in a peer review session.

Whereas *Contexts: Writing and Reading* is designed to teach writing and reading skills, research on basic writers shows that they are usually strong in oral skills. This assignment, then, attempts to employ those oral-aural skills as an impetus and supplement to writing and reading.

CHAPTER NINE   **The Simple Sentence**

Chapter Nine begins Part Two. This unit is intended to provide students with the information and skills they need to analyze sentences, an ability that is essential not only to writing correct sentences but also to comprehending sentences. We also assume that students will continue reading and writing larger units of discourse and accordingly have included reading/writing assignments in each chapter. However, if you prefer not to leave sentence structure until last, there are several effective ways in which you might integrate this instruction into your course:

1. You might use Part Two for individual assignments, selectively assigning sections to students as they seem to need them.

2. You might intersperse the instruction in this unit with that in the first unit.

3. You might teach selectively only those sections of Part Two that you find are needed by your students as you evaluate their writing. (However, we feel that all students would benefit from the instruction on modification, coordination, and subordination.)

4. You might teach the entire unit in the order in which it is given, emphasizing the editing and proofreading of the students' own writing.

However you decide to use this unit, we are not suggesting that you delay until the final few weeks of the course instruction on the use of standard English in written discourse; we assume that you will emphasize proper usage and written conventions throughout.

Chapter Nine is devoted to a detailed explanation of the structure of the simple sentence. Like everything else in this unit, punctuation is taught in the context of syntax rather than lumped together as a set of prescriptive rules for students to memorize.

The exercises in this chapter are of two types: In the first, students are asked to compose original sentences; in the second, they are asked to supply appropriate responses in a cloze passage from which words belonging to a certain syntactic category (e.g., nouns, pronouns) have been omitted. Each of these types of exercises allows students to make choices. Equally important, each allows you to analyze the errors students make to gain insight into their thinking processes. (Mina Shaughnessy's *Errors and Expectations* provides useful examples of error analysis.)

The second part of Chapter Nine is devoted to instruction on editing and proofreading. For the first time, the instruction and exercises focus on errors, the purpose being to help students recognize such errors in their own writing. Students should understand that the goal of this instruction is to teach editing and proofreading, not simply recognition of error.

READING AND WRITING ABOUT *GENDER ISSUES*

Again, the topic of gender issues is one most students are willing to discuss. However, they may not be very clear about just what is involved in gender issues. Often younger students do not seem to understand what all the fuss is about. They tend to be happy with their respective roles, and the interactions they have had with members of the opposite sex thus far may not have resulted in their perceiving any problems. The reading selections in this assignment should provide the background and information students need for a productive discussion.

Students may choose among five different suggestions for writing topics. All of them require informative/persuasive essays that may challenge the students. Extensive discussions, involving small groups as well as the entire class, can help students formulate and articulate their ideas.

The section on revising emphasizes editing for correctness as well as revising in more substantive ways. Letting students work in pairs will probably result in more productive editing.

This assignment is the first one to include specific editing questions. Remind students to read their essays over more than once, focusing first on content issues and then on editing concerns.

CHAPTER TEN   Expanding the Simple Sentence: Modification

Begin this chapter by helping your students see how dramatically a simple sentence can be expanded through modification. Emphasize the use of both modifying words and phrases. Be sure to point out that often the most important information—the *new* information—in a sentence is expressed by modifiers rather than by the essential elements.

The exercises in this chapter emphasize the choices a writer has in expanding a sentence. Encourage experimentation, especially in the sentence-combining exercises. Don't settle for just one response from each student; insist that everyone write a second or even a third combination. We suggest that you work with the sentences orally, letting the students hear how the sentences sound and having them compare one version with another. Discuss how and why each variation subtly affects the meaning of the sentence.

Discuss punctuation and usage in the context of the cloze and sentence-combining exercises. The cloze exercises should provide opportunities to discuss why an adverb rather than an adjective is appropriate in certain sentences, and the sentence-combining exercises should offer ample opportunity to point out how to punctuate sentences that include appositives or participial phrases. You might want to pay specific attention to the problem of fragments, especially those that result from the use of appositives, participial phrases, and prepositional phrases. We include additional instruction on fragments in Chapter Twelve in the discussion of dependent clauses.

READING AND WRITING ABOUT *SOCIAL ISSUES*

The topics, reading selections, and writing suggestions in this chapter and the two that follow are definitely more challenging than those in earlier chapters. These assignments require students to read and write about social issues, educational issues, and ethical issues. Thus, students are expected to come to some conclusions about abstract, complex issues to which they may have previously not given much thought. The discussions you have about these issues in class (or in small groups) can do a great deal to prepare students to write about them. The readings that are included will also help by providing students with information and different perspectives. You might want to provide additional help with the vocabulary in these selections—especially with "Drink Until You Finally Drop" and "Safer Sex."

This assignment on social issues begins with a cubing exercise, which should help students analyze a single issue. However, you may want to begin by asking students to brainstorm (as a class) on different social issues. In other words, ask them to list as many different social issues as they can think of in order to understand how many issues there are that affect us as a society. Then you might spend some time defining the concept of social issue—just what is a social issue. Finally, you can choose one issue to explore in depth by "cubing."

The readings focus on four specific issues—the homeless, alcohol consumption, sexually transmitted diseases, and racism. Encourage students to look at all of these problems from the perspective of both the individual and society. In other words, what effect do these problems have on an individual and what effect do they have on our society? What are the "costs" of each?

Since the suggestions for writing in this chapter would benefit from some research on the part of the students, you might want to suggest that they interview someone (a doctor who treats STDs, a counselor who works with alcoholics, a police officer who deals with vagrants, etc.) or visit someplace (a homeless shelter, a family planning clinic, an AA meeting, etc.) to collect information for their essay.

You might want to organize peer review groups according to the content of students' essays. That is, students who wrote about homelessness can work as a group, those who wrote about discrimination can work in another group, and so forth.

CHAPTER ELEVEN   ## The Compound Sentence: Coordination

The emphasis on coordination in Chapter Eleven should reinforce the instruction on coordinate details provided in Part One. Therefore, establish initially the relationship between coordinate (or compound) elements in a sentence and coordinate elements in a paragraph. It is important that students understand the concept as well as the application of coordination.

Instruction on the compound sentence is a logical outgrowth of the initial emphasis on coordination. Although it is important for students to understand how to write and read compound sentences, it is more important for them to understand the relationships involved in all coordinate elements. Therefore, emphasize the conjunctions that are used to connect the independent clauses in a compound sentence; you might even insist that students memorize them. Be sure your students understand the relationships signaled by both coordinate conjunctions and conjunctive adverbs. Punctuation of the compound sentence is effectively taught in conjunction with its structure. The semicolon invariably causes problems for some students; expect some to overuse it initially.

Again, you may use the exercises in the first part of Chapter Eleven as opportunities to analyze your students' inappropriate responses. You will also find that these exercises provide you with opportunities for additional incidental instruction; for example, you might review the patterns of the simple sentence as you work with the basic clauses used in the sentence-combining exercises, or you might check students' original sentences for subject-verb agreement or pronoun reference.

Instruction on the sentence invariably focuses on writing; the concept of coordination, however, has important applications to reading as well. Include in your discussions as many references to reading as possible. For example, as you review the conjunctions used to connect coordinate elements, discuss how a knowledge of the relationships they signal is essential to reading comprehension.

The last part of Chapter Eleven focuses on the *run-on sentence*, by which we mean any compound sentence that is incorrectly punctuated; thus, our definition of run-on sentences includes fused sentences and sentences that have a comma splice.

READING AND WRITING ABOUT *EDUCATION*

This assignment begins by asking students to apply the reporter's questions—*who, where, what, when, why,* and *how*—to education. You could also begin by asking students to brainstorm as a class on what they consider the most important educational issues, to compare the advantages and disadvantages of public and private education, or to write a journal entry in which they evaluate their own education. Education may not be a topic they are immediately excited about, so this preliminary activity needs to engage their interest and to help them perceive themselves as "experts" on this subject.

The first two readings, by Mike Rose and Thomas Cottle, provide students with the perspectives of two types of non-traditional students. The first is about a Hispanic student who is not academically prepared for college; the second is about returning students—those who have been out of school for a period of time and are now returning to complete their education. Many of your students may also be non-traditional students and can contribute additional perspectives.

The third reading addresses the issue of cheating. Although cheating is also, of course, an ethical issue, discuss it first as an academic problem. Help the students view cheating from the standpoint of teachers and administrators. Then discuss the ethical, and even social, implications of cheating. How does cheating affect the individual who cheats? Others in the class? Society as a whole?

The writing suggestions encourage students not only to use their own experiences and opinions but also to go beyond these to consider their topic from other viewpoints. Again, your students could probably write more effective essays if they interviewed someone who could give them a different perspective or additional information.

As students edit their work, ask them to focus especially on the punctuation of compound sentences.

CHAPTER TWELVE   The Complex Sentence: Subordination

Much of Chapter Twelve is devoted to the complex sentence. Classroom instruction should emphasize the concept of subordination and should relate the subordinate elements of a sentence to the subordinate details of a paragraph.

The complex sentence can be divided into three different types of subordinate clauses: adverb, adjective, and noun. Each type of clause is discussed separately, as are the relationships signaled by the conjunctions used to introduce the clauses and the appropriate punctuation for each.

The exercises in this chapter are more challenging than those in the preceding two chapters. Many are of the same type but more difficult. Some new types are also introduced; for example, students are asked not only to supply appropriate subordinating conjunctions but also to supply subordinate clauses that work with certain conjunctions. Each type of exercise affords opportunities for instruction incidental to the main purpose of constructing and correctly punctuating complex sentences.

The second part of this chapter focuses on editing the complex sentence. Recognition of subordinate clause fragments as well as punctuation of complex sentences is emphasized. You might want to review all types of fragments, which, like run-on sentences, are a particular problem for students who have not learned to recognize sentence boundaries.

READING AND WRITING ABOUT *ETHICAL ISSUES*

This final assignment focuses on ethical issues—the most abstract and complex topic that students have been asked to read and write about thus far. However, the specific issues introduced by the readings should enable students to view ethical issues as those they encounter and deal with every day. The first two readings focus on honesty—first honesty in dealing with money and then honesty in terms of telling the truth, especially in personal relationships. Students will probably have strong opinions on the matter of honesty, but these readings may help them appreciate the complexity of the issue. The third reading focuses on the right-to-die issue—an issue which has become even more complex and controversial in recent years because of the increasing number of people who have AIDS. Placing this emotional issue in this context may enable students to view it from a new perspective.

Asking students to write about ethical issues is a tricky business. They often respond by taking a strong position but not defending it very well. To encourage more thoughtful responses, devote as much time as possible to class discussions of these and other ethical issues so that students can see that other opinions are possible. Group discussions, debates, and interviews (even of other class members) will all help. Most important, insist that students support their assertions with evidence of some sort. Emphasize the persuasive purpose of this essay.

You might ask students to focus especially on complex sentences as they edit their essays. Remind students, however, to consider the *whole* work as they revise—to consider purpose, audience, focus, and development as well as correctness.

PART ONE

From Paragraph to Essay

Context can be defined as the immediate surroundings of a person or thing. Your home, work, and school are the contexts in which you operate in your daily life. But language also has context. Words and sentences usually exist within a larger language context, and, to a great extent, it is this context that determines their meaning. For example, the word *ring* can refer to a piece of jewelry or the sound that a bell makes. Almost every word has different meanings or shades of meaning. You can *make* a bed, a decision, an error, a pie, a new start, or a mess.

To understand words, you must see or hear them in context—in a sentence with other words that give you clues to their meaning. Even sentences are more easily understood in context. The meaning of a given sentence frequently depends on the sentences that come before and after it. For example, read the following sentences to decide what each one "means."

1. The wind and hail damaged the new plant.
2. The young woman made the basket easily.
3. His chest was badly damaged.

The first sentence could be a report of weather damage to a recently planted bush or to a newly built factory. The second sentence could describe a basketball player or a weaver of baskets. And the third sentence could be a medical report or a description of a piece of broken furniture. Without the sentences that come before and after, you cannot be sure what these sentences mean. To communicate clearly, a writer must provide a context for the reader, who then uses that context to determine the writer's meaning.

The need for context is only one of many concerns that readers and writers share. Reading and writing are related processes that require many of the same skills. Furthermore, reading often provides you with information and ideas that you can use when you write. And writing

1

about what you read helps you to understand and remember what you have read.

This book reflects our conviction that reading and writing skills are more effectively developed when they create a context for each other. Some lessons may seem more like reading lessons to you, and others may seem more like writing lessons. (Old habits of thinking of the two separately are hard to break.) But many of the lessons will be so integrated that you will not really be sure whether to think of them as reading lessons or writing lessons. We hope, in fact, that by the end of the book you will not even be concerned about making a distinction because you will have accepted the idea that a reading lesson is also a writing lesson and that a writing lesson is also a reading lesson. When you reach that point, you will have become a better reader and a more effective writer.

CHAPTER ONE
The Reading/Writing Process

As a beginning college student, you are probably much more concerned about *what* you will be reading and writing than about *how* you read and write. We begin this book, however, by looking at the processes—what happens, both physically and mentally, when you read or write. It is not easy to step back and view yourself as a reader or a writer. By the time you are an adult, these processes have become so familiar that you seldom think about them. But one of the most important steps in improving as a writer and reader is becoming aware of what happens as you read and write.

Asked to describe what happens when she writes, Cathy, one of our students, responded, "My writing is a process of thinking, writing, thinking, scratching out, thinking, writing again, and sometimes starting the whole process over." Cathy also commented that, for her, writing was a "struggle with the pen to sort out a complex bundle of words." Her descriptions are both accurate and perceptive. For most of us, writing is a struggle that involves rewriting as well as writing. And each time we write, the process varies a little because it is not an exact process like turning on a computer or solving a math problem by using a specific formula.

The writing process also varies from one person to the next. No two people go through exactly the same process when they write, even if they are writing to the same audience for the same purpose. So when we talk about the process of writing or reading, we are not talking about a precise method but rather about a general pattern. Understanding this general process, even though it is messy and inexact, will help you become a better reader and writer.

In general, effective readers and writers go through three stages when they read or write:

1. Preparation (prereading and prewriting)
2. Reading/writing (processing information)
3. Review (rereading and rewriting)

3

Although most writers and readers go through these three stages in the order in which we have listed them, each stage actually merges with the others. That is, one stage does not have to end completely before another stage begins. Writers and readers move back and forth between the stages, proceeding to one before completing another or returning to an earlier stage before moving forward again. Or they engage in two stages at the same time, as when a writer discovers new ideas while rewriting or discards an idea (thus "rewriting") before beginning to write. In addition, readers and writers usually go through each stage repeatedly. For example, a reader may go over a reading selection several times before understanding it, and a writer may write several drafts before producing one that is satisfactory. As readers, we read and reread, trying to understand the ideas and information provided by the writer. As writers, we write and rewrite, trying to understand our own ideas and communicate them clearly and effectively to our readers. Many rereadings and rewritings may be necessary before this process of making meaning is complete.

Rather than listing these stages in sequential order, as we have above, we can more accurately illustrate them as stages that occur repeatedly in a circular pattern, as in Figure 1.

FIGURE 1

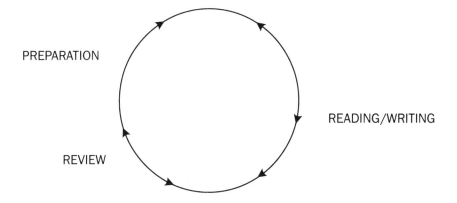

Even though these stages vary each time you read or write, you need to understand them and the ways they relate to one another.

PREPARATION

Your preparation for both reading and writing is of two types: long-term and short-term. Long-term preparation consists of everything you have done and learned in your life. Thus, in one sense, you have been preparing all your life for each reading and writing assignment that you do, because your ability to read and write depends on your prior knowledge and experience. You are able to communicate with others because you have shared similar, though not identical, experiences and backgrounds. For example, when a writer describes feelings of pride or guilt or anger, you understand those feelings because you also have experienced them. And when you write about an awkward or embarrassing incident, you know that most of your readers will understand because they have had similar experiences.

Thus, your previous reading, ideas, feelings, and experiences make you your own best source of information for reading and writing. However, to use your long-term preparation effectively, you need to make this resource available through short-term preparation; that is, you need to tap your memory by using prereading and prewriting strategies.

Prereading Strategies

How do you read the assignments that your instructor gives you in your textbook? Are you a conscientious student who begins with the first sentence of each chapter or essay and reads through to the very last sentence without a pause or a break? If so, you are undoubtedly a very dedicated student, but you are probably not nearly as effective a reader as you can be. You may even sometimes find yourself nodding off or daydreaming, and you may often reach the end of the chapter without understanding or remembering much of what you have read. To become a more effective reader, you need to learn to read *actively* rather than passively. That is, you need to learn to *participate* in the reading process by recreating the writer's meaning in your own mind.

To prepare to read, you should first *survey* the selection to be read in order to gain a general understanding of the subject and main ideas. To survey a reading selection efficiently, look briefly at the title, introduction, main headings, first sentences in paragraphs, and conclusion. Also, note any numbered points, charts, or graphs. Visuals like these often compress information into a form that is easy to understand and remember. This quick preview should give you a fairly accurate idea of the author's subject, purpose, and main ideas. Then, as you begin to read, you will already know something about what the writer is going to say, and you will be recalling from your own experiences and background the information and ideas that you need to comprehend what you are reading.

A second strategy that will help you prepare to read effectively is to *question* yourself about what you are going to read. After you have surveyed the material to be read, establish a definite purpose for reading by turning the title and main headings into questions. For example, if you are reading a chapter in your biology book entitled "The Effect of Photosynthesis on Plant Life," rephrase the title as a question: What is the effect of photosynthesis on plant life? Then read to find the answer. As you encounter different headings in the chapter, rephrase them as questions also. Asking specific questions about a passage before reading it gives you a definite purpose for reading and improves your concentration and comprehension.

Prewriting Strategies

You also need to prepare for writing by using specific strategies. In each chapter you will find a section called Reading and Writing About. In each of these sections we suggest one or two prewriting activities that will help you discover ideas about what you are writing and help you plan and organize those ideas. These prewriting strategies give you the opportunity to think about your subject—to "mull it over"—from various points of view.

As you write your paragraph or essay, you will continue to think about your subject, perhaps changing your mind or modifying your ideas as you write. Sometimes, even when you are not thinking directly about a writing assignment, an idea will come to you. This conscious and unconscious "thinking time" is also part of your preparation for writing.

READING/WRITING

The central part of the reading/writing process involves the construction of meaning. Both readers and writers create ideas out of words. The following strategies enhance this meaning-making process.

Reading

After you have surveyed the reading selection and established a purpose for reading by asking questions about it, read to answer those questions. If the writer has provided accurate clues to the content of the selection and if you have predicted that content successfully, you will find the answers to your questions as you read.

Do not hesitate to reread sentences or paragraphs that you do not understand. Even the best readers must occasionally reread in order to comprehend if the material is difficult or if their minds have wandered.

Also, do not hesitate to vary your rate of reading. Good readers have flexible reading rates that vary, depending on the material being read and their purpose for reading it. For example, if you are reading a mystery novel, you will usually read rapidly. If you are skimming the want ads in the newspaper to locate a job or an apartment, you will probably read even more rapidly. However, if you are reading a textbook to learn complex material or understand difficult ideas, you will need to read more slowly and carefully.

When you read actively, you *respond* to what you are reading. You may agree or disagree, or you may even respond with confusion or anger. But responding helps you to understand and remember.

Some readers find that underlining or taking notes as they read helps them understand what they are reading. Other readers find that initially reading a selection through without writing anything works best for them. They go back and take notes or underline later when they review.

A good compromise for a long textbook chapter is to underline or take notes after each section or subsection. Every sentence seems important as you are first reading it, but this strategy helps you distinguish between important and less important ideas and, thus, prevents you from underlining too much. (Have you seen used books with almost an entire page highlighted in blue or yellow? Extensive highlighting does not help students when they get ready to review.)

You will have to experiment to find the strategies that work best for you, but writing nearly always reinforces reading comprehension and retention.

Writing

Like reading, writing is an act of discovery. Do not hesitate to make changes as new ideas or discoveries come to you. A good writer, like a good reader, is flexible. Do not limit yourself to the ideas you have before you begin to write. Even in the final review stage, you may have new insights that will strengthen your writing, making it more vivid, more interesting, or more readable.

The number of drafts you write depends on how many discoveries you make as you write. The writer who requires several drafts is often a better writer than the one who "gets it right" the first time. Just as an artist shapes and reshapes, colors and recolors, so a writer writes and rewrites until the finished product achieves the purpose for which it is intended.

REVIEW

The final stage of the reading/writing process is *review.* Review involves rereading and rewriting. Readers reread to be sure they comprehend what they have read. Writers rewrite to be sure their readers will comprehend what they have written. As you have already learned, however, the rereading and rewriting stages are not limited to the final part of the process. Readers reread when a passage goes in a direction they have not expected or when relationships among ideas are not clear—in other words, anytime they fail to comprehend what they are reading. Writers rewrite when they realize that a draft is not accomplishing its purpose—sometimes even starting over in the middle of a draft—or when they get fresh ideas or new insights.

Rereading

To review a reading selection, you may repeat your previewing procedure, focusing again on the title, introduction, main headings, and conclusion; you may review your questions to see if you can answer them fully and correctly; or you may review your notes. Occasionally, you may want to reread the entire selection. Or you may choose to take notes on what you have read during the review stage rather than during the initial reading. Remember that the reviewing, whatever form it takes, is as important to comprehension and retention as is the actual reading, so do not omit this important stage of the process. You may, however, want to delay it until a later time or to review quickly when you have finished reading and then to review more carefully just before a class discussion or an exam.

Rewriting

In rewriting, you assume the difficult role of being a reader of your own writing. To rewrite effectively, you must learn to look at your writing objectively—to resee it as your reader will.

Rewriting, like rereading, may occur at any point during the process and may involve a single word or the entire composition. As illustrated in Figure 2, rewriting is itself a process that exists within the larger process of writing:

FIGURE 2

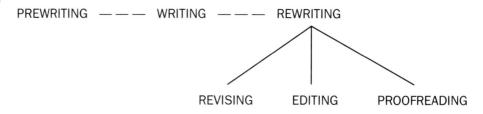

Thus, we use the word *rewrite* to include three different functions: revising, editing, and proofreading. To *revise* means to make important changes in the content, focus, or organization of a draft; to *edit* means to make changes or corrections in sentence structure, usage, and word choice; and to *proofread* means to make minor corrections in the final copy. If you become too concerned with correctness (editing and proofreading) during your early drafts, you may inhibit your writing process. Get your ideas down on paper and organized before you worry about spelling errors and punctuation. Knowing that you can attend to matters of style and correctness on later drafts can free you to think more clearly and creatively on early drafts. Save editing and proofreading primarily for the final stages.

THE WRITING PROCESS AT WORK

Karen, one of our students, produced the following series of drafts in working on an assignment that asked her to write about her hometown. This series illustrates the process that we have been describing. The first draft is a brainstorming list she generated; in it she merely lists some things that come to her mind when she thinks of her hometown, Biloxi, Mississippi.

FIRST DRAFT

Beach and waterfront property; shrimping industry; commercial, traffic, hotels, congested, night clubs, drugs in schools, business scandals; good Catholic schools, Edgewater Mall businesses; sand, Ship Island.

The second draft is a false start, a beginning that seemed to be leading nowhere in particular and so was discarded. But in this draft Karen begins to focus on the beach, an important feature of Biloxi, which is located on the Gulf Coast.

SECOND DRAFT

My hometown is a
place that is very commercial.

Commercial

My hometown ~~has~~ is a very commercial city.
Hotels, businesses and night clubs line up and
down the beachfront. Construction is usually
conducted along the beachfront where ~~cars~~ Cars
sit bumper to bumper. Smelly fumes leak and
corrode the air with, black smoke.
their

In her third draft, Karen continues to focus on the beach and the activities that occur there, developing her ideas further. However, she still is not sure where she is going with these ideas. As a result, her essay lacks a thesis—a main idea to control it. In addition, she lacks a clear idea of why she is writing this essay and for whom—her purpose and audience. At this point, Karen is making progress, but she still needs to make some important decisions about the main point she wants to make and the audience for whom she is writing.

THIRD DRAFT

In Biloxi, ~~my hometown~~, tourists, ~~sunbathers~~, and
fishermen leave the harbors in route to the
Barrier Island.
Boating and sun bathing at any of the islands
is a popular activity along the coast. Yahats
of all sizes travel to the islands for beach and
sun. During the summer, the heat blisters the
sand and bakes the decks. ~~On a boating trip, the
salty air may blow, but it does not stop the~~
The ~~warm salty water off the coast of the islands
also attracts boaters. The water is salty, but
many sunbathers like to swim~~ As the sunbathers
swim in the salty water, they baste in the sun.
~~The salty water attracts the sun so a high sun
protection must be used.~~ After about 2 hours
the sunbathers turn a rosy red color. One can

find these rosy red humans spread out on the white sandy beaches or on top of yahats and shrimp boats!

<u>fishermen</u>
shrimp dirty water
industry / money
oystering
blessing of fleet / June

<u>tourists</u>
(boating)
sun
beach (pollute)
hot (fort)
catch the boat
gambling casino
(Ship Island)

In the next draft, Karen sharpens her focus by limiting her topic to the gambling cruise ships that recently had been approved for the Mississippi Gulf Coast. She also discovers her audience and purpose—to inform residents of the area of this new tourist attraction in Biloxi.

FOURTH DRAFT

A taste of Las Vegas has settled in the backyard of the Mississippi Sound. Gambling ships are now allowed to cruise along the coast. Two years ago, ships were not allowed to pass through the Sound area. Many conflicts occurred between citizens of the coast. Opponents tried to block gambling ships along the Mississippi Gulf Coast with state and federal regulations. Turmoil arose between political leaders and church organizations. Political leaders stressed that ships would boost the economy and tourism of the surrounding area. Church organizations stressed moral values of individuals who gamble along the coast.

Despite efforts to sink operations in the sound, the House of Representatives approved a bill to allow any vessel of 150 feet or more to conduct gambling operations in the sound. The sound is a 8 to 12 mile-wide stretch of water between the beach along U.S. 90 and the barrier islands. This particular bill would allow vessels to operate anywhere in the sound as long as *the boat is moving. Cruise ships as small as 150 feet with a capacity of 200 passengers can now offer the full array of casino games.*

In her final draft, Karen improves her organization, further develops her subject, clarifies vague and imprecise statements, and edits and proofreads her essay. It is apparent in this final draft that Karen's process of writing and rewriting resulted in her finally discovering her subject, purpose, and audience.

FINAL DRAFT

A taste of Las Vegas has settled in the back yard of the Mississippi Sound. The sound is an 8- to 12-mile-wide stretch of water between the Biloxi and Gulfport coastline and the barrier islands. Gambling cruise ships carry casino worshipers through the sound on daily excursions. The tourists of the Biloxi area have a rare opportunity to board one of the many cruise lines available.

Two years ago, gambling ships were not allowed to pass through the sound area. Many conflicts occurred between citizens of the coast over the decision of legalized gambling. Opponents tried to block gambling ships along the Mississippi Gulf Coast with state and federal regulations. Turmoil arose between political leaders and church organizations. Political leaders stressed that ships would boost the economy and tourism of the surrounding area. Many Baptist and Catholic organizations were especially concerned with the gambling issue.

Despite the churches' efforts to sink gambling operations, the House of Representatives approved a bill to allow any vessel of 150 feet or more to conduct gambling operations in the sound. This particular bill would allow vessels to operate anywhere in the sound as long as the boat is moving. Cruise ships as small as 150 feet with a passenger capacity of two hundred can now offer the full array of casino games.

The gambling cruise ships depend on the citizens and tourists of the Mississippi Gulf Coast to support their industry. To keep the ships of entertainment alive, their financial needs must be met. They must be supported by the community and the tourists of the area. The groups of tourists who arrive from the surrounding states show that casino gambling is needed in our area. Hotels and restaurants in the Biloxi-Gulfport area have shown an increase in service since the ships arrived. The gambling ships are significant in the economy of the community. I hope the public supports legalized gambling in Mississippi, because it will bring more tourists to this area.

The three elements that this student discovered during her process of writing—purpose, audience, and subject—are universal elements of good writing, as indicated in Figure 3 on p. 12.

In fact, both writing and reading always occur in a context shaped by these three elements. The processes of reading and writing are, in large part, struggles to discover the answers to the important questions of why, who, and what—purpose, audience, and subject. Writers and speakers produce a text (anything that is written or spoken) by consid-

FIGURE 3

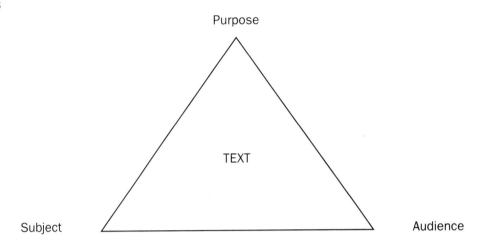

ering purpose (why), audience (who), and subject (what). Readers or listeners should also consider these rhetorical elements as they react to a text, especially if their purpose in reading or listening is to react critically to the text in addition to gaining information or understanding ideas.

An awareness of these issues is important to both reading and writing. Good writers always write with a definite audience and purpose in mind. Similarly, good readers always read with an awareness of the purpose of the writer. Thus, as a writer, you must consider your reader: the person who will read what you are writing. And, as a reader, you must consider the writer: the person who has written what you are reading.

These three elements—purpose, audience, and subject—are basic to the reading/writing situation. Moreover, these elements are so dependent on one another that a change in any one element means there will be changes in the other elements. If a writer's purpose is to inform, the message will be different from one in which the writer's purpose is to entertain. For example, look at the following two paragraphs about airline passengers. Both have the same general subject and could be read by the same general audience. In fact, you might find articles similar to these paragraphs in one of the magazines that airlines supply passengers. However, the two paragraphs differ because one is intended to amuse or entertain and the other is intended to inform. Read the two paragraphs and see if you can determine the author's purpose in each.

PARAGRAPH 1

Once upon a time, people took an airplane only if they were 1) in a hurry, 2) on an expense account, or 3) rich. Today, everyone flies, including large numbers of children. It is not unusual, especially on weekend flights, to find several children flying alone, obviously shuttling between divorced parents. And no flight is complete without several babies, one of whom always cries constantly. Even older children traveling with parents present fellow travelers with some uncomfortable situations. On a recent flight, I found myself seated in the midst of a family of five—three little boys and their parents. They were returning from a trip to Canada and were, understandably, tired and impatient. During the course of the three-hour flight, I traded seats with the youngest boy (who wanted to sit by a window), shared my newspaper with the eldest (a precocious twelve-year-old), and let the mother (a woman of considerable bulk and various possessions) pass by so that she could sit between two of the boys who were fighting. Later I was allowed to help when the youngest of the three lads dumped his entire tray of food on the floor beneath our feet. In between these high points, I learned from the proud mother more about her sons and their various achievements than I really wanted to know. I cannot say that I would prefer to ride a bus from Toronto to Dallas, and I certainly am not villain enough to suggest that children should be checked with the baggage, but I must confess I did not arrive feeling that I was one of a privileged few who fly.

PARAGRAPH 2

Most Americans spend an increasing amount of their time in airplanes and airports. Whereas flying was once considered a privilege, it is now viewed as a chore—one that is tiring as well as boring. In order to make your flights less tiring, you need to learn how to pace yourself so that you arrive at your destination as alert and rested as possible. One of the ways to accomplish this goal is to avoid overeating and overdrinking. Because food is served frequently and because passengers are usually bored, they tend to eat more than they need and to drink more than they should. Thus it is best to avoid the ''snacks'' served on shorter flights if you know that you will be served a full meal on the next leg of your journey. As for beverages, diet drinks and fruit juices have not only fewer calories but fewer side effects than do regular soft drinks or alcoholic beverages. Tea and coffee, without sugar, are fine unless drunk to excess, in which case they may make you nervous or irritable. A bottle of wine with your meal can serve as a before-dinner drink and also make your food more enjoyable. But avoid any excess—calories, caffeine, or alcohol—if you want to arrive feeling well. Another major problem in flying arises from the lack of exercise that accompanies a long trip. It is almost impossible to move around freely, much less get any real exercise, when cramped into an economy-class seat. You should, therefore, take advantage of the time you spend waiting in airports to get some significant exercise. For example, instead of taking escalators, climb stairs; and instead of riding a tram or bus, walk between gates or terminals. If you arrive at your departing gate and still have time to spare, walk around the waiting area, even if you have to walk in circles. Eating and drinking less and exercising more will help you arrive at your destination capable of conducting your business or enjoying your vacation.

Did you decide that Paragraph 1 was intended to entertain or amuse and that Paragraph 2 was intended to inform? Can you imagine the effect on these two paragraphs if we changed the audience so that one was intended for young children and the other for adults? We would have to change either paragraph a great deal to make it suitable for young readers. Each time you read or write you must answer questions about purpose, subject, and audience. In the chapters that follow, and especially in the Reading and Writing About sections that conclude each of the chapters, you will learn how answering these questions can help you to become a better reader and writer.

READING AND WRITING ABOUT—

Reading and Writing

Preparing: Listing, Marking a Text, and Freewriting—

In the following selections, specialists in reading and writing give some good advice. Mortimer J. Adler—noted philosopher, author of *How to Read a Book* (1940, 1972), and editor of the *Encyclopedia Britannica*'s Great Books series—recommends some specific steps to follow during the process of reading. Peter Elbow, author of *Writing Without Teachers* (1973), and *Writing with Power* (1981), and *Embracing Contraries* (1986) describes the strategy of *freewriting*, which can help you prepare to write. In both cases, using the process effectively can help you to read with more understanding and to write more effectively.

Listing ideas can also prepare you to read and write. Before reading these essays, write two brief lists. In one list, jot down what you do to prepare to read an essay or a chapter in a textbook. In the other list, jot down what you do to prepare to write a paragraph or an essay. Then discuss your lists with two or three of your classmates.

HOW TO MARK A BOOK
Mortimer J. Adler

Before you read, survey the following essay by Mortimer Adler; read the introductory paragraph, the main headings, the first sentence of each paragraph, the headings in the numbered lists, and the concluding paragraph. As you survey, turn the title and major headings into *questions* that you can expect the selection to answer. For example, since the title itself suggests a question, it could be rephrased as "How should *I* mark a book?" Write your questions for each of the two major headings in the margins of this textbook.

As you read, search actively for the answers to your questions and *recite* by underlining your answers in your textbook. For example, underline and number the "reasons for marking" that you find in the section with that title.

See paragraph 2.

Remember, too, that in reading actively, you *respond* to what you are reading. In the margins, put a check by at least one statement with which you agree, an *X* by one or two statements with which you disagree, a *?* by any statement that confuses you, and an *!* by an idea that you especially like. Try to show each type of response at least once.

Answers will vary.

1   You know you have to read "between the lines" to get the most out of anything. I want to persuade you to do something equally important in the course of your reading. I want to persuade you to "write between the lines." Unless you do, you are not likely to do the most efficient kind of reading.

Reasons for Marking

(1) 2   Why is marking up a book indispensable to reading? First, it keeps you awake. (And I don't mean merely conscious; I mean wide awake.) In the second place,

(2)   reading, if it is active, is thinking, and thinking tends to express itself in words, spoken or written. The marked book is usually the thought-through book. Finally,

(3)   writing helps you remember the thoughts you had, or the thoughts the author expressed. Let me develop these three points.

3   If reading is to accomplish anything more than passing time, it must be active. You can't let your eyes glide across the lines of a book and come up with an understanding of what you have read. Now an ordinary piece of light fiction, like, say, "Gone with the Wind," doesn't require the most active kind of reading. The books you read for pleasure can be read in a state of relaxation, and nothing is lost. But a great book, rich in ideas and beauty, a book that raises and tries to answer great fundamental questions, demands the most active reading of which you are capable. . . .

4   If, when you've finished reading a book, the pages are filled with your notes, you know that you read actively. The most famous *active* reader of great books I know is President Hutchins, of the University of Chicago. He also has the hardest schedule of business activities of any man I know. He invariably reads with a pencil, and sometimes, when he picks up a book and pencil in the evening, he finds himself, instead of making intelligent notes, drawing what he calls "caviar factories" on the margins. When that happens, he puts the book down. He knows he's too tired to read, and he's just wasting time.

5   But, you may ask, why is writing necessary? Well, the physical act of writing, with your own hand, brings words and sentences more sharply before your mind and preserves them better in your memory. To set down your reaction to important words and sentences you have read, and the questions they have raised in your mind, is to preserve those reactions and sharpen those questions.

6   Even if you wrote on a scratch pad, and threw the paper away when you had finished writing, your grasp of the book would be surer. But you don't have to throw the paper away. The margins (top and bottom, as well as side), the end-papers, the very space between the lines, are all available. They aren't sacred. And, best of all, your marks and notes become an integral part of the book and stay there forever. You can pick up the book the following week or year, and there are all your points of agreement, disagreement, doubt, and inquiry. It's like resuming an interrupted conversation with the advantage of being able to pick up where you left off.

7   And that is exactly what reading a book should be: a conversation between you and the author. Presumably he knows more about the subject than you do; naturally, you'll have the proper humility as you approach him. But don't let anybody tell you that a reader is supposed to be solely on the receiving end. Understanding is a two-way operation; learning doesn't consist in being an empty receptacle. The learner has to question himself and question the teacher. He even has to argue with the teacher, once he understands what the teacher is saying. And marking a book is literally an expression of your differences, or agreements of opinion, with the author.

Ways of Marking

8   There are all kinds of devices for marking a book intelligently and fruitfully. Here's the way I do it:

1. *Underlining:* of major points, of important or forceful statements.

2. *Vertical lines at the margin:* to emphasize a statement already underlined.

3. *Star, asterisk, or other doo-dad at the margin:* to be used sparingly, to emphasize the ten or twenty most important statements in the book. (You may want to fold the bottom corner of each page on which you use such marks. It won't hurt the sturdy paper on which most modern books are printed, and you will be able to take the book off the shelf at any time and, by opening it at the folded-corner page, refresh your recollection of the book.)

4. *Numbers in the margin:* to indicate the sequence of points the author makes in developing a single argument.

5. *Numbers of other pages in the margin:* to indicate where else in the book the author made points relevant to the point marked; to tie up the ideas in a book, which, though they may be separated by many pages, belong together.

6. *Circling of key words or phrases.*

7. *Writing in the margin, or at the top or bottom of the page, for the sake of:* recording questions (and perhaps answers) which a passage raised in your mind; reducing a complicated discussion to a simple statement; recording the sequence of major points right through the books. I use the end-papers at the back of the book to make a personal index of the author's points in the order of their appearance.

9   The front end-papers are, to me, the most important. Some people reserve them for a fancy bookplate. I reserve them for fancy thinking. After I have finished reading the book and making my personal index on the back end-papers, I turn to the front and try to outline the book, not page by page, or point by point (I've already done that at the back), but as an integrated structure, with a basic unity and an order of parts. This outline is, to me, the measure of my understanding of the work.

REVIEWING THE READING   Answers will vary.

See paragraph 1.   1. What is Adler's main point? (Hint: What should readers do in addition to reading "between the lines"?)

2. In his second paragraph Adler gives three reasons for marking a book. If you haven't already done so, underline and number these reasons in your book.

See paragraph 8.   3. Adler also lists several ways of marking a book. What are three of these ways?

See paragraph 9.   4. How does Adler use the end-papers at the front and back of the book?

See paragraph 9.   5. How does Adler measure his "understanding of the work"?

UNDERSTANDING VOCABULARY

Look back through Adler's essay and circle any words that are unfamiliar to you. To help you learn new words like these, try keeping a personal vocabulary list in which you record (1) the unfamiliar word, (2) the context (surrounding words) in which the word is used, and (3) the appropriate definition.

EXAMPLE

Word—*fundamental*
Context—"But a great book, rich in ideas and beauty, a book that
   raises and tries to answer great *fundamental* questions, demands the most active reading. . . ."
Definition—basic, important, essential

Keep your vocabulary list handy as you read the selections in *Contexts* so
that you can record any unfamiliar words that you encounter. Try to use
a few of these new words each week in your writing and speaking.

REACTING CRITICALLY

Look at the list you wrote earlier about what you do to prepare to read an
essay or chapter. Are your usual preparations similar to or different from
Adler's? In what ways does your list resemble or differ from his? Do you
usually "mark a book" as Adler does? Which of his suggestions will be
most helpful to you in your reading and studying, and why? Discuss
your responses with a group of two or three of your classmates.

▨ THE BENEFITS OF FREEWRITING
Peter Elbow

Before you read, think about how you feel about writing. Do you enjoy
writing? Or does writing sometimes bother you? Now, look back at the
list you made about what you do to prepare to write. When you write, do
you sometimes have trouble "getting started"? Even famous writers admit they are frightened by the blank page. Ernest Hemingway, for example, reported that he always continued a sentence or a thought to the top
of the next page so he wouldn't have to face a blank page. One technique
for combating this fear is *freewriting*, which Peter Elbow explains in this
selection from his book *Writing with Power* (1981).

See text annotations.   *As you read,* identify benefits that writers can gain from freewriting.
Number these benefits in the margin.

1   Freewriting is the easiest way to get words on paper and the best all-around
practice in writing that I know. To do a freewriting exercise, simply force yourself
to write without stopping for ten minutes. Sometimes you will produce good
writing, but that's not the goal. Sometimes you will produce garbage, but that's
not the goal either. You may stay on one topic, you may flip repeatedly from one
to another: it doesn't matter. Sometimes you will produce a good record of your
stream of consciousness, but often you can't keep up. Speed is not the goal,
though sometimes the process revs you up. If you can't think of anything to write,
write about how that feels or repeat over and over "I have nothing to write" or
"Nonsense" or "No." If you get stuck in the middle of a sentence or thought, just
repeat the last word or phrase till something comes along. The only point is to
keep writing.

⟨1⟩ 2   Thus, freewriting is the best way to learn—in practice, not just in theory—to
separate the producing process from the revising process. Freewriting exercises
are push-ups in withholding judgment as you produce so that afterwards you can
judge better.

② 3   Freewriting for ten minutes is a good way to warm up when you sit down to write something. You won't waste so much time getting started when you turn to your real writing task and you won't have to struggle so hard to find words. Writing almost always goes better when you are already started: now you'll be able to start off already started.

③ 4   Freewriting helps you learn to write when you don't feel like writing. It is practice in setting deadlines for yourself, taking charge of yourself, and learning gradually how to get that special energy that sometimes comes when you work fast under pressure.

④ 5   Freewriting teaches you to write without thinking about writing. We can usually speak without thinking about speech—without thinking about how to form words in the mouth and pronounce them and the rules of syntax we unconsciously obey—and as a result we can give undivided attention to what we say. Not so writing. Or at least most people are considerably distracted from their meaning by considerations of spelling, grammar, rules, errors. Most people experience an awkward and sometimes paralyzing *translating* process in writing: "Let's see, how shall I say this." Freewriting helps you learn to *just say* it. Regular freewriting helps make the writing process *transparent*.

⑤ 6   Freewriting is a useful outlet. We have lots in our heads that makes it hard to think straight and write clearly: we are mad at someone, sad about something, depressed about everything. Perhaps even inconveniently happy. "How can I think about this report when I'm so in love?" Freewriting is a quick outlet for these feelings so they don't get so much in your way when you are trying to write about something else. Sometimes your mind is marvelously clear after ten minutes of telling someone on paper everything you need to tell him. (In fact, if your feelings often keep you from functioning well in other areas of your life frequent freewriting can help: not only by providing a good arena for those feelings, but also by helping you understand them better and see them in perspective by seeing them on paper.)

⑥ 7   Freewriting helps you to think of topics to write about. Just keep writing, follow threads where they lead and you will get to ideas, experiences, feelings, or people that are just asking to be written about.

⑦ 8   Finally, and perhaps most important, freewriting improves your writing. It doesn't always produce powerful writing itself, but it leads to powerful writing.

REVIEWING THE READING

See paragraph 1.   1.   After defining freewriting, Elbow gives specific directions for freewriting. Underline these directions.

See paragraphs 2–8.   2.   Elbow also lists seven ways that freewriting can improve writing. Underline these benefits of freewriting.

UNDERSTANDING VOCABULARY

Many words have three main parts: a prefix, a root, and a suffix. In the word *freewriting* itself, *write* is the base, or root, word; *-ing* is a suffix; and *free* functions as a prefix. A prefix occurs at the beginning of a word and alters its meaning. Thus, the prefix *re-* added to *writing* would form the word *rewriting*, meaning "to write again." Here are the meanings of five common prefixes:

syn-	=	together
dis-	=	apart, away, aside
trans-	=	across, beyond, through

de-	=	down or away
per-	=	through or by

Use the meanings of these prefixes to help you define the following words from the reading by Elbow. (If you need to, you may use a dictionary.)

1. syntax (paragraph 5)
2. distracted (paragraph 5)
3. transparent (paragraph 5)
4. depressed (paragraph 6)
5. perspective (paragraph 6)

If you wish, add one or two of these words to your personal vocabulary list.

REACTING CRITICALLY

Of the seven benefits of freewriting that Elbow lists, identify *three* that you think might really help *you* improve *your* writing. Could freewriting also create problems for you as a writer? What problems might it create?

Responding in Writing—

According to Elbow, to *freewrite* is to write rapidly for several minutes without stopping and without worrying about form or correctness. You can freewrite about a particular subject, such as people, places, clothes, or heroes. Or you can simply write about whatever comes to mind, repeating words or phrases if you cannot think of something else to write. Usually, this free flow of words loosens up your thoughts, and one idea leads you to another. At the end of five or ten minutes, you may be writing about something entirely different from what you started writing about. Often, writers discover a topic as they write.

Now, freewrite in your journal or notebook about your own writing process.

Revising Your Writing—

Meet with a small group of students and compare your writing process with that of your classmates. How are your processes similar? How are they different? What can you learn from one another?

CHAPTER TWO
General and Specific

The ability to distinguish between general and specific concepts is a skill that is basic to both reading and writing. Something is general or specific only in relation to something else. That is, a general concept is something that is broader, that encompasses more, than something else. For example, a *book* is a more general concept than is a *textbook.* But *book* is less general and, therefore, more specific than *publication.* Consider the following list, which begins with a general concept and becomes increasingly more specific:

> publication
> book
> textbook
> composition textbook
> *Contexts: Writing and Reading*

Rearrange the following list so that it, too, begins with the most general term and ends with the most specific term:

> sports car
> car
> vehicle
> Pontiac Firebird
> 1991 Pontiac Firebird

Did you select *vehicle* as the most general concept and *1991 Pontiac Firebird* as the most specific? And did you figure out that a car is a type of vehicle and, therefore, the concept *car* is more specific than *vehicle,* just as *sports car* and *Pontiac Firebird* are more specific than *car*? If you understand these simple distinctions, you are ready to consider the differences between general and specific words and between general and specific statements.

GENERAL AND SPECIFIC WORDS

A word, or term, can be categorized as general or specific only when it is compared with another word or words. For example, the word *vegetable* is more specific than *plant* but more general than *zucchini.* And the word *car* is more specific than *vehicle* but more general than *sports car.*

You see examples of general and specific relationships every day. For example, a restaurant menu usually classifies specific food choices under general headings. This detailed menu provides you with both general and specific information, including in several instances how the particular types of food are prepared.

EXAMPLE

MEATS	VEGETABLES	DESSERTS
Baked ham	Green beans	Cheesecake
Broiled salmon	Scalloped potatoes	Apple pie
Roast beef	Creamed corn	Chocolate cake
Fried chicken	Sautéed mushrooms	Ice cream

Whatever you are reading or writing, you will need to be able to distinguish between general and specific words. The activities that follow will help you reach this goal.

EXAMPLE

The following list includes one general term and three specific terms:

flower (general)
carnation (specific)
rose (specific)
tulip (specific)

In this group, *flower* is the most general word. *Carnation, rose,* and *tulip* are more specific words because they are types of flowers. The relationship of the general word *flower* to the specific kinds of flowers is diagrammed in Figure 4a.

FIGURE 4a

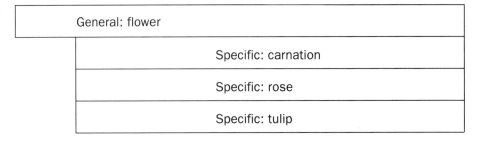

General: flower		
	Specific: carnation	
	Specific: rose	
	Specific: tulip	

■ EXERCISE 2.1   For practice in identifying general and specific words, study the following word groups and circle the most general word in each group.

1. poodle
   (dog)
   collie
   dachshund

2. Chicago
   Boston
   (city)
   Denver

3. cheddar
   Swiss
   mozzarella
   (cheese)

4. (furniture)   5. situation comedies   6. bridge
   couch   (television shows)   poker
   table   soap operas   (card games)
   chair   game shows   gin rummy

■ EXERCISE 2.2   The following list contains three specific words and a blank space for the general word that describes them. Study the specific words in the example below and then write an appropriate general word in the blank space.

EXAMPLE

General: _____**snake**_____
   Specific: cobra
   Specific: rattlesnake
   Specific: copperhead

You might have written *reptile* in the blank because cobras, rattlesnakes, and copperheads are all reptiles. However, *reptile* is actually a broader word than you need because it describes not only cobras, rattlesnakes, and copperheads—all of which are snakes—but also turtles, lizards, and other reptiles besides snakes. The best answer is the word *snake*, which is general enough to include each of the words listed but not so general that it includes other types of reptiles.

Now study each of the following lists of specific words and write an appropriate general word in the blank provided.

1. General: _____**color**_____
   Specific: red
   Specific: blue
   Specific: yellow

2. General: _____**president**_____
   Specific: John Kennedy
   Specific: Harry Truman
   Specific: George Bush

3. General: _____**gem or jewel**_____
   Specific: diamond
   Specific: emerald
   Specific: ruby

4. General: _____**cloth or fabric**_____
   Specific: linen
   Specific: silk
   Specific: cotton

5. General: _____**tree**_____
   Specific: oak
   Specific: maple
   Specific: pine

6. General: _____**fish**_____
   Specific: trout
   Specific: bass
   Specific: salmon

The word groups in these exercises involve two levels of generality. That is, each group has one general word and three words that are equally specific. The following group of words also includes one term that is more general than the others, but the remaining words express different levels of specificity.

EXAMPLE

entertainer (general)
musician (more specific)
vocalist (still more specific)
Madonna (most specific)

FIGURE 4b

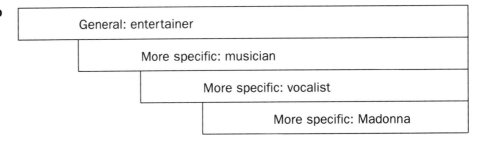

In this example, *entertainer* is the most general word. *Musician* is more specific than *entertainer*, but since musicians can be pianists, violinists, drummers, or even composers or vocalists, the term *vocalist* is still more specific than the term *musician*. But the most specific term is *Madonna*, a particular female vocalist.

EXERCISE 2.3   Study the following group of words to determine the general/specific relationships: America, United States, California, North America. Then write these words in the appropriate spaces below:

EXAMPLE

General: **America** _____

Specific: **North America** _____

More specific: **United States** _____

Most specific: **California** _____

Did you decide that *America* is the most general word, *North America* more specific, *United States* even more specific, and *California* the most specific word? Now, arrange in order from general to specific the words in each of the following groups.

1. math, College Algebra, subject, algebra

General: **subject** _____

Specific: **math** _____

More specific: **algebra** _____

Most specific: **College Algebra** _____

2. blazer, coat, blue blazer, clothes

General: **clothes** _____

Specific: **coat** _____

More specific: **blazer** _____

Most specific: **blue blazer** _____

3. dog, collie, animal, mammal

General: **animal** _____

Specific: **mammal** _____

More specific: **dog** _____

Most specific: **collie** _____

4. sport, football, team sport, professional football

General: **sport** _____

Specific: **team sport** _____

More specific: **football** _____

Most specific: **professional football** _____

5. nonfiction, book, _A Woman Named Jackie,_ biography

General: **book** _____

Specific: **nonfiction** _____

More specific: **biography** _____

Most specific: **_A Woman Named Jackie_** _____

6. Miami-Dade Community College, school, college, community college

General: **school** _____

Specific: **college** _____

More specific: **community college** _____

Most specific: **Miami-Dade Community College** _____

GENERAL AND SPECIFIC STATEMENTS

Thus far in this chapter, you have been learning to distinguish between general and specific words. However, statements as well as words can be classified as general or specific. To be an effective reader and writer, you must also be able to distinguish between general and specific statements.

Like a word, a statement can be viewed as general or specific only in relation to other statements. For example, read the sentences below. Can you determine which one of them is the most general?

1. Luke Skywalker, the hero of *Star Wars* and its sequels, became the hero of many young fans a few years ago.
2. In recent years, young people have admired violent movie heroes such as Dirty Harry and Rambo.
3. Each generation of young people seems to elevate certain movie characters to the status of folk heroes.
4. In past generations, the Lone Ranger and Superman had their loyal followings.

Did you select sentence number 3 as the most general statement? Can you see that the other three sentences about specific heroes support this general statement with several specific statements? The combination of a general statement and specific statements is an important characteristic of paragraphs. The following exercises will give you practice in combining general and specific statements.

■ EXERCISE 2.4

Answers will vary.

The sample exercise below includes three specific statements. In the space provided, write a general statement that expresses the idea supported by the specific statements.

EXAMPLE

General statement: **Craig has made excellent grades in his**

accounting course.

Specific statement: Craig has made 90s on all his accounting quizzes.

Specific statement: He received an *A* on his major project.

Specific statement: He also earned a good grade on his final exam in the course.

Your statement should be general enough to include each of the specific statements but not more general than the specific statements suggest. For example, the statement "Craig made good grades on his accounting tests" is too specific because it doesn't take into consideration that he also made an *A* on his major project. In contrast, the statement "Craig earned good grades in all his classes" is too general because the specific statements refer only to his accounting course. An appropriate general statement, one that encompasses all the specific statements but does not go beyond them, is "Craig has made excellent grades in his accounting course."

Answers will vary.

Now write an appropriate general statement for each of the following groups of sentences.

1. General statement: **Environmental problems are becoming**

    more serious.

    Specific statement: Many of our rivers and lakes are seriously polluted.
    Specific statement: Air pollution is a health threat in many industrial areas.
    Specific statement: Waste disposal poses an increasingly difficult dilemma for cities and towns across the nation.

2. General statement: **In the past, female clothing was**

    often uncomfortable.

    Specific statement: High-heeled shoes with pointed toes tortured the feet of the women who wore them.
    Specific statement: Girdles squeezed women's bodies into unnatural shapes and restricted both physical movement and breathing.
    Specific statement: In even earlier ages, long skirts and layers of petticoats meant that women suffered excessively from the heat in summertime.

3. General statement: **Smoking is harmful to the human body.**

    Specific statement: Smoking can cause permanent stains on teeth.
    Specific statement: Smoking contributes to heart disease.
    Specific statement: Smoking can cause lung cancer.

▓ **EXERCISE 2.5**

Answers will vary.

The example below contains one fairly general statement and spaces for three more specific statements. Write an appropriate specific statement in each of these spaces.

EXAMPLE

General statement: Yesterday's weather was unpleasant.

Specific statement: **The temperature was 10°.**

Specific statement: **Snow fell all day.**

Specific statement: **The wind blew at thirty miles per hour.**

You might have written in these spaces such statements as "The temperature was 10°," "Snow fell all day," and "The wind blew at thirty miles per hour." Many other specific statements are possible for this exercise, but you should be sure that your statements are more specific than the general statement and that they directly support it.

Now, apply what you have learned in this example to each of the sentence groups that follow. For each group, write three specific statements to support the general statement.

Answers will vary.

1. General statement: A fast-food restaurant can offer certain advantages.

   Specific statement: **The food is consistently good.**

   Specific statement: **Service is fast.**

   Specific statement: **Prices are reasonable.**

2. General statement: Country music has become big business.

   Specific statement: **The Country Music Association sponsors award shows on prime-time television each year.**

   Specific statement: **Country music performers command huge salaries.**

   Specific statement: **Millions of records made by country musicians sell each year.**

3. General statement: Computers have changed our lives.

   Specific statement: **We write with computers.**

   Specific statement: **We depend on them for storing and retrieving information.**

   Specific statement: **We even play games on them.**

INTRODUCTION TO OUTLINING

Outlining is a method of organizing ideas by indicating their relationship to one another. Like a diagram, an outline is a blueprint or plan of a completed work. It is a skeleton that allows you to see the essential framework of a piece of writing.

Since an outline visually represents general and specific relationships, you must understand how to distinguish between general and specific concepts in order to outline. For example, *tree, grass,* and *flower* are three general categories. Thus, on an outline, you would arrange them as three equal headings:

EXAMPLE

tree

grass

flower

Then, if you wanted to include some specific examples of each of these three general categories, you could place them under the appropriate headings. For example, if you wanted to list *oak, elm, pine,* and *fir* under *tree,* you would list these four specific types of trees under the general heading *tree.*

EXAMPLE

Tree
   oak
   elm
   pine
   fir

You could also add letters or numbers to your outline to make the relationships clearer.

EXAMPLE

1. Tree
   a. oak
   b. elm
   c. pine
   d. fir

Or you could use a different system of representation, as in Figure 5, as long as you continued to indicate that *tree* is the most general term and that *oak, elm, pine,* and *fir* are specific examples or types of trees.

FIGURE 5

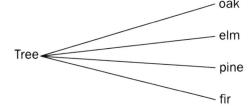

 **EXERCISE 2.6**

See Instructor's Resource Guide for sample outline.

On a separate sheet of paper, continue the outline started above. Add two other main headings—*flower* and *grass*—to the main heading of *tree*. Then organize the following plants under these three headings. Use any format you like for your outline, but be sure that you represent accurately the relationships between the general headings and the more specific types and examples of each.

rose	fir	St. Augustine grass
pine	tulip	red oak
elm	maple	Peace Rose
daisy	orchid	violet
spruce	carnation	pecan
rye grass	bluegrass	white oak
Bermuda grass	oak	American Beauty Rose

Formal and Informal Outlines

Both formal and informal outlines indicate what is important and what is less important and how the various ideas relate to one another. But the purposes of formal and informal outlines differ. An informal outline, such as a planning or study outline, is written for the benefit of the writer himself or herself. Therefore, the forms of informal outlines vary widely. Some are little more than well-organized lists; others are diagrams consisting of circles and arrows or boxes inside boxes. As long as it communicates to the one who wrote it, an informal outline serves its purpose.

Formal outlines, in contrast, are written by a writer for a reader other than himself or herself. The purpose of a formal outline is to provide the reader with information about what has been outlined. Formal outlines are most appropriately used as tables of content. They are frequently included with long reports, research papers, and proposals as a guide to the contents. Since formal outlines must communicate clearly to a reader, the writer must use a traditional form that is familiar to everyone. Look at the following example of a formal outline:

Main idea: Literature has traditionally been divided into three categories.

 I. Fiction
  A. Novel
  B. Short story
 II. Drama
  A. Tragedy
  B. Comedy
   1. Low comedy
   2. High comedy
 III. Poetry

You should be able to determine from this formal outline that the three main types of literature are fiction, drama, and poetry. You should also be able to see that fiction can be divided into the subcategories of novel and short story and that drama can be divided into tragedy and comedy. Further, you can see from this outline that low comedy and high comedy are types of comedy. The numbers and letters assigned to the different entries on the outline and the system of indentation indicate the relative importance of the entries and their relationships to one another.

In an informal outline this same information might be shown as follows:

Main idea: Literature can be divided into three types.
1. Fiction
    Novel
    Short story
2. Drama
    Tragedy
    Comedy (high and low)
3. Poetry

In this informal outline, numbers, indentation, and parentheses are used to communicate the same information about relative importance and relationships that was given in the formal outline. Any number of variations of this type of listing could be used to create an effective informal outline.

Figure 6 contains an example of still another type of informal outline:

FIGURE 6

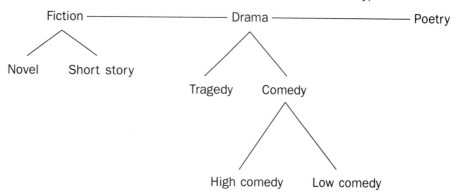

Main idea: Literature can be divided into three types.

An informal outline such as this can also be called a *map* because it provides you with a visual representation of your thinking.

Sentence Outlines

In an outline, either formal or informal, you can use sentences rather than words or phrases. Using what you have learned about general and specific concepts, you can easily construct a simple sentence outline. For example, we can begin an outline with the following general statement:

▇ Even in our modern society, many superstitions exist.

To use the sentence in a formal outline, you could identify it with a Roman numeral and place it at the left margin of the page:

EXAMPLE

I. Even in our modern society, many superstitions exist.

Under this general statement, you could list several specific statements. You could identify these with capital letters. You could also indent them to indicate that they are more specific than the general statement:

EXAMPLE

I. Even in our modern society, many superstitions exist.
   A. Many people believe that certain actions bring good or bad luck.
   B. Others faithfully read horoscopes.
   C. Still others stay home on Friday the 13th.

If you want to include in your outline even more specific details, you could add these details under the appropriate statement.

EXAMPLE

I. Even in our modern society, many superstitions exist.
   A. Many people believe that certain actions bring good or bad luck.
      1. They often avoid walking under ladders to ward off bad luck.
      2. They cross their fingers for good luck.
   B. Others faithfully read horoscopes.
   C. Still others stay home on Friday the 13th.

■ EXERCISE 2.7

Answers will vary.

In the following exercise, construct a simple outline by writing specific examples and details under the general statement that is given.

I. Americans are becoming increasingly health conscious.

   A. **They are modifying their diets.** _____

      _____

      1. **They avoid eating too much fat, salt, or sugar.** _____

      2. **They eat more fresh fruits and vegetables.** _____

   B. **Many Americans are also exercising regularly.** _____

      _____

      1. **Some engage in team sports.** _____

      2. **Others run, walk, or swim.** _____

   C. **Almost everyone is better informed about health.** _____

      _____

      1. **Most people recognize dangerous symptoms.** _____

      2. **Increasing numbers have regular medical examinations.** _____

READING AND WRITING ABOUT—

Memories

Preparing: Writing a Journal—

In both a journal and a diary, you are writing primarily to yourself; that is, you are your own audience. However, a journal is not exactly the same as a diary. A diary is usually a factual record of daily events. In a journal, however, you write not just about what you do but also about what you think, see, and feel. The purpose of a journal is to allow you to discover—to question and explore, to think critically, and to write freely about your thoughts.

You may write in your journal as often as you wish. However, writing in your journal will be easier and more enjoyable if you make at least one entry each week, and you may want to make daily entries. You may be able to use the ideas that you record in your journal in your writing assignments.

Although a journal entry has more structure and order than free-writing, it is similar to freewriting in that its focus is on ideas rather than on correctness. Although most instructors react to journal entries with written comments, they usually do not evaluate them in the same way they evaluate other written assignments. Thus, you should not be overly concerned with correctness. Instead, you should feel free to experiment with your journal writing, trying not only new ideas but also new words, new forms, and new styles of writing.

Now, prepare to read the following selections by thinking about an important memory—perhaps a memory from your youth or childhood. Why is this memory important to you? Freewrite about this memory for five minutes. (Save your freewriting to use in a later writing assignment.)

REMEMBERING MARTIN LUTHER KING, "THE KING"
Tobi Gillian Sanders

Before you read, think about your memories of Martin Luther King. Have you seen and heard him on film? What do you remember most about him? In this selection, Tobi Gillian Sanders, who was a college student living in New York in 1968, records in her journal her reactions to his assassination. These impressions were originally published in *Members of the Class Will Keep Daily Journals* (1971). Sanders was a senior editor at Bantam Books before she was killed in an automobile accident in 1987.

See text annotations.
Details will vary.

As you read, notice how Sanders uses specific details to make her memories real. Underline some of the most effective details.

New York, 4 April 68

1   Martin Luther King, the "King," was killed tonight. After the first shock, what did I think? Something perhaps not seemingly sympathetic: such men die in such ways. "To a man of spirit it is more painful to be oppressed like a weakling than in the consciousness of strength and common hopes to meet a death that comes unfelt." Well done, Martin Luther, well done. Let the people say *Amen.*

2   I can still hear his voice. It was the Negro voice. The deep soulful timbre that only we have. God, how he could move people. "I have a dream that one day on the red clay hills of Alabama, that little black boys and little white boys will walk hand in hand." "We shall overcome."

3   Some say his philosophy died with him. I would say that the kind of man who could implement that philosophy died with him. The climate of the country will never again produce his like. The conditions are gone. Under him the civil rights movement came of age, and the growth cycle doesn't reverse itself. We have passed that point. There won't be a chance for another little black boy in Atlanta, Georgia, to grow up believing in the innate goodness of man. Would he even be encouraged?

*   *   *

New York, 6 April 68

4   Walked through Harlem today. Had to. Had to get where I could feel some currents of compassion. Found them. God, it was sad. The voice of Martin Luther King, blaring from a small record shop and people standing around listening. To hear him again, to hear the deep voice going high and strong in the Baptist church manner, was enough to carry me back. I believed him then—do I believe him now? Do I believe in the brotherhood of Man? What else is there to believe in? What better is there to believe in? They are all so beautiful, the ideals.

5   I have not paid my dues to the cause. I haven't been flogged as heavily and as hard as others like me. There is a gap.

*   *   *

New York, 8 April 68

6   Tonight Marsha and I walked up and down Broadway after the Memorial for Dr. King. Both of us felt I think, the inadequacy of what we had done in our lives, the way we'd lived. For we hadn't done anything and we hadn't lived. Sure, some would offer us the excuse that we're too young to be expected to have done anything. But I think it wasn't that we weren't activists, but that we weren't believers and we weren't thinkers, we had no visions, no dreams. I told Marsha that we had been sheltered, but I think blinded would be more apt. Blinded because, and I speak only for myself here, I had excused myself with "Not me, but my brother."

7   I have taken too long to come home.

8   I acted as if "going home" was what I would do when I finished college, after I had learned certain things, but no. How can you set dates for commitments. That very act would make the idea of a committed life seem a mere choice of career, something one decides after going to the placement office. But it isn't that, it musn't be made that. And I was naive to think of it in those terms. It calls for caring.

*   *   *

New York, 9 April 68

9   Watched the funeral from <u>10:00 to about 5:00. Watched the people. Saw the</u> <u>South in bloom.</u> Remembered all the despair there until hope came and watched hope buried today. It was something I shared in. The church atmosphere was very familiar . . . <u>memories of many church mornings, the heat, the flowery hats,</u> the emotionalism. I had forgotten <u>how eloquent an old black woman's face is,</u> I had forgotten <u>the sounds of the "Southern Negro."</u> I had forgotten the feeling that comes from being surrounded by your own people. I think I've tried to flee from all that. I know that in my last years at home, I refused to attend church and sometimes at gatherings I was repulsed by all that I attempted to remember today. I think I felt that they were taking God much too seriously, a borrowed God at that. They put all their hope in the idea of a "heavenly home": "no matter what happens here, everything will be all right up yonder." Well, I ceased to look up "yonder." It was, I felt, a sad trick. I didn't think there was anything "up yonder" but space, and somehow they knew it too. It was a grand illusion, but not compensation enough for hell on earth.

*   *   *

New York, 11 April 68

10   <u>I've thought about the singing of "We Shall Overcome" at Dr. King's funeral.</u> <u>It was sincere, full-bodied, and emotional.</u> But I know with certainty that that was the last time that song will be sung, that those days of marching and singing are over. And I'm sorry. The movement had beauty to it. There's beauty in going to face unflinchingly those who hate and persecute you. There's beauty in marching to face a man with a gun, a man puzzled because he knows that shooting you is what you dare him to do, and he doesn't want to give you that satisfaction even though he always thought that the worst he could do to you was kill you. But that proves how little he knows about suffering. Your kind of suffering.

11   But that's over. And I'm nostalgic. Enough of the emotionalism and the Bible are ingrained in me to make me that way. It was peculiar to the South, it could only have flowered there; not because of the number of Negroes, not because of the number of injustices. I think the Southern Negro might be a little more patient, more apt to be caught in a dream, more apt to believe the songs he sings, but even he stops.

REVIEWING THE READING   Answers will vary.

See paragraphs 1 and 3.

1. In her entry for April 4, 1968, what is Sanders's first reaction to King's death? What other reactions does she show in the same entry?

See paragraph 4.

2. When Sanders walks through Harlem on April 6, what does she see and hear that reminds her of King?

3. Circle the general statement that reflects the details given in paragraph 6.

See paragraph 9.

4. What specific memories of the South does the funeral on April 9 trigger in Sanders's mind?

See paragraph 11.

5. What does Sanders believe the future holds for black Americans? (See her entry for April 11.)

UNDERSTANDING VOCABULARY

Review the following sentences from the reading to be sure you understand the meanings of the underlined words. Write these words and definitions in your personal vocabulary list.

1. (*April 4*) "I can still hear his voice. It was the Negro voice. The deep soulful <u>timbre</u> that only we have."

    The *context*—the words that come before and after *timbre*—gives you clues to its meaning. *Timbre* is a distinctive tone or sound, in this case the soulful sound of King's voice.

2. (*April 4*) "Some say his philosophy died with him. I would say that the kind of man who could <u>implement</u> that philosophy died with him."

    This word is a verb meaning "to fulfill" or "carry out" a plan or procedure. The prefixes -*im* and -*in* often mean "in." In this case, however, the -*im* is an intensive that completes, or makes stronger, the meaning of its Latin root *plere,* which means "to fill." Thus, *implement* means to "fulfill, to carry into effect."

3. (*April 4*) "There won't be a chance for another little black boy in Atlanta, Georgia, to grow up believing in the <u>innate</u> goodness of man."

    Here, the prefix -*in* carries the same meaning as the word *in.* Therefore, something that is *innate* is "inborn," or in a person from birth.

4. (*April 11*) "But that's over. And I'm <u>nostalgic</u>."

    Sanders's sad, wistful memories of King suggest that *nostalgia* means a longing for a place, person, or time that is gone.

Look up the definition(s) of other unfamiliar words from this selection in your dictionary and add the words to your vocabulary list.

REACTING CRITICALLY

In her grief, Sanders was disillusioned and pessimistic about the survival of Martin Luther King's philosophy. She states that "the kind of man who could implement that philosophy died with him" (paragraph 3). And later, she writes, "I think the Southern Negro might be a little more patient, more apt to be caught in a dream, more apt to believe the songs he sings, but even he stops" (paragraph 11).

Over twenty years later, do you believe Sanders's pessimism was justified? Have other black men and women successfully carried out King's dream? Or is the dream yet to be realized? If the dream is not a reality, is this because supporters have "stopped," as Sanders feared they would, or because of other reasons? Explain your response.

▓ THE CHESS SET

Amy Tan

Before you read, you might like to know that this story is part of *The Joy Luck Club* (1989), a best-selling novel by Amy Tan. The novel describes the changing relationships between four pairs of Chinese American mothers and their daughters. The narrator in this story is Waverly Jong; her mother is Lindo Jong. In this excerpt, Waverly remembers the gifts she and her brother received at an annual Christmas party when they were children.

As you read, notice how Tan makes her memory real to her readers by including specific details about what she saw and felt. Underline impo-tant specific details about the Christmas gifts—especially in the third rand fourth paragraphs.

See text annotations.
Details will vary.

1   My older brother Vincent was the one who actually got the chess set. We had gone to the annual Christmas party held at the First Chinese Baptist Church at the end of the alley. The missionary ladies had put together a Santa bag of gifts donated by members of another church. None of the gifts had names on them. There were separate sacks for boys and girls of different ages.

2   One of the Chinese parishioners had donned a Santa Claus costume and a stiff paper beard with cotton balls glued to it. I think the only children who thought he was the real thing were too young to know that Santa Claus was not Chinese. When my turn came up, the Santa man asked me how old I was. I thought it was a trick question; I was seven according to the American formula and eight by the Chinese calendar. I said I was born on March 17, 1951. That seemed to satisfy him. He then solemnly asked if I had been a very, very good girl this year and did I believe in Jesus Christ and obey my parents. I knew the only answer to that. I nodded back with equal solemnity.

3   Having watched the other children opening their gifts, I already knew that the big gifts were not necessarily the nicest ones. One girl my age got a large coloring book of biblical characters, while a less greedy girl who selected a smaller box received a glass vial of lavender toilet water. The sound of the box was also important. A ten-year-old boy had chosen a box that jangled when he shook it. It was a tin globe of the world with a slit for inserting money. He must have thought it was full of dimes and nickels, because when he saw that it had just ten pennies, his face fell with such undisguised disappointment that his mother slapped the side of his head and led him out of the church hall, apologizing to the crowd for her son who had such bad manners he couldn't appreciate such a fine gift.

4   As I peered into the sack, I quickly fingered the remaining presents, testing their weight, imagining what they contained. I chose a heavy, compact one that was wrapped in shiny silver foil and a red satin ribbon. It was a twelve-pack of Life Savers and I spent the rest of the party arranging and rearranging the candy tubes in the order of my favorites. My brother Winston chose wisely as well. His present turned out to be a box of intricate plastic parts; the instructions on the box proclaimed that when they were properly assembled he would have an au-thentic miniature replica of a World War II submarine.

5   Vincent got the chess set, which would have been a very decent present to get at a church Christmas party, except it was obviously used and, as we dis-covered later, it was missing a black pawn and a white knight. My mother gra-ciously thanked the unknown benefactor, saying, "Too good. Cost too much." At which point, an old lady with fine white, wispy hair nodded toward our family and said with a whistling whisper, "Merry, merry Christmas."

6   When we got home, my mother told Vincent to throw the chess set away. "She not want it. We not want it," she said, tossing her head stiffly to the side with a tight, proud smile. My brothers had deaf ears. They were already lining up the chess pieces and reading from the dog-eared instruction book.

REVIEWING THE READING   Answers will vary.

See underlined details.

1. In this selection, Tan uses specific statements to support more general statements. For each of the general statements given below, identify the specific statement(s) that Tan uses for support.

   a. "Having watched the other children opening their gifts, I already knew that the big gifts were not necessarily the nicest ones" (paragraph 3).

   b. "The sound of the box was also important" (paragraph 3).

   c. "As I peered into the sack, I quickly fingered the remaining presents, testing their weight, imagining what they contained" (paragraph 4).

   d. "My brother Winston chose wisely as well" (paragraph 4).

2. Tan relates this childhood memory to make an important point about people and about society. What is this point?

UNDERSTANDING VOCABULARY

Prefixes such as *bene-* ("good"), *in-* ("in"), *pro-* ("forth, forward"), *re-* ("again"), *sub* ("under"), and *un-* ("not") change the meanings of words. Use your knowledge of these prefixes to define the words below:

1. inserting (paragraph 3)
2. undisguised (paragraph 3)
3. rearranging (paragraph 4)
4. proclaimed (paragraph 4)
5. submarine (paragraph 4)
6. unknown (paragraph 5)
7. benefactor (paragraph 5)

If any words are new to you, add them to your personal vocabulary list.

REACTING CRITICALLY

In the story, the mother "thanked the unknown benefactor, saying, 'Too good. Cost too much.'" But when the family arrived home, the mother "told Vincent to throw the chess set away. 'She not want it. We not want it,' she said." What do these actions tell you about the mother? Why does she contradict herself? How does she really feel? Would you feel the same way?

Responding in Writing—

Reread your freewriting about an important memory. Then write a journal entry telling about this memory and its significance for you. Be sure to use specific words and statements to support your more general points. Remember that in a journal you focus on expressing your ideas, not on usage, spelling, and punctuation.

Revising Your Writing—

Rewrite your journal entry as a paragraph or a brief essay. In your introduction or conclusion, include a statement explaining the significance of this memory. If necessary, reorder your general and specific statements or add more specific statements to make your ideas clearer. Then proofread your paragraph or essay to correct the most obvious errors in usage, spelling, and punctuation.

CHAPTER THREE
Main Ideas

The main idea of a paragraph or of a longer composition, such as an essay or report, is the general statement that is developed and supported by the other, more specific, sentences. Having learned in the last chapter how to distinguish between general and specific statements, you are now ready to learn how to develop a general statement that serves as the main idea of a paragraph.

The paragraphs that we include in this chapter are all individual paragraphs that can stand alone as small compositions. Although most compositions consist of more than one paragraph, we focus in this chapter on single paragraphs so that you can learn to write and identify main ideas. The basic principles of paragraph development are the same whether the paragraph stands alone or is part of a longer composition. Most paragraphs have a main idea that is supported by more specific statements. In later chapters, you will use these basic principles of paragraph structure to compose and read paragraphs that are parts of longer compositions.

As you read the following student paragraph, notice the combination of general and specific statements.

Although the primary use of a root cellar is to store canned goods and produce, at times it is put to other uses. When my grandfather was farming, he often used his root cellar as a place to make wine. The wine was made and stored in the cellar because it was always cool and allowed the wine to ferment slowly and to age properly. This sometimes led neighboring farmers to gather in the cellar and use it as a place to play cards, gamble, and drink wine. By adding electric heating, my father was able to use his cellar to keep newborn baby chickens and baby calves alive through harsh winter nights. My father's friend once used his cellar as temporary living quarters after his home had burned to the ground. My brothers and I often used the cellar as a place to hang deer that we killed during hunting season. We would let the meat hang there for approximately two weeks to give it a chance to age.

Thus, the root cellar remains an integral part of the farming system in Western Colorado.

Ralph Antonelli

1. In the space below, write the general statement that begins this paragraph:

   Although the primary use of a root cellar is to store canned

   goods and produce, at times it is put to other uses.

2. Notice that the other sentences in the paragraph explain in detail the different uses of a root cellar. List below the five uses the writer describes.

   a. **To make and store wine**

   b. **To keep young animals alive in cold weather**

   c. **As a temporary home**

   d. **To hang and age deer**

   e. **As a place for neighbors to gather and socialize**

Answers will vary.

3. Based on the observations you have made about this paragraph, write your own definition of a paragraph in the lines that follow.

   A paragraph consists of a general statement that is supported by

   other related sentences that include more specific details.

4. Did you include in your definition the following characteristics?

   a. The paragraph begins with a general statement.

   b. The paragraph consists of a series of sentences that are all related to the general statement.

   c. The sentences that follow the general statement give specific details about it.

You might define a paragraph as a group of sentences that develops one main idea. The main idea of a paragraph is the general statement that the other sentences support or explain. It is usually stated, often at the very beginning of the paragraph. In the paragraph about the uses of a root cellar, the main idea statement is the first sentence. Another term for main idea statement is *topic sentence*.

A paragraph may be a complete composition in itself, or it may be part of a longer composition. In either case, a well-developed paragraph usually consists of the same three parts that make up any composition: an introduction, a body, and a conclusion. In fact, a well-developed paragraph is a composition in miniature. The introduction to the paragraph is often the topic sentence. The body of the paragraph consists of several sentences that discuss and develop the topic sentence. The supporting statements are more specific than the general statement that serves as the paragraph's topic sentence. These more specific supporting sentences develop the main idea by examining it in more detail. The conclusion of a paragraph is often a general statement that reemphasizes the main idea expressed in the topic sentence.

The diagram in Figure 7 shows the form and proportions of a model paragraph. Notice that the first word in the paragraph is indented several spaces (usually five to eight) from the margin. Notice too that the introduction is brief, consisting only of the topic sentence. The body of the paragraph is much longer than either the introduction or the conclusion. The conclusion, like the introduction, is brief, usually only one or two sentences.

FIGURE 7

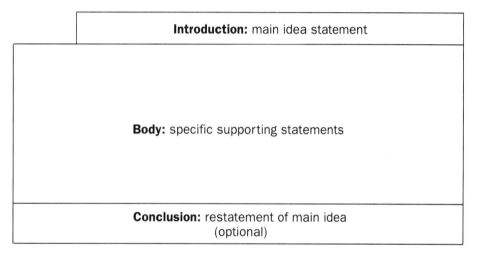

Introduction: main idea statement

Body: specific supporting statements

Conclusion: restatement of main idea
(optional)

This paragraph model is just that—a model, or pattern, to help you in reading and writing paragraphs. Later, in this and future chapters, you will learn about other paragraph patterns. If you observe paragraphs in books, magazines, and newspapers, you will notice that professional writers often write paragraphs that do not follow set patterns. Experienced writers may omit topic sentences, combine patterns, and vary methods of organization to suit their subject and purpose. In learning to write, however, you will find that you can develop your writing—and reading—ability more quickly and easily if you start with a simple and specific model such as this one.

Note: Many magazines and books indicate paragraphing with spacing instead of indentation. Often, as in this textbook, the first paragraph in an essay or section begins at the margin, but additional paragraphs are indented. In writing your own paragraphs and essays, however, you should always indent the first line to show the beginning of a paragraph.

 EXERCISE 3.1   The following student paragraphs follow the pattern of the model paragraph. That is, they begin with a topic sentence, are developed by specific supporting statements, and end with a concluding statement. Read each of the paragraphs, carefully examining the details. Then select—from each group of three sentences—the topic sentence that best expresses

the main idea supported by the details; write the sentence in the space provided.

PARAGRAPH A

1. Life at my mother's house is always hectic.
2. My mother always makes me feel welcome when I go home.
3. My favorite place to go is my mom's.

My favorite place to go is my mom's.
(Topic sentence)

The house is always full of people. My dad's on the couch looking at television, my three brothers are somewhere making lots of noise, and my cousins, Billy and Daniel, seem to always be hanging around somewhere waiting for my mom to finish cooking so they can eat. There's always some kind of activity going on; there's never a dull moment. Children are running around making noise with all kinds of toys, and we're constantly having to throw the cat outside because she's running in the house every time the door opens. However, the best part about being there is we're all together. When I'm depressed about something, sick, or feeling lonely, I go there because I know I'll find peace of mind, even though it's noisy. If there's a problem, I feel like if I can just make it to where my mama is, somehow and some way she'll make it all right. When I get sick, being close to Mama or just in the house around Mama and the family makes the pain a little bit better. When loneliness becomes a problem, I jump in the car and go home because I know I'll find some kind of company, maybe even more than I want. Over all, I love going to my mother's because there's love, understanding, and peace there. Just a word or hug from my family and knowing I can go there when life throws me a curve make me happy.

Emma McNair

PARAGRAPH B

1. France has one of the world's best programs for taking care of the elderly.
2. Old people in our society are not cared for as well as they are in other countries.
3. Old people should be cared for by their children.

Old people in our society are not cared for as well as they are in
(Topic sentence)
other countries.

Here in America, elderly people are usually put into old folks' homes, left by themselves, and forced to live on a fixed income. They are not given a tax break or exempted from taxes. When they get sick, they either pay for treatment themselves, or the bills are paid by their families if the costs exceed what is allowed by Medicare. In other countries, however, the situation is much different. In France, for example, elderly people are given free medical services. In Italy, they are exempted from certain taxes. And in the Far East, old people are considered very knowledgeable. This knowledge is put to good use for the benefit of the entire family. The old people are made to feel that they continue to contribute to the family's well being. Americans might learn from other countries how to improve the lives of their old people.

Robert Stidham

PARAGRAPH C

1. Crying is for sad and happy times.
2. Crying is for women.
3. I hate to see people cry.

Crying is for sad and happy times.
(Topic sentence)

For instance, my mother cried at both my graduation and when she sent me off to college. At graduation she cried in a time of happiness, because if she hadn't burst into tears she would have fainted instead. Also she cried to show me and everyone how proud she was of her only son. When I was sent off to college, it was a different story. Tears came into her eyes and one or two rolled down her cheek in this time of sadness to show me the grief inside of her heart at our departure from each other. I bit my tongue and broke down into tears also.

Albert McRae III

PARAGRAPH D

1. It is difficult to speak on an unfamiliar subject.
2. The ability to speak in public is an asset.
3. Public speaking really makes me nervous.

Public speaking really makes me nervous.
(Topic sentence)

The thought of having to speak to a large audience makes me sick. I hate having more than two people looking at me at the same time. I also dislike being given a specific subject on which to speak, such as the Equal Rights Amendment or some aspect of foreign relations with a strange country. These topics make me nervous because I don't know a lot about them. Another thing that makes me nervous is the thought that I might bore my listeners. When it comes to public speaking, I would rather do something else.

Jim R. Sprague

EXPRESSING MAIN IDEAS AS TOPIC SENTENCES

A topic sentence is the general statement that expresses the main idea of a paragraph. In very simple terms, it tells the reader what the paragraph will be about. As illustrated in the model paragraph, the topic sentence usually, but not always, comes at the beginning of the paragraph. The other sentences in the paragraph relate directly to the topic sentence, explaining, expanding, developing, and supporting it.

Topic and Assertion

An effective topic sentence has two basic parts: *topic* and *assertion.* The topic indicates what the paragraph is about, and the assertion is the point that is being made about the topic. In Paragraph D above, for example, the topic is "public speaking" and the assertion is "really makes me nervous." The assertion makes a statement about the topic. It may express an attitude or opinion ("Recycling should be enforced by law"), or it may simply indicate what is to follow ("There are three reasons why we should recycle"). In other words, the assertion is the point you will make or the idea you will develop in your paragraph.

Note: The topic sentence can not be a specific statement of fact, such as "The temperature of the sun's surface is 11,000° Fahrenheit," because such a statement needs no further development or support.

In each of the three topic sentences below, the topic has been underlined once, and the assertion has been underlined twice.

Computers have changed the way we write.

A college freshman's first semester can be very stressful.

This country needs a national health care program.

In most topic sentences, the grammatical subject of the sentence is the same as the topic, and the predicate of the sentence is the same as the assertion. To express both topic and assertion, therefore, a topic sentence must be a complete sentence. Most topic sentences are in the form of a statement, but they can also be expressed as a question: "How have computers changed the way we write?"

It is important not to confuse topic sentences with the subject or title. Compare the following examples:

Title (subject): College Entrance Exams
Topic sentence: College entrance exams are racially and sexually biased.

Title (subject): Active Learning
Topic sentence: Students learn more when they actively engage in learning.

Title (subject): How to Survive in College
Topic sentence: To survive in college, you must learn to manage stress.

Notice that the titles (or subjects) tell what the paragraph is about but not what you are going to say (assert) about your topic. In other words, the title expresses the topic but not the assertion; a topic sentence expresses both.

■ EXERCISE 3.2   In each of the following topic sentences, underline the topic once and the assertion twice.

1. Learning a foreign language can be difficult for adults.
2. Telephones intrude into the privacy of our daily lives.
3. Movies are often filmed in exotic locations.
4. Financial problems can create stress for college students.
5. Many gun-related accidents involve children.
6. Television commercials communicate forcefully and clearly.
7. Parents of teenage children often feel unappreciated.
8. College dorms frequently have security problems.
9. Driving in a large city requires nerves of steel.
10. Committees often cause more problems than they solve.

Narrowing the Topic Sentence

Notice that the topic sentences in the exercise above are general statements that can be developed by specific details and examples. Since a paragraph is usually less than one page in length, an extremely broad or vague topic sentence is inappropriate. Thus, in deciding on a topic sentence for your paragraph, choose an idea that is general but not *too* general—an idea that you can explain fully in less than a page.

Often a statement that is too general to serve as a topic sentence can be narrowed by the addition of a specific time, place, or person. For example, look at the following sentence:

■ Sports are exciting.

This statement is so broad that it cannot possibly be developed adequately in a single paragraph. If you narrow the statement by specifying a particular type of sporting event or activity, you will have a workable topic sentence:

■ Football is an exciting sport.

If you narrow further, you will have an even more effective topic sentence:

■ The 1991 Super Bowl game kept me on the edge of my chair.

Notice that as you narrow your topic sentence by adding more specific details, it becomes a longer sentence. In general, the more words you use, the more specific your statement will be. Notice also that in the examples above we have made both the topic and the assertion more specific:

TOPIC	ASSERTION
1. Sports	are exciting.
2. Football	is an exciting sport.
3. The 1991 Super Bowl game	kept me on the edge of my chair.

The exercise below will provide you with practice in narrowing statements so that they will be effective topic sentences. As you revise these sentences, keep in mind the following guidelines:

1. A topic sentence should always be a complete sentence.
2. A topic sentence should not merely state a single fact.
3. A topic sentence should be a general statement but should not be too broad or vague.

EXERCISE 3.3

Answers will vary.

Rewrite each broad statement below, narrowing both topic and assertion. You will need to change words and add new words.

1. Education is important.

   An introductory course in political science helps students understand

   the process of electing a president.

2. My friends are very important to me.

   My friend Shawn can almost always cheer me up.

3. Exercise improves health.

   Walking regularly improves the health of heart patients.

4. Our economy is in trouble.

   Unemployment has become a major problem in recent years.

5. Pollution causes serious problems.

   An oil spill (or a specific oil spill) causes serious problems for

   marine life.

6. Television is boring.

   Soap operas are boring because events and characters are so predictable.

7. Teachers require too much homework.

   Professor Miller, my History 121 teacher, is requiring too much home-

   work this week.

8. Modern medicine improves our lives.

Vaccines have eliminated many childhood illnesses.

9. Movies are better (or worse) than ever.

   The special effects of today's science fiction movies are far superior to those of early sci-fi flicks.

10. Fashions change quickly.

    Women's skirt lengths change almost every year.

■ EXERCISE 3.4   Choose one of your narrowed topic sentences from Exercise 3.3 and write a paragraph developing it. In writing your paragraph, follow the model on page 41. Begin with your narrowed topic sentence, add specific supportive details, and end with a conclusion that restates the topic sentence.

IDENTIFYING THE MAIN IDEA IN A PARAGRAPH

Before you can understand what you read, you must be able to identify main ideas and separate them from supporting details. In other words, you must be able to distinguish between the general statements that state the main idea of the paragraph and the specific statements that support the main idea. In most paragraphs the main idea is stated in a topic sentence, or main idea statement. Although this sentence occurs most often at the beginning of the paragraph, it may occur at various other places within the paragraph.

Main Idea as First Sentence

Often, the main idea appears only once in a paragraph. Most frequently, the main idea statement occurs at or near the beginning of the paragraph, usually as the first sentence. Remaining sentences, then, give explanations, examples, and details. This pattern (general to specific) is illustrated in Figure 8 and the sample paragraph. Underline the main idea statement in the paragraph.

FIGURE 8

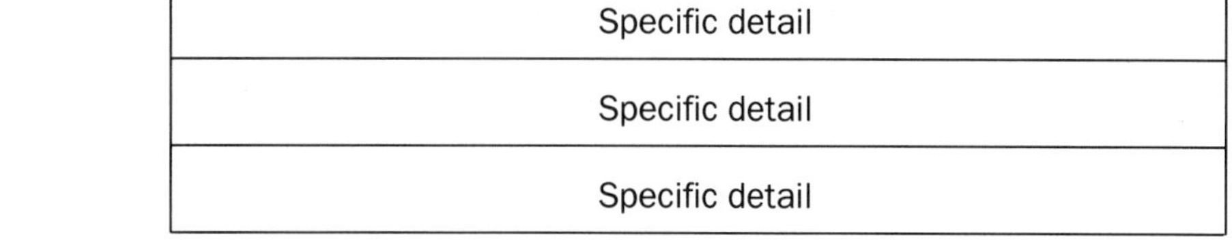

Main idea statement	
	Specific detail
	Specific detail
	Specific detail

The American breakfast has changed dramatically in the past few decades. In the first fifty or sixty years of this century, a typical breakfast consisted of bacon and eggs or cereal. Although some people occasionally liked a gooey donut or a sweet roll for breakfast, most Americans preferred the standard fare—day after day. Since the 1960s, however, breakfasts have become increasingly exotic. Traditional breakfast fare seems rather dull compared with Belgian waffles, French omelettes, or huevos rancheros (eggs topped by a spicy Mexican salsa). Breakfasts have also become healthier. Yogurt, granola, and fruit are considered better for people than bacon and eggs accompanied by buttery hot biscuits smothered in gravy.

Main Idea as Last Sentence

The main idea also occurs frequently as the last sentence of a paragraph. In this case, the paragraph starts with details or examples and concludes with the main idea. This paragraph pattern (specific to general) is illustrated in Figure 9 and the sample paragraph. Underline the main idea statement in the paragraph.

FIGURE 9

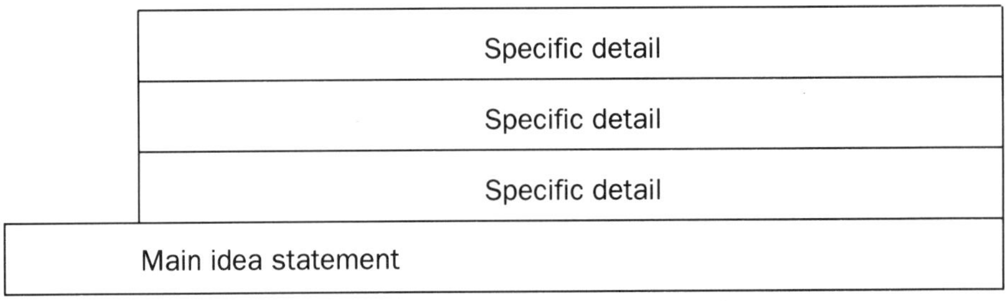

| Specific detail |
| Specific detail |
| Specific detail |
| Main idea statement |

In the early 1980s, prosperity seemed to be our birthright. Jobs were plentiful, money was easy to borrow, and the stock market was on a steady upward course. Then, in the last part of the decade, the economic picture changed. The homeless became a familiar sight on city streets. Some people lost their jobs, and graduates had more difficulty finding employment. And on at least one occasion, the stock market dipped low enough to make even the most optimistic investors nervous. Savings-and-loan associations, banks, and even insurance companies began to fail. By the end of the decade it was clear that the nation was in a significant recession. The 1980s were a time of transition in which the nation moved from economic optimism and prosperity to economic pessimism and hard times.

Main Idea as First and Last Sentence

The main idea is often stated at both the beginning and the end of a paragraph. However, the final statement of the main idea is not merely a restatement of the topic sentence. The last sentence reinforces the main idea, but it also reflects the conclusions that the writer has reached. This pattern (general to specific to general) is illustrated in Figure 10 and the sample paragraph. Underline the main idea statements in the sample paragraph.

FIGURE 10

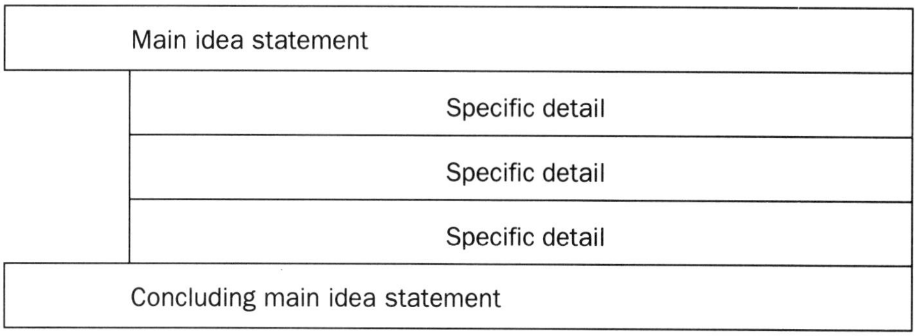

Main idea statement
Specific detail
Specific detail
Specific detail
Concluding main idea statement

The weather in West Texas is completely unpredictable. Winter often brings warm, sunny days while summer and spring may surprise residents with periods of cool, cloudy weather. The wind may blow fiercely one day and be completely calm the next. Drought may plague the region at times, only to be followed by heavy rainfall and even flooding. At one time or another, and in no particular order, West Texans experience blinding dust storms, record-breaking heat waves, tornadoes, hail, thunderstorms, and "blue northers"— those sudden cold spells that sweep across the Panhandle and into the state from the north. The climate throughout West Texas is often dramatic, sometimes disagreeable, but seldom dull.

Main Idea as Second/Middle Sentence

The main idea may also be stated in the second (or even the third or fourth) sentence of a paragraph. In this pattern, the first sentence or sentences serve as an introduction to the main idea, which restricts or narrows the focus expressed in the first sentence(s). Or the first sentence(s) may function as a transition, linking the paragraph to the preceding one. This paragraph pattern (introduction/transition to general to specific) is illustrated in Figure 11 and the sample paragraph that follows. Underline the main idea statement in the paragraph.

FIGURE 11

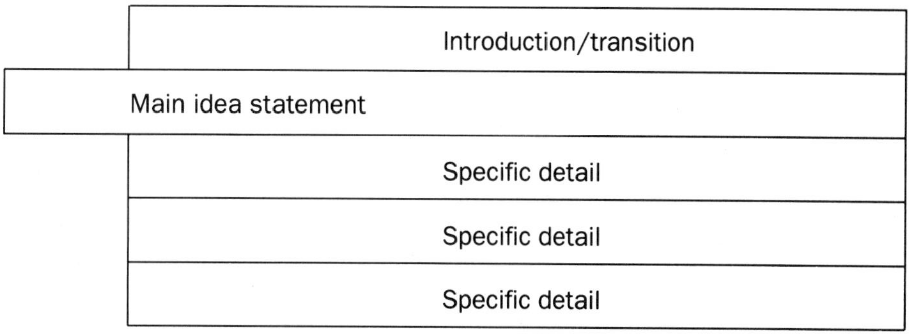

Introduction/transition
Main idea statement
Specific detail
Specific detail
Specific detail

In the past few years, millions of Americans have begun to exercise. Unfortunately, many of these energetic but amateur athletes have sustained serious injuries. Tennis players have ruined their elbows, joggers their knees, and aerobic dancers their ankles. More serious injuries are often sustained by those who play competitive sports such as basketball or football. Even lifting weights involves certain risks to muscle tissue and bones. Although some athletic injuries require only time and rest in order to heal, others result in permanent damage.

EXERCISE 3.5   The students who wrote the following paragraphs placed their main idea statements in various positions. Read each paragraph carefully and underline its main idea statement. Indicate in the space provided which paragraph pattern each student used:

Main idea as first sentence
Main idea as last sentence
Main idea as first and last sentence
Main idea as second/middle sentence

PARAGRAPH A

Football season is the beginning of a confusing and hectic time for me. Having all the children and grandchildren, a group of fourteen people, home for Sunday dinner when the Cowboys are playing is a trying situation. The real fans sit with eyes glued on the television and expect everyone else to watch the game or shut up. The others, who are not as interested in football, laugh and talk even though these activities disturb the hollering, screaming fans. The grandchildren running in and out of the house cause more confusion. As I cook dinner, serve everyone, and referee the children, I begin to feel like the battered football that has been thrown all over the field.

Doris Osborn

Paragraph pattern: **main idea as first sentence**

PARAGRAPH B

I was seventeen when I joined the Marine Corps, along with hundreds of other young people from different parts of the country. After we had completed our entrance physical, we were sworn in. There were nine other guys with me then, all raising their right hands, pledging allegiance to our country and its principles of democracy. I can remember the look in the eyes of these other nine as we lowered our hands and were congratulated. It was a look of belonging and pride. At that moment, I understood for the first time the meaning of the word *camaraderie.*

Michael Luck

Paragraph pattern: **main idea as last sentence**

PARAGRAPH C

Since my father died five years ago, my grandfather and I have become very close to each other. He always gives me helpful advice. Whenever I have a problem that I can't talk over with my mother, I go to my grandfather. And when I need financial help, my grandfather is always willing to help. For example, when I am sick and need medication, my grandfather tells me to get the medication on his drugstore account. My grandfather is always there to give a helping hand. I look upon him as the father that I lost.

Ray C. Walker

Paragraph pattern: **main idea as first sentence**

PARAGRAPH D

James Bond is a character with a style of his own. <u>He is an expert at everything he does.</u> When it comes to a car race, he is A. J. Foyt. When it comes to skiing, there is no one on the slopes who can keep up with him. There is nothing he can't do. When an actor can do all this, the final test is women. Believe it or not, Bond is an expert on that subject too. All he has to do is make eye contact with a woman, and she is his for the night. While all this is taking place, he is constantly being shot at. The funny part about it is that he never gets hit. If I could become Bond for one day, I would fulfill my wildest dreams.

Robert Story

Paragraph pattern: **main idea as second sentence**

PARAGRAPH E

<u>My room indicates the disorganized way I run my life.</u> My bed is very seldom made and is usually a mess. The closet is a storehouse for old books, boxes of junk, and tools that are not arranged in any order at all. My drawers are full of old papers, checks, and other items that should be in some order but aren't. Clothes are usually strung out all over the room, and my book shelf is a mass of confusion with my record albums and tapes mixed with my books and drawing utensils. <u>My room reflects my lifestyle, which is usually disorderly.</u>

Bill McRae

Paragraph pattern: **main idea as first and last sentence**

EXERCISE 3.6 The following paragraphs have all been taken from college textbooks. Read each paragraph carefully and then underline the main idea. In the space provided, indicate the paragraph pattern.

PARAGRAPH A

<u>The assassination of John Kennedy had a profound impact on American society and culture.</u> Because of its suddenness, news of the killing wrenched the American people from the routines of their daily lives. People would later remember exactly what they were doing when they first heard the news. As word of the shooting spread from Dallas, people everywhere crowded around televisions and radios seeking further information. The sophistication of the public media made the assassination a national event, an experience that was shared simultaneously throughout the country and the world. Surveys later revealed that 92 percent of all Americans learned of the assassination within two hours and that more than half of all Americans watched the same television coverage of the event. Millions of citizens were glued to their television sets on November 24 and watched Jack Ruby murder the suspected assassin. <u>As Pearl Harbor had shocked an earlier generation of Americans, the assassination of Kennedy and its aftermath touched the lives of the entire nation.</u>

David W. Noble et al., Twentieth Century Limited

Paragraph pattern: **main idea as first and last sentence**

PARAGRAPH B

Geography comes from a Greek word whose literal meaning is "description of the earth." <u>But modern geography is concerned with people as well as</u>

with the earth, and with relationships and analysis as well as with description. Geographers analyze the physical world and examine relations between places in order to throw light on the patterns and nature of human society. They investigate the interrelationship that exists between people and their physical environment. They examine regional differences, and attempt to account for them. Geographers pick out regional patterns, and try to draw regional lines and identify regional relationships. The earth and its spatial framework, and the pattern of distribution of people and elements on the earth's surface, are studied by geographers to develop a better understanding of the human world. They set people in the framework of the earth they inhabit.

Rhoads Murphey, *Patterns of the Earth*

Paragraph pattern: **main idea as a second sentence**

PARAGRAPH C

One of the tools a wise customer uses is knowing the right time to buy. For instance, you should get linen products, sheets, towels, and blankets during the January White Sale. Each January, merchants reduce the prices of all kinds of household goods, including those made of cotton, wool or other fabrics. Smart consumers wait until January to buy such products. Shop for winter clothes in the spring, tennis rackets in the fall, and skis in the summer. A good time to shop for Christmas cards and wrapping is a week or two after Christmas.

John S. Morton and Ronald R. Rezny, *Consumer Action*

Paragraph pattern: **main idea as first sentence**

PARAGRAPH D

Home information networks will make it possible to receive news from computer terminals in the home. The information will be received when the household wants it and at a reasonable price. Any Touch-Tone telephone now used in homes can, with a minor change, also be used as a computer input terminal. The telephone buttons become the keys of a terminal input device. By keying in a code number, an individual will be able to request from an outside computer storage unit the particular news that he or she is interested in. International events, sports results, business news, and home-making news will all be available. The computer will respond with the requested information in seconds. The news material will be printed on a home printer device. Pictures will be displayed either on a TV set equipped with special devices or on a Picture-phone device.

Beryl Robichaud et al., *Introduction to Data Processing*

Paragraph pattern: **main idea as first sentence**

PARAGRAPH E

Scientists are no exception, but they are devoted to a very specialized cause: the discovery of the nature of nature through basic research. No one else will find the cures for cancers or concern themselves with black holes in space. Cancer research is understandable in the eyes of the general public. It is obviously practical, but black holes may seem to be silly things on which to spend money. The same thing might have been said about the researches of Copernicus. All he did was discover that the earth is not the center of the universe. Although everyone may not consider this fact important, it does have a profound effect on some religious views. <u>Scientists are devoted to the discovery of truth and to expressing it openly for anyone to use.</u>

John W. Harrington, Discovering Science

Paragraph pattern: **main idea as first and last sentence**

PARAGRAPH F

Soap opera was another legacy from radio to television. <u>The soaps in those early days began with some basic dilemma, then spun fantastic plots and subplots around it.</u> Sometimes it took years to work out the details. One of the original stories, "Our Gal Sunday," wandered on through years of elaborate plots based on the theme expressed in every episode: "Can a girl from a little mining town in the West find happiness as the wife of a wealthy and titled Englishman?" The same basic set of characters carried through the months and years, with new ones being added to meet story demands and with old ones disappearing as emphasis shifted.

Robert D. Murphy, Mass Communication and Human Interaction

Paragraph pattern: **main idea as second sentence**

Implied Main Idea

In some paragraphs the main idea or topic sentence is not stated. Rather, it is suggested or *implied* throughout the paragraph. In the sample paragraph below, the main idea is implied rather than stated. Read the paragraph carefully and then state the main idea in your own words. Key words that provide you with clues to the main idea of the paragraph have been italicized.

Answers will vary.

On his *inauguration day, Andrew Jackson* mounted his horse and rode to the White House, followed by *a crowd of* 10,000 visitors. The people *pushed* into the White House, *climbing on delicate furniture* to see the new president. *Excited supporters trod on valuable rugs* with muddy boots, *turned over pieces of furniture,* and *broke expensive glassware.* They *pushed* and *shoved* to get next to the new president, who, after being backed helplessly against a wall, climbed out a back window.

Main idea: **On Andrew Jackson's inauguration day, his excited**

supporters destroyed valuable White House property and even

endangered the president.

Although this paragraph does not have a stated main idea or topic sentence, each sentence is an important detail that suggests or implies the main idea. One way that you could have stated the main idea is that "On Andrew Jackson's inauguration day, his excited supporters destroyed valuable White House property and even endangered the president."

In your reading you will sometimes find paragraphs in which the main idea is implied rather than stated. When you read a paragraph with an implied main idea, you must use the supporting details to help you determine—or infer—the main idea. The main idea you formulate from these details is an *inference*. The process of inferring a main idea from the details within a paragraph is similar to the process of inferring the meaning of an unfamiliar word from its context. In both situations, you use the information given to help you infer what the writer implies.

As a writer, you may occasionally write a paragraph with an implied main idea. If you choose not to include a topic sentence, however, you should keep your main idea clearly in mind, being sure that each detail develops the main idea so clearly that your reader will have no difficulty understanding it.

■ EXERCISE 3.7

Answers will vary.

In the three paragraphs that follow, the main idea is implied rather than stated. Read each paragraph carefully and then state in your own words its main idea:

PARAGRAPH A

He was the only non-American student in the history class. Since most of the discussions focused on American history and culture, he had little to contribute. He was also very shy, especially when he was called on to answer a question. To make matters even worse, he had to work on a group project with three girls, a situation that only increased his normal shyness.

Main idea: **The shy non-American student was uncomfortable in his**

history class.

PARAGRAPH B

In the distant past, writers labored with quill pens and ink, carefully forming each letter by hand. The fountain pen, when it appeared on the writing scene, was viewed as a marvelous convenience. Then the typewriter provided writers with a much more efficient method of writing, a method that for many years was viewed as the ultimate in writing convenience. When the correcting typewriter came along, writers thought they had died and gone to heaven. Today, however, writers who write with computers and word process-ing programs scorn "old-fashioned" typewriters.

Main idea: **Improvements in technology have made writing**

easier.

PARAGRAPH C

Daytime television is dominated by soap operas and silly quiz shows. Newcasts are brief, sports events are rare, and first-run sit-coms are nonex-istent. After the morning shows, which end about the time people's workdays begin, the tube emits the shrieks of quiz show contestants. These ridiculous shows are followed by the high (but seldom serious) drama of the soap operas, with their endless crises and passionate sex. In contrast, nighttime television provides viewers with newscasts, sports events, situation comedies, serious dramas, and documentaries. Viewers can choose from movies, comedies, news stories, musical variety shows, and numerous "specials," all designed to appeal to a more mature, intelligent audience.

Main idea: **Nighttime television is more mature and intelligent**

than is daytime television.

▨ **EXERCISE 3.8**

Answers will vary.

The following paragraphs have been taken from college textbooks. Read each paragraph carefully. The main idea is stated in some of these paragraphs; in others it is implied. In each paragraph underline the main idea statement or words that give clues to the main idea. Then, in the space provided, write the main idea in your own words.

PARAGRAPH A

Some of the resources you have read about—air, water, soil, plants—have been important to people for thousands of years. Some mineral resources have also been important for a long time. For example, early hunters used a certain kind of rock (flint) to make their spearpoints and arrowheads. And people have long valued gold for its beauty. But many other minerals were not resources for early people. They did not know how to use coal or oil. They did not know how to process iron to make tools from it. Therefore none of these minerals were resources for them. Many of the minerals people use today have only become important resources in the past century or two.

Arthur Getis and Judith M. Getis, *Geography*

Main idea: **Many minerals we depend on today have become**

important to us only recently.

Is the main idea stated or implied? **stated**

PARAGRAPH B

As we read a work of literature, at some point we develop a sense of its quality. In the case of fiction, we may decide that the story it tells is "great," "good," or just "so-so," and thus we begin to evaluate. Often our initial response is subjective, based largely on personal tastes and prejudices. Such a reaction is natural; after all, we must start somewhere. No doubt many professional critics first come to an assessment of an author's work by way of preference and bias. But sheer curiosity might get the better of us and make us ask: Why? Why is this story so enjoyable or moving, and that one not quite satisfying? To find out, we need to probe the elements of fiction and study its techniques. We need to examine the parts so that we might gain a fuller understanding and appreciation of the whole.

Anthony Dubé et al., *Structure and Meaning: An Introduction to Literature*

Main idea: **Our first response to a piece of literature is often**

subjective, but we also need to learn how to analyze and

evaluate it objectively.

Is the main idea stated or implied? **implied**

PARAGRAPH C

Obviously, beyond the very necessities for life itself, the distinction between needs and wants is not clear, at least not for society as a whole. . . . If you live in the suburbs or in a rural area where there is no public transportation, you may believe that you need a car. Others might need only a bicycle and occasional taxi fares. You may also believe that you need a college education in order "to succeed." Again, others may well reject this idea. Likewise, some families need a washer and dryer, some don't. Most profess the need for a refrigerator and a stove; others need only a cafeteria meal ticket or a hot plate and a cold cellar. The point is that most things an individual or family considers to be needs are not really vital to life but are simply higher-order wants.

Daniel McGowan, Contemporary Personal Finance

Main idea: **Many of the things that people believe are needs**

are actually only wants.

Is the main idea stated or implied? **stated**

PARAGRAPH D

The Court is neither free to rule on all controversies in American society nor capable of correcting all injustices. Not only do institutional obstacles prevent the Court from considering certain major questions, but even when it has the authority, the Court exercises considerable self-restraint. Judicial restraint can be based on philosophical as well as practical considerations. Many justices believe certain types of questions should not be considered by the Court. Furthermore, the Court often evades those issues on which it can expect little political or public support. John P. Roche states that the Court's power "has been maintained by a wise refusal to employ it in unequal combat."

Robert S. Ross, American National Government

Main idea: **The Supreme Court's power is limited.**

Is the main idea stated or implied? **stated**

PARAGRAPH E

[During the Middle Ages] London's narrow streets were lined with houses and shops, most of them built of wood. Fire was an ever-present danger. The streets were mostly unpaved and during the day were crowded with people, dogs, horses, and pigs. . . . But from the perspective of the twelfth century, London was a great, progressive metropolis. The old wooden bridge across the River Thames was being replaced by a new London Bridge made entirely of stone. Sanitation workers were employed by the city to clear the streets of garbage. There was a sewer system—the only one in England—consisting of open drains down the centers of streets. There was even a public lavatory.

C. Warren Hollister, Medieval Europe: A Short History

Main idea: **During the Middle Ages, London was**

dangerous and filthy, but the people of that time

thought of it as a progressive city.

Is the main idea stated or implied? **implied**

PARAGRAPH F

Facts provide information. They are the necessary ingredients of reasoning. They don't, however, provide all the answers. They don't tell us where we came from or what we're destined for. They don't point a path through life. They don't give us the courage to go on when we feel most like quitting. They don't, and never will, explain the forces of good and evil, or soften the fear of death, or solve any other riddle of life. Unless we are able to recognize and participate in the kinds of truths that present themselves in the metaphorical images of mythology, the answers to these riddles are unknowable. "Myth," observes mythologist Ananda Coomaraswamy, "embodies the nearest approach to absolute truth that can be stated in words."

Peter R. Stillman, *Introduction to Myth*

Main idea: **To understand life, we need the truths**

found in myths as well as the information

supplied by facts.

Is the main idea stated or implied? **implied**

READING AND WRITING ABOUT—

People

Preparing: Mapping—

People are fascinating. We all like to read and write about people we know (or know about). Biographies of famous people hit the best seller list almost immediately. Magazines that promise information about celebrities sell quickly. In your college classes, you will probably be asked to write reports about people who have made significant contributions to a certain discipline or played an important role in history or science. For example, in a history class you might be asked to write a report on Queen Elizabeth, Frederick Douglas, or Franklin Roosevelt. But stories about common people can also be fascinating. The following selections by Claire Fejes, Carl T. Rowan, and Rudolfo A. Anaya are about ordinary people who made a major impression or played an important role in the authors' lives.

When you are writing or reading, you can use a technique called *mapping* to explore your ideas or to help you identify and organize the ideas of another writer. For example, look at Figure 12 to see how one student mapped ideas about her neighbor, Frances Nelson.

FIGURE 12

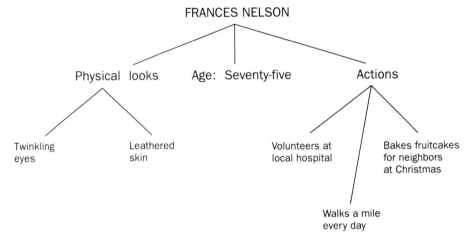

Remember, too, that you can use a map like this to give structure to ideas in your reading—to help you distinguish main ideas from details. Just as a road map helps you to find your destination when you are on a trip, a planning map like this helps you to determine where you want to go in your writing or where you have been in your reading.

Now, begin your own writing map. Think of an interesting person about whom you might like to write. Write the name of this person at the top of a blank sheet of paper. Then branch down with ideas and details about this person. Continue your map until you have several levels of details. Be sure to save your map. You may be able to use it as the basis for a later writing assignment.

▨ BESSIE WHOLECHEESE

Claire Fejes

Before you read, think about a person whose life has been very different from your own. In this selection Claire Fejes, a long-time resident of Alaska, paints both a verbal and a visual portrait of an Athabaskan Indian woman who has lived her entire life in the small village of Galena. Fejes, a professional artist as well as a writer, includes this sketch in her collection *Villagers: Athabaskan Indian Life Along the Yukon River* (1959).

See text annotations. Details will vary.

As you read, try to visualize Bessie Wholecheese. Underline the details that describe her appearance.

1   I asked a woman in the store who would be a good model to paint, and was directed to Bessie Wholecheese's house. Her sprawling log cabin had a front porch stacked with dried fish and miscellaneous tools. A large husky nursing three pups blocked the entranceway. I smelled wood smoke and salmon.

2   I stepped over the pups and greeted Bessie, who invited me in. <u>A pleasant, rounded woman with a strong face and long gray hair, she gave the impression of great inner strength.</u> Geranium plants grew on her windowsill, and her huge room was warmed by a homemade barrel stove, topped with a large teakettle and a five-gallon water can. Her daughter sat rocking her newborn baby beneath a black-velvet wall hanging of Jesus.

3   I told Bessie that I was traveling on the boat and would like to paint her, offering to pay for her time.

4   "What, pay me for sitting still?" she laughed.

5   After we chatted about the boat, the weather and her family, Bessie sat placidly near her stove. I placed my oil box on a chair and sat on another one facing her. Drying socks hung on the line over the stove, and I heard the faint sizzle of rain splattering against a hot chimney pipe. The warm hearth and cozy stillness of her house appealed to me after the noisy boat. <u>Bessie's tranquility and cheerfulness and her solid personality</u> were nourishing for me. She was as she seemed to be. It began to rain harder outside, slapping the window with drops, and the teakettle made a gurgling sound on the hot stove. Her latest grandchild slept peacefully.

6   I painted <u>her curved forms, her full womanly breasts, with her arms folded over her round belly, her sleeves rolled up over her strong forearms. Her shapes contrasted with those of the stove,</u> somehow tied to its symmetry—the woman and the hearth, tied symbolically.

7   Bessie had given birth to twenty-two children, of which eight had died. <u>At fifty-nine,</u> she had twenty-six grandchildren. <u>There was not a wrinkle on her face.</u> All but the last three children had been born in her home with the help of whoever happened to be present. "Once there was a girl here and I told her what to do," she said casually. "I never had no trouble." And yet eight had died, probably of tuberculosis or at childbirth.

8   We established an easy rapport. She appreciated the fact that I was a countrywoman, an Alaskan used to the woods, not a tourist but one who had weathered many northern winters and who understood village life.

9   In contrast to Bessie's home deliveries, her daughter had her baby in the Anchorage Hospital and was in labor twenty-two hours. She did not breast-feed her baby, as Bessie had, but gave him a modern plastic nipple to suck.

10   Bessie did not have much use for doctors. "Nowadays if a girl has a little pain, she runs to the doctor," she said. She believed in her own natural health and in her ability to take care of herself. She ate simply and worked hard, fishing in the summer and through the ice in the winter, chopping wood and usually shooting her own moose.

11   In Bessie's grandmother's time, Indians were considered married when the man moved in and helped the girl's family to hunt. Bessie and Edgar Nollner lived together following the Indian tradition. Edgar, descended from one of the first settlers of Galena, was one of the dog mushers who rushed the diphtheria serum to Nome in the winter of 1925.

12   Together they had filled a big freezer with moose and fish. A practical man, Edgar had built four rafts and a house on oil drums just in case the water threatened to flood again.

13   When I left I thanked her and put some money where Bessie would find it later. The painting had strength and I liked it; I would finish it at home in my studio. I liked the title, too—"Bessie Wholecheese of Galena."

REVIEWING THE READING   Answers will vary.

1. The main idea of this selection is implied rather than stated. Write the main idea in your own words.

See paragraphs, 2, 6, and 7.

2. What physical details does Fejes include about Bessie Wholecheese?

3. What do the details that Fejes gives about the house tell you about Bessie Wholecheese?

See paragraphs 1, 2, and 5.

4. How do the details about Bessie Wholecheese's appearance and her house help you to form an opinion of her character?

UNDERSTANDING VOCABULARY

In paragraph 8, Fejes writes that she and Bessie Wholecheese "established an easy *rapport*." The word *rapport* is a French word which is pronounced RHA-POR, with the final *t* silent. Meaning "a relationship of mutual trust or emotional attraction," *rapport* suggests the important personal connection established between Fejes and her subject Bessie Wholecheese during their brief relationship.

REACTING CRITICALLY

1. Fejes describes Bessie Wholecheese as having "full womanly breasts" and a "round belly." She is surrounded by images of life—geranium plants, nursing pups, her daughter, and her newborn grandchild. Moreover, Fejes ties her symbolically to the hearth—the center of life and warmth in the home. What do these images suggest about what Bessie Wholecheese represents to Fejes?

2. The author Fejes does not tell her reader much about herself except that she is an artist painting a portrait of Bessie Wholecheese. However, she implies a contrast between herself and her subject. How does this contrast contribute to your understanding of Bessie Wholecheese and her life?

▓ UNFORGETTABLE MISS BESSIE

Carl T. Rowan

Before you read, think about a special teacher you have had. In the following essay,* syndicated columnist Carl T. Rowan recalls a special teacher who encouraged him to succeed. Born in 1925 in Ravenscroft, Tennessee, Rowan was formerly a director of the United States Information Agency and an ambassador to Finland. He is the author of several books, including *South of Freedom* (1952), *Wait Till Next Year: The Life Story of Jackie Robinson* (1960), and *Just Between Us Blacks* (1974).

Bracketed annotations may vary.

As you read, bracket [ ] passages that describe Miss Bessie's teaching.

1   She was only about five feet tall and probably never weighed more than 110 pounds, but [Miss Bessie was a towering presence in the classroom. She was the only woman tough enough to make me read *Beowulf* and think for a few foolish days that I liked it.] From 1938 to 1942, when I attended Bernard High

---

*Reprinted with permission from the March 1985 *Reader's Digest*. Copyright © 1985 by The Reader's Digest Assn. Inc.

School in McMinnville, Tenn., [she taught me English, history, civics—and a lot more than I realized.]

2   I shall never forget the day she scolded me into reading *Beowulf.*

3   "But Miss Bessie," I complained, "I ain't much interested in it."

4   [Her large brown eyes became daggerish slits. "Boy," she said, "how dare you say 'ain't' to me! I've taught you better than that."]

5   "Miss Bessie," I pleaded, "I'm trying to make first-string end on the football team, and if I go around saying 'it isn't' and 'they aren't,' the guys are gonna laugh me off the squad."

6   "Boy," she responded, "you'll play football because you have guts. [But do you know what *really* takes guts? Refusing to lower your standards to those of the crowd. It takes guts to say you've got to live and be somebody fifty years after all the football games are over."]

7   I started saying "it isn't" and "they aren't," and I still made first-string end—and class valedictorian—without losing my buddies' respect.

8   [During her remarkable 44-year career, Mrs. Bessie Taylor Gwynn taught hundreds of economically deprived black youngsters—including my mother, my brother, my sisters and me.] I remember her now with gratitude and affection—especially in this era when Americans are so wrought-up about a "rising tide of mediocrity" in public education and the problems of finding competent, caring teachers. [Miss Bessie was an example of an informed, dedicated teacher, a blessing to children and an asset to the nation.]

9   Born in 1895, in poverty, she grew up in Athens, Ala., where there was no public school for blacks. She attended Trinity School, a private institution for blacks run by the American Missionary Association, and in 1911 graduated from the Normal School (a "super" high school) at Fisk University in Nashville. Mrs. Gwynn, the essence of pride and privacy, never talked about her years in Athens; only in the months before her death did she reveal that she had never attended Fisk University itself because she could not afford the four-year course.

10   At Normal School she learned a lot about Shakespeare, but most of all about the profound importance of education—especially, for a people trying to move up from slavery. ["What you put in your head, boy," she once said, "can never be pulled out by the Ku Klux Klan, the Congress or anybody."]

11   [Miss Bessie's bearing of dignity told anyone who met her that she was "educated" in the best sense of the word. There was never a discipline problem in her classes. We didn't dare mess with a woman who knew about the Battle of Hastings, the Magna Charta and the Bill of Rights—and who could also play the piano.]

12   [This frail-looking woman could make sense of Shakespeare, Milton, Voltaire, and bring to life Booker T. Washington and W. E. B. DuBois. Believing that it was important to know who the officials were that spent taxpayers' money and made public policy, she made us memorize the names of everyone on the Supreme Court and in the President's Cabinet. It could be embarrassing to be unprepared when Miss Bessie said, "Get up and tell the class who Frances Perkins is and what you think about her."]

13   Miss Bessie knew that my family, like so many others during the Depression, couldn't afford to subscribe to a newspaper. She knew we didn't even own a radio. [Still, she prodded me to "look out for your future and find some way to keep up with what's going on in the world."] So I became a delivery boy for the Chattanooga *Times.* I rarely made a dollar a week, but I got to read a newspaper every day.

14   [Miss Bessie noticed things that had nothing to do with schoolwork, but were vital to a youngster's development. Once a few classmates made fun of my frayed, hand-me-down overcoat, calling me "Strings." As I was leaving school, Miss Bessie patted me on the back of that old overcoat and said, "Carl, never fret about what you *don't* have. Just make the most of what you *do* have—a brain."]

15   Among the things that I did not have was electricity in the little frame house that my father had built for $400 with his World War I bonus. [But because of her inspiration, I spent many hours squinting beside a kerosene lamp reading Shakespeare and Thoreau, Samuel Pepys and William Cullen Bryant.]

16   No one in my family had ever graduated from high school, so there was no tradition of commitment to learning for me to lean on. Like millions of youngsters in today's ghettos and barrios, [I needed the push and stimulation of a teacher who truly cared. Miss Bessie gave plenty of both, as she immersed me in a wonderful world of similes, metaphors and even onomatopoeia. She led me to believe that I could write sonnets as well as Shakespeare, or iambic-pentameter verse to put Alexander Pope to shame.]

17   In those days the McMinnville school system was rigidly "Jim Crow," and poor black children had to struggle to put anything in their heads. Our high school was only slightly larger than the once-typical little red schoolhouse, and its library was outrageously inadequate—so small, I like to say, that if two students were in it and one wanted to turn a page, the other one had to step outside.

18   Negroes, as we were called then, were not allowed in the town library, except to mop floors or dust tables. But through one of those secret Old South arrangements between whites of conscience and blacks of stature, [Miss Bessie kept getting books smuggled out of the white library. That is how she introduced me to the Brontës, Byron, Coleridge, Keats and Tennyson. "If you don't read, you can't write, and if you can't write, you might as well stop dreaming." Miss Bessie once told me.]

19   [So I read whatever Miss Bessie told me to, and tried to remember the things she insisted that I store away. Forty-five years later, I can still recite her "truths to live by,"] such as Henry Wadsworth Longfellow's lines from "The Ladder of St. Augustine":

20   *The heights by great men reached and kept*
      Were not attained by sudden flight,
      But they, while their companions slept,
      Were toiling upward in the night.

21   [Years later, her inspiration, prodding, anger, cajoling and almost osmotic infusion of learning finally led] to that lovely day when Miss Bessie dropped me a note saying, "I'm so proud to read your column in the Nashville *Tennessean*."

22   Miss Bessie was a spry 80 when I went back to McMinnville and visited her in a senior citizens' apartment building. Pointing out proudly that her building was racially integrated, she reached for two glasses and a pint of bourbon. I was momentarily shocked, because it would have been scandalous in the 1930s and '40s for word to get out that a teacher drank, and nobody had ever raised a rumor that Miss Bessie did.

23   I felt a new sense of equality as she lifted her glass to mine. Then she revealed a softness and compassion that I had never known as a student.

24   ["I've never forgotten that examination day," she said, "when Buster Martin held up seven fingers, obviously asking you for help with question number seven,

'Name a common carrier.' I can still picture you looking at your exam paper and humming a few bars of 'Chattanooga Choo Choo.' I was so tickled, I couldn't punish either of you.''']

25   Miss Bessie was telling me, with bourbon-laced grace, that I never fooled her for a moment.

26   When Miss Bessie died in 1980, at age 85, hundreds of her former students mourned. [They knew the measure of a great teacher: love and motivation. Her wisdom and influence had rippled out across generations.]

27   Some of her students who might normally have been doomed to poverty went on to become doctors, dentists and college professors. Many, guided by Miss Bessie's example, became public-school teachers.

28   ["The memory of Miss Bessie and how she conducted her classroom did more for me than anything I learned in college," recalls Gladys Wood of Knoxville, Tenn., a highly respected English teacher who spent 43 years in the state's school system. "So many times, when I faced a difficult classroom problem, I asked myself, *How would Miss Bessie deal with this?* And I'd remember that she would handle it with laughter and love."]

29   No child can get all the necessary support at home, and millions of poor children get *no* support at all. [That is what makes a wise, educated, warm-hearted teacher like Miss Bessie so vital to the minds, hearts and souls of this country's children.]

REVIEWING THE READING   Answers will vary.

1. Reread the first paragraph carefully. What is the main idea of this paragraph—and also of Rowan's entire essay? Underline this main idea.

2. Underline the topic sentence, or main idea, of paragraph 14. What example supports this topic sentence?

See paragraphs 1, 4, and 12.

3. What does Miss Bessie look like?

See paragraphs 22–25.

4. What incident reveals Miss Bessie's compassion and understanding to Rowan years after he was her student?

5. What qualities make Miss Bessie an outstanding teacher? (Name at least three.) What details support each quality?

6. In your opinion, what is the most important "lesson" that Miss Bessie teaches her students?

UNDERSTANDING VOCABULARY

Rowan's essay includes several words that may be unfamiliar to you. For instance, the following paragraph includes several words that may be difficult for you:

> Years later, her inspiration, *prodding,* anger, *cajoling* and almost *osmotic infusion* of learning finally led to that lovely day when Miss Bessie dropped me a note saying, "I'm so proud to read your column in the Nashville *Tennessean.*"

Now, reread the following revision of this paragraph with more familiar words substituted for the difficult ones:

> Years later, her inspiration, *pushing,* anger, *begging,* and almost *osmosis-like exchange* of learning finally led to that lovely day when Miss Bessie

dropped me a note saying, "I'm so proud to read your column in the Nashville *Tennessean.*"

Add to your vocabulary list one or two of these words—or any other words that you would like to remember from the reading.

REACTING CRITICALLY

1. Sometimes you need to use information stated in a reading to help you "fill in gaps" for information that is not stated. When you use this process, you are *inferring* information or *drawing conclusions.* What information does Rowan include to help you infer what conditions were like for blacks in Tennessee in the 1930's and 1940's.

2. Coincidentally, the characters described by both Fejes and Rowan share the same name—Bessie. What other qualities do these women share? In what ways are they different?

A CELEBRATION OF GRANDFATHERS
Rudolfo A. Anaya

Before you read, think about your own grandfather, your grandmother, or some older person who is important to you. In the following selection and in his award-winning novel *Bless Me, Ultima* (1972), Rudolfo A. Anaya has written with understanding and sensitivity about older people. Here, he remembers and describes his own grandfather.

Text annotations will vary.

As you read, underline passages that reveal the appearance and actions of Anaya's grandfather.

1   *"Buenos días le de Dios, abuelo."* God give you a good day, grandfather. This is how I was taught as a child to greet my grandfather, or any grown person. It was a greeting of respect, a cultural value to be passed on from generation to generation, this respect for the old ones.

Main Idea

2   The old people I remember from my childhood were strong in their beliefs, and as we lived daily with them we learned a wise path of life to follow. They had something important to share with the young, and when they spoke the young listened. These old *abuelos* and *abuelitas* had worked the earth all their lives, and so they knew the value of nurturing, they knew the sensitivity of the earth. The daily struggle called for cooperation, and so every person contributed to the social fabric, and each person was respected for his contribution. . . .

3   My grandfather was a plain man, a farmer from Puerto de Luna on the Pecos River. He was probably a descendant of those people who spilled over the mountain from Taos, following the Pecos River in search of farmland. There in that river valley he settled and raised a large family.

4   Bearded and walrus-mustached, he stood five feet tall, but to me as a child he was a giant. I remember him most for his silence. In the summers my parents sent me to live with him on his farm, for I was to learn the ways of a farmer. My uncles also lived in that valley, the valley called Puerto de Luna, there where only the flow of the river and the whispering of the wind marked time. For me it was a magical place.

5   I remember once, while out hoeing the fields, I came upon an anthill, and before I knew it I was badly bitten. After he had covered my welts with the cool

mud from the irrigation ditch, my grandfather calmly said: "Know where you stand." That is the way he spoke, in short phrases, to the point.

6   One very dry summer, the river dried to a trickle, there was no water for the fields. The young plants withered and died. In my sadness and with the impulse of youth I said, "I wish it would rain!" My grandfather touched me, looked up into the sky and whispered, "Pray for rain." In his language there was a difference. He felt connected to the cycles that brought the rain or kept it from us. His prayer was a meaningful action, because he was a participant with the forces that filled our world, he was not a bystander.

7   A young man died at the village one summer. A very tragic death. He was dragged by his horse. When he was found I cried, for the boy was my friend. I did not understand why death had come to one so young. My grandfather took me aside and said: "Think of the death of the trees and the fields in the fall. The leaves fall, and everything rests, as if dead. But they bloom again in the spring. Death is only this small transformation in life."

Main Idea

8   These are the things I remember, these fleeting images, few words.

9   I remember him driving his horse-drawn wagon into Santa Rosa in the fall when he brought his harvest produce to sell in the town. What a tower of strength seemed to come in that small man huddled on the seat of the giant wagon. One click of his tongue and the horses obeyed, stopped or turned as he wished. He never raised his whip. How unlike today when so much teaching is done with loud words and threatening hands.

10   I would run to greet the wagon, and the wagon would stop. *"Buenos días le de Dios, abuelo,"* I would say. This was the prescribed greeting of esteem and respect. Only after the greeting was given could we approach these venerable old people. *"Buenos días te de Dios, mi hijo,"* he would answer and smile, and then I could jump up on the wagon and sit at his side. Then I, too, became a king as I rode next to the old man who smelled of earth and sweat and the other deep aromas from the orchards and fields of Puerto de Luna.

11   We were all sons and daughters to him. But today the sons and daughters are breaking with the past, putting aside *los abuelitos.* The old values are threatened, and threatened most where it comes to these relationships with the old people. If we don't take the time to watch and feel the years of their final transformation, a part of our humanity will be lessened.

12   I grew up speaking Spanish, and oh! how difficult it was to learn English. Sometimes I would give up and cry out that I couldn't learn. Then he would say, *"Ten paciencia."* Have patience. *Paciencia,* a word with the strength of centuries, a word that said that someday we would overcome. *Paciencia,* how soothing a word coming from this old man who could still sling hundred-pound bags over his shoulder, chop wood for hours on end, and hitch up his own horses and ride to town and back in one day.

13   "You have to learn the language of the Americanos," he said. "Me, I will live my last days in my valley. You will live in a new time, the time of the *gringos.*"

14   A new time did come, a new time is here. How will we form it so it is fruitful? We need to know where we stand. We need to speak softly and respect others, and to share what we have. We need to pray not for material gain, but for rain for the fields, for the sun to nurture growth, for nights in which we can sleep in peace, and for a harvest in which everyone can share. Simple lessons from a simple man. These lessons he learned from his past which was as deep and strong as the currents of the river of life, a life which could be stronger than death.

15   He was a man; he died. Not in his valley, but nevertheless cared for by his

sons and daughters and flocks of grandchildren. At the end, I would enter his room which carried the smell of medications and Vicks, the faint pungent odor of urine, and cigarette smoke. Gone were the aroma of the fields, the strength of his young manhood. Gone also was his patience in the face of crippling old age. Small things bothered him; he shouted or turned sour when his expectations were not met. It was because he could not care for himself, because he was returning to that state of childhood, and all those wishes and desires were now wrapped in a crumbling old body.

16   *"Ten paciencia,"* I once said to him, and he smiled. "I didn't know I would grow this old," he said. "Now, I can't even roll my own cigarettes."

17   I would sit and look at him and remember what was said of him when he was a young man. He could mount a wild horse and break it, and he could ride as far as any man. He could dance all night at a dance, then work the *acequia* the following day. He helped neighbors, they helped him. He married, raised children. Small legends, the kind that make up every man's life.

18   He was 94 when he died. Family, neighbors, and friends gathered; they all agreed he had led a rich life. I remembered the last years, the years he spent in bed. And as I remember now, I am reminded that it is too easy to romanticize old age. Sometimes we forget the pain of the transformation into old age, we forget the natural breaking down of the body.

19   Real life takes into account the natural cycle of growth and change. My grandfather pointed to the leaves falling from the tree. So time brings with its transformation the often painful, wearing-down process. Vision blurs, health wanes; even the act of walking carries with it the painful reminder of the autumn of life. But this process is something to be faced, not something to be hidden away by false images. Yes, the old can be young at heart, but in their own way, with their own dignity. They do not have to copy the always-young image of the Hollywood star. . . .

20   I returned to Puerto de Luna last summer, to join the community in a celebration of the founding of the church. I drove by my grandfather's home, my uncles' ranches, the neglected adobe washing down into the earth from whence it came. And I wondered, how might the values of my grandfather's generation live in our own? What can we retain to see us through these hard times? I was to become a farmer, and I became a writer. As I plow and plant my words, do I nurture as my grandfather did in his fields and orchards? The answers are not simple.

21   "They don't make men like that anymore," is a phrase we hear when one does honor to a man. I am glad I knew my grandfather. I am glad there are still times when I can see him in my dreams, hear him in my reverie. Sometimes I think I catch a whiff of that earthy aroma that was his smell, . . . Then I smile. How strong these people were to leave such a lasting impression.

22   So, as I would greet my *abuelo* long ago, it would help us all to greet the old ones we know with this kind and respectful greeting: *"Buenos días le de Dios."*

REVIEWING THE READING   Answers will vary.

1. What main point does Anaya make about his grandfather?

2. Underline the topic sentence, or main idea, of paragraph 2. How does this main idea suggest the main idea of the essay?

3. Underline the main idea of paragraph 7, which occurs in the grandfather's statement.

4. Can you picture Anaya's grandfather in your mind? What does he look like?

5. What kind of person was Anaya's grandfather? What specific actions and words reveal his character?

6. Anaya's grandfather taught him several important lessons. What is one of these?

See paragraphs 12 and 16.

7. How do Anaya and his grandfather change places?

8. Anaya uses the grandfather's occupation of farming in a metaphorical or symbolic way in the essay. That is, he explains certain areas of life by comparing them to farming.

    a. What comparison does Anaya make in paragraph 7?

    b. What comparison does he suggest in paragraph 18?

UNDERSTANDING VOCABULARY

If you don't know Spanish, the Spanish words in this selection probably seem very "foreign" to you. And yet many English words trace their origins to the same sources as Spanish words. Nearly all Spanish words and many English words come from Latin sources. For example, the Spanish word *buenos* ("good") and the English words *benefit* ("good deed, advantage") and *benevolence* ("good will") come from similar sources. Moreover, the Spanish word *Dios*, which means "God," comes from the same source as the English word *deity*, also meaning "God." The Spanish word *días* (paragraphs 1 and 10) and *paciencia* (paragraphs 12 and 14) should also remind you of English words that you know. What are these words?

Notice also that the endings of Spanish nouns indicate whether the word is masculine or feminine. For example, *hijo* ("son"), *abuelo* ("grandfather"), and *gringo* ("American"–negative connotation) end in the masculine *o* whereas *abuelita* ("grandmother") ends in the feminine *a*. With these words, the masculine and feminine word endings are clearly related to the gender, or sex, of the grandfather and grandmother. However, the endings of many Spanish words have no connection to gender. For example, *acequias* ("irrigation ditches") and *paciencia* ("patience") both have feminine endings even though the male farmers worked the irrigation ditches and both men and women needed patience.

REACTING CRITICALLY

In your opinion, what different purposes did Anaya have in writing his essay? Remember that when you consider a writer's purpose(s), you must also consider the intended audience. Meet with a group of your classmates and make a list of these purposes. Then try to determine Anaya's *primary* purpose, giving reasons for your conclusion.

Responding in Writing

Use one of the following assignments as the basis for a paragraph or essay about an interesting person you know.

1. Write a description of an interesting person for a reader who has never met the person. You may want to write about a person from the mapping that you did at the start of this lesson. Or you may decide

to write about someone else—a person you met traveling, a fellow student or employee, or a teacher or some other person from your past. Be sure, though, to choose someone you have actually observed or can observe. As you write, answer these questions:

a. What does this person look like?

b. Describe this person's personality or character. How does he or she talk and act?

c. What is especially interesting, unusual, or significant about this person?

2. In his essay "Unforgettable Miss Bessie," Carl T. Rowan describes an ordinary person who is an extraordinary teacher and citizen. Have you had an outstanding teacher in high school or elementary school? Write a paragraph or brief essay nominating this teacher for an Outstanding Teaching Award.

   After stating your main idea, include three or four reasons that explain why this teacher should win an award. Be sure to support each reason with specific examples and details from your experience and observations. Remember that your purpose is to convince your audience—the judges—to give the teaching award to your nominee.

Revising Your Writing

As you revise your paragraph or essay, ask yourself these questions:

1. Is my main idea clearly stated? Is it narrow enough? Does it have both topic and assertion?

2. Have I supported my main idea with specific details or reasons? Do I need to add, delete, or rearrange details or reasons?

3. Do I have a clear sense of my purpose and audience?

You may want to exchange papers with a classmate and use these questions to evaluate each other's papers before you revise.

After you revise your paper, edit and proofread it for errors in usage, spelling, and punctuation. To help you "see" errors more easily, try one of these techniques:

1. Read your paper aloud.

2. Type your paper.

3. Read your sentences backward, one at a time, beginning with the last and working forward. (If you are using a word processor, begin reading at the end of your document and scroll backwards.)

4. Use a pointer (finger, pen, pencil, or cursor) to force yourself to look at each word on the page.

CHAPTER FOUR
Supporting Main Ideas

Well-written paragraphs have a main idea that is either stated in a topic sentence or clearly implied. To communicate convincingly, however, writers must also use facts and details that support the main idea. Read the following paragraph carefully, noticing the details that are used to support the main idea.

> It was a land tortured by weather. There were wet springs when days of pouring rain put creeks out of banks and washed away cotton and corn. At times, before the water could drain off, dust storms blew down from the western plains, clouding the sky and making mouths gritty. Summers were long, hot, dry—worst in the dog days of August, when creeks ran low and scummy and the earth cracked in the sun. The people learned to be grateful for the first cool days of fall, and to bundle up in hard winters when blue northers swept down across Kansas and Oklahoma. They shivered in their shacks and said there was "nothing between them and the North Pole but a bobbed-wire fence."

William Owens, *This Stubborn Soil*

Identify three specific details from this paragraph that support the main idea that the land was tortured by weather.

Answers will vary.

1. <u>**pouring rain put creeks out of banks**</u>

2. <u>**summers were long, hot, dry**</u>

3. <u>**blue northers swept down across Kansas and Oklahoma**</u>

These specific details about the weather make the main idea vivid and meaningful. The details tell us *how* the land was tortured by the weather. We learn that it was not floods, hurricanes, or earthquakes that the people feared but heat, dust storms, rain, and "blue northers."

FACTUAL AND SENSORY DETAILS

Notice the types of details that are included in the above reading. All of the details are much more specific than the general statement that expresses the main idea (the topic sentence). However, different types of specific details are used. Some are *factual* (dust storms came from the western plains and northers from Kansas and Oklahoma), which help the reader by giving him or her explicit, exact information. Factual details answer such questions as who, what, when, where, why, how, and how many. Often these details provide names, dates, places, numbers, measurements, or statistics. Other details are descriptive (gritty mouths, scummy creeks, cracked earth). Notice that the descriptive details are all *sensory*, appealing to sight, hearing, smell, taste, or touch. These details help the reader not only to visualize but also to hear, feel, smell, and taste what the writer is expressing. Poetry is full of these sensory details, but good prose is also enriched by their use.

A good descriptive paragraph has an effective balance of the two types of details—sensory and factual. Readers often need both types to comprehend fully the main idea. If we read only the general statement that expresses the main idea ("It was a land tortured by weather"), we know very little about the land or what kind of weather the people who lived there endured. The details that support the main idea, however, give us a vivid image of the effects the weather had on the people and land. If we had only the details, on the other hand, we would not be sure exactly what the author was saying about the land. The details without the main idea may leave us wondering what the point of the paragraph is. Thus, good writers and good readers are always concerned about the important relationship between general (main) ideas and specific (supporting) details. Look at the examples below:

EXAMPLES

A. General statement—The clerk looked tired and irritable.
   Factual detail—She had been working behind the busy perfume counter for ten hours.
   Sensory detail—Her feet ached, her voice was almost gone, and she thought that she could not stand another indecisive Christmas shopper.
B. General statement—The fight left the boxer badly injured.
   Factual detail—Four of his front teeth were missing.
   Sensory detail—Purple bruises marked his face, and his eyes were swollen shut.
C. General statement—It was a hot night.
   Factual detail—The temperature never dropped below 90°.
   Sensory detail—The slight breeze that stirred the curtains felt warm on my sweaty skin.

In the examples given above, the general statements are all rather vague and abstract. A tired clerk may be any number of different people in a variety of situations, a boxer may be injured in several different ways, and a hot night in Florida is not the same as a hot night in

Maine. The details that support these general statements communicate to the reader specifically what the writer means. The factual details help the reader *understand* the writer's meaning; the sensory details help the reader *experience* the writer's meaning. Working together, the two types of details enable the writer to communicate more exactly and effectively.

EXERCISE 4.1   First write a sentence using factual details to develop the general statement that is provided. Then, using sensory details, write a second sentence that develops the same general statement.

EXAMPLE

Child-care programs often fail to provide adequate care for the children who are left in their charge. (general)

a. Some employ only two care givers for as many as ten or twelve infants. (factual)

b. Others are located in dilapidated old buildings that are hot in summer and cold in winter. (sensory)

1. The unabridged dictionary was enormous.

   a. **It was over nine hundred pages long.** _____

   _____

   b. **The librarian could hardly lift it.** _____

   _____

2. The math section of the exam must have been very difficult.

   a. **Only five of the thirty students completed it.** _____

   _____

   b. **The others left the testing center looking limp and exhausted.** ___

   _____

3. The young athlete became an outstanding quarterback.

   a. **In his first season as a pro, he completed over 70 percent of the**

   passes he attempted. _____

   _____

   b. **Like homing pigeons, his long, soaring passes found the**

   receiver's hands. _____

   _____

4. The lawyer worked very hard.

   a. She seldom left the office before eight o'clock in the evening.

   _____

   _____

   b. Her days were a blur of letters, briefs, and telephone calls.

   _____

   _____

5. Traffic on the freeway has become a serious problem.

   a. Over 100,000 cars travel the freeway each weekday.

   _____

   _____

   b. Thousands of motorists fume in frustration as they slowly inch

   their way to work each morning.

   _____

6. The florist keeps his shop well stocked.

   a. He has seven different varieties of iris and three types of roses.

   _____

   _____

   b. The shop is a riot of bright reds, yellows, and purples and is

   filled with fragrant odors.

   _____

7. The train sped down the track.

   a. At times it reached speeds of eighty-five and ninety miles an

   hour.

   _____

   b. Passengers heard the steady hum of the wheels and saw

   telephone poles whizzing by.

   _____

8. The waiter was busy.

   a. **During one five-minute period, he served five customers and took three new orders.**

   b. **Without appearing to dash about, he seemed to be everywhere at once.**

9. It was a cold November.

   a. **The snow was two feet deep, and the temperature remained below freezing every day.**

   b. **People's breath froze in midair as they slogged to work through the crusty snow.**

10. Computers have changed our lives.

    a. **The stock market and the federal government use computers to keep records and make projections.**

    b. **The low hum of computers has become so common that few of us even hear it.**

Coordinate Details

One way to develop the main idea of a paragraph is to use coordinate, or equally specific, details. For example, the supporting details in the paragraph below are coordinate.

(1) Mexico offers visitors a world of contrasts. (2) Its pyramids and ancient ruins give us a glimpse of the past while its modern cities provide us with the best of today's technology. (3) Its mountains offer cool weather and majestic peaks while, only a few miles away, its beaches tempt us with brilliant sun and white sand. (4) Its elegant restaurants serve the most sophisticated continental cuisine while, across the street or down the block, sidewalk vendors sell the simplest of native foods. (5) Thus the traveler to Mexico is faced with a series of delightful decisions.

In this paragraph, the main idea, which is stated in sentence (1), is supported by three equally specific, or coordinate, supporting details: sentences (2), (3), and (4). Sentence (5) concludes the paragraph and reinforces the main idea. This paragraph can be diagrammed as shown in Figure 13.

FIGURE 13

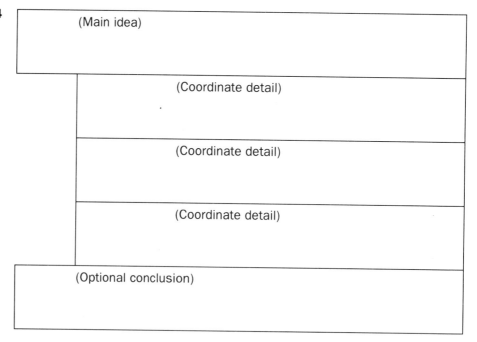

| Main idea (sentence 1) |
| Coordinate detail (sentence 2) |
| Coordinate detail (sentence 3) |
| Coordinate detail (sentence 4) |
| Conclusion (sentence 5) |

EXERCISE 4.2   Write a paragraph telling what you do in the morning to get ready to go to class or to work. Develop your paragraph with factual and sensory details that are coordinate, or equally specific. Use the block form below (Figure 14) to write your rough draft. You should write a different sentence in each block.

Student paragraphs will vary.

FIGURE 14

| (Main idea) |
| (Coordinate detail) |
| (Coordinate detail) |
| (Coordinate detail) |
| (Optional conclusion) |

Expanding Coordinate Details

Another important way to support the main idea of a paragraph is to expand coordinate details. That is, you may use two, three, or more major supporting details that are coordinate, or equally specific, and then develop each of the coordinate details further by adding more specific details.

This pattern is illustrated for you in the paragraph below. This paragraph contains three major coordinate details, each of which is further supported by a more specific detail. As you read the paragraph, try to decide which sentences express the major coordinate points and which express the more specific details.

(1) My father's death, which occurred when I was nine years old, had several important effects on me. (2) First of all, I felt great sadness and loneliness. (3) For the first few months, my loneliness was so great that I often dreamed that my father would miraculously return. (4) In addition, throughout the rest of my childhood, I was afraid of losing someone else whom I loved. (5) Whenever my mother was away from home, I was always nervous until she returned. (6) Finally, the loss of my father caused me to develop a greater sense of responsibility. (7) For example, I believed that with my father gone I was responsible for helping my mother with her chores. (8) My father's death, therefore, left me lonely, frightened, and responsible—a young child with adult feelings.

In this paragraph, the main idea is stated in sentence (1); the major coordinate details are stated in sentences (2), (4), and (6); the more specific supporting details occur in sentences (3), (5), and (7); and sentence (8) briefly summarizes the paragraph. This paragraph pattern can be diagrammed as shown in Figure 15.

FIGURE 15

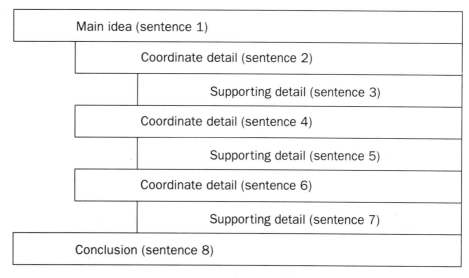

A variation of this pattern is illustrated in the following paragraph, which also contains three major coordinate details. However, in this pattern, each coordinate detail is supported by not one but two specific details. As you read the paragraph, try to determine which sentences contain the major coordinate details and which contain the more specific supporting details.

(1) The older woman who returns to school faces a number of problems. (2) For one thing, upon enrolling in college, she immediately becomes a minority. (3) She is no longer surrounded by her peers—other women who have shared experiences—but by young people, many of whom are the ages

of her own children. (4) Very often, the only person in a class who is her age is the instructor (and even he or she may be much younger). (5) In addition, an older woman who re-enters the academic world assumes the double burden of managing a household while being a student. (6) She may still have children at home or a husband who makes demands on her time. (7) If she is divorced or widowed, she faces problems such as managing finances, maintaining a car, and mowing the lawn. (8) Finally, a woman middle-aged or older who decides to complete her education faces the challenge of developing a new image of herself—one that is not related to her roles as wife and mother. (9) This problem may prove to be the most difficult of all, for it is not easy to assume a new identity, especially if the former one has been comfortable and secure. (10) To make the transition from housewife to student, a woman must think of herself as an individual rather than as a person whose identity depends on her relationships to other people. (11) Although her maturity may well prove to be an asset as she continues her studies, the older co-ed initially finds herself in a challenging situation.

In this paragraph, the main idea is stated in sentence (1); the major coordinate details are stated in sentences (2), (5), and (8); more specific supporting details are stated in sentences (3) and (4), (6) and (7), and (9) and (10); and the concluding statement comes in sentence (11). This paragraph can be illustrated as shown in Figure 16.

FIGURE 16

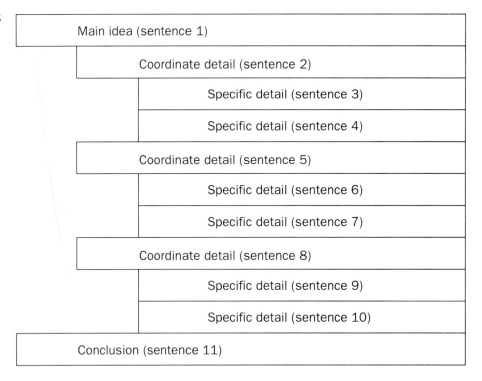

EXERCISE 4.3   Write a paragraph telling what you like about your favorite place to eat—a cafeteria, a restaurant, or your home. Use both factual and sensory details, and develop your paragraph according to the model you have just studied. Use two or three coordinate details, developing each with one or, better yet, two more specific details. Use the block form shown in Figure 17 to write your rough draft. You should write a different sentence in each block, but you may not need to use all of the blocks.

Student paragraphs will vary.

FIGURE 17

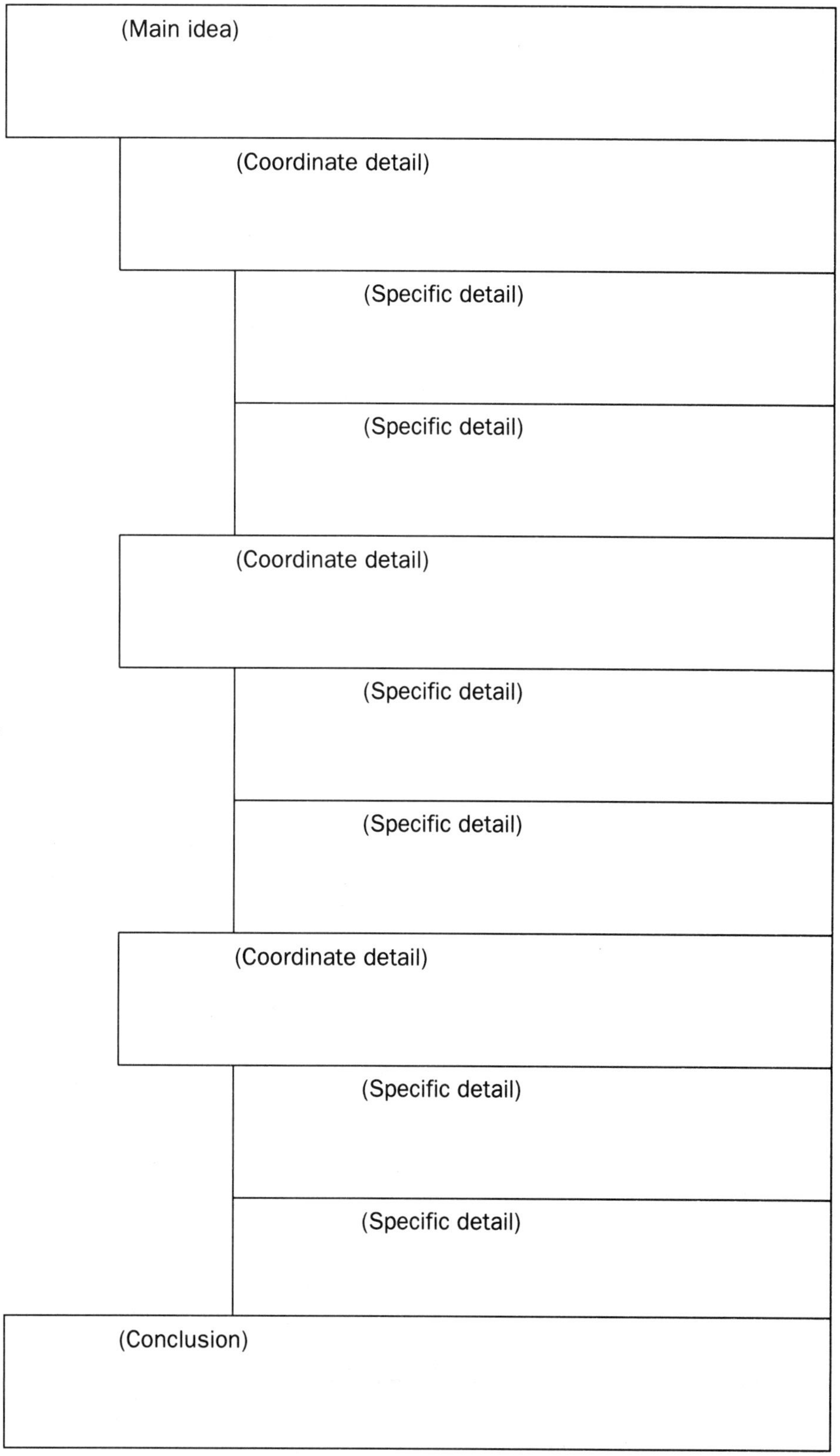

(Main idea)

(Coordinate detail)

(Specific detail)

(Specific detail)

(Coordinate detail)

(Specific detail)

(Specific detail)

(Coordinate detail)

(Specific detail)

(Specific detail)

(Conclusion)

Increasingly Specific Details

Another way to develop the main idea of a paragraph is to use a series of increasingly specific details. In this pattern, each detail is more specific than the one before it. An example of this pattern is found in the following paragraph:

> (1) Clothes make the woman as well as the man. (2) Many business and professional women are realizing that clothes are an asset not just to their appearance but also to their careers. (3) A female lawyer or doctor must select clothes that inspire confidence in her clients or patients. (4) Well-cut suits or dresses, and tasteful accessories help reflect the image of competence that people expect in doctors and lawyers.

In this paragraph the main idea, which is stated in sentence (1), is a general statement about clothes and women. Sentence (2) is more specific, narrowing to the effect that clothes have on the careers of business and professional women. Sentence (3) is still more specific, focusing on women in two particular professions, medicine and law. Finally, sentence (4) cites specific types of clothing that are appropriate for female doctors and lawyers to wear to work. (See Figure 18.)

FIGURE 18

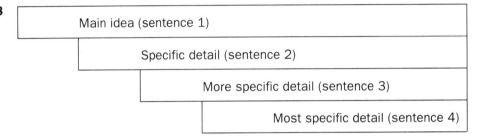

Main idea (sentence 1)

Specific detail (sentence 2)

More specific detail (sentence 3)

Most specific detail (sentence 4)

EXERCISE 4.4

Student paragraphs will vary.

Write a paragraph describing your favorite clothing—what you most enjoy wearing. Develop your paragraph with factual and sensory details that are increasingly specific. Use the following block form (Figure 19) to write your rough draft. Write a different sentence in each block.

FIGURE 19

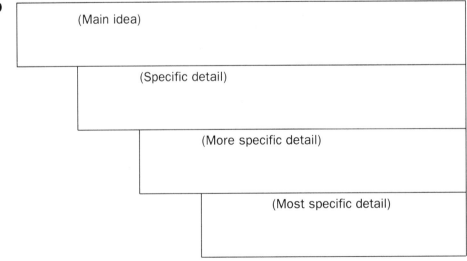

(Main idea)

(Specific detail)

(More specific detail)

(Most specific detail)

■ **EXERCISE 4.5**   The following paragraphs were written by freshman English students.
Read each paragraph and then answer the questions that follow.

Answers will vary.

PARAGRAPH A

On a sunny Sunday afternoon the sandy beach attracts several different
types of visitors. Young mothers go to the beach to take their children to
swim and surf in the warm water. Teen-age girls go to lie down on the sandy
beach to get a sun tan and to watch the beauty of the blue water. Young men
and teen-age boys go to play on the sand dunes with their four-wheel-drive
trucks to see which truck doesn't get stuck. Others, like me, just go to watch
the pretty girls sun bathing on the sand dunes.

Paul Noyola

1. What is the main idea of the paragraph?

   On a sunny Sunday afternoon the sandy beach attracts several different

   types of visitors.

2. Are the supporting details equal or unequal in importance? In other
   words, are the details coordinate? Or are some more specific than
   others?

   Details are equal (coordinate).

3. In the space below, briefly list three supporting details.

   a. **Young mothers take their children to swim and surf.**

   b. **Teen-age girls go to get a tan and watch the water.**

   c. **Young men and teen-age boys go to play on the sand with their four-**

   wheel-drive trucks.

PARAGRAPH B

The computer is a workhorse. It is generally capable of working twenty-
four hours a day. It does not ask for raises, breaks, or time off from work. A
computer will do thousands of tasks exactly the same way, in most cases
without any mistakes. It is also much faster than humans. Computers are
also able to perform dangerous, boring, or routine jobs. Of course, there are
some computer errors or equipment failures, but not as many as we might
think. In fact, most computer errors are caused by the users themselves, not
by the computer.

Christy Till, adapted

1. What is the main idea of the paragraph?

The computer is a workhorse.

_____

2. What are the five coordinate details in the paragraph?

a. **It is generally capable of working twenty-four hours a day.**

_____

b. **It does not ask for raises, breaks, or time off from work.**

_____

c. **A computer will do thousands of tasks exactly the same way, in**

   most cases without any mistakes.

d. **It is also much faster than humans.**

_____

e. **Computers are also able to perform dangerous, boring, or routine**

   jobs.

PARAGRAPH C

Two of the benefits of the computer are quickness and accuracy. Many different functions can be performed at the same time, thus increasing speed. For example, a computer can transmit the contents of an entire encyclopedia in a few seconds. A computer can also perform repetitive functions with flawless accuracy. For example, if a robotic arm is used to make a weld on cars at an automobile factory, the weld can be performed without the slightest variation. These characteristics of the computer help business increase productivity, which is one of the main objectives of the computer.

Royce Lee Brooks, Jr., _adapted_

1. What is the main idea of this paragraph?

Two of the benefits of the computer are quickness and accuracy.

_____

2. This paragraph includes both major coordinate details and more specific supporting details. What are the two major coordinate details in the paragraph?

a. **Many different functions can be performed at the same time,**

   thus increasing speed.

b. **A computer can also perform repetitive functions with flawless**

   accuracy.

3. Each major coordinate detail is developed by a more specific supporting detail. Fill in the diagram in Figure 20 to show the relation
   ships among the sentences in this paragraph.

FIGURE 20

Two of the benefits of the computer are quickness and accuracy.

Many different functions can be performed at the same time, thus increasing speed.

For example, a computer can transmit the contents of an entire encyclopedia in a few seconds.

A computer can also perform repetitive functions with flawless accuracy.

For example, if a robotic arm is used to make a weld on cars at an automobile factory, the weld can be performed without the slightest variation.

These characteristics of the computer help businesses increase productivity, which is one of the main objectives of the computer.

■ EXERCISE 4.6   The following paragraphs were taken from freshman textbooks. Read each paragraph and then answer the questions that follow it.

PARAGRAPH A

How do you write a rough draft? There is no simple way to do it; there are several approaches, including no doubt some which no one has tried yet. You will find some writers who say they begin by writing and rewriting their introduction until they get their thesis, purpose, and plan stated clearly and their relationship with their readers established. They believe that once they get the opening in reasonably good shape they can write the rest of the paper relatively easily. You will find other writers who state that they try to write the end of their paper first in the belief that it is easier to write the rest once they know the final idea they want to lead up to. You will find still others who say that they begin anywhere they can in the hope that once they start writing they can more easily pull their best ideas from the unconscious. They are all right—up to a point. Writers write rough drafts just about any way they can.

Thomas E. Pearsall and Donald H. Cunningham, *The Fundamentals of Good Writing*

1. What is the main idea of this paragraph?

   There are several approaches to writing rough drafts.

2. In the spaces below, rewrite in your own words the major supporting ideas.

   a. **Some writers begin their rough draft by writing and rewriting**

      their introduction.

   b. **Others write the conclusion of their paper first.**

   c. **Still others begin wherever they can in order to get started.**

PARAGRAPH B

Against Britain's armies of well-trained regulars, the Patriots seemed ill-matched. For one thing, the soldiers of the Continental Army had little experience in military tactics and fighting in open battle. Their training had been limited largely to frontier warfare against the Indians and the French. Their officers, too, had little experience compared to British officers. What is more, the Continental Army was loosely organized. Patriots had joined up, not because they had been ordered to do so, but of their own free will. Such volunteers felt free to return to their homes whenever their short terms of service were finished. As a result, the leaders of the army could hardly tell from day to day how many troops were under their command. Also, the colonies had no real navy. Against the strongest navy in the world the Americans could send not one first-class fighting ship.

Howard B. Wilder et al., *This Is America's Story*

1. What is the main idea of this paragraph?

   Against Britain's armies of well-trained regulars, the Patriots

   seemed ill-matched.

2. This paragraph includes both coordinate and more specific supporting details. How many major coordinate details does it include?

   three

3. What are the coordinate details?

   a. **The Continental Army was inexperienced.**

   b. **The Continental Army was poorly organized.**

   c. **The colonies did not have a real navy.**

4. What more specific details support the first coordinate detail?

   a. **Their training was limited primarily to frontier fighting.**

   b. **Colonial officers were not as experienced as British officers.**

5. What more specific details support the second coordinate detail?

   a. **Colonists had joined the army voluntarily.**

   b. **These volunteers felt free to return home.**

   c. **Leaders could not predict the size and content of their army.**

PARAGRAPH C

The North and South were also divided on the issue of federal regulation of commerce. The North, which derived much of its income from commerce, wanted the federal government to be able to make protective commercial regulations and to use a low tariff on imports as a source of revenue. On the other hand, the South, which made its money by exporting staple produce, such as tobacco and rice, feared that a government with the power to regulate commerce might legislate high export duties on such items. The South therefore demanded that all acts regulating commerce be passed by a two-thirds majority in Congress. The South also demanded assurance that Congress would not interfere with the slave trade.

Rebecca Brooks Gruver, *An American History*

1. What is the main idea of the paragraph?

   The North and South were divided on the issue of federal regulation

   of commerce.

2. How many major coordinate details does the paragraph contain?

   two

3. What are the coordinate details?

   a. **The North . . . wanted the federal government to be able to make**

      protective commercial regulations and to use a low tariff on imports

      as a source of revenue.

   b. **The South . . . feared that a government with the power to regulate**

      commerce might legislate high export duties.

4. Which coordinate detail is supported by more specific details?

   the second

5. In your own words, write one of these specific supporting details.

   (Answers will vary.)

OUTLINING SUPPORTING DETAILS

An outline is essentially a visual representation of general and specific relationships. General statements form the main headings of an outline, and specific statements form the subheadings. But, to outline, you must determine the relationships among the various supporting statements.

Since coordinate ideas are equal, they should be represented on your outline in the same (parallel) manner. If there are more specific details, these should be parallel to one another but subordinate to the more general statements. For example, social sciences, physical sciences, and humanities are three general categories of subjects you study in college. On an outline, therefore, you would arrange them as three equal, or coordinate, headings:

EXAMPLE

Social sciences
Physical sciences
Humanities

If you included some specific examples of each of these three general categories, you would arrange them under the appropriate headings. For example, if you wanted to list psychology, sociology, and anthropology under social sciences, you would list these equally specific examples in a coordinate pattern.

EXAMPLE

Social sciences
Psychology
Sociology
Anthropology

The numbers and letters you use in your outline should reinforce the relationships among the details.

EXAMPLE

I. Social sciences
   A. Psychology
   B. Sociology
   C. Anthropology

If you add additional details that are even more specific, you should indicate that these details are subordinate to the others but are coordinate to one another. For example, you could add two specific types of psychology courses and indicate this further level of subordination as shown in the formal outline below:

EXAMPLE

I. Social sciences
   A. Psychology
      1. Abnormal psychology
      2. Experimental psychology
   B. Sociology
   C. Anthropology

■ EXERCISE 4.7

Answers will vary.

Complete the formal outline below by adding the names of specific courses under the appropriate general headings. If necessary, use your college catalog to find this information.

I. Social science
   A. Psychology
      1. Abnormal Psychology
      2. Experimental Psychology
   B. Sociology

      1. **Sociology of the Family** _____

      2. **Sociology of Poverty** _____

   C. Anthropology

      1. **Cultural Anthropology** _____

      2. **Physical Anthropology** _____

II. Physical science

   A. **Biology** _____

      1. **Botany** _____

      2. **Zoology** _____

   B. **Chemistry** _____

      1. **Organic Chemistry** _____

      2. **Inorganic Chemistry** _____

III. Humanities

   A. **Art History** _____

   B. **American Literature** _____

   C. **Introduction to Philosophy** _____

Planning Outlines and Maps

Remember, however, that not all outlines have to be formal. If you are using an outline to plan what you are going to write, you can use any form that communicates clearly to you. Planning outlines can assume a variety of forms as long as they accurately communicate the relationships that exist among the different items of information. For example, you could use the informal outline or map in Figure 21 to represent the same information that is in the example formal outline on p. 85.

You could also communicate the same information in another way, as indicated in Figure 22 on p. 87.

The form that a planning outline or map takes depends on you, since you are the one who will be using it. Some people call these planning outlines "scratch" outlines because they can be little more than scratches on a paper if the writer who makes them understands what those scratches mean.

FIGURE 21

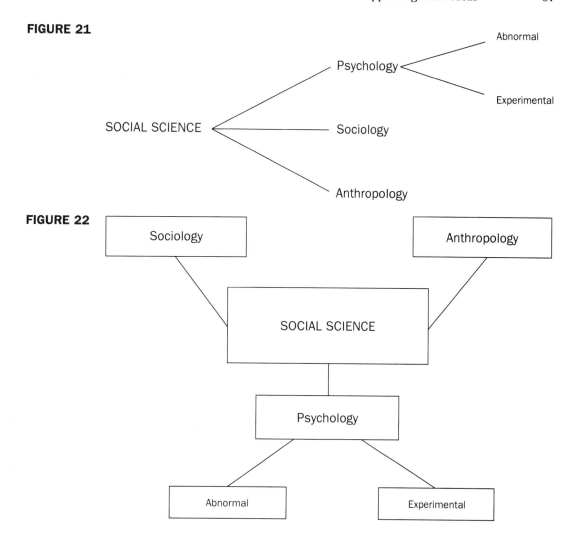

FIGURE 22

■ EXERCISE 4.8   On a sheet of paper, make an informal planning outline or map of a paragraph explaining to a new college student the different disciplines under which college courses are organized. If necessary, use your college catalog to find this information. You will need to indicate the same relationships between the general categories and specific courses that you used in the formal outline on page 86, but choose a different format—one similar to the informal outlines illustrated in Figures 21 and 22 or one that you make up yourself.

Outlines will vary.

RELEVANT AND IRRELEVANT DETAILS

In writing a paragraph, you should be sure that each detail you select supports—or is relevant to—the main idea. Details that do not support the main idea will distract and confuse your readers. A paragraph that includes only details that support its main idea has unity. You can make your paragraphs clearer to your reader if you make sure that they are unified.

In order to check a paragraph for unity, you can turn the main idea into a question and then check to see if each detail answers this question. If a detail does not answer the main idea question, it is probably irrelevant—off the subject—and should be omitted. The unity of the following paragraph, for example, is destroyed because it includes a supporting detail that does not develop the main idea statement. To determine which detail should be omitted, turn the main idea into the question "Why do I feel uncomfortable every time I walk into my sociology class?" Then read each detail to see if it answers this question.

Every time I walk into my sociology class I feel uncomfortable. First of all, I am the only non-American student in the class. Most of the discussions are about American culture, which I know very little about. The class is quite interesting, though. I very seldom speak in class because of my poor English. When we work in groups, I usually sit quietly and do not say anything because I am the only guy in our group. The majority of the class is girls, and I'm usually shy when it comes to being around girls. Another problem is that the teacher usually just calls on students to answer questions, so I try to hide behind someone who is taller and bigger than I am. The worst thing is that this is my second try for the class, so the teacher tries to ask me the questions. I hope the discomfort I have in this class will soon be over.

Peter Garangmaw

Did you see that the sentence "The class is quite interesting, though" does not answer the question that was asked? It does not develop the main idea of the paragraph and should therefore be omitted.

EXERCISE 4.9   Each of the following paragraphs includes an irrelevant sentence. Read each of these paragraphs carefully. Then turn the main idea into a question and check each sentence to determine whether or not it answers the question. In the spaces below the paragraphs, write your question and the sentence which does not belong.

PARAGRAPH A

"Sesame Street" is an educational and entertaining show for young kids. "Sesame Street" helps the kids to learn their ABCs, numbers, and small words such as cat, dog, and bird. The show has Muppets and people dressed up in costumes to keep the kids happy while they are learning. The show also has small cartoon characters with funny sounding voices to keep the child's eyes glued to the television while the character is spelling out words for the child to learn. The "Electric Company," which airs on most public broadcasting stations right after "Sesame Street," is also a good show for children. Children will enjoy "Sesame Street" even if it is educational.

Kevin Pannell

1. What question did you ask?

   Answer will vary.

2. What sentence does not belong?

   The "Electric Company," which airs on most public broadcasting

   stations right after "Sesame Street," is also a good show for children.

PARAGRAPH B

Each day a similar drama occurs in my history class. Just before class all the students are chatting to their friends about whom they met or what they did the day before. Once the professor enters the room, however, it becomes quite silent, except for the rustle of paper as the students prepare to jot down notes from the lecture. The professor soon begins to give notes with a deep voice like that of a sergeant in the army. Most students write busily, trying to remember everything that is important. However, not all students take notes. One guy daydreams about the miniskirted blonde who sits next to him. Another guy sits with his head on his desk, moaning because he drank too much at his fraternity party the night before. He belongs to the Beta fraternity, but the most popular fraternity on campus is the Kappa Alpha fraternity. Soon the bell rings, and once again the classroom is filled with the buzzing of students talking as they leave for their next classes.

1. What question did you ask?

    Answer will vary.

    _____

2. What sentence does not belong?

    He belongs to the Beta fraternity, but the most popular fraternity on

    campus is the Kappa Alpha fraternity.

    _____

READING AND WRITING ABOUT—

Places

Preparing: Observing, Listing, and Clustering—

Good writers are also close observers. They see and experience the world around them in such a way that they can share it with others. Moreover, they understand—or at least think about—the significance of the people, places, and events they observe.

Think about a place you would like to write about. You may choose this place because it is familiar or comfortable, because it is new or different, or because you like or dislike it.

Visit this place in person and observe it closely, listing specific details as you notice them. What do you see, hear, feel, taste, and touch as you observe this place? How do you react to this place? Why do you react as you do? Don't worry about the order in which you list the details you observe. At this point, you are merely gathering information for future use. For example, suppose you have chosen to write about Fifth Avenue in Manhattan on Christmas Eve. Your list of observations might include the following:

lights	expensive shops
decorations	skyscrapers
concrete	Christmas trees
crowds	furs
wind	tinsel
shoppers	marble
cars	voices
horns	cold
jewelry	trash
music	vendors
street people	gasoline fumes
St. Patrick's	odor of chestnuts
Tiffany's	taxis

Once you have made a fairly long list, look back over it. Do some of your details seem more important or more interesting than others? Are some related to one another? Draw lines connecting those that are related. Do these connecting lines indicate any relationships you had not thought of before? Can you identify one particular cluster, or group, of related details that interests you more than the others? Look, for example, at the details that have been connected in the list below. Do you see a relationship among these details?

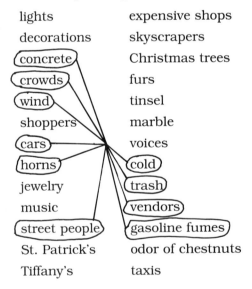

lights	expensive shops
decorations	skyscrapers
concrete	Christmas trees
crowds	furs
wind	tinsel
shoppers	marble
cars	voices
horns	cold
jewelry	trash
music	vendors
street people	gasoline fumes
St. Patrick's	odor of chestnuts
Tiffany's	taxis

After you have examined your list to identify connecting or related details, you should be able to make a statement that expresses the main ideas suggested by these related details. In the list above, for example, we have connected details related to the unpleasant aspects of life on a busy street in mid-Manhattan rather than to the glitter and excitement that also are found in this place, especially at Christmas time. We can express the idea suggested by this relationship in the following statement:

■ In the midst of the glamour and excitement of Manhattan on Christmas Eve, Fifth Avenue also has a harsh reality.

Notice that this main idea also makes a *significant* point about the place being observed.

In the following selections, notice the close observations that Eudora Welty and Anna Quindlen have made of the places that they describe. In addition, the details that these authors include suggest a special significance about each of these places.

■ THE LITTLE STORE
Eudora Welty

Before you read, think about a place you liked to visit when you were a child. In the following selection, Mississippi novelist and short-story writer Eudora Welty records her childhood memories of visiting a little store in her neighborhood.

As you read Welty's description of an early twentieth-century general store, try to relate her experience to your own. Although you may not have visited a store like this one, you may remember visiting a place that was interesting and exciting to you when you were a child.

1   Our Little Store rose right up from the sidewalk; standing in a street of family houses, it alone hadn't any yard in front, any tree or flowerbed. It was a plain frame building covered over with brick. Above the door, a little railed porch ran across on an upstairs level and four windows with shades were looking out. But I didn't catch on to those.

2   Running in out of the sun, you met what seemed total obscurity inside. There were almost tangible smells—licorice recently sucked in a child's cheek, dill-pickle brine that had leaked through a paper sack in a fresh trail across the wooden floor, ammonia-loaded ice that had been hoisted from wet croker sacks and slammed into the icebox with its sweet butter at the door, and perhaps the smell of still-untrapped mice.

3   Then through the motes of cracker dust, cornmeal dust, the Gold Dust of the Gold Dust Twins that the floor had been swept out with, the realities emerged. Shelves climbed to high reach all the way around, set out with not too much of any one thing but a lot of things—lard, molasses, vinegar, starch, matches, kerosene, Octagon soap (about a year's worth of octagon-shaped coupons cut out and saved brought a signet ring addressed to you in the mail. Furthermore, when the postman arrived at your door, he blew a whistle). It was up to you to remember what you came for, while your eye traveled from cans of sardines to ice cream salt to harmonicas to flypaper (over your head, batting around on a thread beneath the blades of the ceiling fan, stuck with its testimonial catch).

4   Its confusion may have been in the eye of its beholder. Enchantment is cast upon you by all those things you weren't supposed to have need for, it lures you close to wooden tops you'd outgrown, boy's marbles and agates in little net pouches, small rubber balls that wouldn't bounce straight, frazzly kite-string, clay bubble-pipes that would snap off in your teeth, the stiffest scissors. You could contemplate those long narrow boxes of sparklers gathering dust while you waited for it to be the Fourth of July or Christmas, and noisemakers in the shape of tin

frogs for somebody's birthday party you hadn't been invited to yet, and see that they were all marvelous.

5   You might not have even looked for Mr. Sessions when he came around his store cheese (as big as a doll's house) and in front of the counter looking for you. When you'd finally asked him for, and received from him in its paper bag, whatever single thing it was that you had been sent for, the nickel that was left over was yours to spend.

6   Down at a child's eye level, inside those glass jars with mouths in their sides through which the grocer could run his scoop or a child's hand might be invited to reach for a choice, were wineballs, all-day suckers, gumdrops, peppermints. Making a row under the glass of a counter were the Tootsie Rolls, Hershey Bars, Goo-Goo Clusters, Baby Ruths. And whatever was the name of those pastilles that came stacked in a cardboard cylinder with a cardboard lid? They were thin and dry, about the size of tiddlywinks, and in the shape of twisted rosettes. A kind of chocolate dust came out with them when you shook them out in your hand. Were they chocolate? I'd say rather they were brown. They didn't taste of anything at all, unless it was wood. Their attraction was the number you got for a nickel.

7   Making up your mind, you circled the store around and around, around the pickle barrel, around the tower of Cracker Jack boxes; Mr. Sessions had built it for us himself on top of a packing case, like a house of cards.

8   If it seemed too hot for Cracker Jacks, I might get a cold drink. Mr. Sessions might have already stationed himself by the cold-drinks barrel, like a mind reader. Deep in ice water that looked black as ink, murky shapes that would come up as Coca-Colas, Orange Crushes, and various flavors of pop, were all swimming around together. When you gave the word, Mr. Sessions plunged his bare arm in to the elbow and fished out your choice, first try. I favored a locally bottled concoction called Lake's Celery. (What else could it be called? It was made by a Mr. Lake out of celery. It was a popular drink here for years but was not known universally, as I found out when I arrived in New York and ordered one in the Astor bar.) You drank on the premises, with feet set wide apart to miss the drip, and gave him back his bottle.

9   But he didn't hurry you off. A standing scales was by the door, with a stack of iron weights and a brass slide on the balance arm, that would weigh you up to three hundred pounds. Mr. Sessions, whose hands were gentle and smelled of carbolic, would lift you up and set your feet on the platform, hold your loaf of bread for you, and taking his time while you stood still for him, he would make certain of what you weighed today. He could even remember what you weighed the last time, so you could subtract and announce how much you'd gained. That was goodbye.

REVIEWING THE READING   Answers will vary.

1. The overall impression, or main point, of Welty's essay is implied rather than stated. What is it?

2. The second paragraph is developed with sensory details. Underline these details. To what senses do they appeal?

3. In the third paragraph, Welty lists a number of factual details about the contents of the store. Underline these details.

4. Paragraphs 6 and 8 combine factual and sensory details effectively.

In paragraph 6, for example, instead of simply saying that the glass counter contained a row of candy, Welty gives the names of the particular candies (factual details). And she describes the pastilles (small flavored tablets or lozenges) as "thin and dry," tasting of wood (sensory details). Now, reread paragraph 8, underlining factual details and circling sensory details.

UNDERSTANDING VOCABULARY

1. Welty's description of the little Mississippi store is vivid and realistic. One way she achieves this realism is by including regional terms used primarily by Southerners. For example, *croker sack* is a regional term meaning "gunny sack" or "burlap bag."

2. Did you find any other words that you could not define from the context? Compare your list of unfamiliar words with the lists of one or two of your classmates. Then look these words up and add them, along with their pronunciation and definition, to your personal vocabulary list.

REACTING CRITICALLY

Welty describes the "Little Store" from the point of view of a child. How do you suppose an adult would have reacted to the store? Would an adult have seen, smelled, or tasted the same things? Why or why not? Is Welty's description idealized or realistic?

CITY KID

Anna Quindlen

Before you read, think about where you like to live. Are you a city person or a country person? At present, do you live in a rural area, a small town, a suburb, or a large city? Would you prefer to live somewhere else? Why or why not? In this selection from her collection of articles *Living Out Loud* (1988), Anna Quindlen admits she is a true "city kid." Quindlen is the author of the novel *Object Lessons* (1991) and has a regular column in the *New York Times.*

Annotations may vary. *As you read,* circle Quindlen's reasons for living in the city and underline her reasons for leaving the city. Does she want to stay or to leave?

1   In the city neighborhood in which I live, stoop sitting is the primary summer spectator sport. One night, I found myself doing it with my father. Together we looked out on the vista of brick row houses, ten-family tenement buildings, and dozens of other stoops filled with other families. Across the street three elderly women were watching from their windows, pillows cushioning the sills; a group of men were fixing the transmission of a beaten-up Plymouth, and a wiffle-ball game was under way with pieces of corrugated cardboard box serving as bases.

2   My father leaned back and said philosophically, "Your grandfather worked hard all his life so that none of his grandchildren would ever have to live like this." I knew he was right. America is a country that loves lawns, and I have become a city kid. When my parents were growing up, success could be measured by how far you managed to travel from the tenements and the cement

stoops. Lots of my friends have measured their success by whether they have managed to stay.

3   For many of us, these are the crunch years for setting up homes and setting down roots, when people dig in their heels or get out. In my neighborhood, the moving vans have been lumbering by like prehistoric beasts, dragging out antique bureaus and brass beds, taking them to places of grass and trees and lawn furniture.

4   These are places where the schools are good. The schools here aren't. Much of the green on our streets comes from glittery pieces of broken beer bottle. At 2:00 A.M. you can wake bolt upright to the sound of rap music, coming from big shiny boxes with detachable speakers, music so loud it sounds as if it's coming from the clock radio next to the bed.

5   So people leave—usually for the sake of the children. You can open the door and let them outside and not worry that they'll be run over by beer trucks, these people say. You can let them go sledding in winter and swimming in summer and in between they can burn leaves at the curb and catch whirligigs that spin down from the maple trees and split them and stick them to the bridges of their noses. They can trick-or-treat and go caroling. There will be a basketball hoop at the end of every driveway.

6   It sounds wonderful. Perhaps my kids would love it. Certainly their father thinks they would. It's just not for me. I grew up in the suburbs; I know about catching lightning bugs and putting them in an empty peanut butter jar with holes punched in the top, and having a permanently scuffed place in your backyard where home plate always is. I'm not going to say it's sterile and awful, and dull people live there. That's not true. It's just that, like the perfectly nice guy you meet on a blind date who would be great for your friend Carol but could move to Indianapolis for all you care, the suburbs and I have no chemistry. The first time I walked down Broadway, something deep inside me just said "Yes."

7   My "Yes" should be subordinated to what is best for my children, according to one school of thought. I may actually spend a few grades in that school—if I decide that its opinion does not reflect a Tom Sawyer fantasy about children that is way off base. My children seem to like some of the same things about the city streets that I do: the people constantly eddying around them, the shifting play of color and movement, the 78-rpm metabolism in a 33⅓ world. Maybe they would prefer a yard, and the smell of the grass when it's just been mowed. There is a certain pathos to the fact that it is a big deal excursion for them to visit the lawn at the local college on the hill.

8   Those are the philosophical considerations. For lots of people we know, the decision to move has been financial. It's pretty chilling to discover that real estate is a primary determinant of family size in New York, and that the only-child phenomenon is to some extent a byproduct of the one-bedroom apartment. Some people have told me the only way they would have room for two is to move to the suburbs. Some simply said that they did not want to answer any more questions from their three-year-olds about why disheveled strangers were calling them Satan the Devil Incarnate the Son of Richard Nixon.

9   So someday the van may come to our house for what I can't help thinking of as the longest trip of our lives. My kids will play with other kids who are just like them, on streets that are just like ours and just like the one where I played with kids just like me. Perhaps my chemistry, my metabolism, will change. Not long ago my closest friend, who was a city person as sure as I was, moved to a place out in the suburbs for business reasons. We agreed that she'd have to tolerate

it. Instead she bloomed. "It's so quiet and peaceful," she said happily over the phone. Exactly. That's my problem, right there.

REVIEWING THE READING   Answers will vary.

1. Quindlen states her main idea in the second paragraph and implies it in the concluding paragraph. State this main idea in your own words.

2. The first paragraph of this essay captures the reader's attention by relating a brief anecdote (a little story) about what Quindlen observed from her porch stoop one summer night. What details does she give to try to interest her readers?

3. Paragraphs 4 to 7 are particularly strong in both factual and sensory details. What are three factual details used in these paragraphs? What are three sensory details? To what various senses does Quindlen appeal?

4. List the reasons that Quindlen's family and friends give for leaving the city to move to the suburbs. Then make another list of the reasons why Quindlen prefers to remain in the city.

UNDERSTANDING VOCABULARY

1. In paragraph 7, the phrase "78-rpm metabolism [life processes] in a 33⅓ world" is a metaphor, or a comparison in which one of the things being compared is only suggested. To what is Quindlen comparing the speed of a record turntable? What is she saying with her comparison? (Note: A 78 rpm record makes 78 rotations per minute instead of the slower 33⅓.)

2. Do you need to add *metabolism* or any other words from Quindlen's essay to your personal vocabulary list? Take a few minutes to review all the words you have added to your list. Then work with a partner on these words.

REACTING CRITICALLY

In the last paragraph, Quindlen writes, "That's my problem, right there." But Quindlen *implies* this problem rather than directly stating it. What is her problem? In comparison to Welty in "The Little Store," does Quindlen idealize her surroundings or view them realistically?

Responding in Writing—

Write a description of a place that holds a special interest or significance for you. Try to observe this place before you write about it. (You may be able to use your prewriting.) If possible, write about the place you have chosen as it appears (or appeared) at a particular time. For example, just as Quindlen wrote about how her street looked as she viewed it from her front stoop on a summer night, you might write about a Kansas farm at daybreak, a New Orleans restaurant at noon, or a Boston shipyard or marketplace in the late afternoon.

Think of the main point or impression you want to make about this place, and be sure to make this point clear. You may state your main point near the beginning or the end of your essay, or you may imply it throughout. Remember to use specific factual and sensory details that support your main point.

The following specific assignments about place are based on the writing and thinking activities you worked on earlier in this chapter. Choose one as the basis for your essay:

1. Write a paragraph or essay about the place that you observed earlier. Look over your prewriting list to find details you can use and to discover the "point" you want to make about this place.

2. Write a paragraph or essay about a place you visited when you were a child. What did you notice about this place at the time? What did you see, hear, touch, smell, or taste? If you had first visited this place as an adult, would your point of view have been different?

3. Write an essay in which you explain the type of place that is "home" to you. Do you like to live in the country? The suburbs? The city? What are the major reasons for your choice? That is, why do you prefer this kind of home environment? What specifically do you like about this place? How does it appeal to your senses? In your essay, try to convince readers who have never seen the place to buy a home in the same area.

Revising Your Writing

Remember that some of the best writing that you do is rewriting. Exchange drafts with a classmate. Then answer the following questions about your classmate's draft.

1. What is the main idea or overall impression of the essay? Is it clearly stated or implied? How or where is the main idea expressed?

2. Does the paragraph or essay include specific details or reasons? Are the details both factual and sensory? (Do you as a reader have a sense of how the place looks, sounds, feels, smells, and tastes?) Which details are most effective? What details need to be added, omitted, or rearranged?

3. Does the writer have a clear sense of purpose and audience? What is the writer's purpose? Who is the audience? How can the writer make the purpose clearer to the audience?

When you and your partner have read each other's drafts, use your partner's responses to help you revise your draft.

Finally, edit and proofread your revised draft. Your editing will be more successful if you reread your paragraph or essay several times, concentrating on one feature, such as spelling, in each separate reading. When you have edited your paragraph or essay so that it is as clear and correct as possible, write or type your final copy and proofread it to be sure you have written exactly what you intended to write. Remember to read word by word during the proofreading stage.

CHAPTER FIVE
Reading and Writing Essays

Thus far in this book our primary concern has been the paragraph. But, as a college student, you are frequently required to read and write longer compositions, especially essays. Your knowledge of paragraph structure will be very helpful to you as you begin to work with essays because the basic structure of an essay is the same as that of a paragraph. An essay, like a paragraph, consists of an introduction, a body, and a conclusion. However, an essay is composed of a series of related paragraphs, whereas a paragraph consists of a series of related sentences.

A good essay is composed of *well-developed paragraphs*, which in turn develop the main idea of the essay. Many readers and writers make the mistake of ignoring the structure of the paragraph once it is part of an essay. Although the paragraphs that make up the body of an essay may not be able to stand alone as compositions, they often have essentially the same structure as a paragraph that is meant to stand on its own. Therefore, as you read and write essays, you will continue to use your knowledge of paragraphs.

The essay diagrammed in Figure 23 on p. 98 consists of five paragraphs: an introductory paragraph, three body paragraphs, and a concluding paragraph. The number of paragraphs varies widely from one essay to another. Some essays are very brief; others are quite long. But the five-paragraph essay serves as a convenient model.

INTRODUCTION: STATEMENT OF THESIS

Essays, like paragraphs, develop one main idea. The main idea of an essay is called a *thesis statement*, and it is expressed in the introduction, usually at the end of the introduction. Like the main idea of a paragraph, a thesis is a general statement. The general statement that serves as a thesis for an essay is often more general than the topic sentence of a paragraph but not so general as a thesis of a book.

FIGURE 23

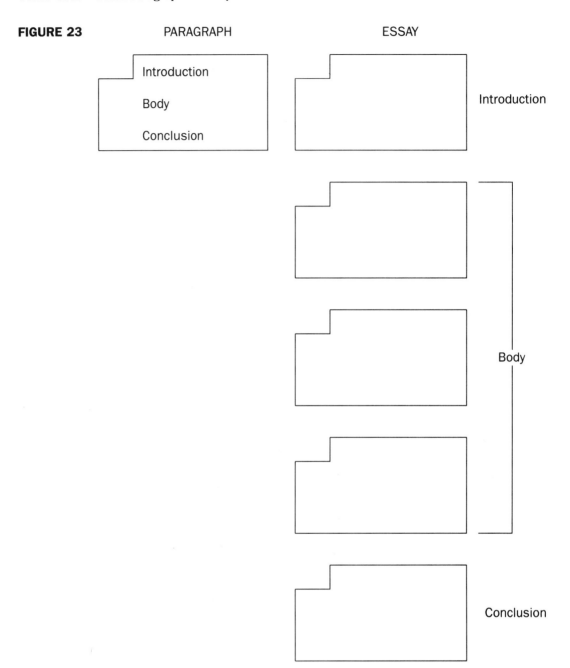

EXAMPLE

Topic sentence of a paragraph: My sixth-grade teacher was a strict
   disciplinarian.

Thesis of an essay: Discipline problems created a poor environment for learning in my high school.

Thesis of a book: One of the major problems with the U.S. system
   of education is its failure to deal effectively with discipline problems.

Notice that the topic sentence of the paragraph is limited to a particular person (sixth-grade teacher) and to a specific aspect of that person (role as disciplinarian). The paragraph that develops this topic

sentence will not merely describe the sixth-grade teacher but will focus on how he disciplined the class. In contrast, the thesis of the essay is broad enough to include a discussion of several problems that contributed to lack of discipline in the high school, but it is limited to a particular high school at a particular time and to the experience of one person. The essay that develops this thesis will not discuss every aspect of the writer's high school experience—just the problems associated with discipline in the school. The thesis of a book, however, is much broader, allowing for a complex, complete discussion of how the problem of discipline affects the entire school system of the United States.

Thus, the general statement that serves as the controlling idea of an essay should not be *too* general. In fact, many times the same idea that served as the topic sentence of a paragraph can be used effectively as the thesis of an essay. A very broad, vague, overly general statement is inappropriate as the thesis of an essay. If you narrow your main idea so that your focus is fairly limited, you will have less difficulty writing your essay and will write a better essay.

As a reader, you should look carefully at the introduction of an essay to determine the thesis. Although not all writers place the thesis statement in the introduction, most writers—especially writers of textbooks, newspapers, magazines, and reports—include in their introduction a thesis statement that explains clearly the point they wish to make. It is a good idea, therefore, to read the introduction very carefully, looking especially for the thesis statement. Since everything else in the essay will be related to the thesis, you must identify it before you can understand the essay as a whole.

Occasionally, a writer will not include a thesis statement. At least, he or she will not express the main idea in a single sentence that can be identified as a thesis. Just as a paragraph may have an implied rather than a stated topic sentence, an essay may have an implied rather than a stated thesis. But every essay has a main idea; if there is no stated thesis, you should formulate in your own words what you think the writer's thesis is. Read the introduction several times if necessary to determine what the subject is and what the writer is going to say about that subject. You may not understand clearly the remainder of the essay unless you begin your reading with a clear idea of the writer's thesis. You may also want to return to the introduction after you have read the entire essay (or chapter or article) in order to review the thesis statement. Sometimes after you have read an essay, its thesis statement will have more meaning. Reviewing the thesis after you have read an essay will also help you remember the essay's main points.

Writing Introductions

An introduction serves as a contract between a writer and his or her readers. In the introduction, a writer makes specific commitments that must then be fulfilled. The most important of these is the thesis statement, which commits the writer to a specific focus. In effect, it provides the reader with an accurate expectation of what the writer plans to do— the main idea that the writer plans to develop.

In general, a good introduction accomplishes three purposes:

1. It attracts the reader's interest.
2. It provides the reader with background information.
3. It focuses the reader's attention on the main idea of the essay.

For example, the following paragraph could serve as an introduction to an essay on the discipline problems that affected one person's high school education.

Background information

From 1982 to 1986, I attended an inner-city high school in Chicago. The school was located in an area that was rapidly changing from residential to commercial. It was an old, respected school that had educated the children of the families in the neighborhood for over fifty years. Many of the teachers were dedicated, competent professionals, who had taught in this school all of their professional lives. Others were inexperienced, young teachers who were encoun-

Transition

tering their first students. However, neither the experienced nor the inexperienced teachers were able to handle the undisciplined, unmotivated students who

Thesis statement

attended the school in the 1980s. As a result, discipline problems created a poor environment for learning in the high school.

Notice that the writer devotes several sentences to background information, supplying the reader with a context for what is to follow. The sentence about the problems the teachers had in controlling the students serves as a transition, focusing the reader's attention on the thesis statement that follows. The writer and the reader are now ready to explore this thesis statement in the body of the essay.

As a writer, you want your introduction to be not only clear but also interesting. A dull or trite introduction can discourage a reader from continuing to the main part of the essay. But attempts at cuteness and cleverness often fail, resulting in an introduction that is not only unclear but also embarrassingly inappropriate.

SUGGESTIONS FOR WRITING EFFECTIVE INTRODUCTIONS

1. Be clear and direct. (Clarity is more important than cleverness.)
2. Provide the background information your reader needs to understand your subject.
3. Avoid trite expressions, such as "in the world today" or "for as long as man has existed."
4. End your introduction with a clear statement of your thesis.

BODY: DEVELOPMENT OF THESIS

The body of a unified, coherent essay consists of a number of related paragraphs that develop the thesis. The individual sentences within each paragraph support the main idea (topic sentence) of the paragraph, and the paragraphs support the main idea (thesis) of the essay (see Figure 24).

A writer develops the topic sentence of a paragraph by discussing,

FIGURE 24

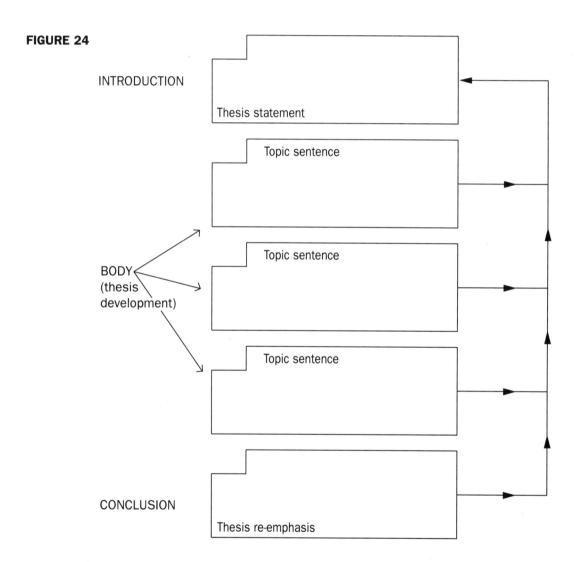

INTRODUCTION

Thesis statement

Topic sentence

BODY
(thesis
development)

Topic sentence

Topic sentence

CONCLUSION

Thesis re-emphasis

explaining, and expanding the idea that it expresses. A writer develops the thesis of an essay in the same way. Both topic sentences and thesis statements are general statements that must be supported by specific facts, details, and examples. In an essay, a writer usually devotes a paragraph to each *major* supporting point. Each of these supporting points is directly related to the thesis and helps develop it. But each major supporting point is also developed individually as a paragraph.

SUGGESTIONS FOR WRITING EFFECTIVE BODY PARAGRAPHS
1. Keep your thesis in mind at all times; each paragraph in the body of your essay should support and develop your thesis.
2. Structure each paragraph so that it has a topic sentence (stated or implied) that is fully developed by supporting details.
3. Avoid paragraphs of only one or two sentences. (Such paragraphs are usually underdeveloped or unnecessary.)
4. Vary the structure of the paragraphs in the body of your essay so that the topic sentence is not always the first sentence.
5. Vary the number of paragraphs in your essays. (Every essay does not have to have exactly five paragraphs.)

CONCLUSION: RE-EMPHASIS OF THESIS

The conclusion of an essay, like the conclusion of a paragraph, gives the reader a sense of completion. Conclusions usually refer to the introduction or, at least, re-emphasize in some way the thesis stated in the introduction. Often the conclusion briefly summarizes the thesis and the major supporting points. A good conclusion always confirms the audience's understanding of what they have read by reminding them of the writer's purpose. Like introductions, conclusions often provide readers with an overview.

For example, the paragraph below would effectively conclude the essay on discipline problems in the Chicago high school.

Recently I visited my parents in Chicago and drove past my old high school. Now a warehouse for textbooks, the building looks abandoned and dilapidated. Crude, obscene messages remain scrawled on the walls, and many of the windows are broken or missing. Evidently, the discipline problems finally defeated the valiant but discouraged teachers. I am glad the school is now closed, for learning had become impossible in that environment.

Conclusions should not be cute or trite or obvious. The best conclusions are appropriate, clearly written, and straightforward. They do not strain for an effect they cannot achieve (such as humor, cleverness, or brilliance). If you have not written a good essay, your conclusion cannot save it; however, a good essay can be damaged by an ineffective or inappropriate conclusion.

Writing Conclusions

Just as an introduction can be viewed as a contract between you and your reader, a conclusion reassures your reader that you have fulfilled your contract. Your closing paragraph should leave your reader with a sense of completion—with the feeling that you have done what you intended to do and have finished what you had to say.

Several different types of conclusions accomplish this purpose:

1. *Restatement of main idea.* The main idea may be re-emphasized or reinforced. If you choose this type of conclusion, however, be

sure not to merely repeat your thesis. You should vary the wording so that your conclusion is not too similar to your introduction, and you should also try to get beyond your thesis statement—to express an appropriate conclusion and to give your reader a sense of closure.

2. *General impression.* If your essay is basically a description of an experience or of some person, place, or thing, an effective conclusion might consist of a statement of the dominant impression you have attempted to convey. For example, if your essay about your high school is largely a description of what occurred to you when you were there, you might conclude with what you remember most clearly about the whole experience.

3. *Evaluation.* An essay may also conclude with a judgment based on the information presented. For example, you might end an essay on your high school by evaluating whether the experience was essentially negative or positive.

4. *Recommendation.* An essay can be concluded with a suggestion for some action the writer feels should be taken. This type of conclusion is especially appropriate if the main idea is a controversial statement or one that is persuasive in nature. For example, you might conclude your essay about your high school's discipline problems by recommending that a new administration be hired or a new school board be elected.

5. *Prediction.* Even though a conclusion is the final part of an essay, it can be used to make a prediction on the basis of the major points made in the essay. This prediction should be closely related to the content of the essay, giving a reasonable explanation of what may happen. For example, you might predict in the conclusion to your essay about your high school's problems that the school will be closed in the near future.

6. *Implications.* In a conclusion you can discuss the implications of the arguments and evidence you have presented. In other words, you can explain why what you've written is important.

Regardless of the type of conclusion you choose for your essay, the conclusion should re-emphasize your thesis. It should also be a clear signal to your reader that you have completed what you had to say. Following are some suggestions that will be helpful to you in writing conclusions.

SUGGESTIONS FOR WRITING EFFECTIVE CONCLUSIONS

1. Do not contradict the point you have made.
2. Do not introduce a new topic or new information.
3. Do not conclude with a cliché (such as "You can't teach an old dog new tricks").
4. Do not apologize for lack of knowledge, ability, or resources.
5. Do not use obvious transition words or phases such as *in conclusion, in summary,* and *as I have attempted to show.* You may, however, use less obvious transition words, such as *therefore, finally,* and *consequently.*

6. Do make your conclusion brief and to the point.
7. Do make the tone (serious, humorous, clever, straightforward, and so on) consistent with the overall tone of your essay.

FROM PARAGRAPH TO ESSAY

Read the following paragraph, which compares two different cities. Note especially the topic sentence and the major supporting points.

> <u>Moving from Detroit, Michigan, to Hobbs, New Mexico, was not easy.</u> First, I had to get used to the change in climate. Even though the weather in Michigan is not ideal, it was what I had known all my life, and I was used to the dampness and the cold in winter and the dampness and the heat in the summer. In Hobbs, any moisture evaporates immediately. And it is sometimes difficult to tell winter from summer since the two seasons are so much alike. My next problem was adjusting to life in a small town. Detroit is a busy, industrial city that never sleeps. Hobbs never wakes up. It is so quiet and small that I felt at first as though I were living on the fringe of civilization. But the biggest problem I had was the difference in time. I don't mean just the fact that Detroit is on Eastern Standard Time and Hobbs is on Mountain Standard Time. I mean fast versus slow. Everyone in Detroit is on the move—in a hurry, rushed, afraid of being late. In Hobbs, on the other hand, no one really cares what time it is. No one seems concerned about getting places on time, much less early. But now that I have lived in Hobbs for a year, I find that I too am slowing down. Moreover, I have found that I haven't left civilization. I've just moved to a different type—a drier, warmer, quieter, slower one.

EXERCISE 5.1   Answer the following questions about the paragraph you have just read.

1. What is the main idea of the paragraph?

   Moving from Detroit, Michigan, to Hobbs, New Mexico, was not

   easy.

2. Is the main idea expressed in a topic sentence? **yes**
3. Underline the topic sentence.
4. What are the major supporting points developed in the paragraph?

   a. **First, I had to get used to the change in climate.**

   b. **My next problem was adjusting to life in a small town.**

   c. **But the biggest problem I had was the difference in time.**

Now read the following essay, which has the same main idea as the paragraph you have just read. As you read, notice that the main difference between the paragraph and the essay is that the writer uses different paragraphs for each of the three major supporting points in the essay and that she uses many more details and examples to support each major point. Notice also that the author contrasts Hobbs with Detroit in each of the three paragraphs that make up the body of the essay. This pattern of organization is typical of many comparison/contrast essays.

1   I was born in Detroit, Michigan, and had lived there all of my life until I married and moved with my husband to Hobbs, New Mexico. The morning that my parents took us to the airport, they cried as if I were leaving the country and moving to a foreign land. Although I felt some apprehension, I thought that surely there could not be much difference between one state or city and another. After all, both Detroit and Hobbs are in the United States. People in both places speak English, eat hamburgers, and wear blue jeans. I felt confident that my life would be much the same. It did not take me long to discover, however, that moving from Detroit to Hobbs was not easy.

2   First, I had to get used to the change in climate. Even though the weather in Michigan is not ideal, it was what I had known all my life. I was used to the dampness and the cold in winter and the dampness and heat in summer. I accepted mildew and frizzy hair as facts of life. In Hobbs, any moisture that accidentally occurs immediately evaporates. Even in the early morning there is no dew on the grass, and a rainfall is a major event, celebrated and talked about for days. Fog and mist are absolutely unheard of. Day after day the sun shines brightly, even relentlessly, drying out everything. In fact, it is sometimes difficult to tell winter from summer because the two seasons are so much alike.

3   My next problem was adjusting to life in a small town. Detroit is a busy, industrial city that never sleeps. Hobbs never wakes up. It is so quiet and small that I felt at first as though I were living on the fringe of civilization. Instead of several major newspapers, a variety of local radio and television channels, and a choice of big name entertainers and shows, Hobbs has one daily newspaper, a small radio station, and a few movies. By ten o'clock at night almost everyone is at home. And everyone knows everyone else. In Detroit, I could go all over the city and never see anyone I knew—not even a familiar face. In Hobbs, I rarely see anything but familiar faces. A stranger in town is the source of real excitement—a cause for speculation and curiosity. In Hobbs I don't dare go to the supermarket (there are only a few) with my hair in curlers, for I am sure to see people I know. In Detroit I could be anonymous when I chose; in Hobbs I am part of a small, even intimate community.

4   But the biggest problem I had was the difference in time. I don't mean just the fact that Detroit is on Eastern Standard Time and Hobbs is on Mountain Standard Time. I mean fast versus slow. Everyone in Detroit is on the move—in a hurry, rushed, afraid of being late. In Hobbs, on the other hand, no one really cares what time it is. No one seems concerned about getting places on time, much less early. For example, soon after we arrived in Hobbs we were invited to a party. Conditioned by years of living in Detroit, where everyone strives to be punctual, my husband and I arrived at the party on time. The door was opened by a surprised hostess, who, dressed in a robe, was straightening the living room and preparing some last-minute snacks for the party. She very graciously invited us in and explained that the other guests would be arriving soon. (''Soon'' turned

out to be almost an hour later.) We sat uncomfortably in the deserted living room as the hostess finished dressing and preparing the food. When the other guests finally arrived, an hour after the appointed time, the party began, although guests continued to arrive late into the evening. I now realize that when people in Hobbs say a party begins at a certain time, they don't really mean at that exact time. The attitude toward time is so relaxed that it is almost impossible to be *late*. People just aren't terribly concerned with being punctual.

5   I have now lived in Hobbs for a year, and I find that I am slowing down, too. I don't drive as fast as I did; I don't worry if I am a few minutes late; and I certainly don't arrive at parties on time. I am also getting used to the climate. On a recent trip back to Detroit I was terribly conscious of the humidity and nearly froze because the weather was so cold and damp. Moreover, I have discovered that moving to Hobbs has not meant that I left civilization. I've just moved to a different type of civilization—one that is drier, warmer, quieter, and slower.

■ EXERCISE 5.2   Answer the following questions about the essay you have just read.

1. What is the main idea of the essay? **Moving from Detroit to Hobbs**

   was not easy.

2. Is the main idea expressed in a thesis statement? **yes**

3. Underline the thesis statement.

4. What are the major supporting points developed in the essay?

   a. **First, I had to get used to the change in climate.**

   _____

   b. **My next problem was adjusting to life in a small town.**

   _____

   c. **But the biggest problem I had was the difference in time.**

   _____

5. Does each of these major supporting points serve as a topic sentence of a paragraph?

   yes

6. Underline each of the topic sentences that expresses a major supporting point.

7. Compare these topic sentences with the three major supporting points of the original paragraph. Are they the same supporting points?

   yes

Answers will vary.   8. List below several details the writer uses in the essay but not in the paragraph.

   a. **In Detroit she accepted mildew and frizzy hair as facts of life.**

   _____

b. **In Hobbs there is no morning dew, and a rainfall is a major event.**

_____

c. **Hobbs has only one daily newspaper, a small radio station, and a few**

movies. _____

d. **In Hobbs no one arrives at a party on time.** _____

_____

READING AND WRITING ABOUT—

Work

Preparing: Questioning and Interviewing—

When newspaper reporters cover an event or do an interview, they often use the technique of *questioning* to be sure they get all the information they need. You will find that these "reporters' questions" can also help you to select a topic and to gather information. You can remember them as the *5-W questions* and *how?*

To help you prepare to read and write about the topic of work, use these questions to *interview* a partner about his or her career goals. Then have the partner use the same questions to interview you. Take notes on your interviews and then exchange notes at the end of the interview session.

1. *What* career do you plan to pursue?
2. *When* did you decide on this career or line of work?
3. *Where* do you want to work?
4. *Who* influenced you in your decision?
5. *Why* did you choose this career?
6. *How* do you plan to prepare for your future career?

PREPARATION FOR LIFE
Susan Allen Toth

Before you read, think about your own work experiences. What kinds of jobs have you held? What did you learn from these jobs? In the following selection from her book *Blooming: A Small-Town Girlhood* (1981), Susan Allen Toth describes her own work experience as a teen-ager in Ames, Iowa, and its effects on her today.

As you read, notice that Toth's essay is clearly structured with an introduction and a conclusion that indicates her thesis and four body paragraphs. Underline the topic sentences of paragraphs 2, 3, and 4; underline the phrases that suggest the main idea of paragraph 5.

Annotations may vary.

1   "No allowance this week, Jennie, twice you didn't get your bed made," I say regretfully but firmly, in my best parental voice of authority and responsibility. "I know," she answers cheerfully. "That's okay. I don't really need the money anyway." She is probably right, I think gloomily as I chalk up one more defeat for the Protestant work ethic. With two grandmothers, a weekend present-giving father, and an indulgent mother, why should she feel the need to earn money? What, besides a dog, does she want that she hasn't got? My attempts at starting Jennifer on an allowance have been a failure. Current child-care experts offered me two opinions: give money but don't require chores, because children should simply expect to help around the house anyway; give money and require chores, because children need to learn the connection between work and money. Anyone who grew up in Ames when I did would have unhesitatingly chosen the second approach. But I have become out-of-date.

2   In Ames everyone worked. Fathers had jobs and mothers were homemakers, a word religiously observed in a town whose college was famed for its Division of Home Economics. Some mothers had outside jobs, not for pleasure but because they needed the money. Everyone knew that Mrs. McCallum clerked at the Hy Valu because her husband drank, Mrs. Olson managed the Dairy Dreme because her husband had deserted their family, my mother taught because she was a widow and had to support two daughters. A few other women, mainly faculty wives, worked even though they were securely married, but they were idiosyncratic individuals who somehow made their own rules and were not judged by ours.

3   As soon as I can remember, my friends and I wanted to get jobs. We looked forward to being sixteen, the magic age when most employers would be able to put us legally on their payrolls. Until then, we had to scrabble furiously for what summer and after-school jobs we could dig up in a small town whose work force did not usually expand at the times we were available. All girls babysat. Boys mowed lawns, raked leaves, shoveled walks, and delivered papers. In junior high school, we all detasseled corn in the summer. But by high school, we began to look more seriously for jobs that might "lead to something," jobs that seemed more important, jobs that offered what our high-school vocational counselor portentously called "preparation for life." As a sixteen-year-old reporter on the Ames *Daily Tribune*, I did a photo feature on teenagers' summer jobs, ostentatiously lugging my large black box camera around town to interview my friends. Kristy ran the elevator between the basement, first, and second floors of Younkers; Jack washed dishes at the Iowa State Union cafeteria; Emily was a carhop at the A&W Root Beer Stand; Patsy clerked at her aunt's fabric store; Charlie was cutting and hauling sod on an outlying farm. Kristy told me, confidentially, that her job was numbingly dull; Jack was planning to quit in a few weeks, when he'd saved enough for golf clubs; Emily hated the rude jibes she had to endure with her tips; Patsy didn't get along with her old-maid aunt; and Charlie said his job was about as much fun as football practice, and a lot dirtier. But we were all proud of ourselves, and the Ames *Daily Tribune* was proud, too: my pictures ran on the front page, a visible testament to the way the younger generation was absorbing the values of its elders.

4   Besides the prestige that went with holding a job, a public acknowledgment that we were almost ready to enter the grown-up world, we of course wanted the money. All of us had small allowances, and we sighed together with agonized desire when we window-shopped on Saturday afternoons. Most of us schemed and planned from junior high on how to stretch our baby-sitting money, detas-

seling pay, and allowances into an annual first-day-of-school outfit and a formal for the Christmas Dance. In August I both sewed and plotted about how to spend my summer's accumulated earnings. At first my atlas and guide was the August issue of *Seventeen,* then, by the end of high school, the college issue of *Mademoiselle.* Thick as catalogues, bulging with advertisements, they offered page after page of tempting photographs, models I knew I'd never really resemble but whose clothes might just make me passable at a distance. Ames had never seen such exotic outfits: Bermuda shorts with raccoon jackets flung over them, blazers, Chanel suits. Eagerly I read the copy, absorbing the ease, the self-confidence the models exuded. ''Jenny Blair, a senior at Southwest High, will enter Penn in the fall. Here she dashes to a tennis date in a crisp skirted outfit in white pique. Note the casual fling of her silk jacquard scarf.'' I didn't know anyone who had a tennis outfit. Since I didn't play tennis myself, I was able to pass over Jenny Blair without too much envy. But the next page! ''Scotty Wales will party tonight in this red striped jersey two-piece pull-on outfit. Later she can wear the top with her gray flannel slacks.'' Scotty, who was sixteen, according to the text, looked more like twenty: smooth, sleek, gleaming red lipstick. I noted the price of the red striped wool jersey: $35. Almost half my budget of $77.40, counting the bonus I'd get from having stuck the whole detasseling season. Over many long hot afternoons, I made notes, added figures, shuffled priorities, folded back pages until my fingers were black with newsprint. Occasionally I asked my mother's advice. ''That seems awfully like the striped dress you have, dear,'' she'd say discouragingly. Or, ''That is nice, but my, it's expensive. I wouldn't spend all that money if I were you.'' Finally, ''Maybe you'll have time to make a new dress.''

5   Money, money, money. How I wanted it then, as I tried to reduce my shopping list to the size of my budget. In the end I never bought anything from the magazines anyway. Their world was too remote from mine, and I settled for what I could find on sale downtown in Ames. Years later, when I was married, I suddenly had access to a joint income that was more than enough to permit an occasional extravagance. I soon opened a charge account at Peck & Peck, where I'd vainly dreamed hours away on college afternoons. Browsing there one day, I saw a handsome plaid wool suit that cost more than I had ever paid before, and bought it. I never wore it much. It didn't matter to me like the orange print cotton dress with a tucked midriff I'd bought one fall at Younkers for $14.98. I'd tried on a whole rack that day, consulted my friends, thought my purchase over for two days; when I decided to take the orange dress home, I carefully paid out money from my small horde saved from clearing dishes at the Memorial Union, baby-sitting, and assisting at playground dramatics. I didn't have to ask my mother's permission to charge it. I wore that dress till deodorant rotted its armpits. It was a tangible proof of my earning power and my growing independence.

6   Aside from basic money management, what did I actually learn from all my summer and after-school jobs? Each one may have given me some small skills, but the cumulative effect was to deepen my belief that work was the essential aspect of grown-up life. Even now, I am sometimes filled with anxieties at the prospect of stretches of free time. When I do not immediately rush to fill that time with work, I have to fight off guilt, struggling mentally against a picture of a Real Grown-up shaking a finger at me, someone with the droning voice of our high-school career counselor, but with firm overtones of former employers, teachers, even my mother. ''This,'' the voice beats relentlessly into my ear, ''is your preparation for life.''

REVIEWING THE READING   Answers will vary.

1. Toth begins her essay with an anecdote (a little story) about her daughter Jennie. Do you think this beginning is effective? Why or why not?

See paragraphs 1 and 6.

2. Restate Toth's thesis in your own words.

3. Paragraphs 2, 3, and 4 all have stated topic sentences. What are they?

4. In paragraph 5, the topic sentence, or main idea, is implied. State this main idea in your own words.

5. What are two specific details that Toth uses to support the topic sentence of paragraph 2?

6. Paragraph 4 includes an effective mix of factual and sensory details. What are three factual details from this paragraph? What are three sensory details?

See paragraph 6.

7. What did Toth learn from her work experience? That is, how did her work as a teen-ager help "prepare her for life"?

UNDERSTANDING VOCABULARY

Often you will encounter two or more new words that look and sound similar. For example, study the following pairs of words from Toth's essay:

1. *portentously* (paragraph 3) and *ostentatiously* (paragraph 3)
2. *accumulated* (paragraph 4) and *cumulative* (paragraph 6)

You can learn to distinguish between these words by using what you know about one to help you understand the other. Be careful, however, not to substitute the meaning of one word for that of a different but related word.

The suffixes of *portentously* and *ostentatiously* make these words look and sound similar. The first suffix, *-ous*, makes the base words into adjectives, and the second suffix, *-ly*, changes the words into adverbs. However, though these suffixes make the words sound similar, their roots and actual meanings are quite different. A *portent* is "an omen or a prophecy," so *portentously* means "in an ominous or foreboding manner." An *ostentation* is a "pretentious display" or a "showing off," so *ostentatiously* means "in a pretentious or showy manner."

In contrast, the roots of *accumulated* and *cumulative* are similar, whereas their affixes are quite different. Both words derive from the Latin root *cumulus*, meaning "to heap." The prefix *a-* (*ad-*) adds the meaning of "in addition," and the various suffixes alter the uses of the words. Thus, the *-ed* ending makes *accumulated* a past-tense verb, whereas the *-tive* suffix makes *cumulative* an adjective. *Accumulated*, therefore, means "to have piled up or collected"; *cumulative* means "enlarging or increasing by addition, piling up."

In addition, the word *detasseling* may look strange to you. A tassel is the pollen-bearing corn silk that protrudes from the end of an ear of corn when it is ready to be picked. This tassel must be removed before the corn can be shelled. Since the prefix *de* means "from" or "away," to *detassel* is to remove the tassel.

Record these words and their definitions in your vocabulary list. If you encountered other unfamiliar words in Toth's essay, you may also want to record them and their definitions.

REACTING CRITICALLY

The second paragraph describes job opportunities available to women in Toth's home town in the 1950s. How do job opportunities for women differ today? What new fields have been opened to women? Are women given equal pay, respect, and opportunity for advancement? Why or why not? Do men and women differ in their attitudes toward their work? If so, how?

OUT OF COLLEGE, OUT OF WORK
Stephen Sherrill

Before you read, think about what it would be like to be out of work. Have you ever lost a job or known someone who did? How did you or that person feel? In the following selection, Stephen Sherrill, a free-lance writer from New York City, describes his own feelings and reactions when he found himself in this situation.

As your read, notice that Sherrill weaves into his story about his visit to the unemployment office some of his thoughts on his generation and how it compares to the generation(s) before him. Underline the thesis that he states in the first paragraph.

See text annotation.

1   One of the things my classmates and I were not told at our college graduation four years ago was what papers we would need for a visit to the unemployment office. Luckily, however, in addition to being told that we were the future, etc., we were told to always be prepared. Thus, when I made my first visit a few months ago, all of my papers were in order. I had suspected that getting "processed" would be time consuming, and I was right. But that was OK; I wanted it that way. Like graduation ceremonies and funeral services, applying for unemployment insurance is one of those lengthy rituals whose duration almost seems designed to make one sit and think. It's a valuable time to take stock.

2   What I was not prepared for was the TV crew facing me as I walked in. The "MacNeil/Lehrer" news team was doing a story on white-collar unemployment, and they had come to the right place. I had expected the office to be like a great mixing pool, like the Department of Motor Vehicles. But the people in the endless line ahead of me—with their trenchcoats and folded newspapers—looked like the same ones I used to fight with for a seat on the Wall Street-bound subway train every morning when we all had jobs. Like them, I did my indicted-mobster-leaving-the-courthouse imitation, evading the cameras as I inched ahead in line. After finally reaching the front, and giving the clerk evidence of the life and impending death of Wigwag magazine, where I was a writer, I was told to sit down in the next room and wait.

3   The next room looked exactly like a college classroom (when I squeezed into a seat I realized I'd forgotten how uncomfortable school desks are). Looking around me, I was struck by the number of people in the room who were, like me, twentysomething—not the middle-aged crowd I'd expected. But after giving it some thought, it made more sense. I knew that, along with seemingly every other industry, Wall Street and the big law firms were trimming down after the fat years

of the '80s: last hired, first fired, sit down in the next room and wait. So here we were, members of the generation accused by our older siblings of being mercenary and venal, back in the classroom again, only this time having to raise our hands with questions like, "I didn't get the little pink form in my information booklet." Who among us would have guessed it in the heady days of 1986?

4   In truth, I was never that proud of my generation. I too had been scornful of those who happily graduated to fast, easy money. And although I had rejected that route myself, that suddenly seemed irrelevant. At this perverse reunion I found myself feeling a kinship with my new daylong classmates, squirming in their desks around me, who had embraced the '80s. Most of these wunderkinder were now counting themselves lucky to have found their little pink forms.

5   Like most of them, my notions of college and post-college life were formed by watching the '60s generation. To be young, energetic and full of conviction seemed important and exciting. The world had listened to them and we looked forward to our turn. There were many of us who would have liked to help stop a war, disrupt political conventions, take over deans' offices or volunteer in the South for civil rights. We would have welcomed the chance for a few years of world-changing before settling down to more responsible (i.e. lucrative) activities, as so many of the thirtysomething crowd, now with kids and mortgages, had done.

6   *Bicycle Messenger* But we had graduated into a different world—one so harsh and competitive that a *Republican* president would soon declare the need for something "kinder and gentler." AIDS, skyrocketing tuition, disappearing federal grants, the lack of so easy a common cause as peace and love (or hating hatred) and a dazzling job market offering salaries that, when offered to people so young with four years of loan indebtedness, left virtually no other choices. We weren't in the '60s anymore—we never had been. Those who hadn't realized this by graduation quickly found out that student-loan officials don't grant deferments for time spent "finding" oneself.

7   When comparing themselves to us, members of the '60s generation, while using their own college years to rationalize their recent, less than idealistic choices, imply that we younger "careerists" didn't pay our dues before joining them in their 20th-story offices. Ironically, though, depending on the severity of the recession, my generation may ultimately come to resemble our grandparents' generation more than the one we always wanted to be a part of. When I talk to my friends about job prospects and we compare our experiences at various unemployment offices (one ex-co-worker had *two* camera crews to dodge) I wonder if we, like our grandparents in the '30s, will be permanently shaped by these few years. Will we one day say, "Son, when I was your age, in the Great White-Collar Depression, we didn't fool around after college. We took whatever office-temp or bicycle messenger work we could get and we were *grateful*."

8   My name was soon called and, along with several others, I filed into another classroom for a 90-minute lecture on how unemployment insurance works—sort of a "Principles of Bureaucracy 101." The last item on my day's agenda was figuring out how to leave while avoiding the only people in the room with jobs: the camera crew. (I began to wonder if their eagerness was due to spending the day with a bunch of former job-holders.) When we all finally left the office, most of us had been there for about 3 hours. But we were not the irritated, impatient New York crowd one would expect—we had lots of time on our hands and we were learning how to deal with having even more. We were at last getting the long-awaited "year off," albeit a crueler and less gentler version. Although we can't

be quite as free and easy as our counterparts were 20 years ago—we have to mail in our coupons every week, and we've promised to look for work—<u>this may be the only chance for a coming of age my generation will get.</u>

REVIEWING THE READING   Answers will vary.

1. Study the title of Sherrill's essay. Notice that he uses the same word, *out*, for different effects. How do you react to the phrase "out of college" as opposed to the phrase "out of work"?

2. Sherrill's essay begins with an introduction that captures his reader's interest and states his thesis, and it ends with a conclusion that restates his thesis. Underline words and phrases that suggest this thesis. Then write it in your own words.

See paragraphs 3 and 4.   3. Sherrill uses several comparisons in his essay. What similarities does he find between the college classroom and the unemployment office? What differences does he see?

4. In paragraphs 4 to 7, Sherrill compares his generation—the generation of the 1980s—to the generation of the 1960s. In his opinion, how were the lives and opportunities of these generations similar and/or different?

See paragraph 7.   5. Sherrill says that his generation may ultimately come to be more like which other generation? Why?

See paragraph 8.   6. Although Sherrill is not happy to be out of work, he does find one advantage in his situation. What is this advantage?

UNDERSTANDING VOCABULARY

Our language is constantly changing, with new words being formed every day. Many of these new words are compounds of words already in existence. Compound words may be written as one word (*trenchcoat*, paragraph 2), as a hyphenated word (*white-collar*, paragraph 2), or as two words (*news team*, paragraph 2).

1. When two or more words are temporarily combined to make a new descriptive word, these words are usually hyphenated if they appear before the word they are describing. Thus, Sherrill writes the unusual compound "indicted-mobster-leaving-the-courthouse imitation" when he wants to describe a particularly dramatic imitation. Circle other compound, hyphenated words you find occurring before

See text annotations.   the words they describe.

2. A popular television show of the 1980s used the unusual compound "Thirtysomething" as its title. What effect does the compounding have on the meaning of this word? How and where does Sherrill refer

See paragraphs 3 and 5.   to this compound or variations of it?

3. In paragraph 4, Sherrill uses the word *wunderkinder*. This word is composed of two German words meaning "wonder" and "children." What does the German compound mean? How does this meaning fit the context in which Sherrill uses it?

REACTING CRITICALLY

Sherrill calls the economic recession in which he is caught "the Great White-Collar Depression." With a group of classmates, discuss the Great

Depression of the 1930s. Have you read about or heard an older friend or family member describe the Great Depression? How are economic conditions today similar to those of the Great Depression? How do they differ?

Responding in Writing—

Use one of the following specific assignments as the basis of an essay on your career goals or work experience.

1. Write an essay discussing your career goals. Before you begin writing your draft, reread the prewriting that you saved from your interview. You may find the answers to the *what, when, where,* and *who* questions helpful in writing your introduction. However, to determine your thesis and develop the body of your essay, you will probably want to focus on the answers to the *why* or *how* questions, developing them further with examples and details.

2. Susan Allen Toth describes the jobs that women and teen-agers held in her home town during the 1950s. Using your own personal experiences and observations, write an essay comparing job opportunities "then and now" for *either* women or teen-agers. (To help you structure your essay, review the organization of the essay on pp. 105–106 comparing Detroit, Michigan, and Hobbs, New Mexico.)

3. Stephen Sherrill's essay explains how the national economy caused his own personal work situation to change and considers the effect that this change had on his life. In an essay, discuss (a) how your work situation or career goals have changed due to altered personal interests or to forces beyond your control, or (b) the effects that the loss of a job can have on an individual and his or her family. Are all of these effects negative? In your conclusion, you might discuss what, if anything, can be done to combat the negative effects or to extend the positive effects.

Revising Your Writing—

Now that you have a draft of your essay, reread it carefully and decide how you want to revise it. At this point, you are playing the role of reader rather than writer. Use the following questions to analyze and evaluate your own essay:

1. What is the main idea of your essay?
2. Is your main idea expressed in a thesis statement?
3. If your answer to question 2 is "yes," underline the thesis statement in your draft.
4. What major supporting points do you develop in your essay?

    a. _____

    b. _____

c. _____

d. _____

5. Does each of your major supporting points serve as a topic sentence of a paragraph?

6. In your draft, underline each topic sentence that expresses a major supporting point.

7. List two or three details from each of your supporting paragraphs. Do you need more details in any of these paragraphs? What other details could you add?

8. Does your concluding paragraph restate your main idea or provide a clear general impression, evaluation, recommendation, or prediction? Which type of conclusion have you used?

CHAPTER SIX
Arranging and Connecting Ideas

For a piece of writing to be comprehensible to a reader, it must be unified and coherent. That is, the ideas must be logically arranged and connected so that a reader understands why they occur as they do. A written composition is coherent if the different ideas in it function as a unit, or whole, and not as a series of individual, unconnected sentences or paragraphs. In the following sections of this chapter, you will learn more about coherence—how ideas relate to one another—and the signals that writers and readers use to communicate about these relationships.

ARRANGEMENT

Writers achieve coherence primarily by using a pattern of arrangement that is familiar to readers. The most common pattern of arrangement is the simple general-to-specific pattern, in which a writer begins with a general idea and supports it with specific details. But additional patterns are often needed. Three of the most frequently used patterns are time order, space order, and order of importance. You are already familiar with these patterns, but the following reviews and exercises will help you see how writers and readers use them to communicate effectively.

Time Order

Most narratives (compositions that tell a story, relate a series of events, or describe a process) are arranged in chronological order; that is, they are arranged in the order in which the events of the narrative occurred. Compositions arranged in chronological order often include references to the time of day, day of the week, or specific dates. Or they include signal, or transition, words such as *first, then, next,* and *last* to indicate the passage of time. The following paragraph is arranged in chronological order:

The beginning of each school term marks a period of rebirth for college campuses. Before the term begins, the campus is strangely vacant and quiet. Then students begin to move into the dorms, carrying suitcases, trunks, and boxes from their cars to their assigned rooms. Shouts of laughter, yells of greeting, and squeals of excitement ring across the campus as students resume their interrupted relationships and establish new ones. Meanwhile, maintenance crews move busily around the campus trimming, repairing, painting, and generally refurbishing the campus and buildings. A few days later, teachers arrive, coming to their offices to plan for their classes, going to the library to complete a last bit of research, exchanging stories with colleagues. Finally, on the day classes begin, commuting students flood the campus, fighting for parking spaces, joining resident students as they scurry to classes, and generally adding to the growing sense of confused activity. A new semester has begun, and the campus is alive once more.

EXERCISE 6.1   Each of the following groups of sentences may be rearranged in a logical paragraph based on time order. Study each group of sentences, looking for the logical time sequence and for other transitional clues. More than one arrangement may be possible for the sentences in each group, but decide what you believe is the best order and number the sentences accordingly.

PARAGRAPH A

TOPIC SENTENCE: I was impressed by a television commercial I saw when I was little.

__3__   The camera then moved slowly up the Native American's body, showing his clothes and markings.

__1__   In the beginning of this commercial, the camera was focused on pieces of trash lying on the roadside—cans, bottles, candy wrappers, and cigarette butts.

__5__   Then, the camera completed its journey, showing the pain and disturbance clearly visible in his face.

__2__   With a pause after each item of trash, to let it sink in, the camera slowly moved to a pair of moccasin-covered feet.

__4__   When the camera reached the lower part of his face, I noticed the drops of tears rolling down his fleshy, strong cheeks.

__6__   The Native American's tears were falling because of the contamination of the land.

Dave McNish, *adapted*

PARAGRAPH B

TOPIC SENTENCE: Motion pictures became another form of amusement for the American people.

__5__   A second landmark was in 1927, when Al Jolson's *The Jazz Singer* successfully introduced motion pictures with sound.

__8__   The widespread popularity of television after World War II reduced the number of moviegoers.

__1__   Pioneered in America by Thomas Edison, the earliest motion pictures were different from those we see today.

__9___ However, through the years to the present, "going to the movies" has continued to be the favorite recreation of millions of Americans.

__2___ In these early movies, the film flickered and was dim; the motions of the actors were quick and jerky; and the actors' facial expressions as they showed fear, joy, or sadness would seem rather silly to us.

__3___ But the movies improved rapidly.

__6___ Then, during the 1930s, pictures in color added to the enjoyment of moviegoers.

__7___ In the thirties and forties, as many as 100 million people went to the movies each week.

__4___ In 1915, the success of *Birth of a Nation* encouraged the building of silent-movie theaters in cities and towns throughout the country.

Adapted from Howard B. Wilder et al., *This Is America's Story*

Space Order

Many compositions, especially those that describe places or people, are arranged in space order; that is, the objects or details are arranged in the order in which they are observed in space. In a description of a room, for example, the writer may describe objects from left to right, from floor to ceiling, or from the outside walls to the center of the room. Compositions arranged by space order often include references to directions, such as *right, left, up, down, east, west, under, over, beyond, in front of, behind,* and so on. The following paragraph illustrates space order.

The view from the front door was breathtaking. Immediately in front of the house, to the west, was a small dirt road, and beyond this road the land dropped sharply so that the entire valley was visible. This broad valley was cut down the center by the Snake River, a curving blue-white scar across the pale green sage brush that covered most of the valley. On the far side of the valley, sandstone cliffs rose abruptly from the gently rolling valley floor. Rising above the cliffs were the distant mountains, majestic peaks crowned with snow and ice.

EXERCISE 6.2   Each of the following groups of sentences may be arranged in a logical paragraph based on space order. Study each group of sentences, looking for the logical spatial sequence. More than one arrangement may be possible for the sentences in each group, but in Paragraph A the best arrangement is from the house outward, and in Paragraph B the best order is from bottom to top. Number the sentences in the order in which they should be arranged in a paragraph.

PARAGRAPH A

TOPIC SENTENCE: Skillful landscaping distinguishes the professor's white stucco house.

__4___ A low trellis separates these flowers from the evenly manicured lawn, which is broken only by a circular planter filled with more geraniums and centered with a fountain.

___2___ In front of the brick wall of the courtyard is a carefully shaped box hedge.

___5___ At the edge of the street, this lawn drops sharply three feet to a street-level sidewalk.

___1___ Directly in front of the house is a small brick courtyard in which cacti and yucca plants have been attractively arranged.

___3___ Next to this hedge grow rows of brightly colored flowers—red geraniums and white periwinkles.

PARAGRAPH B

TOPIC SENTENCE: College Hall was one of the oldest and most used buildings on campus.

___2___ The maps that covered the dusty chalkboards of classrooms on that floor reflected the history courses that occupied them.

___3___ Above, on the second floor, was the English Department, one of the largest departments on campus.

___5___ The third floor of the building housed the overflow from the English Department plus the Sociology Department.

___1___ On the first floor, the History Department coexisted peacefully with the Dean's office.

___6___ On this top floor were also most of the classrooms used by English and Sociology.

___4___ Two programs related to the English Department, the computer lab and writing center, were also on this floor.

Order of Importance

The details in a composition may also be arranged according to order of importance. That is, writers may begin with the most important supporting point and end with the least important; however, more frequently, writers begin with the least important point and end with the most important. The latter pattern allows a writer to build to a high point, or climax. In either arrangement, writers may help their readers by emphasizing the points with signal words such as *first* and *second* or with descriptive phrases such as *more important* and *most important*. As you read the following paragraph, notice how the details progress from the least important to the most important:

Several considerations should influence your choice of a career. First, you should choose a career that will provide the lifestyle you want. If living in an expensive house and driving a big car are your goals, you should not decide to be a schoolteacher or a paramedic. Although it is possible to make a good living in these professions, most teachers and paramedics make rather modest salaries, especially at the beginning of their careers. Second, and more important, you should choose a career for which you have an aptitude. Even though you may love art, if you have no talent as an artist, you will not be successful. Finally, and most important, you should choose a career you will enjoy. Deciding to be a mechanic because you are good at repairing cars is not wise if you do not find car maintenance interesting or enjoyable. Becoming a lawyer is a mistake if you do not enjoy writing briefs or researching legal issues. You will spend countless hours working at whatever career you choose. Those hours will be more rewarding and less tiring if they are spent in work you enjoy.

■ **EXERCISE 6.3**   Each of the following groups of sentences may be arranged in a logical paragraph based on order of importance. Study each group of sentences, looking for a logical order, for signal words, and for clues of repetition. More than one arrangement may be possible for the sentences in each group, but you should determine the best order and number the sentences accordingly.

PARAGRAPH A

TOPIC SENTENCE: During the Middle Ages, England had a very strict class structure based on the manor, a self-supporting landed estate.

2 Above the serf and below the lords was a large group of freemen, including tenants, shop owners, craftsmen, clergymen, soldiers, and lesser nobles.

4 Finally, at the very top of the class structure was the king, to whom the nobleman owed his allegiance.

1 The least important member of the class system was the serf, a servant who was bound to the soil of the manor and to the nobleman who owned it.

3 Near the top of the hierarchy was the lord who owned the estate.

PARAGRAPH B

TOPIC SENTENCE: All organisms can be classified on the basis of their specializations into more or less well-defined types of categories.

3 Within a phylum, the next highest rank is the class.

1 Within the living world as a whole, the highest taxonomic rank usually recognized is the kingdom.

4 Using criteria of likenesses and differences among and within groups, one may recognize orders within a class, families within an order, genera within a family, and species within a genus.

5 The species normally is the lowest unit.

2 The next highest rank within the kingdom is the division, or the phylum.

Adapted from Paul Weisz, *The Science of Biology*

TRANSITION

Ideas within a composition are held together primarily by logical arrangement. One idea usually follows another because readers and writers have agreed that certain arrangements, or patterns, are logical. For example, it is "logical" to discuss how to dress for an interview before discussing what to say (time order), to describe the front of a house before describing the rear of the house (space order), and to consider the most important reason for choosing to attend a certain college after you have considered the less important reasons (order of importance). But readers often need help to see your logic. Even though you arrange your ideas in a familiar, logical pattern, a reader may not perceive the pattern or the logic without assistance. The assistance a writer gives a reader is called *transition*.

Transition can be defined as the clues, or signals, a writer provides to help a reader see the connections between ideas. If the connections between the ideas are obvious, transitions are usually not needed; if they are less obvious, clear transitions become essential. In general, good writers are sensitive to the needs of their readers and give them as much assistance as possible.

The three basic methods of indicating transition are (1) repetition of key words and ideas, (2) repetition of structure, and (3) use of transition words and phrases to signal the appropriate relationships.

Repetition of Key Words and Ideas

One of the most common means of providing transition is to repeat key words or ideas. This repetition reinforces the main idea and connects supporting details to the main idea and to one another. In writing, you may reinforce, clarify, or elaborate a key word or idea by (1) repeating the same word, (2) using a more specific word or phrase for the same idea, (3) using a word or phrase with a similar meaning (a synonym), or (4) substituting a pronoun. Below you will find examples of each of these types of repetition:

1. *Repetition of exact word:* The *sea* can be beautiful, but the *sea* can also be dangerous.
2. *Repetition through more specific words:* In literature, *birds* often appear as symbols. For example, the *robin* may symbolize hope and the *raven* death.
3. *Repetition through synonyms:* The candidate made an *attempt* to convince voters, but his *try* was unsuccessful.
4. *Repetition through pronouns:* The *professor* started her lecture on the Constitution, but *she* was unable to finish it before the bell rang.

Much of the coherence of the following paragraph comes from the effective use of various types of repetition to reinforce the main topic, "dangerous chemicals." Key words or phrases that repeat or reinforce this topic have been boxed for you. In addition, marginal notes indicate how the author has used repetition to make the paragraph cohere, or "stick together."

Topic sentence	(1) For the first time in the history of the world, every human being is now
Key phrase	subjected to contact with dangerous chemicals from the moment of concep-
Repetition through pronoun	tion until death. (2) In the less than two decades of their use, the synthetic
Repetition through synonym	pesticides have been so thoroughly distributed throughout the animate and

Repetition through pronouns	inanimate world that they occur virtually everywhere. (3) They have been recovered from most of the major river systems and even from streams of groundwater flowing unseen through the earth. (4) Residues of these chemicals linger
Repetition through more specific phrase	
Repetition through pronouns	in soil to which they may have been applied a dozen years before. (5) They have entered and lodged in the bodies of fish, birds, reptiles, and domestic and wild animals so universally that scientists carrying on animal experiments
Repetition through related word (synonym)	find it almost impossible to locate subjects free from such contamination.
Repetition through pronoun	(6) They have been found in fish in remote mountain lakes, in earthworms burrowing in soil, in the eggs of birds—and in man himself. (7) For these
Repetition through exact word	chemicals are now stored in the bodies of the vast majority of human beings,
Repetition through pronoun	regardless of age. (8) They occur in the mother's milk, and probably in the tissues of the unborn child.

Rachel Carson, *Silent Spring*

As you read the paragraph above, did you notice that the writer has reinforced the key words "dangerous chemicals" with all four types of repetition of key words or ideas? If she had used only one type of repetition—repetition through exact words or through pronouns, for example—the paragraph would be repetitious and dull. To see how different the effect would have been, reread the paragraph and substitute the exact word *chemicals* for each boxed word. You will discover that it is not just repetition but repetition with variation that provides the most effective transition.

EXERCISE 6.4   The coherence of the following paragraph comes primarily from the effective use of repetition. Study the paragraph and underline all the words and phrases that refer to the subject "language."

Americans speak many languages. There is English, our mother tongue and the official language of the United States, which most of us speak more or less well. But there are other languages that many of us also speak. Spanish, Chinese, and Japanese, for example, are increasingly spoken in this country. In addition, there are different dialects spoken in the major geographical regions of the country. Southern English is not the same language as the Northeastern and Midwestern varieties of English. And Cajun English differs from every other language spoken in this country. Then there are the jargons that characterize different <u>language</u> communities. For example, lawyers speak their own <u>version of</u>

<u>English</u>, whereas teen-agers, truck drivers, and musicians speak still <u>others</u>.

Thus, although we speak of <u>English</u> as our <u>official language</u>, it is really only our

<u>common language</u>.

Repetition of Structure

Repetition of structure can also improve transition and coherence. When as writers we present information in obviously similar, or parallel, structures, we help our readers focus on our ideas and on the relationships among those ideas. In contrast, when we present related details and ideas in forms that have different, or nonparallel, structures, our awkward or unclear presentation of those ideas may keep our readers from understanding them. For example, which sentence below is easier to read and understand?

1. A successful pilot must have education, experience, and is courageous.
2. A successful pilot must have education, experience, and courage.

Do you agree that the second sentence is clearer? The first sentence is awkward because the writer has not used parallel forms in a situation in which the reader expects similar forms or structures to be repeated. In contrast to the first sentence, which shifts from noun forms (*education* and *experience*) to an adjective (*courageous*), the second sentence clearly emphasizes three necessary attributes of a pilot by repeating them in parallel noun forms.

As a writer, you can add coherence by repeating parallel (1) word forms, (2) phrases, (3) clauses, and (4) sentences. As a reader, you can use such repetition of structure to help you identify important supporting details and their relationships to one another. Examples of the four major types of structural repetition are given below:

1. *Repetition of word form:* The coach *fired* the punter, *traded* a running back, and *hired* a new wide receiver. (repetition of verbs of similar structure)
2. *Repetition of phrases:* The child looked everywhere for the missing ball—*in the closet, behind the door,* and *under the bed.* (repetition of phrases of similar structure)
3. *Repetition of clauses:* It was obvious *that I had failed* and *that she had succeeded.* (repetition of clauses of similar structure)
4. *Repetition of sentences: I was tired. I was hungry. I was lost.* And, suddenly, *I was afraid.* (repetition of sentences of similar structure)

Now read aloud the following paragraph. As you read, notice how the writer repeats similar structures to make his paragraph more coherent, more readable, and more rhythmic. As you read the paragraph, notice especially the repetition of the word *it* and the repeated structure of *it* plus a verb, which occurs throughout the paragraph. The repeated, parallel structures have been underlined and noted for you in the margins.

Repetition of phrases
from dawn
to dusk
to dawn

Repetition of sentences
It trembles
It moves
It is

Repetition of "who"
clauses
who gaze
who jump
who lumbers
who cross
. . . smash,
. . . shortchange,
. . . get jammed

(1) In New York from dawn to dusk to dawn, day after day, you can hear the steady rumble of tires against the concrete span of the George Washington Bridge. (2) The Bridge is never completely still. (3) It trembles with traffic. (4) It moves in the wind. (5) Its great veins of steel swell when hot and contract when cold; its span often is ten feet closer to the Hudson River in summer than in winter. (6) It is an almost restless structure of graceful beauty which, like an irresistible seductress, withholds secrets from the romantics who gaze upon it, the escapists who jump off it, the chubby girl who lumbers across its 3,500-foot span trying to reduce, and the 100,000 motorists who each day cross it, smash into it, shortchange it, get jammed up on it.

Gay Talese, "New York"

By repeating the same structures, the writer is able to emphasize the various activities of the different people who use the bridge. Indeed, his repetition of structure creates a rhythm that reminds us of traffic rushing back and forth across the bridge. By repeating similar structures but varying the content of those structures, you can make your writing clearer and more interesting for your reader. Moreover, you can improve the sound and rhythm of your writing and learn to be more aware of the rhythms in your reading.

■ **EXERCISE 6.5**   The following paragraph also makes effective use of repetition of structure. Read the paragraph aloud and listen to its rhythm. Then reread the paragraph and look for structures that are repeated. Finally, fill in the blanks in the outline that follows the paragraph.

On Wednesday morning at quarter past five came the earthquake. A minute later the flames were leaping upward. In a dozen different quarters south of Market Street, in the working class ghetto and in the factories, fires started. There was no opposing the flames. There was no organization, no communication. All the cunning adjustments of a twentieth century city had been smashed by the earthquake. The streets were humped into ridges and depressions, and piled with the debris of fallen walls. The steel rails were twisted into perpendicular and horizontal angles. The telephone and telegraph systems were disrupted. And the great water mains had burst. All the shrewd contrivances and safeguards of man had been thrown out of gear by thirty seconds' twitching of the earthcrust.

Jack London, "San Francisco Earthquake"

1. Repetition of phrases

   a. In **a dozen different quarters** _____

   b. in **the working class ghetto** _____

   c. in **the factories** _____

2. Repetition of sentence structures and "no" phrases

   a. There **was no opposing the flames.** _____

   b. There **was no organization,** _____

      no communication. _____

3. Repetition of sentence structures

   a. All **the cunning adjustments of a twentieth century city had been**

      smashed by the earthquake. _____

      _____

   b. All **the shrewd contrivances and safeguards of man had been**

      thrown out of gear by thirty seconds' twitching of the earthcrust.

      _____

4. Repetition of sentence structures, phrases, and word forms

   a. The streets **were humped into ridges and depressions,**

      and **piled with the debris of fallen walls.** _____

   b. The steel rails **were twisted into perpendicular and horizontal angles.**

      _____

   c. The **telephone** and **telegraph systems were disrupted.**

      _____

   d. And **the great water mains had burst.** _____

      _____

Transition Signals

Probably the most common type of transitional device is the use of specific transition words and phrases to indicate relationships within and between sentences and paragraphs. These words and phrases signal changes and thus alert readers to "shift gears" or to take a new direction. For example, the word *however* signals contrast, and the words *next* and *then* signal progression.

Transition within the following paragraph is clear because signal words indicate specific relationships among ideas. As you read the paragraph, be sure you understand the appropriateness of each signal word. The signal words have been underlined for you, and the relationships that they indicate have been noted for you in the margin.

Comparison	Just as the fear of nuclear destruction seems to be fading, a new fear
Comparison	confronts Americans—the fear of AIDS. Like our fear of a nuclear holocaust, our
Contrast	fear of AIDS is fueled by the fact that it is potentially so destructive and yet is so
Contrast	abstract. We know that AIDS is capable of killing multitudes, but it is unreal to us
Cause and effect/result	because we cannot see it or feel it or touch it. Therefore, we seek to give it a
	name or a face—a reality with which we can deal. Unfortunately, the name we
	most often give it is *homosexual*. We want to blame someone, to identify a real
Contrast	enemy instead of having to deal with a faceless abstraction that cannot feel our
Comparison	rage. Similarly, we gave our fear of nuclear destruction the name of *Communist*.
	We are, it seems, more comfortable with hate than with fear.

This passage is easy to read because the writer has made effective use of signal words.

As readers, we know to expect a contrasting idea when we see the word *nevertheless*, a similar idea when we see *and*, and a condition when we see *if*. Therefore, these words help us to "guess" or predict the general idea or type of idea that follows them. Such words help us understand the content of the passage well enough that we are not surprised and confused as we read through it. If we read the signal incorrectly, or if the writer gives us a faulty signal, we must go back and reread to comprehend the passage.

Just as readers take advantage of signal words to predict the content of a passage, writers use signal words to help guide readers from one idea to another. However, you do not want to add too many signal words or inappropriate ones. You should arrange your sentences and paragraphs so that one idea follows another in some type of logical progression. The signal words you use should serve primarily to reflect and reinforce the order of arrangement you have chosen. The following lists suggest some of the most common signal words and phrases. Notice that they are divided into categories on the basis of the type of development or order of arrangement with which they can be used.

TIME ORDER

first	until	last
second	while	finally
third, etc.	when(ever)	immediately
now	then	suddenly
before	soon	gradually
after(ward)	sometime(s)	meanwhile
later	next	

SPACE ORDER

where(ever)	within	at the top
behind	outside	at the bottom
before	around	to the north
under	upon	to the south
in	in front	to the east
out	in back	to the west
over	to the left	up/down
above	to the right	through

ORDER OF IMPORTANCE   ADDITION

first	foremost	and
second	especially	in addition
third, etc.	less/least	furthermore
then	important	moreover
next	finally	also
more important	last	
most important		
primarily		

ILLUSTRATION

for example	to illustrate	that is
for instance	such as	

COMPARISON/CONTRAST

however	on the contrary	although
but	on the one hand/	though
yet	on the other hand	even though
nevertheless	instead of	whereas
like	still	in contrast
likewise	rather	or/nor
similarly	just as	while
as	like	

CAUSE AND EFFECT/RESULT   CONDITION

therefore	hence	as if
consequently	thus	if
accordingly	since	
as a result	because	
so	for	

▨ EXERCISE 6.6

Answers will vary.

For practice in using signal words, read the following paragraphs carefully and then write appropriate signal words in the blanks. (The category of signal word is indicated in parentheses under each blank.) Be sure to read the paragraphs through completely before you start to fill in the blanks, and reread as many times as necessary to determine the relationships among words and ideas.

Some influences on consumer behavior can be directly observed and measured, ___**while**___ others must be inferred. ___**For example**___, the
(contrast)   (illustration)
impact of a retailer placing a large "sale" sign in the window of his or her store can be an important influence in triggering the start of the purchase decision process for consumers walking by the store. Many of these consumers will notice the sign ___**and**___ quickly begin the
(addition)
problem recognition stage, stopping and entering the store to obtain information about the sale item. The sign is, ___**thus**___, a very
(cause and effect)
direct influence on consumer behavior.

Many consumers, especially those between the ages of twelve and thirty, have been observed in recent years wearing short-sleeved shirts with alligators on them. ___**If**___ they are asked why they bought
(condition)
that kind of shirt, they may cite the quality of the materials or the shirt's excellent fit. Many students of consumer behavior, ___**however**___,
(contrast)
would attribute the choice of the particular shirt to such social factors as a desire for prestige and acceptance by one's peers. It is extremely difficult to measure these influences, ___**so**___ their importance can
(cause and effect)
only be inferred, ___**but**___ they are no less important to an un-
(contrast)
derstanding of consumer behavior. Marketers must thoroughly understand both inferred and direct influences on consumer behavior, which include demographic factors, marketing mix factors, and situational factors.

Thomas C. Kinnear and Kenneth L. Bernhardt, *Principles of Marketing*

READING AND WRITING ABOUT—

Heroes

Preparing: Brainstorming and Journal Writing—

You have probably read about famous legendary heroes such as King Arthur, Joan of Arc, and Odysseus. You have also seen fictional television shows and movies about popular culture heroes such as Superwoman, Batman, and Dick Tracy. But heroes also exist in history and in contemporary life. In fact, every society has its heroes—individuals who represent the best its people can offer. And the heroes a particular society chooses can tell us much about the values of that society.

To prepare you to read and write about this subject, *brainstorm* about the topic "heroes." That is, make a list of people whom you consider to be heroes. Don't worry about the order in which you list these heroes. At this point, you are merely retrieving ideas from your memory and recording them.

When you finish your brainstorming, read and think about your list. Then select one of the "heroes" you listed and write a journal entry about this person.

■ LARGER THAN LIFE
Phil Sudo

Before you read, think about how you would define the word *hero.* Do you think of both men and women as heroes? What actions do you consider heroic? Who are our "American heroes"? In the following selection, published in *Scholastic Update* in November 1990, Phil Sudo defines the word *hero* and explores its cultural applications.

Annotations may vary.   *As you read,* underline Sudo's definitions of *hero.*

1   When Nelson Mandela visited the United States in June, cheering throngs of Americans hailed him as a hero. His decades-long struggle against South Africa's system of racial separation, unwavering through years of imprisonment, was inspiring not only to South Africans, but to freedom-loving people in this country as well.

2   Imagine if Iraqi leader Saddam Hussein were to visit the United States. The crowds would still turn out—only they'd be hostile. Many here view him as a murderous, ruthless dictator. And yet, in his own part of the world, Hussein is as big a hero as Mandela is in South Africa.

3   How can Mandela and Hussein—one admired in this country, the other despised—*both* be heroes? . . .

4   *Courage and Loyalty*   The word "hero" comes from the Greek word *heros,* meaning to protect or to serve. Originally, the term applied only to mythical

figures—gods or semidivine beings, such as Hercules and Perseus, who excelled in battle and embodied such values as courage and loyalty. The ancient Greeks developed an entire tradition of literature around such heroes; in classic epics like the *Iliad* and the *Odyssey,* Homer spun tales of the brave Odysseus and other warriors, whose adventures were first passed down orally, then later through the written word.

5   The notion of heroes was not unique to the West. Other early societies, such as China and India, developed similar traditions, around heroes such as Kuan Ti and epics like the *Mahabharata.*

6   Over time, historians began to look upon real people as heroes—Simón Bolívar, Sun Yat-sen, George Washington—larger-than-life individuals who founded countries or dedicated their lives to liberation. These were the rare men and women who embodied, as one historian wrote, "the perfect expression of the ideal of a group, in whom all human virtues unite."

7   Learning the tales of these greats helps forge values and a cultural identity. When you read the story of George Washington cutting down a cherry tree and saying. "I cannot tell a lie," you learn the value of honesty in American society. In Japan, when schoolchildren read the tale of the *47 Ronin,* a band of samurai who stick together through years of hardship to avenge their master's death, they learn the value of loyalty and group togetherness. . . .

8   In this country, some educators believe our heroes are too one-sided. U.S. history books, they say, are filled with the accomplishments of white European males to the exclusion of women and minorities.

9   In fact, many Americans today are beginning to question the very definition of a "hero." These days, we bestow the honor mainly on sports figures, movie stars, musicians, and comedians. "The word 'hero' is a debased word," says Michael Lesy, a professor at Hampshire College in Amherst, Mass., and author of the soon-to-be-published book *Rescues.* It has become confused with "celebrity," "role model," and "idol," he says. . . .

10   *What Makes a Hero?*   But if there is argument over what constitutes a "hero," few among us fail to admire heroic acts. Thwarting a robbery, rescuing a drowning man, pulling a child from a burning house—these are all unquestionable acts of heroism. And while the brave souls who perform them may never become famous or reap rewards, they are certainly heroes.

11   In fact, the one trait of heroes that transcends all cultural boundaries, Lesy says, is the willingness to risk one's life for the good of others. "It's not an American trait, it's not Japanese, it's not Iraqi, it's the bottom-line of the human species," he says.

12   Consider the words of Nelson Mandela: "I have cherished the idea of a democratic and free society. It is an ideal which I hope to live for and to achieve. But if needs be, it is an ideal for which I am prepared to die."

13   And these words from slain civil rights leader Martin Luther King, Jr.: "If a man hasn't found something he will die for, he isn't fit to live."

14   *Potential Within Us All*   We hail these men as heroes because their courage gives us strength, their ideals give us vision, and their spirit enlarges our own. But keep in mind that, extraordinary as these heroes may seem, they are still human beings like you and me. And as such, they demonstrate that within all of us, there is the potential to become heroes ourselves.

15   Look around you, at your friends, your family, your school. Is there someone among them that you'd call a hero? Probably so.

16   Now take a look in the mirror. What do you see?

17   What do you *want* to see?

REVIEWING THE READING   Answers will vary.

See paragraph 4.

1. Sudo lists several mythical heroes. What qualities make these figures heroic?

See paragraph 9.

2. According to Michael Lesy, why do many people question the meaning of heroism today?

3. Each of the following passages contains parallel, or repeated, structures. Underline the repetition in these sentences.

   a. "Thwarting a robbery, rescuing a drowning man, pulling a child from a burning house—these are all unquestionable acts of heroism."

   b. "Consider the words of Nelson Mandela: 'I have cherished the idea of a democratic and free society. It is an ideal which I hope to live for and to achieve. But if needs be, it is an ideal for which I am prepared to die.' "

   c. "Look around you, at your friends, your family, your school."

See paragraphs 11–13.

4. According to Sudo, what is the ultimate test of a hero? What examples does he give of this kind of commitment?

UNDERSTANDING VOCABULARY

Review the definitions of *hero* that you underlined in this essay. You should have underlined not only the Greek derivation of the word in the fourth paragraph but also several other defining phrases. Write your own definition of *hero,* being sure to enclose within quotation marks any phrases that you quote from the article.

REACTING CRITICALLY

1. Sudo states that "in his own part of the world, Hussein is as big a hero as Mandela is in South Africa." What qualities does Hussein have that could make him a hero to the people in his country?

2. According to Sudo, "Some educators believe our heroes are too one-sided. U.S. history books, they say, are filled with the accomplishments of white European males to the exclusion of women and minorities." Do you agree or disagree? Explain why.

3. How are heroes and celebrities similar? How are they different? Can someone be both? Why or why not? Give examples to support your position.

■ CHRISTA MCAULIFFE: AN ORDINARY HERO
Mike Pride

Before you read, think about the idea of women as heroes. How many women did you list in your earlier brainstorming about heroes? Also, think about the tragic explosion of the *Challenger* shuttle in 1986. Did you see the explosion on television? What was your reaction? Now, several years later, which astronaut do you remember most clearly from this tragic event? Why do you remember this person more clearly than the others? In this essay, Mike Pride, editor of Christa McAuliffe's hometown newspaper, remembers his town's hero.

As you read, notice how Pride uses his journal entries to unify his essay and to emphasize the contrast between a day of happiness and a day of sorrow. Underline each quotation from his journal.

See paragraphs 1 and 8.

1   In the journal I keep, the entry for July 20, 1985, begins: "Yesterday was an incredible day to be editor of the local paper." The day before at the White House, Christa McAuliffe, from my hometown, Concord, N.H., had been named the teacher in space. Near the end of my journal entry is this quotation from her: "I think the students will say that an ordinary person is contributing to history, and if they can make that connection, they are going to get excited about history and about the future."

2   Christa made the future—space—an area we covered in the small newspaper I edit. From before that July day until the moment she disappeared in a pink-white puff on the newsroom television screen, we helped her neighbors follow her odyssey. Last week we had a different job. There had been a death in the family, and we groped, with our readers, for what it meant.

3   Christa made Concord proud. The people in our city saw in her the best that we have to offer. Concord is a family town, and it cares about education. A mother, a wife and a teacher, Christa spoke out for her profession. She was robust and confident; she played volleyball and loved the outdoors. She was a volunteer in a city that seems at times to be run by volunteers. She also taught what Roman Catholics used to call a catechism class. She let no one forget that when she was growing up, teaching was one of the few fields open to women. She was a role model, bringing home the message again and again: if I can do this, think what you can do.

4   And she became a media darling. In front of a semicircle of TV cameras, she would describe deadpan how the shuttle's toilet worked. The people of Concord, of course, knew that Christa was not performing for the media. The camera didn't lie, and Christa didn't act. This was the real *her.* Whether she was waving Paul Giles's baton to conduct Nevers' Band—it dates back to the Civil War—or chatting with her son's hockey teammates at the Everett Arena, she was the same vibrant, positive person the rest of America saw on TV.

5   *Crazy About Christa*   It is assumed in our society that people who capture the nation, as Christa had, go on to fame and fortune. Those who knew her best knew that Christa had no such intention. She would have used her celebrity to advocate causes she believed in, but she could hardly wait to get back to her classroom at Concord High. She had chosen the profession and chosen Concord, and her selection as teacher in space had done nothing but affirm those choices.

6   If Christa liked Concord, Concord was crazy about Christa. It made her the grand marshal in a parade. It gave her a day. Her high school sent her off to Houston with a banner that read "Good luck from the Class of '86 . . . Mrs. McAuliffe . . . Have a blast!" A committee made big plans for her homecoming. New Year's Eve, the city featured ice sculptures of rocket ships and stars on the New Hampshire State House lawn.

7   Bob Hohler, our paper's columnist, became Christa's shadow, sending back dispatches from Washington, Houston, and, finally, Cape Canaveral. Her beam-

ing face graced our front page countless times, floating weightless during train-ing, dwarfed by *Challenger* before an earlier launch, grinning with her husband, Steve. Her story always seemed too good to be true, and too American. No one is really the girl next door. No one rides in a parade down Main Street on a bright, sunny Saturday afternoon. No one equates a modern venture with the pioneers crossing the plains in Conestoga wagons.

8   In the journal I keep, the entry for Jan. 28, 1986, begins: <u>"What a tragic day for Concord."</u> Tears have flowed in my city for days—long, wearying days. Words have flowed, too, in verse, in letters to the editor, on radio talk shows.

9   *Intense and Personal*   All the media people who have interviewed me and others at the newspaper want to know how it feels here. Our pain is more intense and personal, I tell them, but we know we are not alone; nearly every-one I know was consoled by a call from someone. Ordinary people, the kind McAuliffe's mission had intended to reach, have called from out of the blue. One man from Alberta, Canada, told me that his family felt terrible and needed to speak with someone here because if they felt that bad, he said, we must feel much worse.

10   I thought at first that Christa's death would be hardest on the children. They had learned all about the shuttle, and in an age without heroes, they had found one in her. Most had witnessed the dreadful moment. Yet times like these remind us that children are resilient. Age robs us of the instinct to go forward without a backward glance. I even suspect now that we have tried too hard to make our children feel what we want them to feel. It is the adults in Concord who still have swollen eyes and stricken looks. They comprehend what was lost, and what was lost was a part of them. It is not a myth to say that everyone in town knew Christa. She was easy to meet, easy to talk to. Even those who never had the chance felt as though they had.

11   Since we picked up Christa McAuliffe's trail, our town has traversed from the green, fertile days of midsummer to the cold heart of winter. The subtle daily changes of nature have played tricks on us; sometimes, at this time of year, it can seem as if summer might never come again.

12   Many people have compared Christa's death with the assassination of John F. Kennedy, the inspiration of her youth. There are differences, but for the people of Concord—even for the nation as a whole—the comparison is valid. She stood for what was best in us at a time when we wanted to believe that the American spirit was reborn. That makes her death hard.

REVIEWING THE READING   Answers will vary.

1. Christa McAuliffe called herself "an ordinary person . . . contributing to history." How was McAuliffe "an ordinary person"? How was she an extraordinary person?

2. In paragraph 2, Pride writes "there had been a death in the family." Explain this statement. What family does Pride mean?

See paragraphs 1 and 8.

3. In his journal entries, Pride underscores the effect of Christa McAu-liffe's death on him and on Concord by effectively contrasting their pride in her selection as an astronaut and their horror at her death. In addition, he uses the technique of repetition—repeating the struc-ture of his statement but varying its content—to emphasize this con-trast. If you have not already done so, underline these two parallel passages in your book.

4. Repeated, or parallel, sentences in the third paragraph emphasize McAuliffe's contributions to the town of Concord. For example, Pride writes *"She was* robust and confident." Find and underline other sentences in the paragraph that follow this same structural pattern.

5. Pride also uses effective parallelism within sentences. Underline the parallel, or repeated, structures in these sentences:

    a. "A mother, a wife and a teacher, Christa spoke out for her profession."

    b. "If Christa liked Concord, Concord was crazy about Christa. It made her the grand marshal in a parade. It gave her a day."

    c. "Her story always seemed too good to be true, and too American. No one is really the girl next door. No one rides in a parade down Main Street on a bright, sunny Saturday afternoon. No one equates a modern venture with the pioneers crossing the plains in Conestoga wagons."

    d. "It is not a myth to say that everyone in town knew Christa. She was easy to meet, easy to talk to."

UNDERSTANDING VOCABULARY

In his second paragraph, Pride writes, "From before that July day until the moment she disappeared in a pink-white puff on the newsroom television screen, we helped her neighbors follow her odyssey." Do you know the meaning of the word *odyssey*? The origin of this word can be traced back to Odysseus, a mythical Greek hero. Because of Odysseus's epic quest for his homeland, the word *odyssey* now means "a personal journey or search."

REACTING CRITICALLY

1. Pride asserts that "in an age without heroes, they [the school children] had found one in her [Christa McAuliffe]." Are we living in a time and a place "without heroes"? Explain your answer.

2. In his article "Larger Than Life," Phil Sudo calls attention to the small number of women who are considered to be heroes in America's history. Why are so few women considered heroes? How many female heroes can you name? Are a female hero and a heroine the same? Why or why not? Is Christa McAuliffe a hero or a heroine?

▓ PRIME-TIME HEROES
Eric V. Copage

Before you read, think about your television "heroes." How do their lives differ from your life? In what ways are they the same? How many of these television heroes are black? Do you think television effectively portrays black heroes? Can people identify with heroes of racial and ethnic backgrounds different from their own. Why or why not? Eric V. Copage, an editor of the *New York Times Magazine* and the author of *Kwanzaa: An African-American Celebration of Culture and Cooking,* considers these questions in the following essay.

Annotations may vary.   *As you read,* circle the names of the television heroes that Copage had as a child.

1   No one told me that because I am black I couldn't be Superman. No one told me I couldn't be Peter Gunn, the wild, wild James West or John Drake, Secret Agent Man.

2   These television paladins of yesteryear came up during a recent dinner conversation. A companion told me a black friend of his, roughly my age, had felt hobbled by the lack of African-American heroes and the prevalence of negative stereotypes on television during his childhood. While I knew that television programs could adversely affect self-esteem, I also knew, through my own experience, that it needn't be that way. And as my 4-year-old son and 16-month-old daughter hurtle through the world, I know I must do my best to nurture them the way I was nurtured.

3   When I was growing up, virtually all the main characters on TV were white. But that didn't prevent me from being lost in space with Billy Mumy or diving under the sea with Lloyd Bridges. When "I Spy" premiered in 1965, the precedent of Bill Cosby's starring role was lost on my 10-year-old mind. I watched because Scotty (Cosby) and Kelly (Robert Culp) were so cool that they could wisecrack in the face of death, which was the same reason I admired John Steed and Emma Peel—"The Avengers"—played by Patrick Macnee and Diana Rigg, both of whom, of course, were white.

4   It's not that I was oblivious to color. I remember feeling an emotional dissonance between ending the pledge of allegiance at school "with liberty and justice for all," and going home to see TV news footage of blacks fire-hosed for demanding to eat and walk where ever they chose. In the integrated and white middle-class neighborhoods of Los Angeles, racial epithets had been hurled at me. Yet the racial violence seemed distant and surrealistic, and I never went home crying as a result of a racist remark.

5   Rather, the reality of my home was the most powerful one I had. The adults in my life told me I could do anything if I was determined and resourceful. Granted, being middle-class made this easy to accept. But the people who gave me this advice had come from backgrounds that were far from middle-class. My father, for instance, grew up during the Depression in the ghettos of Chicago, yet managed to become a successful real-estate broker and never dwelt on the disadvantages dealt him. My mother, a housewife and sometime actress, grew up poor but didn't seem alienated from society.

6   And when, as a youngster, I'd tell my father my big plans for the future—to buy the company that made Colgate toothpaste and change the name to Copage—he'd just give me a sly smile that seemed to say proudly, "That's my boy," as any middle-class father would. I was expected to be ambitious because there was an intrinsic pleasure in excelling, not because I had to prove anything to whites.

7   Even the Watts riots of 1965 failed to convince me that to be black was to be helpless and hopeless in America. My father owned a hamburger stand in Watts as an investment, and hired local teen-agers to work at the counter. They didn't dress as I did, and they sure didn't take the music, karate and acrobatics classes children in my neighborhood routinely attended. Yet I believed that if these teen-agers continued to work hard and look for opportunities, they could make better lives for themselves, as my father had for himself.

8   Over the next two years, however, a sense of otherness took root in me. In my mostly white junior high school, I was asked whether I preferred being called Negro or black. I began hearing chants of "black is beautiful." That being black

was to be somehow tragic and full of rage was played out on the TV news, where I saw black Americans talking about revolution and shooting clenched-fist salutes in the air. In the midst of this, I began to doubt myself and the values I had grown up with. I feared I might be an "Oreo."

9   This conflict was brought into vivid relief for me in 1968. I was 13 when my 6-year-old brother, Marc, was tapped to play the part of Corey Baker in "Julia," the half-hour sitcom that starred Diahann Carroll as a widowed nurse trying to raise her young son (my brother). Julia was middle-class, beautiful and smart, and lived with her son in an integrated apartment building.

10   Being the first series since "Beulah" in 1950 to star a black woman, "Julia" received a fair amount of publicity, and more than a fair amount of vitriol. Black activists and some white television critics said the series, produced and written by whites, was "unrealistic" because it did not address the black rage blazing across America's inner cities.

11   But for me, "Julia" was as real as television gets, no more sanitized or hyperbolized than "I Love Lucy" or "The Patty Duke Show." And besides, the show, with its black characters functioning without pathology in a "white" world, was enough like my life to seem grounded in reality. Were the show's critics charging that my family had forsaken our blackness? Yes, I avidly listened to Bach and Beethoven, but to Charlie Parker and Miles Davis as well. True, when my grandmother cooked chitlins, I shut the kitchen door to contain the stench, but did that make me less black?

12   For years after that I had a knee-jerk response to television's depiction of black people and black family life: Was the "social reality" that was not a part of "Julia" more "black"?

13   Still, the fact is that no black person ever complained to me about the life depicted on "Julia." On the contrary, in our conversations about the show, blacks of my acquaintance seemed proud. Certainly, I reasoned, seeing Greg Morris as the expert technician on "Mission: Impossible" or Denise Nicholas as a concerned and conscientious school counselor on "Room 222" could inspire a black child to reach beyond his social limitations.

14   Recognizing the power of television made me restless for further change. Sidekick status was just not good enough. Why didn't James Earl Jones play Chief Ironside and get chauffeured by some trusty white soul? Why couldn't Captain Kirk be black? And speaking of the Enterprise, why hadn't it ever run into black aliens?

15   As my friend and I walked to his bus stop after that recent dinner party, we talked about how the depiction of blacks has changed over the past 25 years. Today my children routinely see black judges, lawyers, obstetricians and cops on "Sesame Street," "The Cosby Show" and "Mister Rogers's Neighborhood." This is good. And with Cosby, Oprah Winfrey and Quincy Jones, blacks are beginning to control their own images. That is even better.

16   But a parent's encouragement, regardless of his or her economic or social circumstance, is more powerful than any cathode-ray-tube hero. Besides, throughout America's history, its good will toward blacks has always come sporadically, been slow to gather force and quick to dissipate. Television has been a mirror of that. As my friend boarded the bus and waved goodbye, I thought I'd continue to teach my children what I had been taught: that they needn't see a black become President or win the Indy 500 on television before feeling they can do it in real life.

REVIEWING THE READING   Answers will vary.

1. Review the names of Copage's television heroes that you have circled. What qualities do these heroes have in common?

2. What is Copage's thesis? State it in your own words.

3. The title of this article focuses reader attention on television heroes. However, by following Mortimer Adler's suggestion of "reading between the lines," we discover that the hero that Copage admires most is not a television personality but an ordinary person whom he knows very well. Who is this ordinary hero? Why is that person a hero to Copage?

See paragraphs 5 and 6.

See paragraphs 9 and 10.

4. Why did Copage identify with the situation comedy "Julia"? What inner conflict "was brought into vivid relief" for Copage after this show aired? How did Copage resolve his conflict?

5. Like Sudo and Pride, Copage uses effective parallel structure (repetition of similar structures). Underline the parallel structures in paragraphs 1 and 14.

6. Copage also uses transition effectively. Read the following paragraph from the essay, filling in the transition words. Do not look back at the original paragraph until you have completed the entire paragraph. Remember that more than one transition can work in the same place.

_____**Rather**_____ , the reality of my home was the most powerful one I

had. The adults in my life told me I could do anything _____**if**_____

I was determined and resourceful. Granted, being middle-class made

this easy to accept. _____**But**_____ the people who gave me this advice

had come from backgrounds that were far from middle-class. My father,

_____**for instance**_____ , grew up during the Depression in the ghettos of Chi-

cago, _____**yet**_____ managed to become a successful real-estate broker

_____**and**_____ never dwelt on the disadvantages dealt him. My

mother, a housewife _____**and**_____ sometime actress, grew up poor

_____**but**_____ didn't seem alienated from society.

UNDERSTANDING VOCABULARY

1. In paragraph 8 Copage uses the term "Oreo." Derived from a popular cookie composed of two chocolate wafers filled with a white cream, this term has come to mean "black on the outside and white on the inside."

2. The words that we use every day come from many sources—from various languages and from many disciplines—art, literature, history, science, and so on. Three of the words in this reading come from very different sources.

a. The word *paladin* (paragraph 2) comes from history. A paladin was once one of the twelve peers of the court of Charlemagne, an eighth-century king of France. Today, the word means "a perfect example of chivalry," or a "heroic champion."

b. The word *surrealistic* (paragraph 4) comes from art. The artistic movement of surrealism flourished in the early twentieth century, especially in France; its goal was to transform society by liberating the unconscious. Thus, *surrealistic* means "dreamlike."

c. The word *vitriol* (paragraph 10) comes from chemistry. Its chemical definition is "a sulfuric acid," and the word now has a more general meaning of "bitterness, harshness, or abrasiveness."

Add to your vocabulary journal these and any other words from the reading that you would like to learn.

REACTING CRITICALLY

1. According to Copage, one of his companion's black friends had "felt hobbled by the lack of African-American heroes and the prevalence of negative stereotypes on television during his childhood." How would you evaluate television's portrayal of blacks today? Which black characters are portrayed as heroes on television today?

2. Review again the names of Copage's heroes. How many of them are black? How many are white? As a child, did Copage, an African American himself, distinguish between black and white heroes? Did you? Why or why not?

Responding in Writing—

Use one of the following assignments as the basis for an essay about heroes.

1. Review your brainstorming and freewriting. Who is your personal hero? Why is this person heroic? Write an essay nominating this person for a Medal of Heroism. (This medal may be awarded either to a hero who is dead or to one who is alive.) Remember that your purpose is to convince the judges to give the medal to your nominee, so be sure to support your argument.

2. Write an essay defining the word *hero*. You may use quotations from Sudo's article to support your opinion, but the overall definition should be yours, not his. Use specific examples from your experience, observations, and reading as well as examples from Sudo's article.

3. In an essay, answer the question "Can a hero be a celebrity?" How do you view celebrities—people who are well known in music, movies, and sports, for example? Are some of your heroes celebrities? Why or why not? Support your answer with one extended example or several shorter ones. Your essay should be directed to a general audience, perhaps the readers of your local newspaper.

4. As Sudo points out, few women are considered to be heroes in U.S. history. Can you think of a woman whom you consider to be a hero? Write an essay about this person.

5. Write an essay about a minority hero in America—an African American, a Hispanic American, an Asian American, or a member of some other minority group. What has this person contributed to his or her culture? What has he or she contributed to American life as a whole?

6. Mike Pride calls Christa McAuliffe an "ordinary" person, and Eric V. Copage seems to admire his "ordinary" father more than all the television heroes he watched. Can an ordinary person be a hero? Why or why not? Write an essay about an "ordinary person" whom you consider to be a hero.

Revising Your Writing—

Meet with a group of your classmates and answer the following questions about one another's drafts.

1. What is the purpose of the essay? Who is the audience? Does the essay succeed in achieving its purpose and communicating to its audience? Why or why not?

2. What is the thesis? Is it clearly stated or implied? Where is it stated or implied? Does the thesis need to be revised? In what way?

3. What are the major supporting points and details? What other details could be added? Should any details be omitted because they do not support the main idea? If so, which one(s)?

4. How are the supporting examples arranged in the entire essay (time order, space order, order of importance)? How are details arranged within the individual paragraphs? What arrangement might be more effective?

5. What forms of transition does the paragraph or essay contain? What additional transitions, if any, are needed?

6. How does the essay conclude? Is this conclusion effective? How could it be improved?

After you have revised your essay, edit it for problems in sentence structure, punctuation, spelling, and word choice. Remember to edit for one problem at a time. Then proofread your essay for minor errors and omissions.

CHAPTER SEVEN
Developing Ideas

The traditional methods of developing ideas are almost as old as language itself. Even before writing was invented, people used these familiar methods to explore and develop their ideas. They are, essentially, methods of thinking—ways of approaching and exploring a topic which enable you to expand your knowledge. Learning to use these common methods of development will improve your ability to generate information and support a topic when you write and to recognize familiar patterns of thought and development when you read.

Most paragraphs, and certainly most longer pieces of writing, such as essays, are combinations of different methods of development; for example, a story, which is primarily narration, often includes description. In fact, we seldom find any single method of development in isolation. However, in studying these methods, we will examine them first individually.

NARRATION

Most simply, narration is a story. It is probably the oldest and is certainly the best known of all methods of development. We have all had experiences with stories—listening to them, telling them, watching them on television or movie screens—even before we learned to read and write. Since a narrative is a sequence of events, it can be a historical account, a scientific process, or a case study as well as a novel or short story. A narrative relates what happened. It can tell what happened to you, to someone else, or to something else. A novel tells you what happened to the characters in the story. Your history text tells you what happened at Valley Forge or during the Great Depression. And your biology text tells you what happens when trees lose their leaves or a cell divides.

The following paragraphs illustrate three different kinds of narration:

Eight children were there at play, seven sisters and their brother. Suddenly the boy was struck dumb; he trembled and began to run upon his hands and feet. His fingers became claws, and his body was covered with fur. Directly there was a bear where the boy had been. The sisters were terrified; they ran, and the bear after them. They came to the stump of a great tree, and the tree spoke to them. It bade them climb upon it, and as they did so it began to rise into the air. The bear came to kill them, but they were just beyond its reach. It reared against the tree and scored the bark all around with its claws. The seven sisters were borne into the sky, and they became the stars of the Big Dipper.

N. Scott Momaday, *The Way to Rainy Mountain*

When they arrived at Love Field, Congressman Henry Gonzalez said jokingly, "Well, I'm taking my risks. I haven't got my steel vest yet." The President, disembarking, walked immediately across the sunlit field to the crowd and shook hands. Then they entered the cars to drive from the airport to the center of the city. The people in the outskirts, Kenneth O'Donnell later said, were "not unfriendly nor terribly enthusiastic. They waved. But were reserved, I thought." The crowds increased as they entered the city—"still very orderly, but cheerful." In downtown Dallas enthusiasm grew. Soon even O'Donnell was satisfied. The car turned off Main Street, the President happy and waving, Jacqueline erect and proud by his side, and Mrs. Connally saying, "You certainly can't say that the people of Dallas haven't given you a nice welcome," and the automobile turning on to Elm Street and down the slope past the Texas School Book Depository, and the shots, faint and frightening, suddenly distinct over the roar of the motorcade, and the quizzical look on the President's face before he pitched over, and Jacqueline crying, "Oh, no, no. . . . Oh, my God, they have shot my husband," and the horror, the vacancy.

Arthur M. Schlesinger, Jr., *A Thousand Days*

After paralyzing the tarantula, the wasp cleans herself by dragging her body along the ground and rubbing her feet, sucks the drop of blood oozing from the wound in the spider's abdomen, then grabs a leg of the flabby, helpless animal in her jaws and drags it down to the bottom of the grave. She stays there for many minutes, sometimes for several hours, and what she does all that time in the dark we do not know. Eventually she lays her egg and attaches it to the side of the spider's abdomen with a sticky secretion. Then she emerges, fills the grave with soil carried bit by bit in her jaws, and finally tramples the ground all around to hide any trace of the grave from prowlers. Then she flies away, leaving her descendant safely started in life.

Alexander Petrunkevitch, "The Spider and the Wasp"

The first of these narratives is a Kiowa myth that explains how the Big Dipper came to be. This myth is the most familiar type of narrative—one that tells a simple story. The second tells of the assassination of President Kennedy, and the third is an account of how a wasp kills a spider and attaches her egg to its dead body. All three narratives tell "what happened" in a clear, interesting way. Below are some of the reasons these are good narratives.

1. ***All three narratives include a lot of specific details.*** They are not just a series of general statements but include "telling" details that

help you create vivid images of what happened. For example, the Kiowa myth about the Big Dipper doesn't just say that the boy became a bear. The story provides you with specific details about the boy's fingers becoming claws and his body becoming covered with fur. The historical account of President Kennedy's death includes the words of several people who were present, describes the weather and the crowds, and gives the specific route (including street names) that the president's motorcade followed. Finally, the story of the spider and the wasp provides very graphic, almost gruesome details about how the wasp kills the spider, sucks its blood, grabs a leg in her jaws, and then drags her prey into a "grave."

2. *The specific details in these narratives are arranged so you can follow them easily.* In most narratives, the details are arranged in chronological order—that is, according to the order in which they occurred. For example, in the myth you learn that the boy became a bear before you learn that the bear chased his sisters or that they climbed a tree, which carried them up into the sky. In the account of President Kennedy's death, you are given signals that emphasize the passing of time. For example, the author uses terms such as *when, then, immediately,* and *soon* to indicate the sequence in which the events occurred. Similarly, the author of the narrative about the spider and the wasp uses words such as *eventually, then,* and *finally* to emphasize that the events being described occurred in a certain order.

3. *All of these narratives make a point or have a purpose.* Although they do not have a stated topic sentence, each has an implied topic sentence—an idea that underlies and gives significance to the sequence of events. The myth explains the Kiowa's belief about how the Big Dipper came into existence. The account of Kennedy's assassination emphasizes the suddenness and unexpectedness of the loss that his death represented. And the story of the spider and the wasp illustrates the close, natural relationship between life and death. Although narratives may be told just to entertain, they frequently serve another purpose. They illustrate a point, explain a process, develop an idea, or provide information.

In the past you have probably thought of narration only as a way of entertaining or being entertained, but as a college student you need to broaden your understanding of this important method of development. Although you will continue to enjoy stories for their own sakes, you should also learn to see them as ways of developing ideas and persuading readers.

■ **EXERCISE 7.1**

Answers will vary.

Think of something that happened to you that caused you to be angry. Write below a sentence in which you explain what happened:

I was angry when _____

_____

_____

Now list below what happened—the specific events that led to your anger. Be careful to list them in the order in which they occurred:

_____

_____

_____

_____

Now think for a moment about what happened to you and why it made you angry. Was it the only time this sort of thing made you angry, or do you frequently respond with anger when something similar happens? Do you think your anger was justified, or were you later sorry that you became angry? Can you reach some conclusion, or generalization, about this incident and why it made you angry? Write your generalization on the lines below:

_____

_____

_____

Revise the generalization you have written above and use it as the topic sentence for a paragraph in which you tell what happened when you became angry. Be sure to include all the steps or incidents you listed above, but as you write your paragraph, develop each part of your narrative by including as many specific details as possible. The details you include will help your reader understand why you felt angry.

DESCRIPTION

Like narration, description is a common method of development. We can describe how a character in a story looks, how a glass of wine tastes, how a headache feels, how garbage stinks, or how a symphony sounds. Description can be part of many different types of writing—fiction, poetry, history, science, biography, philosophy, and business. Description is used heavily in advertising copy and technical manuals, but it can also be found in the most sophisticated novel and the simplest story, in the most formal speech and the most casual conversation.

Effective description suggests images to the reader. It provides the reader with sense impressions—sights, sounds, smells, tastes, and feelings. To describe something effectively, you must be a good observer. You must see people, places, objects, and events with a sharp eye and be able to relate your impressions, using both sensory and factual details. Thus, writing an effective description involves more than using many adjectives and adverbs. It requires noticing, selecting, and ordering details so that they effectively communicate to a reader.

Although description, even more than the other methods of development, is seldom found in isolation, the following paragraphs are primarily descriptive:

She saw green fields wrapped in the thickening gloom. It was as if they had left the earth, those fields, and were floating slowly skyward. The afterglow lingered, red, dying, somehow tenderly sad. And far away, in front of her, earth and sky met in a soft swoon of shadow. A cricket chirped, sharp and lonely; and it seemed she could hear it chirping long after it had stopped.

Richard Wright, ''Long Black Song,'' in *Uncle Tom's Children*

Another time I saw another wonder: sharks off the Atlantic coast of Florida. There is a way a wave rises above the ocean horizon, a triangular wedge against the sky. If you stand where the ocean breaks on a shallow beach, you see the raised water in a wave is translucent, shot with lights. One late afternoon at low tide a hundred big sharks passed the beach near the mouth of a tidal river in a feeding frenzy. As each green wave rose from the churning water, it illuminated within itself the six- or eight-foot-long bodies of twisting sharks. The sharks disappeared as each wave rolled toward me; then a new wave would swell above the horizon, containing in it, like scorpions in amber, sharks that roiled and heaved. The sight held awesome wonders: power and beauty, grace tangled in a rapture with violence.

Annie Dillard, *Pilgrim at Tinker Creek*

These descriptive paragraphs focus on very different subjects and serve different purposes, but both enable you to share the writers' experiences—to see what they saw, hear what they heard, and feel what they felt. Below are some of the elements that make these descriptions effective.

1. *Like the narrative paragraphs, descriptive paragraphs are very detailed.* The writers use specific details to make their descriptions as vivid as possible. You are told precisely where the writer stood ("where the ocean breaks on a shallow beach") when she viewed the sharks. And you are told specifically how the cricket sounded ("sharp and lonely") when it chirped. Each of these writers provides you with the specific details you need to translate the image into one you "understand."

2. *The descriptions include factual as well as sensory details.* For example, in the description of the sharks, the writer tells us that she saw "a hundred . . . sharks" and that their "six- or eight-foot-long bodies" were "twisting."

3. *The writers do not rely exclusively on visual details.* Although each of the descriptions includes many visual details, the other senses are not ignored. In the first paragraph, the writer who is describing the fields includes the sound of the cricket chirping as well as the sight of the sky. In the second paragraph, the writer tells you not only what she saw but how she felt. ("The sight held awesome wonders: power and beauty, grace tangled in a rapture with violence.")

4. *The writers also use comparisons to help readers visualize what they are describing.* For example, in the first paragraph, the writer states that the fields look "as if they had left the earth." And in the second paragraph, the writer compares the sharks to "scorpions in amber."

5. *The writers arrange their supporting details in some familiar or*

logical order. You can recognize or visualize the details because you are familiar with the patterns of arrangement used. Descriptive details can be arranged spatially (according to their actual arrangement in space), chronologically (according to a time sequence), or in order of importance (according to their importance in the mind of the writer).

Both of these paragraphs use chronological order. In the description of the green fields, even though no action is involved, the scene changes as the woman watches it, and the writer presents the details in the order in which the woman viewed them—first the green fields, appearing to float upward, then the red afterglow on the horizon, and finally the chirping of the cricket. Similarly, the description of the sharks is chronological. The writer describes what she saw in the sequence in which it occurred.

6. ***In both of these paragraphs, the description is used to support a main idea.*** In the description of the green fields, the main idea (the woman's loneliness and sadness) is implied. The description of the sharks begins with a clearly stated topic sentence: "Another time I saw another wonder." The author then describes the "wonder" she saw. Like narration, description is often used to support an implied, rather than a stated, main idea, but both methods of development can be used effectively to support and develop an idea.

EXERCISE 7.2   Look around you at the classroom in which you are sitting. Study not only its appearance but also how it feels and smells and sounds. list below details—both factual and sensory—about the classroom.

Answers will vary. _____

_____

_____

_____

_____

_____

_____

Now determine the appropriate arrangement for your details. You might arrange them spatially—floor to ceiling, front to back, right to left. Or you might arrange them chronologically, in the order in which you experience them as you walk in the door and through the room. Or you might simply list them in order of importance—putting what you consider most important first and least important last.

Next, determine the main idea you wish to communicate. You may state this idea as a topic sentence or merely use it as the controlling idea of your paragraph. Write it below.

Answers will vary.

_____

_____

_____

_____

_____

Now write a paragraph in which you use the details you have listed above to support your main idea.

ILLUSTRATION

Main ideas are frequently developed by illustration, or example. Examples give readers specific instances of the general idea expressed in the topic sentence. Sometimes a single example can adequately develop a topic sentence; at other times, several brief examples are needed. In either case, illustration is an effective method of development that is commonly used, especially in informative writing.

Below is a paragraph that is developed by a series of specific examples.

In an attempt to recruit older students, many schools have extended their definition of ''services'' to include housing. Chatham College, a small liberal arts school in Pittsburgh, for example, renovated a separate dorm for older students in 1986. Berry Hall is attractive, convenient and—at $375 a month for singles, including ten cafeteria meals a week—affordable. The University of California at Santa Cruz offers subsidized housing for couples and families as well as support services for its older student population. And Eckerd College, strategically located in St. Petersburg, Florida, has opened a 140-unit older persons' condominium right on campus. A majority of those living there are members of the college's Academy of Senior Professionals in which older students, besides taking their own classes, offer guidance or employment counseling to younger students.

Anne Bianchi, ''Re-entry 101: A Syllabus for the Returning Student''

Rather than a series of examples, you can also use a single extended example to illustrate a point. An extended example is often a brief narration or a description. Notice in the paragraph below that the writer uses the act of climbing stairs to illustrate subconscious knowledge.

English grammar is just one of many things you know subconsciously far better than you know consciously. When you walk up a flight of stairs, for example, you can do so without having to think about how to do it. You can climb stairs while carrying on a conversation, while composing a love sonnet, even while walking in your sleep. Although many hundreds of muscles are finely coordinated in the task of climbing stairs, you perform it errorlessly and even gracefully, and without any apparent mental effort. Yet if you or I were asked to describe how we climb stairs, we would do it very inaccurately at best: ''Let's see,'' we might say. ''First you bring the right leg up and bend the knee. You point the toe up, shift your weight forward, and bring the sole down on the next step. Then. . . .'' Of course you would not have begun to describe which muscles you use when you bend the knee. Your description is a long way from capturing the directions your brain gives to your body as you move. The fact is that unless you are a highly trained physiologist, you do not ''know'' much about how you climb stairs. And yet in another sense you ''know'' how to do it quite well, since you do it all the time. Your conscious knowledge of the task cannot come close to matching what you know sub-consciously.

Richard Veit, Discovering English Grammar

■ EXERCISE 7.3   Working with a small group of your classmates, think of a problem (complicated registration procedures, restrictions on parking, strict attendance policy, poorly lighted parking lots, and so on) that exists on your campus. Write a general statement that clearly expresses this problem. Then, as a group, decide on a single, extended example that develops your main idea. Your example can be narrative or descriptive or both.

COMPARISON/CONTRAST

Another way writers develop their ideas is by comparing or contrasting something that is unfamiliar with something that is familiar. For example, a writer may compare something new, such as a computer's storage capacity, to something well known, such as a human's memory. Often, such comparisons are quite brief, only a sentence or two or perhaps just a phrase or word. At other times, an entire paragraph or even a longer piece of writing may be developed through the use of comparison or contrast. Both of the paragraphs below use comparison/contrast as their primary method of development, but they are not organized in the same way.

■   Some people say the business about the jolly fat person is a myth, that all of us chubbies are neurotic, sick, sad people. I disagree. Fat people may not be chortling all day long, but they're a hell of a lot *nicer* than the wizened and shriveled. Thin people turn surly, mean and hard at a young age because they never learn the value of a hot-fudge sundae for easing tension. Thin people don't like gooey soft things because they themselves are neither gooey nor soft. They are crunchy and dull, like carrots. They go straight to the heart of the matter while fat people let things stay all blurry and hazy and vague, the way things actually are. Thin people want to face the truth. Fat people know there is no truth. One of my thin friends is always staring at complex, unsolvable problems and saying, ''The key thing is. . . .'' Fat people never say that. They know there isn't any such thing as the key thing about anything.

Suzanne Britt, ''That Lean and Hungry Look''

This comparison/contrast paragraph is organized in an alternating pattern. That is, the writer alternately discusses one subject (fat people) and the other (thin people). Notice that she is careful to give approximately the same attention to each subject so that the result is a balanced view.

Now read the next comparison/contrast paragraph, noticing especially how it is organized:

▨   If I've learned anything over the years, it's that when confronted with a new situation, one does best to face it with as much information as possible. I learned this deceptively simple lesson from the births of my two children. The first was for me a lonely and frightening experience, one I went through unrehearsed, *unprepared.* I was swept along, passively, in a sea of pain. The second birth was completely the opposite. My husband, Tom Hayden, and I studied birthing with Femmy DeLyser, childbirth educator and the author of the *Workout Book for Pregnancy, Birth, and Recovery.* With Femmy's help, I was *prepared* for what lay in store. Along with Tom, I planned for the birth, visualized it, and exercised for it. The pain was no less, the process was no faster—that can be a matter of one's genes or heredity—but the preparation meant not losing control. It gave me the ability to ride atop rather than be submerged by the pain. The nature of the experience was completely transformed.

Jane Fonda, *Women Coming of Age*

This comparison/contrast paragraph is organized in a divided pattern. That is, the writer discusses first one subject (her first experience with childbirth) and then the other (her second experience with childbirth). Notice that she introduces her second subject very clearly: "The second birth was completely the opposite."

▨ EXERCISE 7.4   Reread the paragraph that compares fat and thin people. Notice especially the alternating pattern of the supporting sentences. Rewrite the paragraph, changing the alternating pattern to a divided pattern. Read the resulting paragraph and decide whether you prefer this arrangement to the original.

CLASSIFICATION

Classification is another useful method of development. In classification, you organize information by placing things into groups with other things that have similar characteristics. When you classify a subject, you divide it into categories. Thus, only plural subjects can be classified. For example, you can classify students, colleges, computers, pizzas, cars, and television shows, but you can't classify a single student, college, computer, pizza, car, or television show.

Classification is used not only by writers but also by a variety of other people for a variety of different reasons. Scientists and technical writers are fond of classification; so are sociologists and psychologists. Teachers tend to classify students (as bright, dull, irritating, impossible), and students like to classify teachers (as hard, easy, interesting, impossible). Classification can be serious or humorous, but good classification always makes a point. The point, or main idea, developed by the classification may be stated or implied, but it should be clear to the reader. Often, the main idea of a paragraph developed by classification merely states the system of classification. For example, if you are classifying types of plants, you might have a topic sentence similar to this one:

▨   Although plants come in all shapes and sizes, they can all be divided into two groups—those that are easy to grow and those that are not.

This topic sentence not only identifies your categories but also implies that plants should be selected on the basis of how much care they require.

To develop a system of classification, you must first determine a basis for classifying; that is, you need a criterion on which to base your classification. For example, you can classify people according to their occupations, their physical features, their personalities, or their incomes. You can classify cities according to their size, climate, cost of living, or crime rate. However, you must be sure to classify on the basis of a single criterion. For example, you can classify cars according to how much they cost or where they are made but not according to both of these criteria at the same time.

COST

1. Luxury cars
   a. Cadillac
   b. Mercedes Benz
   c. BMW
2. Economy cars
   a. Ford Escort
   b. Toyota Corolla
   c. Chevrolet Cavalier

ORIGIN

1. American cars
   a. Cadillac
   b. Ford
   c. Chevrolet
2. Foreign cars
   a. Mercedes Benz
   b. BMW
   c. Toyota

Classification nearly always involves other methods of development, especially description, comparison/contrast, and illustration. But it is also frequently used as the primary method of developing a paragraph or longer piece of writing. For example, the following paragraph is developed primarily by classification, but the writer also uses several other methods of development:

> There are medium friends, and pretty good friends, and very good friends indeed, and these friendships are defined by their level of intimacy. . . . We might tell a medium friend, for example, that yesterday we had a fight with our husband. And we might tell a pretty good friend that this fight with our husband made us so mad that we slept on the couch. And we might tell a very good friend that the reason we got so mad in that fight that we slept on the couch had something to do with that girl who works in his office. But it's only to our very best friends that we're willing to tell all, to tell what's going on with that girl in his office.
>
> Judith Viorst, "Friends, Good Friends"

Can you identify the criterion on which this writer bases her classification of friends?

level of intimacy

Notice the paragraph's topic sentence. It is very direct, identifying both the main idea and the basis for classification. The sentences that follow, which describe each of the three kinds of friends, develop this topic sentence so that, by the end of the paragraph, you can infer the author's attitude toward her subject. Write in your own words the point you think the writer wants to make about friends:

Answers will vary.

Our relationships with our friends are determined primarily by

the degree of intimacy we share.

What other methods of development does the writer use in this paragraph?

description, illustration, comparison/contrast

■ EXERCISE 7.5

Answers will vary.

On a separate sheet of paper, make a list of as many types of college students as you can think of.

Now, see if you can classify these different types of students into three categories. Write the names of your categories below and then list under them appropriate subtypes or examples.

Category 1 _____

    a. _____

    b. _____

Category 2 _____

    a. _____

    b. _____

Category 3 _____

    a. _____

    b. _____

Write below a topic sentence in which you state your subject and the categories you have identified:

Answers will vary.

Next, write a paragraph in which you develop this topic sentence by briefly describing each of the categories of students you have identified.

CAUSE AND EFFECT

Another method of developing a main idea is to explore its causes or effects. Like the other methods of development, cause and effect is not just a way of writing but also a way of thinking. In our culture, we commonly think in terms of what caused something or what effects something will have. For example, we say that smoking causes lung cancer. In other words,

smoking = cause
lung cancer = effect

In developing a main idea, you can consider either causes or effects or both. The important thing is that you explore the relationship between the cause and effect. Thus, you can begin with a cause and explain its effect, or you can begin with the effect and explore the cause. With cause and effect, you are always moving between the two. Sometimes this movement is clearly in one direction or the other:

cause → effect
effect → cause

The paragraphs below are developed primarily by explaining cause and effect. In one of them, the writer moves from cause to effect. In the other, the writer begins with the effect and then discusses the cause. As you read the two paragraphs, see if you can determine which is which.

■   Once I shot an Iguana. I thought that I should be able to make some pretty things from his skin. A strange thing happened then, that I have never afterwards forgotten. As I went up to him, where he was lying dead upon his stone, and actually while I was walking the few steps, he faded and grew pale, all colour died out of him as in one long sigh, and by the time that I touched him he was grey and dull like a lump of concrete. It was the live impetuous blood pulsating within the animal, which had radiated out all that glow and splendour. Now that the flame was put out, and the soul had flown, the Iguana was as dead as a sandbag.

Isak Dinesen, "The Iguana," in *Out of Africa*

■   I passed all the other courses that I took at my university, but I could never pass botany. This was because all botany students had to spend several hours a week in a laboratory looking through a microscope at plant cells, and I could never see through a microscope. I never once saw a cell through a microscope. This used to enrage my instructor. He would wander around the laboratory pleased with the progress all the students were making in drawing the involved and, so I am told, interesting structure of flower cells, until he came to me. I would just be standing there. "I can't see anything," I would say.

James Thurber, "University Days," in *My Life & Hard Times*

Did you decide that the paragraph about the iguana begins with cause ("Once I shot an Iguana") and that the paragraph about failing botany begins with effect ("I could never pass botany")? The writer of the first paragraph tells us the *effects* of killing the iguana; the writer of the second paragraph tells us *why* he failed botany (because he could not see through a microscope).

Notice that both of these paragraphs, although they are developed primarily by cause and effect, also include narration and description. The iguana paragraph also uses comparison ("he was grey and dull like a lump of concrete").

EXERCISE 7.6   Write a paragraph in which you discuss some of the causes of high school dropout. Then write another paragraph in which you discuss the effects that dropping out of school can have on a young person's life. Finally, combine these two paragraphs into one in which you explore both the causes and the effects of this problem.

DEFINITION

The last method of development we will discuss, definition, is not really a different method so much as it is a combination of all the other methods. Your main concern in defining a subject is to explore the subject's "whatness." In other words, when you define something, you are telling what it is. You can define a subject by describing, illustrating, comparing, or classifying it. You can even define a subject by telling a story about it or analyzing its causes or effects. In definition, you use any and all of the other methods to explain your subject.

Formal definitions, the kind found in dictionaries, are usually brief. A formal definition places the subject (or term) into a class (as in classification) and then tells how it differs from the other members of that class (as in contrast). For instance, we can define a lullaby by placing it in the general category of songs and then specify the characteristics that make it different from other songs. We might arrive at the definition that "a lullaby is a song that is used to encourage sleep."

However, not all definitions are formal definitions. Longer definitions, sometimes called *extended definitions*, are not limited to the specifications of the formal definition. When you define a subject, you are free to use any methods of development that will help your reader arrive at a clear understanding of your subject. You can describe it (using both factual and sensory details), give an example of it, compare or contrast it with something else, or classify it. For example, an extended definition of *lullaby* might include a description of how a lullaby sounds (soothing), an example ("Rock-a-bye-baby in the tree top"), or a comparison with another type of music (rock-and-roll). As you read the following definitions, notice the different methods of development used in each:

Robotics is the science that deals with the construction, capabilities, and applications of robots. Most robots are used to perform tedious, dangerous, or otherwise undesirable work in factories. . . . These industrial robots can work where humans cannot, and do not need protective devices. They never need time off; a typical industrial robot is up and running 97 percent of the time! And the quality of work never suffers. Further, management never has to contend with sick, tired, or bored robots. The machines never complain, go on strike, or ask for higher wages.

Steven L. Mandell, *Introduction to Computers*

Falling in love is an experience that almost everyone has at least once and usually several times. To fall into love is to fall into a profound set of emotional experiences. There may be a range of physical symptoms such as dry mouth, pounding heart, flushed face, and knotted stomach. The mind may race, and fantasy, especially about the loved one, is rampant. Motivation to work, play, indeed for anything except the lover, may fall to zero. As the love feelings develop, strong feelings of passion may occur.

In fact, passionate love is essentially the same as romantic love, except that the focus is more specifically on the emotional intensity and sexual passion.

Clyde Hendrick and Susan Hendrick, *Liking, Loving, & Relating*

In the appropriate spaces below, list the different methods of development you identified in each of the definitions:

1. Robotics

description, comparison/contrast

_____

2. Falling in love

description, comparison/contrast, cause and effect

_____

EXERCISE 7.7   Choose a subject to define. Your subject does not have to be an object; it can be an action, an emotion, an event, a type of person, or anything else that interests you and that you know enough about to define for a reader. Once you have selected your subject, think about the different methods you might use to define it. Can you describe it, compare or contrast it with something or someone else, illustrate it, discuss its causes or effects, and so on? Decide which of the methods would explain your subject most clearly to a reader and write a paragraph using at least two different methods of development.

RECOGNIZING DIFFERENT METHODS OF DEVELOPMENT

As a reader, you will use your knowledge of the different methods of development to understand what you read. Recognizing a familiar pattern of development helps you anticipate how writers are going to present their ideas or information and therefore helps you understand them better. The following exercise will give you practice in recognizing different methods of development.

EXERCISE 7.8   Read the following paragraphs carefully. Then (1) write the main idea of the paragraph in your own words and (2) state its primary pattern of organization (narration, description, illustration, comparison/contrast, classification, cause and effect, or definition). If you discover that other patterns of organization have been used to support the primary pattern, **Answers will vary.**   list them in parentheses.

PARAGRAPH A

So Grant and Lee were in complete contrast, representing two diametrically opposed elements in American life. Grant was the modern man emerging; beyond him, ready to come on the stage, was the great age of steel and machinery, of crowded cities and a restless burgeoning vitality. Lee might have ridden down from the old age of chivalry, lance in hand, silken banner fluttering over his head. Each man was the perfect champion of his cause, drawing both his strengths and his weaknesses from the people he led.

Bruce Catton, *Grant and Lee: A Study in Contrasts*

Main idea: **Grant and Lee were opposites.**

Method(s) of paragraph development: **comparison/contrast**

(description)

PARAGRAPH B

Melody is that element of music which makes the widest and most direct appeal. It has been called the soul of music. It is generally what we remember and whistle and hum. We know a good melody when we hear it and we recognize its unique power to move us, although we might be hard put to explain wherein its power lies. The world has always lavished a special affection upon the creators of melody; nothing is more intimately associated with inspiration, not only in the popular mind but also among musicians.

Adapted from Joseph Machlis, *The Enjoyment of Music*

Main idea: **Melody is the most appealing element of music.**

Method(s) of paragraph development: **definition**

(cause and effect)

PARAGRAPH C

If the system involves the use of a computer, one or more computer programmers may be asked to write a computer program for a particular procedure. For example, a computer programmer may be asked to write a program for computing the gross and net pay for each pay period. Another programmer may be asked to program the procedure for the preparation of paychecks and employee earnings statements. Another may be asked to program the procedure for preparing the quarterly tax reports required by the federal government. Each of these programs will be part of the payroll data processing system.

Beryl Robichaud et al., *Introduction to Data Processing*

Main Idea: **Each particular procedure requires a different**

computer program.

Method(s) of paragraph development: **illustration**

PARAGRAPH D

The main types of crime in the United States can be conveniently classified into four principal categories: crimes of violence; crimes against property; crimes without victims; and white-collar and corporate crime. Our information about crime comes primarily from the annual reports of the Federal Bureau of Investigation (FBI), which compiles data provided by local police forces. The FBI regards crimes of violence and crimes against property as the most serious offenses. These acts—homicide, robbery, rape, aggravated assault, burglary, larceny, auto theft, and arson—are known as the eight "crime index" offenses, and the FBI reports concentrate on them.

Ian Robertson, *Sociology*

Main idea: **There are four types of crime: crimes of violence, crimes against property, crimes without victims, and white-collar and corporate crime.**

Method(s) of paragraph development: **classification**

PARAGRAPH E

One night a moth flew into the candle, was caught, burnt dry, and held. I must have been staring at the candle, or maybe I looked up when a shadow crossed my page; at any rate, I saw it all. A golden female moth, a biggish one with a two-inch wingspread, flapped into the fire, dropped abdomen into the wet wax, struck, flamed, and frazzled in a second. Her moving wings ignited like tissue paper, like angels' wings, enlarging the circle of light in the clearing and creating out of the darkness the sudden blue sleeves of my sweater, the green leaves of jewelweed by my side, the ragged red trunk of a pine; at once the light contracted again and the moth's wings vanished in a fine, foul smoke. At the same time, her six legs clawed, curled, blackened, and ceased, disappearing utterly. And her head jerked in spasms, making a spattering noise; her antennae crisped and burnt away and her heaving mouthparts cracked like pistol fire. When it was all over, her head was, so far as I could determine, gone, gone the long way of her wings and legs. Her head was a hole lost to time. All that was left was the glowing horn shell of her abdomen and thorax—a fraying, partially collapsed gold tube jammed upright in the candle's round pool.

Annie Dillard, "Death of a Moth," in *Pilgrim at Tinker Creek*

Main idea: **One night a moth flew into the flame of a candle and burned up.**

Method(s) of paragraph development: **cause and effect (narration, description)**

PARAGRAPH F

Hiroshima was a fan-shaped city, lying mostly on the six islands formed by the seven estuarial rivers that branch out from the Ota River; its main commercial and residential districts, covering about four square miles in the center of the city, contained three-quarters of its population, which had been reduced by several evacuation programs from a wartime peak of 380,000 to about 245,000. Factories and other residential districts, or suburbs, lay compactly around the edges of the city. To the south were the docks, an airport, and the island-studded Inland Sea. A rim of mountains runs around the other three sides of the delta.

Adapted from John Hersey, *Hiroshima*

Main idea: **Hiroshima was shaped like a fan.**

Method(s) of paragraph development: **description**

PARAGRAPH G

Despite these common assumptions, television highlighted not the candidates' words but their manner of presentation. Radio listeners, who were not distracted by visual appearances, reacted favorably to Nixon's speeches. But the television cameras accentuated the vice president's heavy "five o'clock shadow" and dark eye sockets. His makeup dripped, and his body movements seemed stiff. Suffering from a severe cold, he looked unhealthy, if not unsavory. In contrast, Kennedy brought a dramatic flair to the television screen. He seemed comfortable and confident. The television format, by projecting the candidates as equals, added to Kennedy's national reputation. Subsequent polls indicated that the debates may have influenced as many as four million voters; of these, Kennedy gathered three-quarters.

David W. Noble et al., *Twentieth Century Limited*

Main idea: **The televised debate helped Kennedy and hurt Nixon because**

Kennedy looked better than Nixon.

Method(s) of paragraph development: **comparison/contrast**

(illustration, description)

PARAGRAPH H

On week days Polk Street was very lively. It woke to its work about seven o'clock, at the time when the newsboys made their appearance together with the day laborers. The laborers went trudging past in a straggling file—plumbers' apprentices, their pockets stuffed with sections of lead pipe, tweezers, and pliers; carpenters, carrying nothing but their little paste-board lunch baskets painted to imitate leather; gangs of street workers, their overalls soiled with yellow clay, their picks and long-handled shovels over their shoulders; plasterers, spotted with lime from head to foot. This little army of workers, tramping steadily in one direction, met and mingled with other toilers of a different description—conductors and "swing men" of the cable company going on duty; heavy-eyed night clerks from the drug stores on their way home to sleep; roundsmen returning to the precinct police station to make their night report, the Chinese market gardeners teetering past under their heavy baskets. The cable cars began to fill up; all along the street could be seen the shop keepers taking down their shutters.

Frank Norris, McTeague

Main idea: **During the week, Polk Street was very busy.**

_____

Method(s) of paragraph development: **description (narration)**

_____

PARAGRAPH I

I have always wondered why my own best friends were so important to me; but it wasn't until recently that something happened to make me really understand my relationship with my best friends. My father died, and this was a crisis for me. Most of my friends gave me their condolences. But my best friends did more than that: they actually supported me. They called long distance to see how I was and what I needed, to try and help me work out my problems or simply to talk. Two of my best friends even took time from their spring break and, along with two other best friends, attended my father's memorial service; none of my other friends came. Since then, these are the only people who have continued to worry about me and talk to me about my father. I know that, whenever I need someone, they will be there and willing to help me. I know also that, whenever they need help, I will be ready to do the same for them.

Howard Solomon, Jr., "Best Friends," in Subject and Strategy

Main idea: **Best friends are important because they**

are supportive.

Method(s) of paragraph development: **cause and effect (illustration)**

READING AND WRITING ABOUT—

Television

Preparing: Cubing—

A helpful method for generating, or creating, ideas is a variation of free-writing called *cubing.* Cubing encourages you to consider a topic— an object, event, person, place, or idea—from six different points of view. That is, you examine the topic from the six sides of an imaginary cube:

1. ***Describe it.*** Look at the subject closely and describe what you see—colors, shapes, sizes, and so forth.
2. ***Compare it.*** What is it similar to? What is it different from?
3. ***Associate it.*** What does it make you think of? What comes into your mind? These may be similar or different things, events, times, places, people. Just let your mind go and see what associations you have for this subject.
4. ***Analyze it.*** Tell how it's made, what class it fits, its causes, or its effects.
5. ***Apply it.*** Tell what you can do with it, how it can be used. You might even give examples.
6. ***Argue for or against it.*** Go ahead and take a stand. Use any kind of reasons you want to—rational, silly, or anywhere in between.

Adapted from Gregory Cowan and Elizabeth Cowan, *Writing*

With the help of this prewriting technique, you will be able to focus on ideas before reading about them and to see possibilities for writing in the most unlikely subjects. For example, the following cubing of a clock suggests two or three interesting possibilities for writing:

1. *Describe it:* The clock is about three inches square and light ivory in color with a white face. The white face has black numbers with a black minute hand and a black hour hand. The turquoise second hand constantly turns clockwise, and a little gold alarm hand is nearly hidden under the other larger hands. The brand name *General Electric* is written in small black letters on the lower portion of the inner circle of numbers. The time is . . .

2. *Compare it:* This small alarm clock can be compared with a much larger clock, with the battery clock over our mantel, for instance, or with a large grandfather clock in a beautiful wooden cabinet. Of course, this little clock costs only a fraction of the price of a grandfather clock. The little alarm clock can also be compared with a smaller timepiece, such as a pocket watch or a wristwatch. Size doesn't necessarily make a smaller timepiece less expensive; however, a small wristwatch may cost as much as a grandfather clock. And yet the inexpensive alarm clock can tell time just as accurately as . . .

3. *Associate it:* The clock reminds me of deadlines, of unfinished tasks, of getting up in the morning before I am ready to get up. It also reminds me of sleepless nights looking at the clock ticking away beside my bed, of jerking awake and looking at it in the middle of the night when the phone rings with emergency calls from the hospital about sick parents. The clock can be beneficial, but I have mostly negative associations about . . .

4. *Analyze it:* The clock itself can be broken down into its various parts: its outer covering, the clock face and its parts, the inner gears, and the cord that connects it to its life force of electricity. Perhaps, though, the clock suggests a more interesting analysis—that of time itself, of what time means to me and other people I know, of how important time is in our country as compared with countries in South America or Europe, for example.

5. *Apply it:* To apply the clock, I must think about how I use it. I check the clock when I wake up in the morning to see how long I can snooze before I get up. I check it when I go to bed at night to see how long I have to sleep. When it is in sight, I look at it before I check my watch.

6. *Argue for or against it:* A clock is necessary to my life, but sometimes I would like to throw it out the window! I get tired of deadlines, of rushing from one class to another, from one meeting to another. Sometimes I wish I could get rid of all these deadlines and go back to a life of more natural rhythms—one where I could determine my life instead of the clock's determining it. Yet as I think about it, a baby's life is one of natural rhythms but of no real purpose other than existence, and I wouldn't want to go back to that kind of life. So I guess I need the clock even though I don't really like it.

From this cubing, you could write a narrative of the events surrounding a particular emergency call, a comparison of different kinds of timepieces, or a cause-and effect essay about how you react to deadlines. Now, practice the cubing technique by applying it to the topic *television.* Spend approximately three minutes on each angle. As in your regular freewriting, just try to get your ideas down on paper without worrying about form or correctness. When your instructor gives you the signal to switch points of view, stop—even in midsentence—and switch to the new point of view. When you finish your cubing exercise, you will be surprised not only at how much you have written but also at what interesting ideas you have discovered. Your instructor may ask you to read and discuss your cubings in pairs or small groups.

▨ WHY I QUIT WATCHING TELEVISION
P. J. O'Rourke

Before you read, think about your attitude toward television. Does watching television serve a useful purpose, or is it a waste of time? How many hours a day do you spend watching television? In the following essay,* P. J. O'Rourke explains why he quit watching television and then provides a humorous account of how not watching television affected his life. O'Rourke was the editor of the *National Lampoon* during the 1970s. His books include *Parliament of Whores: A Lone Humorist's Attempts to Explain the Entire U.S. Government* and *Give War a Chance.*

As you read, try to determine O'Rourke's main point about television. In spite of his title, has he *really* "quit watching television"? In addition, circle any unfamiliar words that you encounter.

Annotations will vary.

1   I remember the exact moment I quit watching television. It was 10 years ago. I had a girlfriend who was a compulsive viewer. We were at her apartment on a Sunday afternoon, sitting on the couch, and I was . . . Well, I was nuzzling her ear, making little kissy noises, and generally acting like a boyfriend. Then, all of a sudden, I experienced one of those devastating realizations: She was watching a *Star Trek* rerun over my shoulder.

---

* Reprinted with permission from *Parade* and the author, copyright © 1985.

2   We had a big fight. I'm still wondering where our relationship went wrong. She's still wondering if Captain Kirk got beamed up in time to escape from the Klingons.

3   I was tired of watching television anyway. TV was too dumb. And TV was too much trouble. Not too much trouble to watch, of course, but there was too much trouble on the screen. Every show seemed to be about murder, theft, car chases or adultery. I was living in Manhattan at the time, and if I wanted to see those things, I could look out my window. Even comedy shows like *M*A*S*H* were about people getting blown apart. I figured there was enough real tragedy every day. Why get four more hours of it on TV every night? I gave my television set away.

4   TV is such a waste of time, I thought. I never considered how else I'd fill my evenings and weekends. It turns out there are worse things to do with time than waste it; more expensive things, anyway.

5   In my newfound leisure hours, I fixed up my apartment. This cost $12,000–$600 for the do-it-yourself remodeling and $11,400 for the carpenters, painters and plasterers to repair the damage I'd done. I also took up downhill skiing and paid $1,500 for equipment when I probably could have gotten somebody to break my leg for free. And I began to read. This sounds worthwhile, but anyone who worries about the lewdness and mayhem on TV ought to peek into *The Satyricon* by Petronius or *Gargantua and Pantagruel* by Rabelais or some Shakespeare plays or even the Old Testament. Most of my reading, though, wasn't quite so brainy. I read paperbacks like *Murder for Brunch*. It's hard to call these more intellectual than *The Gong Show*.

6   Without a TV set (and with a new girlfriend), I had time for conversation. But a lot of conversations, if they go on long enough, turn into arguments. What's dumber—watching *Family Feud* or arguing about whether to get a TV so we *could* watch *Family Feud?*

7   Not having a TV is supposed to bring families closer together. I didn't have a family, so this didn't help me.

8   Not having a TV turns out to be more strange than virtuous. I don't see any trend-setting shows like *Miami Vice,* so I don't know what to wear. I still dress like John Cameron Swayze. Without TV advertising, I don't understand new consumer products. Styling mousse, for instance—is it edible? And since, as a spectator, I'm limited to home teams, I've lost interest in most professional sports. I'm honestly not sure what the Seattle Seagulls are. They may be a girls' field hockey team, for all I know. (Editor's note: They're the Sea*hawks*—a football team.)

9   *People* magazine, newspaper gossip columns and friends' conversations are filled with names that mean nothing to me—"Prince," "Sting," "Peewee," "Appollonia." Sounds like a litter of puppies. And the celebrities I do recognize are mystifying. Imagine Mr. T completely out of *The A-Team* context: What kind of character could he possibly play?

10   Lack of a television set has more severe effects too. No TV means no VCR. That is, I actually paid to see *Flashdance* and couldn't even fast-forward through the parts where Jennifer Beals has all her clothes on. Furthermore, I'm getting fat. When you don't have to wait for a commercial to get up and get a sandwich and a beer, you can get up and get a lot more beer and sandwiches.

11   So maybe television isn't so bad for us as it's supposed to be. To research this story, I borrowed my next-door neighbor's TV—or, rather, I borrowed his whole TV room, since televisions are connected to cables now, so you can get 100 silly channels instead of five or six. I watched some shows at the start of the new season; *Hell Town, Hometown, Crazy Like a Fox, Stir Crazy,* etc. There were a few

surprises. On MTV, I saw the video of a song I thought was a tender love ballad. It turns out to be sung by guys in leather underwear chasing a girl through a sewer.

12   But, mostly, television was just the same. It was kind of comforting to see Johnny Carson again, a little grayer but with the same slack gags. Most of the shows are still violent, but I live in New Hampshire these days, and we don't have as much murder, theft or car-chasing (and not even as much adultery) as some might like. The shows are still dumb, but I'm 10 years older, and I've forgotten how perfect everything is in the television world. The people are all pretty. The pay phones all work. And all the endings are hopeful. That's not so bad. Most of us real people are a bit homely, a lot of our endings are hopeless. TV's perfect world was a relief. So I was sitting, comfortable as a pig, in my neighbor's armchair, punching remote-control buttons with my snout.

13   But I didn't enjoy it. No, sir. Not me. I've spent a whole decade acting superior to everybody because I don't watch television. I'm not about to back down and start liking it now. (Though I might drop in next door about 8 tonight. That's when *Amazing Stories* comes on.)

REVIEWING THE READING   Answers will vary.

See paragraphs 1–3; 11–13.

1. According to O'Rourke, why did he quit watching television? At the time the essay was written, had he *really* quit watching television? How do you know?

See paragraphs 6, 8–12.

2. The overall structure of the essay is based on the method of cause and effect. Which paragraphs detail the effects of not watching television? What are two or three of these effects?

3. O'Rourke uses other methods of paragraph development besides cause and effect.

See paragraph 1.

a. Which paragraph(s) is based primarily on narration?

See paragraphs 5, 6, 8–12.

b. Which paragraphs combine illustration with cause and effect?

4. A writer's attitude toward his or her subject is expressed in the *tone* of the writing. Tone can be light or serious, humorous or ironical, happy or sad. What is the tone of O'Rourke's essay?

UNDERSTANDING VOCABULARY

How many unfamiliar words did you circle while reading this essay? Did you circle *compulsive, devastating* (paragraph 1), *lewdness,* and *mayhem* (paragraph 5)? You should be able to figure out the meanings of the first two words from the context of paragraphs 1 and 2. However, if you have not read the books O'Rourke mentions in paragraph 5, you cannot use the context to define the last two words. *Lewdness* means "vulgar, indecent"; *mayhem* means "senseless destruction or injury of people and/or property." If these words are new to you, add them to your personal vocabulary list.

REACTING CRITICALLY

In paragraphs 8 and 9, O'Rourke makes several allusions, or references, to items of popular culture—to fashions, consumer products, sports, musical performers, and other celebrities—that a television viewer would understand. Do you think it is as important to be able to recognize allusions to popular culture as it is to be able to recognize allusions to literature, mythology, and history? Why or why not?

◼ THE TROUBLE WITH TELEVISION

Robert MacNeil

Before you read, think about the title of this essay. Do you agree or disagree that there is "trouble with television"? What problems can television cause? In the following essay, Robert MacNeil, the co-anchor of the *MacNeil/Lehrer NewsHour* on the Public Broadcasting Service, discusses the negative effects that he fears television has on its viewers. MacNeil presented a longer version of this essay in a speech delivered on November 13, 1984, at the President's Leadership Forum at the State University of New York at Purchase, New York.

Annotations will vary.   *As you read,* underline phrases that suggest MacNeil's thesis and purpose.

1   It is difficult to escape the influence of television. If you fit the statistical averages, by the age of 20 you will have been exposed to at least 20,000 hours of television. You can add 10,000 hours for each decade you have lived after the age of 20. The only things Americans do more than watch television are work and sleep.

2   Calculate for a moment what could be done with even a part of those hours. Five thousand hours, I am told, are what a typical college undergraduate spends working on a bachelor's degree. In 10,000 hours you could have learned enough to become an astronomer or engineer. You could have learned several languages fluently. If it appealed to you, you could be reading Homer in the original Greek or Dostoyevsky in Russian. If it didn't, you could have walked around the world and written a book about it.

3   The trouble with television is that it discourages concentration. Almost anything interesting and rewarding in life requires some constructive, consistently applied effort. The dullest, the least gifted of us can achieve things that seem miraculous to those who never concentrate on anything. But television encourages us to apply no effort. It sells us instant gratification. It diverts us only to divert, to make the time pass without pain.

4   Television's variety becomes a narcotic, not a stimulus. Its serial, kaleidoscopic exposures force us to follow its lead. The viewer is on a perpetual guided tour: 30 minutes at the museum, 30 at the cathedral, 30 for a drink, then back on the bus to the next attraction—except on television, typically, the spans allotted are on the order of minutes or seconds, and the chosen delights are more often car crashes and people killing one another. In short, a lot of television usurps one of the most precious of all human gifts, the ability to focus your attention yourself, rather than just passively surrender it.

5   Capturing your attention—and holding it—is the prime motive of most television programming and enhances its role as a profitable advertising vehicle. Programmers live in constant fear of losing anyone's attention—anyone's. The surest way to avoid doing so is to keep everything brief, not to strain the attention of anyone but instead to provide constant stimulation through variety, novelty, action and movement. Quite simply, television operates on the appeal to the short attention span.

6   It is simply the easiest way out. But it has come to be regarded as a given, as inherent in the medium itself; as an imperative, as though General Sarnoff, or one of the other august pioneers of video, had bequeathed to us tablets of stone commanding that nothing in television shall ever require more than a few moments' concentration.

7   In its place that is fine. Who can quarrel with a medium that so brilliantly packages escapist entertainment as a mass-marketing tool? But I see its values now pervading this nation and its life. It has become fashionable to think that, like fast food, fast ideas are the way to get to a fast-moving, impatient public.

8   In the case of news, this practice, in my view, results in inefficient communication. I question how much of television's nightly news effort is really absorbable and understandable. Much of it is what has been aptly described as "machine-gunning with scraps." I think the technique fights coherence. I think it tends to make things ultimately boring and dismissible (unless they are accompanied by horrifying pictures) because almost anything is boring and dismissible if you know almost nothing about it.

9   I believe that TV's appeal to the short attention span is not only inefficient communication but decivilizing as well. Consider the casual assumptions that television tends to cultivate: that complexity must be avoided, that visual stimulation is a substitute for thought, that verbal precision is an anachronism. It may be old-fashioned, but I was taught that thought is words, arranged in grammatically precise ways.

10   There is a crisis of literacy in this country. One study estimates that some 30 million adult Americans are "functionally illiterate" and cannot read or write well enough to answer a want ad or understand the instructions on a medicine bottle.

11   Literacy may not be an inalienable human right, but it is one that the highly literate Founding Fathers might not have found unreasonable or even unattainable. We are not only not attaining it as a nation, statistically speaking, but we are falling further and further short of attaining it. And, while I would not be so simplistic as to suggest that television is the cause, I believe it contributes and is an influence.

12   Everything about this nation—the structure of the society, its forms of family organization, its economy, its place in the world—has become more complex, not less. Yet its dominating communications instrument, its principal form of national linkage, is one that sells neat resolutions to human problems that usually have no neat resolutions. It is all symbolized in my mind by the hugely successful art form that television has made central to the culture, the 30-second commercial: the tiny drama of the earnest housewife who finds happiness in choosing the right toothpaste.

13   When before in human history has so much humanity collectively surrendered so much of its leisure to one toy, one mass diversion? When before has virtually an entire nation surrendered itself wholesale to a medium for selling?

14   Some years ago Yale University law professor Charles L. Black, Jr., wrote: ". . . forced feeding on trivial fare is not itself a trivial matter." I think this society is being force-fed with trivial fare, and I fear that the effects on our habits of mind, our language, our tolerance for effort, and our appetite for complexity are only dimly perceived. If I am wrong, we will have done no harm to look at the issue skeptically and critically, to consider how we should be resisting it. I hope you will join with me in doing so.

REVIEWING THE READING   Answers will vary.

1. Although the primary method of development in this essay is cause and effect, MacNeil also uses several other methods of development to achieve his purpose. For example, find at least one paragraph developed by illustration.

See paragraph 2.

2. Paragraphs 8, 9, and 14 are developed through cause and effect. Analyze these paragraphs, finding the cause(s) and effect(s) in each.

3. Paragraph 7 of MacNeil's essay is the fulcrum—the central point in the essay. In this paragraph, MacNeil uses an effective persuasive technique by admitting the opposing viewpoint—that a place exists for television's "escapist entertainment." However, with his transition word *but*, he immediately introduces the major point, or main idea, that he will develop throughout the remainder of the essay. What idea does he introduce in this sentence?

See paragraphs 7 and 14.

4. Although MacNeil begins his essay with a general statement that looks and sounds like a thesis, this statement is not his thesis. In fact, he builds toward his thesis throughout his entire essay. Write this thesis in your own words.

5. In his last paragraph, MacNeil not only clarifies his thesis but also states his purpose. What is his purpose?

UNDERSTANDING VOCABULARY

Several different types of context clues can help you define words you encounter in your reading. The four most frequently used types of clues can all be found in MacNeil's essay. Use the clues and explanations provided in the passages below to define the underlined words.

1. *Restatement:* "But television encourages us to apply no effort. It sells us instant <u>gratification</u>. It diverts us only to divert, to make the time pass without pain" (paragraph 3). From the meaning of *divert* ("to entertain or amuse") and the remaining explanation about passing time without pain, you can tell that *gratification* means "satisfaction, contentment, happiness."

2. *Contrast:* "Television's variety becomes a narcotic, not a <u>stimulus</u>" (paragraph 4). If you know that a narcotic is a drug that dulls the senses, then you know that the opposite meaning (and thus the definition of *stimulus*) is "something that excites the senses."

3. *Example:* "But it has come to be regarded as a given, as inherent in the medium itself; as an <u>imperative</u>, as though General Sarnoff, or one of the other august pioneers of video, had bequeathed to us tablets of stone commanding that nothing in television shall ever require more than a few moments' concentration" (paragraph 6). The example of General Sarnoff's "command" suggests that an *imperative* is "an order or command," "something that is absolutely necessary."

4. *Synonym:* "Consider the casual assumptions that television tends to cultivate: that complexity must be avoided, that visual stimulation is a substitute for thought, that verbal precision is an <u>anachronism</u>. It may be old-fashioned, but I was taught that thought is words" (paragraph 9). The synonym *old-fashioned* tells you that an *anachronism* is "something that occurs out of its proper time," often something that is old-fashioned.

If one or more of these words is new to you, add the word(s) and definition(s) to your personal vocabulary list.

REACTING CRITICALLY

1. The figures that MacNeil gives about average television viewing times suggest that television is *addictive*, or habit forming. Are you addicted to television, or do you know someone who is? Does the television addict you know watch only certain types of shows or just whatever happens to be on at the time? What are the immediate effects of television addiction? What are the long-range effects?

2. According to MacNeil, television news can be described as "machine-gunning with scraps." Explain this metaphor. What effect does this type of news reporting have on viewers?

3. MacNeil believes that television's tendency to sell "neat resolutions to human problems that usually have no neat resolutions" is symbolized by the television commercial. In your opinion, what effects do these commercials have on their viewers? Do commercials present an unrealistic and even stereotyped view of life? Give examples.

▓ TELEVISION FANTASIES
Peggy Charren and Martin Sandler

Before you read, think about the effect of television on the way you and other viewers see the world around you. For example, is your understanding of the structure and functioning of a police department, a law office, a courtroom, or a hospital strongly influenced by what you have seen on television? In the following selection from their book *Changing Channels: Living (Sensibly) with Television* (1982), Peggy Charren and Martin Sandler discuss the influence of television on viewer expectations.

Annotations will vary.

As you read, look for Charren and Sandler's thesis. Underline words, phrases, and sentences that suggest this thesis.

description

1   The world according to television is a world of extremes. There are very few shades of gray in TV's world of fantastic feats, crucial moments, and urgent emotions. Most television characters are either beautiful or ugly, benevolent or ruthless. In TV's world neither the people nor the situations are average, for average is dull and dull doesn't draw ratings.

cause and effect

2   For people who watch a lot of TV, programs set up expectations that life and the process of everyday living resemble what they see on their sets. When our day-to-day existence turns out to be not as simple, not as neatly packaged, not as happy, as that portrayed on TV, frustration and tension are often the result. When the real world doesn't mesh with expectations set by watching TV, we believe there is something wrong with us. This is particularly true for those who have limited life experiences. For these viewers, television provides almost all of the information they receive about people with lifestyles different from their own.

cause and effect (illustration)

3   The world of television is one in which, according to a study by George Gerbner, policemen, doctors, lawyers, judges and law-breakers outnumber all other working people combined. On TV there are almost no clerical workers, salespeople, artists, or engineers. And blue collar workers, the largest segment of the working force in the real world, are nearly invisible. The result is that heavy TV-watchers and children come to know more about spies, coroners, and small-

town sheriffs than they do about those who carry out the basic tasks in American society.

comparison/contrast 4 (illustration)

In the world of television, police and private detectives alike fill their days with devil-may-care car chases, shoot-ups, and amorous adventures. The real world is far less glamorous: police handle plenty of traffic violations and domestic problems, and private detectives chase debtors, look for missing people, and shadow straying husbands and wives. Television's private eyes regularly solve crimes and bring criminals to justice; most real private detectives have little to do with the actual solving of major crimes.

comparison/contrast 5

And, of course, TV's men in blue always get their man, with a speed unprecedented in the annals of real life, since loose ends must be neatly tied by the close of the thirty- or sixty-minute segment. What of the long hours, mundane tasks, and many frustrations that plague real-life law enforcers, what of the bad guys who never get caught? Where are they on TV? . . .

cause and effect 6

The typical action-adventure shows that feature private detectives, police, or other law enforcement agencies are put together by highly skilled writers, producers, and technicians. Actual police or FBI buildings are shown. Locales around the world are used and identifiable landmarks are featured. Official badges and uniforms are commonplace. Often we are told that the episode is based on some actual case (only the names have been changed to protect the innocent), and at the end of some of these programs we are even informed as to what sentence was given to the "actual criminals." All of this gives an air of authenticity to these series, increasing problems for viewers who have difficulty distinguishing between the truth and the fantasy world of TV.

cause and effect 7 (illustration)

These misconceptions cause trouble in the real world of lawyer's offices and courtrooms. Lawyers around the country report increased difficulty conveying to clients just what they as lawyers can and cannot accomplish. If Perry Mason can wrap up a case successfully in an hour, why can't they? And many legal officials are concerned that jurors will expect clearcut resolutions of cases as a result of TV lawyers' freeing their clients by breaking down witnesses on the stand and then pointing to the actual criminal before the startled eyes of judge and jury.

REVIEWING THE READING   Answers will vary.

See text annotations.
1. Is Charren and Sandler's thesis stated or implied? What is this thesis?

2. "Television Fantasies" explains how unrealistic television shows (the causes) produce unrealistic expectations (the effects) in viewers. The primary method of development in the essay, then, is cause and effect. However, the authors use a variety of methods of development in the individual paragraphs within the essay. Determine the method(s) of development used in each of the seven paragraphs in the essay and write the method(s) in the margin beside each paragraph.

See paragraphs 4–7.
3. According to the authors, what specific aspects of life are misrepresented or oversimplified by television?

UNDERSTANDING VOCABULARY

At least four words from this essay—*benevolent* (paragraph 1), *amorous* (paragraph 4), *unprecedented* (paragraph 5), and *misconceptions* (paragraph 7)—may be unfamiliar to you. An analysis of word parts, however, can help you define each of these words. Use the meanings of the following roots and affixes to define the four words listed above:

PREFIXES	ROOT	SUFFIXES
bene- = good, well	*amor* = love	*-ed* = past tense (*v.*)
con- = with, together	*ced* = go	*-ous* = full of (*adj.*)
mis- = bad, wrong	*cep* = take	*-tion* = act of (*n.*)
pre- = before	*vol* = wish	*-ent* = characterized
un- = not		by (*adj.*)

Add to your personal vocabulary list these and other words that you would like to learn from the readings in this chapter.

REACTING CRITICALLY

1. Compare the purpose and tone of MacNeil's essay with the purpose and tone of the essay by Charren and Sandler. Which is more serious? Which is more persuasive?

2. Charren and Sandler state in paragraph 5 that problems appear to be easily resolved on television because "loose ends must be neatly tied by the close of the thirty- or sixty-minute segment." What effect does this apparently easy resolution have on the viewer's—especially the young viewer's—perception of life? Do some shows give a more realistic picture of life? Give examples of such shows.

Responding in Writing

Select one of the following assignments as the basis of an essay about television. If possible, write your rough draft on a word processor.

1. Use the cubing from your prewriting exercise to help you narrow the topic of "television" and to decide on a particular method of development. For example, you might *compare* two family shows; you might *classify* television dramas into various types; you might *analyze* the effects of television commercials on viewers; or you might *argue* for or against retaining a new and controversial program in the prime time line-up. Remember that even if you base your essay on one primary method of development, you may develop individual paragraphs within the essay by other methods. Give your essay a clearer purpose and context by writing to a particular audience. For example, you might write to persuade the director of programming at a national network or at your local television station to agree with your stand on a controversial program.

2. In pointing out that television is a source of information about popular culture, O'Rourke implies an educational purpose to television. Write an essay to parents in which you argue that television is or is not educational. Be sure to include specific reasons and examples.

3. The authors of both "The Trouble with Television" and "Television Fantasies" focus on the negative aspects of television programming. Write an essay in which you argue that television can have positive effects.

4. Charren and Sandler argue that television does not present a realistic view of life. Write an essay agreeing or disagreeing with Charren and Sandler. Be sure to support your argument with specific reasons and examples.

Revising Your Writing—

Meet with a group of two or three classmates and answer the following questions about one another's essays:

1. What is the purpose of the essay? Who is the audience? Does the essay achieve its purpose and communicate to its audience? Why or why not?

2. What is the main idea of the essay? Is it clearly stated or implied? Where is it stated or implied? Does it need to be revised? If so, in what way?

3. What is the primary method of development? What other methods of development are used? Are these the most effective methods of development for the writer's purpose and audience? What other methods could be used?

4. Does the essay include enough effective support (such as details, examples, causes, and effects)? What are the most effective details? What additional support could be added? Does the essay contain any details that should be omitted because they do not support the main idea? If so, which details should be omitted?

5. Does the essay include clear transitions? What are they? If not, where and how could transitions be provided or improved?

6. How does the essay conclude? Is this conclusion effective? If not, how could it be made more effective?

After you have revised, edit your work for problems in sentence structure, punctuation, spelling, and word choice. Remember that reading or scrolling backwards a sentence at a time helps you to see errors better.

CHAPTER EIGHT
Studying and Reacting to Ideas

The reading process varies significantly, depending on the purpose of the reader and what is being read. Browsing through the funny pages of the Sunday newspaper is not the same as reading a novel, and scanning the classified ads for a used car is not the same as reading a chapter of a textbook. Sometimes you read strictly for pleasure; other times you read for information. Reading includes browsing, skimming, studying, scanning, and memorizing. Efficient readers are aware of these different types of reading and adjust their rate and manner of reading to accommodate their purposes. In this chapter, you will learn more about how to read when your primary purpose is studying.

OUTLINING TO STUDY

Outlining can be an important aid to reading when your purpose is to learn the material being read. If you outline what you read, you force yourself to focus on your reading task and to analyze the content and structure of what you are reading. Because it involves writing, outlining also reinforces learning and retention. Furthermore, an outline provides you with a written record of the most important ideas from your reading—a record that can be invaluable when the time comes for a written assignment or a test.

Study outlines are informal outlines that help you understand and remember what you read. Study outlines, like planning outlines, do not have to conform to any one format or any specific restriction. They can be as informal and individual as you want to make them. They can also be visual diagrams or maps (see pp. 30–31 for examples).

A useful study outline is one that is still comprehensible to you weeks or even months after you have written it, so your outline needs to be clear and complete. A useful study outline is also comprehensive and accurate; it includes all of the important ideas and does not distort their meaning. If you have not previously constructed study outlines, you may find the following general guidelines helpful.

1. Read the *entire* passage carefully.
2. Determine the author's main idea and state it in your own words.
3. Decide on the major subdivisions. (Be sure that all of the major supporting points are of equal importance.)
4. Under each major division, list the more specific supporting points. (Do *not* include too many minor details.)

GUIDED PRACTICE

Use the guidelines above to outline the following paragraph:

1. Read the *entire* passage carefully.

Comedy is usually defined as the opposite of tragedy. One reason definitions of comedy are rarely given is that there are two distinct types of comedy, and these two types are very different. The first type, low comedy, is loud, uninhibited, occasionally physical, and often vulgar. For example, slapstick comedy is considered low comedy. The second type, high comedy, is sophisticated, subtle, and usually romantic. The situation comedies so popular with television viewers are an example of high comedy. Because these two types of comedy are so different, it is difficult to define comedy.

Answers will vary.

2. Determine the author's main idea and state it *in your own words.*

There are two different types of comedy.

Answers will vary.

3. Decide on the major subdivisions. (Be sure these major points are of equal importance.)

First major point: **The first type is low comedy.**

Second major point: **The second type is high comedy.**

4. Under each major division, list the more specific supporting points. (Do *not* include minor details or, as a rule, examples.)

Specific supporting points under first major point:

loud, uninhibited, occasionally physical, and often vulgar

Specific supporting points under second major point:

sophisticated, subtle, and usually romantic

Your outline probably does not include information from either the first or last sentence of the paragraph. Since the first sentence is not the topic sentence but merely an introduction to the main idea (which is stated in the second sentence), it has no information that needs to be included. The last sentence serves as a conclusion and restates the main idea, so it, too, contains no new information. You may have also omitted the examples of the two types of comedy. However, if these examples helped you understand the difference between the two types, you may have included them as minor supporting points.

Now you are ready to construct your outline. Use any format or arrangement with which you are comfortable, but be sure that you (1) indicate the order in which the points on your outline occur and (2) show the appropriate relationships among major and minor supporting points.

When you have completed your outline, you may want to compare it with those of your classmates. Notice that the same basic outline can assume many different forms.

▓ EXERCISE 8.1

Outlines will vary.

Thesis statement See *Instructor's Resource Guide* for sample outline.

Using the guidelines given above, outline the following paragraphs. We have provided a thesis statement for you.

▓ **Thesis:** The origins of modern chemistry can be traced back to ancient civilizations.

1   The earliest attempts to explain natural phenomena led to fanciful inventions—to myths and fantasies—but not to understanding. Around 600 B.C., a group of Greek philosophers became dissatisfied with these myths, which explained little. Stimulated by social and cultural change as well as curiosity, they began to ask questions about the world around them. They answered these questions by constructing lists of logical possibilities. Thus, Greek philosophy was an attempt to discover the basic truths of nature by thinking things through, rather than by running laboratory experiments. The Greek philosophers did this so thoroughly and so brilliantly that the years between 600 and 400 B.C. are called the "golden age of philosophy."

2   During this period, the Greek philosophers laid the foundation for one of our main ideas about the universe. Leucippus (about 440 B.C.) and Democritus (about 420 B.C.) were trying to determine whether there was such a thing as a smallest particle of matter. In doing so, they established the idea of the atom, a particle so tiny that it could not be seen. At that time there was no way to test whether atoms really existed, and more than 2,000 years passed before scientists proved that they do exist.

3   While the Greeks were studying philosophy and mathematics, the Egyptians were practicing the art of chemistry. They were mining and purifying the metals gold, silver, and copper and were making embalming fluids and dyes. They called this art *khemia*, and it flourished until the seventh century A.D., when it was taken over by the Arabs. The Egyptian word *khemia* became the Arabic word *alkhemia* and then the English word *alchemy*. A major goal of the alchemists was to transmute (convert) "base metals" into gold. That is, they wanted to transform less desirable elements such as lead and iron into the element gold. The ancient Arabic emperors employed many alchemists for this purpose, which, of course, was never accomplished. The alchemists also tried to find the "philosopher's stone" (a supposed cure for all diseases) and the "elixir of life" (which would prolong life indefinitely). Unfortunately they failed in both attempts, but they did have some lucky accidents. In the course of their work, they discovered acetic acid, nitric acid, and ethyl alcohol, as well as many other substances used by chemists today.

4   The modern age of chemistry dawned in 1661 with the publication of the book *The Sceptical Chymist*, written by Robert Boyle, an English chemist, physicist, and theologian. Boyle was "skeptical" because he was not willing to take the word of the ancient Greeks and alchemists as truth, especially about the elements that make up the world. Instead, Boyle believed that scientists must start from basic principles, and he realized that every theory had to be proved by experiment. His new and innovative scientific approach was to change the whole course of chemistry.

Adapted, Alan Sherman, Sharon Sherman, and Leonard Russikoff,
Basic Concepts of Chemistry

SUMMARIZING

Many of the skills you use in outlining are also used in writing a summary—a concise restatement of a reading selection. To summarize, you must have a good understanding of what you have read and be able to identify clearly the main idea and the major supporting points. Then you must restate these ideas in your own words. Thus, summarizing, like outlining, requires both reading and writing skills.

Guidelines to Follow in Summarizing

Reading the Selection

Summarizing requires two important reading skills: (1) finding the main idea and (2) determining major supporting points. Neither of these skills is new to you. You simply need to see how they apply to summarizing. Below are some suggestions for how to read a selection you plan to summarize.

1. *Read through the entire selection before you start to summarize.* If you try to summarize as you read, you will very likely fail to recognize the major ideas, and your summary will be too long and inclusive.

2. *Identify the author's main idea.* If the main idea is expressed in a topic sentence, you might want to underline this sentence.

3. *Determine the major supporting points and their relationship to the main idea.* Again, underlining may be helpful.

Writing the Summary

After you have read through the selection carefully and have gone back over it to determine the main idea and major supporting details, you are ready to begin writing your summary. The length of a summary depends on the length of the original selection. For example, a summary of a thirty-page textbook chapter might be several pages long. In summarizing a paragraph, however, you would probably write only one sentence, or two or three at most. A good rule of thumb is that your summary should be approximately one-third the length of the original.

Writing a summary requires all of the writing skills you have studied so far. In addition, here are several specific suggestions that may prove helpful.

1. *If you know the title and author of the selection you are summarizing, include them in your summary.* You may combine this information and the main idea statement in one sentence. (See example in Guided Practice below.)

2. *Include only the author's main ideas and the important supporting details.* Do not insert your own ideas or unimportant details.

3. *Write in your own words.* Use the author's ideas but not the author's words unless you include a direct quotation.

4. *Be brief and to the point.* The whole idea of summarizing is to condense the main ideas of the original into as few words as possible.

GUIDED PRACTICE

To summarize, you first need to read through the entire passage and then go back and identify the main idea and major supporting points. We have underlined the main idea in the following paragraph.

> Children display an amazing ability to become fluent speakers of any language consistently spoken around them. Every normal human child who is not reared in virtual isolation from language use soon comes to speak one or more languages natively. The child's learning of his native language is not dependent on special tutoring. Parents may spend many hours "reinforcing" every recognizable bit of their child's verbal activity with a smile or some other reward, or trying by means of "baby talk" to bridge the gap between their mature language competence and the child's immature one. But there is no particular reason to believe that such activity has any bearing on the child's ultimate success in becoming a native speaker of his parents' language. Children can pick up a language by playing with other children who happen to speak it just as well as they can through the concentrated efforts of doting parents. All they seem to need is sufficient exposure to the language in question.

> Adapted from Ronald W. Langacker, *Language and Its Structure*

One possible summary of this passage follows:

> In *Language and Its Structure,* Ronald W. Langacker points out that children learn to speak any language that is spoken around them without any special instruction.

■ EXERCISE 8.2   Read the following paragraphs and write a summary of each:

Answers will vary.

PARAGRAPH A

American men don't cry because it is considered unmasculine to do so. Only sissies cry. Crying is a "weakness" characteristic of the female, and no American male wants to be identified with anything in the least weak or feminine. Crying, in our culture, is identified with childishness, with weakness and dependence. No one likes a crybaby, and we disapprove of crying even in children, discouraging it in them as early as possible. In a land so devoted to the pursuit of happiness as ours, crying really is rather un-American. Adults must learn not to cry in situations in which it is permissible for a child to cry. Women being the "weaker" and "dependent" sex, it is only natural that they should cry in certain emotional situations. In women, crying is excusable. But in men, crying is a mark of weakness. So goes the American credo with regard to crying.

Ashley Montagu, *The American Way of Life*

Summary: **Ashley Montagu points out that in America crying is considered unmasculine if not un-American. Although women and children are allowed to cry on occasion, men are taught that crying is a sign of weakness.**

PARAGRAPH B

Let me put this in another way. It is true that there are bad teachers—teachers who do not prepare for class, who are arbitrary, who subject their students to sarcasm, who won't tolerate (let alone encourage) questions and criticism, or who have thought little about education. But there are also bad students. By "bad students" I do not mean students who get low grades. Instead, I mean students who do not participate sufficiently in their own education and who do not actively demand enough from their teachers. They do not ask questions in class or after class. They do not discuss the purposes of assignments with their teachers. They do not make the teacher explain the importance and significance of the subject being studied. They do not go to office hours. They do not make the teacher explain comments on papers handed back to the student. They do not take notes on the readings. They just sit in class, letting the teacher do all the work. Education can only be a cooperative effort between student and teacher. By actively participating in these and other ways, you play your proper and necessary part in this cooperative process.

Jack W. Meiland, *College Thinking: How to Get the Best Out of College*

Summary: **In *College Thinking: How to Get the Best Out of College*, Jack W. Meiland defines "bad students" as those who are not actively engaged in their own education. Rather than participating in classes and communicating with their teachers, these students are passive and uninvolved in the process of learning.**

PARAGRAPH C

I believe that it is an increasingly common pattern in our culture for each one of us to believe, "Every other person must feel and think and believe the same as I do." We find it very hard to permit our children or our parents or our spouses to feel differently than we do about particular issues or problems. We cannot permit our clients or our students to differ from us or to utilize their experience in their own individual ways. On a national scale, we cannot permit another nation to think or feel differently than we do. Yet it has come to seem to me that this separateness of individuals, the right of each individual to utilize his experience in his own way and to discover his own meaning in it—this is one of the most priceless potentialities of life. Each person is an island unto himself, in a very real sense; and he can only build bridges to other islands if he is first of all willing to be himself and permitted to be himself.

Adapted from Carl Rogers, *On Becoming a Person*

Summary: **According to Carl Rogers in *On Becoming a Person*,**

most people in our society think that others "must feel and think and

believe" as they do. They have difficulty allowing family members, business

associates, or other nations to be different. However, every individual has a

right and a responsibility to "be himself."

PARAGRAPH D

For thousands of years human beings have communicated with one another first in the language of dress. Long before I am near enough to talk to you on the street, in a meeting, or at a party, you announce your sex, age and class to me through what you are wearing—and very possibly give me important information (or misinformation) as to your occupation, origin, personality, opinions, tastes, sexual desires and current mood. I may not be able to put what I observe into words, but I register the information unconsciously; and you simultaneously do the same for me. By the time we meet and converse we have already spoken to each other in an older and more universal tongue.

Alison Lurie, *The Language of Clothes*

Summary: **Alison Lurie points out in *The Language of Clothes* that clothes**

are a form of communication because they tell us a great deal about the

person who is wearing them.

Summarizing Essays

Writing a summary of a longer composition, such as an essay or a textbook chapter, is similar to writing a summary of a paragraph. Whether you are summarizing a paragraph or a longer passage, you must read through the entire selection and identify both the author's main idea and major supporting details. In summarizing a paragraph, you look for a stated or implied *topic sentence;* in summarizing an essay or chapter, you look for a stated or implied *thesis statement.* In writing a summary of a paragraph, you determine the major supporting details; in writing a summary of an essay, you determine the main ideas of each paragraph.

GUIDED PRACTICE

In the passage below, we have identified the thesis and underlined the main supporting points.

Thesis: Between married partners, there are three main types of loneliness.

1   Loneliness is seldom alleviated by marriage. People who marry each other so they will stop being lonely often discover that the most excruciating loneliness of all is shared with another.

2   There are three main types of loneliness. First, there is the loneliness of the individual who simply has not learned how to get along with people. When such lonely people marry each other, each one has high expectations of his spouse. Neither realizes that the other is paralyzed by the same limitations as he is. As a result, both of them wind up lonelier than ever. The TV and movie play *Marty,* where a shy, inarticulate man meets a shy, inarticulate woman and they find happiness together, is about on a par with *Cinderella* when it comes to realism.

3   A second type of loneliness is found in people who are the very opposite of those in the first group. They have bright personalities and well-developed social skills and are obsessed with the desire to be popular at all costs. Such people make good sales and advertising personnel and social leaders. Many of them give the appearance of being ''sexy,'' when in reality they may be sexually unskilled or frigid, even though they may have had a number of affairs with the opposite sex. This type of person finds it difficult to be intimate with anyone whom he does not feel to be his inferior. The fact remains, however, that in marriage—as in relations with people in general—unless one person can deal with another on a basis of equality, he will be lonely, no matter how outgoing and what a good mixer he may appear to be.

4   A third kind of loneliness is seen in the type of person who must be best in whatever it is he does. Many successful people in the arts, industry and business fall into this category. Often they are kind and loving only to those who can be useful to them. People of this sort trust no one to do anything well, suspecting that almost everyone—even their spouses—will stand in the way of their headlong rush toward success. They require virtually every-thing and everyone to revolve around themselves. If they are glamorous or powerful enough, they may be able to get mates who will put up with this for a while. However, such marriages usually don't last, and they try again and again, drifting from one marriage to another, becoming more and more sus-picious and more and more lonely.

Adapted from William J. Lederer and Don D. Jackson,
"Types of Loneliness," in *The Miracles of Marriage*

EXERCISE 8.3   In the space below, write a one-paragraph summary of the passage you have just read. The first sentence of your summary (the topic sentence) should include the authors' names, the title of the reading selection, and

Summaries will vary.

the main idea. Write your summary in your own words. If you include specific phrases from the passage, be sure to enclose them in quotation marks. Your summary has been started for you:

"Types of Loneliness" by William J. Lederer and Don D. Jackson

states that **even married people can be lonely. The authors identify three**

types of loneliness common among married couples: (1) the loneliness

that results when one or both partners are very shy, (2) the loneliness that

results when one partner can be intimate only with someone he or she

considers inferior, and (3) the loneliness that results when one partner is

driven to be successful and is considerate only of the people who can

be of help in reaching this goal.

USING GRAPHICS TO IMPROVE READING

Textbooks often include a variety of graphics, or visual representations, in addition to words and photographs. Textbook writers use charts, graphs, tables, diagrams, and illustrations to reinforce and supplement the information they are providing in the text. For example, in the first chapter of this text we include several diagrams to help you understand (visualize) the reading and writing processes. And in the section on taking essay exams in this chapter, we provide you with a pie chart that clearly shows how you should budget your time when you are taking an essay exam (see p. 184). The purpose of graphics is to present information in a form that is easily understood by a reader.

If you ignore the graphics that a writer includes, you are failing to take advantage of a useful reading strategy. Although a picture may not be worth a thousand words, it is worth a few minutes of your time. Examining a chart, graph, or diagram can provide you with a new way of perceiving the information presented in the text as well as with additional information. Moreover, graphics are an excellent means of "testing" your comprehension. If you cannot interpret a graphic, you probably need to reread the section of the text to which it refers.

Most graphics are self-explanatory. In fact, they are designed to be as simple and explicit as possible. However, if you have not worked with graphics very much before, you may find the following guidelines helpful:

1. Examine the graphic carefully after you have read the explanation of it in the text.

2. Read the title and/or explanation of the graphic that is usually provided just above or below it.

3. Examine all the figures and words included in the graphic (especially those that appear along the top, bottom, and sides of the graphic).

4. Summarize in your own words the information provided by the graphic.

5. Compare your summary with the explanation provided in the text.

The following paragraph from a psychology text discusses Ebbinghaus's Curve of Forgetting, which explains how rapidly we lose information that we have learned. Below the paragraph is a line graph that illustrates this concept. Read the paragraph and then examine the line graph, noticing especially how one reinforces the other.

The course of forgetting   The systematic study of forgetting was also begun by Ebbinghaus. To measure forgetting, he devised the *method of savings*, which involves computing the difference between the number of repetitions needed to learn a list of words and the number of repetitions needed to relearn it after some time has elapsed. This difference is called the **savings.** If it took Ebbinghaus ten trials to learn a list and ten more trials to relearn it, there would be no savings, and forgetting would have been complete. If it took him ten trials to learn the list and only five trials to relearn it, there would be a savings of 50 percent. As you can see in the graph below, Ebbinghaus found that some savings existed even thirty-one days after the original learning. In general, savings declines (and forgetting increases) as time passes. However, the most dramatic drop in what people retain in long-term memory occurs during the first nine hours, especially in the first hour. After this initial decline, the rate of forgetting slows down considerably.

LINE GRAPH

Ebbinghaus's Curve of Forgetting

Ebbinghaus found that most forgetting occurs during the first nine hours after learning, especially during the first hour. After that, forgetting continues, but at a much slower rate (Ebbinghaus, 1885).

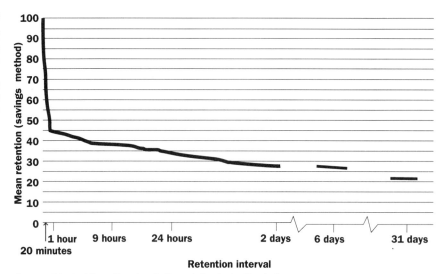

Source: Adapted from Douglas A. Bernstein et al., *Psychology.*

■ EXERCISE 8.4   Now examine the following two common types of graphics and answer the questions that accompany each.

BAR GRAPH

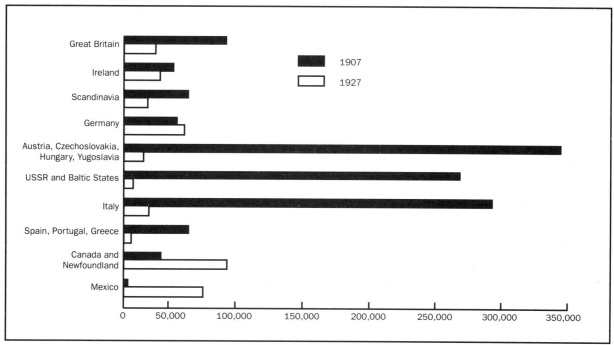

Source: Mary Beth Norton et al., "Immigration, 1907 and 1927," *A People and a Nation: A History of the United States.*

1. From what country (or countries) did the greatest number of immigrants come in 1907? **Austria, Czechoslovakia, Hungary, Yugoslavia**

    In 1927? **Canada and Newfoundland**

2. Approximately how many immigrants came from Germany in 1927?

    65,000 to 70,000

3. In 1907, the second largest group of immigrants came from what country? **Italy**

4. Did Ireland send more immigrants to the United States in 1907 or in 1927? **1907**

5. Which countries sent more immigrants to the United States in 1927 than in 1907? **Germany, Canada and Newfoundland, and Mexico**

TABLE   Per Capita Public School Expenditure, by States, 1985

State	Average per Pupil	Rank	State	Average per Pupil	Rank
Alabama	$2,241	49	Montana	3,968	11
Alaska	6,867	1	Nebraska	3,128	31
Arizona	2,801	40	Nevada	2,998	34
Arkansas	2,344	47	New Hampshire	2,964	36
California	3,291	26	New Jersey	5,220	3
Colorado	3,398	24	New Mexico	3,278	28
Connecticut	4,477	6	New York	5,226	2
Delaware	4,155	7	North Carolina	2,588	45
District of Columbia	4,753	5	North Dakota	3,249	30
Florida	3,409	21	Ohio	3,315	25
Georgia	2,692	42	Oklahoma	3,264	29
Hawaii	3,596	17	Oregon	3,963	12
Idaho	2,290	48	Pennsylvania	4,002	10
Illinois	3,517	18	Rhode Island	4,097	9
Indiana	2,638	44	South Carolina	2,650	43
Iowa	3,409	21	South Dakota	2,813	39
Kansas	3,668	16	Tennessee	2,349	46
Kentucky	2,792	41	Texas	3,287	27
Louisiana	2,821	38	Utah	2,182	51
Maine	3,038	33	Vermont	3,783	15
Maryland	4,101	8	Virginia	3,043	32
Massachusetts	3,889	13	Washington	3,437	19
Michigan	3,434	20	West Virginia	2,866	37
Minnesota	3,408	23	Wisconsin	3,880	14
Mississippi	2,205	50	Wyoming	4,809	4
Missouri	$2,993	35			

Source: U.S. Bureau of the Census, *Statistical Abstract of the United States, 1986* (Washington, D.C.: U.S. Government Printing Office, 1986). Reprinted, Ian Robertson, *Sociology.*

1. In 1985, which state had the greatest per capita public school expenditure? **Alaska**

   What was the average per capita expense in this state? **$6,867**

2. In 1985, which state had the lowest per capita public school expenditure? **Utah**

   What was the average per capita expense in this state? **$2,182**

3. Where does Illinois rank in per capita public school expenditure?

   18

TAKING ESSAY EXAMS

Much of what you have already learned in this chapter can help you when you are taking an essay exam. For example, essay exam questions often ask you to outline the steps in a process or to summarize something you have read.

Below is a list of the common types of instructions you may encounter when taking an essay exam. Each type of instruction has been defined for you:

Analyze. Discuss the various elements of an issue or an event, as in analyzing causes or effects.

Compare. Examine specific events, beliefs, individuals, qualities, or problems to show similarities. (Differences may also be mentioned.)

Contrast. Examine specific events, beliefs, individuals, qualities, or problems to show differences.

Discuss. Examine and analyze in detail a specific issue or problem, considering all sides of the issue.

Enumerate. Although you may answer this type of question in paragraph form, you should answer concisely, listing items instead of discussing them thoroughly. Some instructors prefer items listed and numbered in columns.

Explain. Clarify and interpret fully, showing how and why a certain event occurred or a certain belief developed. Often this requires a discussion of causes and effects, as in the question, "Explain the causes. . . ."

Illustrate. Present a clear, complete example to clarify your answer.

Relate. Show connections and relationships among ideas, individuals, or events.

Summarize. Present the main ideas in concise, summary form.

Trace (*narrate*). Describe the progress, sequence, or development of events or ideas.

Understanding the terms in the preceding list will help you get started on your essay. The following guidelines can also help you perform more successfully on essay examinations:

1. ***Read through the entire examination.*** Pay close attention to the directions and note whether you are to answer all questions or only a specified number. Reading through the entire test gives you an overview of the information to be covered and may prevent unnecessary and time-consuming overlapping in your answers. As you read each question, you may want to jot down ideas and examples in the margin so you will not forget them later.

2. ***Budget your time.*** After reading through all of the questions, determine the total time for the test, the total number of questions to be answered, and the point value for each question. Then quickly plan how you will use your time, allowing a short planning period and a review period but saving the bulk of your time for actually answering the questions. Considering the point value of each question, divide your total time into blocks. On p. 184 is an illustration of how you might budget your time for a one-hour examination with four test questions, each of different point values:

FIGURE 25

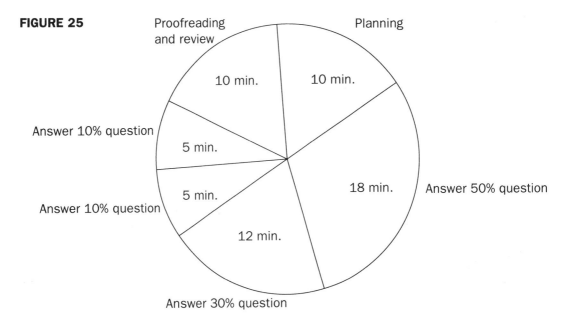

Proofreading and review — 10 min.
Planning — 10 min.
Answer 10% question — 5 min.
Answer 50% question — 18 min.
Answer 10% question — 5 min.
Answer 30% question — 12 min.

3. *Analyze the question carefully.* Circle or underline key words such as *compare*, *explain*, or *summarize*, and be sure you understand what each key word requires of you. Also be sure to notice whether the question contains more than one part.

4. *Follow directions.* Be sure you understand the directions, and then follow them closely. If you have been asked to list, don't discuss; if you have been asked to discuss, don't list.

5. *Plan your answer to each question.* Use scratch paper or the inside cover of your test booklet to make a rough outline of the ideas you intend to discuss.

6. *Answer each question clearly, directly, and completely.* Give your thesis or main idea in the first sentence. If there are two or more subpoints to your answer, you may indicate this in your thesis. (Example: The Native Americans of North and South America differed in their civilizations, their governments, their religions, and their property concepts.) As you develop your thesis, include specific and thorough support, but don't ramble. In a short essay question, your thesis can probably be developed in a paragraph; a longer essay question may require a short essay of three or more paragraphs. In either case, pay close attention to transition and include a concluding statement.

7. *If you don't remember the answer to a question, leave a blank space for it.* Return to it after you have finished the other questions. You might remember the answer before you finish the exam. (Sometimes there are clues in other questions.) It is also a good idea to leave wide margins and blocks of blank space after each answer so you can add information you remember later.

8. *Proofread your answers.* Rereading your answers will give you a chance to catch careless mistakes in spelling and punctuation. Reviewing your answers may also jog your memory and help you think of points that did not occur to you earlier. If so, you will be glad you left extra time and space to add to your answers.

■ EXERCISE 8.5   The ability to predict essay questions can help you prepare more effectively for your examinations. Review the chapter readings listed below and write a possible essay examination question for each.

1. The History of Chemistry (Exercise 8.1, p. 173)
2. Types of Loneliness (p. 178)

After you have written your questions, exchange them with one or more classmates. Did you predict the same questions? Which ones would your instructor be most likely to give on an actual examination?

■ EXERCISE 8.6   Write the answer to one of your essay examination questions.

DRAWING CONCLUSIONS

When a writer does not state the main idea in a thesis or topic sentence, you must use the information provided in the passage to form your own conclusion. Using the information that is available to you plus your own logic, you must *infer* the main idea—that is, you must draw a conclusion.

GUIDED PRACTICE

In the following reading selection, the main idea is not stated in a topic sentence. However, the writer has given you the information you need to draw a conclusion about the main idea.

1   ■   They didn't say anything about this in the books, I thought, as the snow blew in through the gaping doorway and settled on my naked back.

2   I lay face down on the cobbled floor in a pool of nameless muck, my arm deep inside the straining cow, my feet scrabbling for a toe hold between the stones. I was stripped to the waist and the snow mingled with the dirt and the dried blood on my body. I could see nothing outside the circle of flickering light thrown by the smoky oil lamp which the farmer held over me.

3   No, there wasn't a word in the books about searching for your ropes and instruments in the shadows; about trying to keep clean in a half bucket of tepid water; about the cobbles digging into your chest. Nor about the slow numbing of the arms, the creeping paralysis of the muscles as the fingers tried to work against the cow's powerful expulsive efforts.

4   There was no mention anywhere of the gradual exhaustion, the feeling of futility and the little far-off voice of panic.

5   My mind went back to that picture in the obstetrics book. A cow standing in the middle of a gleaming floor while a sleek veterinary surgeon in a spotless parturition overall inserted his arm to a polite distance. He was relaxed and smiling, the farmer and his helpers were smiling, even the cow was smiling. There was no dirt or blood or sweat anywhere.

6   That man in the picture had just finished an excellent lunch and had moved next door to do a bit of calving just for the sheer pleasure of it, as a kind of dessert. He hadn't crawled shivering from his bed at two o'clock in the morning and bumped over twelve miles of frozen snow, staring sleepily ahead till the lonely farm showed in the headlights. He hadn't climbed half a mile of white fell-side to the doorless barn where his patient lay.

James Herriot, *All Creatures Great and Small*

Answers will vary.

Using the facts and details that are given in this reading selection, what conclusion can you logically draw?

Experience is the best teacher.

■ EXERCISE 8.7

Answers will vary.

Below are three paragraphs in which the main ideas are not stated. Read each one, studying the information that is given to draw an appropriate conclusion.

PARAGRAPH A

Hands stained and brow dripping perspiration, the young man struggled to complete the task before him. He had been working for hours, and his body ached with exhaustion. His back hurt from hours of bending over his task; his head hurt from the intense concentration and mental effort he had expended; and his hand hurt from gripping the tool with which he was working. Furthermore, his mind had never felt so fatigued—so utterly depleted. Moaning to himself, he picked up his leaking pen and bent once more over his smudged paper. He must go on. The essay was due in the morning.

Conclusion: **Writing is hard work.**

PARAGRAPH B

Henry VIII became king of England in 1509. His first wife was Catherine of Aragon, who was unable to give him a male child. Dissatisfied with Catherine, Henry became interested in Anne Boleyn, for whom he challenged the Church and divorced Catherine. Ann, too, failed to bear him a male child, so she was charged with adultery and beheaded. Next, Henry married Jane Seymour, who gave him a male heir, Prince Edward, and then conveniently died. Later, Henry married Anne of Cleves on the strength of her portrait. Being disappointed in the real Anne, however, he bought her off and sent her away to a remote castle. He then married Catherine Howard, a pretty young woman who was unfaithful to him and who, not surprisingly, was beheaded for her infidelity. Finally, Henry married Catherine Parr, a young widow to whom he remained happily married until his death.

Conclusion: **Henry VIII married and disposed of his wives casually and**

callously when they did not please him.

PARAGRAPH C

Several model communities were organized in America in the 1800s. In the 1820s Robert Owen founded New Harmony, a community in which all property was cooperatively owned and which did not allow religious worship or marriage; however, internal problems caused the community to be abandoned after only a few years. Brook Farm was organized in 1841 by several New England thinkers and writers, but the community did not succeed economically. In the 1840s, forty model communities were set up by Charles Fourier, but all of them failed, partly because they were made up of intellectuals from the city who soon became dissatisfied with rural farm life. The Oneida community, established by John Humphrey Noyes, was more successful; nevertheless, popular resentment of its practice of communal marriages caused its breakup. The only model utopian or religious community to experience any lengthy success was the Shaker community founded by Mother Ann Lee.

Conclusion: **Most nineteenth-century model communities were**

unsuccessful.

_____

CRITICAL READING AND WRITING

Of the different types of reading, critical reading is the most demanding. Browsing through a magazine or reading a mystery novel makes very few demands on your intellect because you are reading primarily for pleasure. Reading for information requires more mental effort, for you must be sure in these instances that you understand what you are reading. Often too, when you read for information, you must try to remember what you read, so you are striving not only to comprehend but also to retain what you read. Critical reading takes you a step beyond literal comprehension. When you read critically, you are attempting not only to comprehend but also to *evaluate* the significance of the writer's assertions. The step from comprehension to evaluation is not an easy one. It requires first that you understand what you read on a literal level and then that you judge the validity of the ideas and information you have read. Ultimately, however, all educated people need to be able to read critically—to react intellectually as well as emotionally to what they read.

Every educated person also needs to be able to express his or her critical reaction in writing. Critical writing requires that you *understand* what you read, *evaluate* the information and ideas in what you read, and then *express* your evaluation clearly and coherently so that a reader can understand not only your ideas but also those of the author to whom you are responding. As you can see, critical reading and writing require that you use all of the skills you have been studying in this book. You must be able to identify and draw conclusions about main ideas, summarize those ideas for your reader, and then clearly express your own ideas.

Here are some guidelines for critical reading and writing.

1. Read the selection carefully, underlining the main ideas and key words and phrases.
2. Summarize the selection (be as brief but as clear as possible), stating the author and title and the author's purpose, main idea, and major supporting points.
3. Evaluate the main ideas in the selection. Be sure that you:
    a. state whether you agree or disagree with the main ideas.
    b. state your reasons for agreeing or disagreeing.

c. state the strengths and weaknesses of the selection.

d. evaluate how well the author achieves the purpose of the selection.

4. Carefully read and revise what you have written to be sure it is clear, well organized, and adequately developed. Make changes and corrections where they are needed.

These guidelines should be useful to you in any assignment that requires critical reading and writing. However, the skill of reading and writing critically is one that is developed slowly as you gain experience with reading and writing. There is no formula or set of rules that can automatically give you these complex skills. Most of all, critical reading and writing require *thinking*—a skill that cannot be acquired instantly. The more you think seriously about what you read and write, the more accomplished you will become as a critical reader and writer.

GUIDED PRACTICE

To illustrate how you might use these guidelines, we have included below a brief essay, which we have annotated (underlined the important ideas), summarized, and evaluated.

1   Baltimore Maryland. I was waiting for breakfast in a coffee shop the other morning and reading the paper. The paper had sixty-six pages. The waitress brought a paper place mat and a paper napkin and took my order, and I paged through the paper.

2   The headline said, "House Panel Studies a Bill Allowing Clear-Cutting in U.S. Forests."

3   I put the paper napkin in my lap, spread the paper out on the paper place mat, and read on: "The House Agriculture Committee," it said, "is looking over legislation that would once again open national forests to the clear-cutting of trees by private companies under government permits."

4   The waitress brought the coffee. I opened a paper sugar envelope and tore open a little paper cup of cream and went on reading the paper: "The Senate voted without dissent yesterday to allow clear-cutting," the paper said, "Critics have said clear-cutting in the national forests can lead to erosion and destruction of wildlife habitats. Forest Service and industry spokesmen said a flat ban on clear-cutting would bring paralysis to the lumber industry." And to the paper industry, I thought. Clear-cutting a forest is one way to get a lot of paper, and we sure seem to need a lot of paper.

5   The waitress brought the toast. I looked for the butter. It came on a little paper tray with a covering of paper. I opened a paper package of marmalade and read on: "Senator Jennings Randolph, Democrat of West Virginia, urged his colleagues to take a more restrictive view and permit clear-cutting only under specific guidelines for certain types of forest. But neither he nor anyone else voted against the bill, which was sent to the House on a 90 to 0 vote."

6   The eggs came, with little paper packages of salt and pepper. I finished breakfast, put the paper under my arm, and left the table with its used and useless paper napkin, paper place mat, paper salt and pepper packages, paper butter and marmalade wrappings, paper sugar envelope, and paper cream holder, and I walked out into the morning wondering how our national forests can ever survive our breakfasts.

Charles Kuralt, "Down with the Forests," in *Dateline America*

The first paragraph of the following response summarizes Kuralt's essay, identifying his thesis and his two major points. The second paragraph evaluates the essay, giving the reader's reasons for agreeing with Kuralt's stand but pointing out an omission or weakness in the essay.

Main Idea

Summary

     In his essay "Down with the Forests," Charles Kuralt points out that *our widespread use of paper products is a serious threat to our national forests.* He argues that Americans use huge, and probably unnecessary, quantities of paper products; he also argues that this dependence on paper is one reason the government is reluctant to pass laws that prohibit the destruction of entire forests. Kuralt not only implicitly argues against legislation that allows "clear-cutting" in U.S. forests but also indirectly blames American consumers for their thoughtless overuse of paper.

Agreement

Reasons for agreement

Overall strength/weakness

     I agree with Kuralt's basic argument that our forests are in danger and with his implied argument that Americans use too many paper products. By describing in detail how much paper we use in a typical breakfast served in a restaurant, Kuralt dramatically illustrates how we waste paper. Because my own experience confirms that of Kuralt, I too realize that we use a lot of paper products—probably more than we need. Moreover, since paper is made from forests, it is obvious that our extravagant use of paper is directly related to the destruction of forests and perhaps specifically to the loss of our national forests. However, although Kuralt's essay does identify a potentially serious problem, it does not go beyond identification to suggest possible solutions.

■ EXERCISE 8.8   Using the guidelines provided on pages 187–189, read the following selection from *Future Shock* by Alvin Toffler. Then write a paragraph in which you evaluate Toffler's ideas. Be sure that your paragraph includes a summary of the main ideas, a statement of whether you agree, and the reasons for your opinion.

1   Our attitudes toward things reflect basic value judgments. Nothing could be more dramatic than the difference between the new breed of little girls who cheerfully turn in their Barbies for the new improved model and those who, like their mothers and grandmothers before them, clutch lingeringly and lovingly to the same doll until it disintegrates from sheer age. In this difference lies the contrast between past and future, between societies based on permanence, and the new, fast-forming society based on transience.

2   That man-thing relationships are growing more and more temporary may be illustrated by examining the culture surrounding the little girl who trades in her doll. This child soon learns that Barbie dolls are by no means the only physical objects that pass into and out of her young life at a rapid clip. Diapers, bibs, paper napkins, Kleenex, towels, non-returnable soda bottles—all are used up quickly in her home and ruthlessly eliminated. Corn muffins come in baking tins that are thrown away after one use. Spinach is encased in plastic sacks that can be dropped into a pan of boiling water for heating, and then thrown away. TV dinners are cooked and often served on throw-away trays. Her home is a large processing machine through which objects flow, entering and leaving, at a faster and faster rate of speed. From birth on, she is inextricably embedded in a throw-away culture.

3   The idea of using a product once or for a brief period and then replacing it, runs counter to the grain of societies or individuals steeped in a heritage of poverty. Not long ago Uriel Rone, a market researcher for the French

advertising agency Publicis, told me: "The French housewife is not used to disposable products. She likes to keep things, even old things, rather than throw them away. We represented one company that wanted to introduce a kind of plastic throw-away curtain. We did a marketing study for them and found the resistance too strong." This resistance, however, is dying all over the developed world.

4   Thus a writer, Edward Maze, has pointed out that many Americans visiting Sweden in the early 1950's were astounded by its cleanliness. "We were almost awed by the fact that there were no beer and soft drink bottles by the roadsides, as, much to our shame, there were in America. But by the 1960's, lo and behold, bottles were suddenly blooming along Swedish highways. . . . What happened? Sweden had become a buy, use and throw-away society, following the American pattern." In Japan today throw-away tissues are so universal that cloth handkerchiefs are regarded as old fashioned, not to say unsanitary. In England for sixpence one may buy a "Dentamatic throw-away toothbrush" which comes already coated with toothpaste for its one-time use. And even in France, disposable cigarette lighters are commonplace. From cardboard milk containers to the rockets that power space vehicles, products created for short-term or one-time use are becoming more numerous and crucial to our way of life.

5   We develop a throw-away mentality to match our throw-away products. This mentality produces, among other things, a set of radically altered values with respect to property. But the spread of disposability through the society also implies decreased durations in man-thing relationships. Instead of being linked with a single object over a relatively long span of time, we are linked for brief periods with the succession of objects that supplant it.

Adapted from Alvin Toffler, *Future Shock*

READING AND WRITING ABOUT—

Manhood and Womanhood

Preparing: Telling Stories—

For centuries, people have told stories to explain everything from how the world began to where evil came from to what love is. To entertain or make a point, you often tell stories to your friends or family. But you may not have thought that these stories could be used in writing. When a student writer is "stuck" for something to write, a good writing tutor or teacher often simply says, "Well, tell me about it." And the ideas start flowing.

So let's use your oral storytelling skills to help you prepare for writing. Think for a few minutes about the topics "manhood" and "womanhood," which are the focus of the essays by Robert Bly and Sara Davidson in this assignment. What are men like? What are women like? What inner qualities and needs do men and women share? What qualities and needs are different? Then try to think of a story that illustrates manhood or womanhood for you. Your story may be a personal experience, an observation, or a complete fantasy. Finally, meet with a group of two or three of your classmates and tell your stories orally.

◼ THE WEDDING DRESS: WHAT DO WOMEN WANT?

Sara Davidson

Before you read, think about the question "What do women want more than anything?" How would you answer this question? In the following reading, American novelist and journalist Sara Davidson provides one possible response. This selection is taken from *Real Property* (1980). Davidson is also the author of *Loose Change* (1977), a description of what life was like for young middle-class women during the sixties.

As you read, look for the story's answer to the question "What do women want?" Underline key words and phrases that help to answer this question.

Annotations will vary.

1   Danielle Laurent was about to be married, at the age of thirty-three. "Is this your first marriage?" people asked, as she drove around Jerusalem on her motor scooter, ordering flowers and cakes.

2   "Yes."

3   *"Mazel tov!"*

4   Danielle was a French Jew, raised in Paris, but for seven years she had been living in Jerusalem, teaching literature at the Hebrew University. Her fiancé was a professor of physics, thirty-six, also new to marriage. A week before the wedding, Danielle invited friends to come to the home of her aunt, Simone, to spend the evening sewing the wedding dress.

5   I happened to be visiting Jerusalem and was invited. "Please, make an effort," Danielle had said. "I need you."

6   Simone's small house in Abu Tor, overlooking King David's Tower, was filled with women, professional women, ranging from twenty-six to thirty-five. Four were American, one was Spanish, one was Romanian, two were French and three were native Israelis. None was legally married at the time, except Simone.

7   At seventy, Simone is still a beauty, tall and erect, wearing her gray hair in a chignon. Simone has had two lengthy marriages, raised four children and enjoyed a career as a concert violinist. She lived in a villa outside Paris until her first husband died, at forty-two. Her children were away at school by then, so Simone, long a Zionist, immigrated to Israel, where she fell in love with her current husband, Moshe.

8   "I am someone who has lived by love, in love, all my life," she told me as she sat on the couch, her feet propped on pillows. "I have to be an example to the girls."

9   It had been Simone's idea to have the young women sew Danielle's dress by hand, from fabric Simone had bought in India: white silk, with delicate gold embroidery. As we came in, she made us wash our hands and cover our laps with sheets, so the fabric would not be soiled.

10   It was peaceful, sewing together, keeping a watchful circle around Danielle. But there was also a feeling of irony and self-mocking: we were not girls of sixteen, believing in the dress as a passport to the golden land.

11   Simone asked that we go around the circle and take turns telling stories and legends. Danielle, who was first, shook her head no. Her long dark hair covered her eyes as she bent over her sewing. For years, Danielle had been telling herself that what she wanted more than anything was to have a partner, a ''permanent ally,'' and a house full of children. All through her twenties, she had given priority to her work, and assumed she would never have the patience to care for infants. But around the time she turned thirty, it became painful to walk past a children's store. She began to long, to ache for someone to share life with. For thirteen years she had been a waif, fending for herself and traveling across three continents; now that was to change. But could she adjust? Would the love she felt abide?

12   ''Sara, you must provide us with a story,'' Simone said. For a moment, I could think of nothing that seemed appropriate; then I remembered an Arthurian legend I had heard from a friend, Winifred Rosen, who was adapting the tale for a children's book.

13   I began to relate the story, as best I could, from memory. ''In the time of King Arthur and the Round Table, the King was out riding in the forest when he was surprised by a strange knight in full battle dress. The knight drew his sword, but the King said, 'Wait. I'm not armed, you can't do this, it would violate our honor code.' So the knight, whose name was Sir Gromer Somer Joure, had to relent. He made the King promise that he would return to the same spot, alone and unarmed, one year later. The King's life would be spared only if he brought back the answer to this riddle: What do women want, more than anything?''

14   Danielle interrupted the story. ''That's what Freud is supposed to have asked. 'What do women want, dear God?' '' Simone laughed. ''The question did not originate with Freud. It recurs through the ages.'' She turned to me. ''What did King Arthur do?''

15   ''He rode back to the palace and met his nephew, Sir Gawain, who was, you know, the most beautiful and perfect knight in all the kingdom. He told Sir Gawain his plight, and Sir Gawain said, 'Don't worry, I'll ride in one direction, you'll ride in the other, and we'll ask every man and woman we meet, what do women want?'

16   ''So the two of them rode off, and for a year, they asked every person, high and low, wise and simple, what do women want? They were given hundreds of answers.''

17   I stopped to ask the women in Simone's sitting room, ''How would you answer if you had to, 'What do women want more than anything?' ''

18   They paused in their stitching.

19   ''Love.''

20   ''A child.''

21   ''Respect.''

22   ''To be worshiped.''

23   The Romanian lady said, ''I think women want to be men.''

24   Simone smiled, as if she knew none of the above would have saved the King.

25   I continued: ''At the end of the year, Sir Gawain and the King each had a book full of answers. But King Arthur knew he did not have the right answer, and he was prepared to meet his fate, when he saw a woman approaching. This woman was the ugliest hag in creation. She was fat and wrinkled; she had a big nose with snot dripping and hairs sprouting from her face. She gave off a terrible odor. Her teeth were like tusks. She had warts and pus oozing from her eyes. Her name was Dame Ragnell. She rode straight up to the King and said, 'Sir, I alone have

the answer that will save you. I'll tell you on one condition: that you give me Sir Gawain as my husband.'

26   "The King was horrified. 'I can't give you Sir Gawain.' He would rather have died than commit his nephew to such a fate. But Sir Gawain insisted he would marry the hag, gladly, if it would save the King's life.

27   "So King Arthur accepted the terms. 'Now, tell me, what do women want more than anything?'

28   "Dame Ragnell said, 'Sovereignty.' "

29   I paused in my story. We looked at each other, silently, covered with yards of white silk. Everyone seemed to sense instantly how satisfying the answer was.

30   "When King Arthur returned to meet Sir Gromer Somer Joure, he told him the answer, and his life *was* spared. Overjoyed, he rode back to the palace, but he found Dame Ragnell waiting to be married. And she wanted a grand wedding, with all the royal court. After the ceremony, Dame Ragnell gave a little tug at Sir Gawain's sleeve and croaked, 'My lord, I'm your wife now, you have certain duties . . .' "

31   There were groans in the room.

32   "Sir Gawain could barely bring himself to look at her hairy snout, but he was bound by honor. He screwed up his courage, shut his eyes and turned to kiss her, and as he did, she was transformed into the most beautiful, delicate, sensuous creature he had ever dreamed of seeing. They spent the night making love, and as the sun was rising, Dame Ragnell said, 'My beauty will not hold all the time, so you must make a choice. Either have me beautiful by day, when the world can see, and ugly at night; or ugly by day and beautiful in your bed.' "

33   I said to the women, "Which would you choose, if you were Gawain?"

34   The Spanish woman said, "Beautiful by day." But she was quickly outvoted. Danielle said, "If he was a wise man, he would have her beautiful for him alone." Simone abstained, and asked me to continue.

35   "What Sir Gawain said was this: 'My lady, I leave it up to you.' And at that, she became beautiful all the time."

36   Cheers broke out; cakes were passed around. Danielle clapped her hands. "He was a very wise man." Simone, quieting the group, said, "You know, sovereignty is not a problem when you rule alone in your kingdom, but when two sovereign people want to merge their domains . . ." She looked pointedly at her niece. "Ah, that is the riddle you have yet to answer."

REVIEWING THE READING   Answers will vary.

a. See paragraphs 19–23.
b. See paragraph 28.
c. See paragraph 36.

1. The title of the essay asks the same question that King Arthur must answer: "What do women want?"

    a. How do Danielle's friends answer this question?
    b. How does Dame Ragnall answer it?
    c. What paragraph suggests the answer isn't so simple?

2. Notice that Davidson's essay sets up a frame for her story, or a context in which the Arthurian story can logically be told. What is this frame? How is this actual situation related to the story that Sara tells?

a. See paragraph 13.
b. See paragraphs 13, 15–16, and 24–28.
c. See paragraph 30.

3. The Arthurian legend that Sara tells to her friends follows a common story pattern: the quest. A quest usually has three parts—a separation, a test, and a return with some life-saving knowledge.

    a. What causes King Arthur to begin his quest?

b. What is the object of his quest—the test that he must pass? How does he achieve the object of his quest?

c. What happens to King Arthur when he returns with the object of his quest?

See paragraphs 32–35.   4. King Arthur is not the only knight who is tested in this story. What is Sir Gawain's test? How does he pass that test?

UNDERSTANDING VOCABULARY

1. Sara's story about King Arthur's search for the answer to the question "What do women want?" revolves around the meaning of the word *sovereignty*. In your own words, what does *sovereignty* mean? What clues to its meaning are provided in the story? Where do these clues occur?

2. Several other words from Davidson's essay may be new to you. For example, *mazel tov* (paragraph 3) means "good luck." Do you know the meanings of *chignon, Zionist, waif,* and *abstained*? Look up the definition(s) of these or other unfamiliar words in the essay. Add the words and definitions to your personal vocabulary list.

REACTING CRITICALLY

1. Would you have responded to Dame Ragnell as Sir Gawain did? Why or why not?

2. When Sara's story is finished, Simone poses this riddle for Danielle: " 'You know, sovereignty is not a problem when you rule alone in your own kingdom, but when two sovereign people want to merge their domains . . .' She looked pointedly at her niece. 'Ah, that is the riddle you have yet to answer.' " In your opinion, how can two independent people "merge their domains" in a successful or meaningful relationship?

3. You can use the same procedure outlined in the "Critical Reading and Writing" section (pp. 187–189) to help you react to this essay. Do you agree with Davidson's thesis? Why or why not? What are the strengths of the selections? What are its weaknesses? How successful is Davidson in supporting her thesis and achieving her purpose?

▓ IRON JOHN: THE NEW AMERICAN MAN
Robert Bly

Before you read, think about the qualities that you associate with the ideal man. Is he soft and sensitive? Is he firm and decisive? Is he both? Is he in tune with nature? With himself? In the following selection from his book *Iron John: A Book About Men* (1990), Robert Bly explores the developing nature of the American man. Bly is also a prominent American poet and critic—the author of more than fifteen books of poetry and the founder of the literary magazine *Fifties* (*Sixties*, etc.). His collection of poems *The Light Around the Body* won the National Book Award for 1967.

As you read, notice that Bly uses complex words in the first part of his essay but simple, everyday words in the second part—the story of "Find-

Annotations will vary.

ing Iron John." As you read, circle any words that you cannot define from the context of the reading. Some of these words may be defined for you in the glossary in the *Understanding Vocabulary* section, but you may need to look up the definitions of others in a dictionary.

1   We talk a great deal about "the American man," as if there were some constant quality that remained stable over decades, or even within a single decade.

2   The men who live today have veered far away from the Saturnian, old-man-minded farmer, proud of his introversion, who arrived in New England in 1630, willing to sit through three services in an unheated church. In the South, an expansive, motherbound cavalier developed, and neither of these two "American men" resembled the greedy railroad entrepreneur that later developed in the Northeast, nor the reckless I-will-do-without-culture settlers of the West.

3   Even in our own era the agreed-on model has changed dramatically. During the fifties, for example, an American character appeared with some consistency that became a model of manhood adopted by many men: the Fifties male.

4   He got to work early, labored responsibly, supported his wife and children, and admired discipline. Reagan is a sort of mummified version of this dogged type. This sort of man didn't see women's souls well, but he appreciated their bodies; and his view of culture and America's part in it was boyish and optimistic. Many of his qualities were strong and positive, but underneath the charm and bluff there was, and there remains, much isolation, deprivation, and passivity. Unless he has an enemy, he isn't sure that he is alive.

5   The Fifties man was supposed to like football, be aggressive, stick up for the United States, never cry, and always provide. But receptive space or intimate space was missing in this image of a man. The personality lacked some sense of flow. The psyche lacked compassion in a way that encouraged the unbalanced pursuit of the Vietnam war, just as, later, the lack of what we might call "garden" space inside Reagan's head led to his callousness and brutality toward the powerless in El Salvador, toward old people here, the unemployed, schoolchildren, and poor people in general.

6   The Fifties male had a clear vision of what a man was, and what male responsibilities were, but the isolation and one-sidedness of his vision were dangerous.

7   During the sixties, another sort of man appeared. The waste and violence of the Vietnam war made men question whether they knew what an adult male really was. If manhood meant Vietnam, did they want any part of it? Meanwhile, the feminist movement encouraged men to actually look at women, forcing them to become conscious of concerns and sufferings that the Fifties male labored to avoid. As men began to examine women's history and women's sensibility, some men began to notice what was called their *feminine* side and pay attention to it. This process continues to this day, and I would say that most contemporary men are involved in it in some way.

8   There's something wonderful about this development—I mean the practice of men welcoming their own "feminine" consciousness and nurturing it—this is important—and yet I have the sense that there is something wrong. The male in the past twenty years has become more thoughtful, more gentle. But by this process he has not become more free. He's a nice boy who pleases not only his mother but also the young woman he is living with.

9   In the seventies I began to see all over the country a phenomenon that we might call the "soft male." Sometimes even today when I look out at an audi-

ence, perhaps half the young males are what I'd call soft. They're <u>lovely, valuable people</u>—I like them—they're not interested in harming the earth or starting wars. There's <u>a gentle attitude toward life</u> in their whole being and style of living.

10   But many of these men are <u>not happy.</u> You quickly notice the lack of energy in them. They are <u>life-preserving but not exactly life-giving.</u> Ironically, you often see these men with strong women who positively radiate energy.

11   Here we have a finely tuned young man, ecologically superior to his father, sympathetic to the whole harmony of the universe, yet he himself has little vitality to offer.

12   The strong or life-giving women who graduated from the sixties, so to speak, or who have inherited an older spirit, played an important part in producing this life-preserving, but not life-giving, man.

13   I remember a bumper sticker during the sixties that read "WOMEN SAY YES TO MEN WHO SAY NO." We recognize that it took a lot of courage to resist the draft, go to jail, or move to Canada, just as it took courage to accept the draft and go to Vietnam. But the women of twenty years ago were definitely saying that they preferred the softer receptive male.

14   So the development of men was affected a little in this preference. Nonreceptive maleness was equated with violence, and receptive maleness was rewarded.

15   Some energetic women, at that time and now in the nineties, chose and still choose soft men to be their lovers and, in a way, perhaps, to be their sons. The new distribution of "yang" energy among couples didn't happen by accident. Young men for various reasons wanted their harder women, and women began to desire softer men. It seemed like a nice arrangement for a while, but we've lived with it long enough now to see that it isn't working out.

16   I first learned about the anguish of "soft" men when they told their stories in early men's gatherings. In 1980, the Lama Community in New Mexico asked me to teach a conference for men only, their first, in which about forty men participated. Each day we concentrated on one Greek god and one old story, and then late in the afternoons we gathered to talk. When the younger men spoke it was not uncommon for them to be weeping within five minutes. The amount of grief and anguish in these younger men was astounding to me.

17   Part of their grief rose out of remoteness from their fathers, which they felt keenly, but partly, too, grief flowed from trouble in their marriages or relationships. They had learned to be receptive, but receptivity wasn't enough to carry their marriages through troubled times. In every relationship something *fierce* is needed once in a while: both the man and the woman need to have it. But at the point when it was needed, often the young man came up short. He was nurturing, but something else was required—for his relationship, and for his life.

18   The "soft" male was able to say, "I can feel your pain, and I consider your life as important as mine, and I will take care of you and comfort you." But he could not say what he wanted, and stick by it. *Resolve* of that kind was a different matter.

19   In *The Odyssey*, Hermes instructs Odysseus that when he approaches Circe, who stands for a certain kind of matriarchal energy, he is to lift or show his sword. In these early sessions it was difficult for many of the younger men to distinguish between showing the sword and hurting someone. One man, a kind of incarnation of certain spiritual attitudes of the sixties, a man who had actually lived in a tree for a year outside Santa Cruz, found himself unable to extend his arm when it held a sword. He had learned so well not to hurt anyone that he couldn't lift the

steel, even to catch the light of the sun on it. But showing a sword doesn't necessarily mean fighting. It can also suggest a joyful decisiveness.

20   The journey many American men have taken into softness, or receptivity, or "development of the feminine side," has been an immensely valuable journey, but more travel lies ahead. No stage is the final stop.

Finding Iron John

21   One of the fairy tales that speak of a third possibility for men, a third mode, is a story called "Iron John" or "Iron Hans." Though it was first set down by the Grimm brothers around 1820, the story could be ten or twenty thousand years old.

22   As the story starts, we find out that something strange has been happening in a remote area of the forest near the King's castle. When hunters go into this area, they disappear and never come back. Twenty others go after the first group and do not come back. In time, people begin to get the feeling that there's something weird in that part of the forest, and they "don't go there anymore."

23   One day an unknown hunter shows up at the castle and says, "What can I do? Anything dangerous to do around here?"

24   The King says: "Well, I could mention the forest, but there's a problem. The people who go out there don't come back. The return rate is not good."

25   "That's just the sort of thing I like," the young man says. So he goes into the forest and, interestingly, he goes there *alone,* taking only his dog. The young man and his dog wander about in the forest and they go past a pond. Suddenly a hand reaches up from the water, grabs the dog, and pulls it down.

26   The young man doesn't respond by becoming hysterical. He merely says, "This must be the place."

27   Fond as he is of his dog and reluctant as he is to abandon him, the hunter goes back to the castle, rounds up three more men with buckets, and then comes back to the pond to bucket out the water. Anyone who's ever tried it will quickly note that such bucketing is very slow work.

28   In time, what they find, lying on the bottom of the pond, is a large man covered with hair from head to foot. The hair is reddish—it looks a little like rusty iron. They take the man back to the castle, and imprison him. The King puts him in an iron cage in the courtyard, calls him "Iron John," and gives the key into the keeping of the Queen.

REVIEWING THE READING   Answers will vary.

See paragraphs 1, 3, 15, and 20.

See paragraphs 5–10 and 20.

1. What is Bly's thesis, or main idea? Is it stated or implied?

2. Summarize Bly's essay (paragraphs 1 to 20), not including the story "Finding Iron John." In preparing to write your summary, notice that Bly describes the men of the 1950s, 1960s and 1970s. Underline words and phrases that describe the men of each of these decades. According to Bly, what does the future hold for the American man?

3. How does Bly's essay about the changing concepts of American manhood help prepare you to interpret the story of Iron John?

4. Like Davidson's story of King Arthur, Bly's story about finding Iron John also involves a quest. What is this quest? Is it completed?

UNDERSTANDING VOCABULARY

1. Whereas Robert Bly uses a number of complex words in his analysis of the development of American manhood, his illustrative story

"Finding Iron John" uses only simple, concrete words. Why are simple, concrete words so effective in the tale of Iron John?

2. Although you can usually build your vocabulary more effectively by focusing on a few words at a time in your reading or writing, we have provided the following glossary of definitions for several of the more complex words in Bly's analysis of manhood. Use these definitions to help you review any passage that was unclear to you because of an unfamiliar word.

aggressive: bold, hostile, assertive
callousness: lack of feeling, insensitivity, cold-heartedness
cavalier: a gentleman or nobleman who is gallant and carefree
deprivation: need, poverty, being without
ecologically: concerned with ecology, or the relationship between living things and their environments
entrepreneur: a businessperson who operates on a large scale, often originating new ideas; a "wheeler-dealer"
incarnation: a personification or embodiment of something
introversion: directing one's interest and thoughts inward
matriarchal: ruled by one or more women; womanly
nurturing: caring, nourishing, as in a parent's relationship to a child
phenomenon: a curious event or happening
psyche: the soul or mind, conscious or unconscious
receptivity: open-mindedness
remoteness: act of being distant, aloof, withdrawn
resolve: determination or will
Saturnian: related to the Roman god Saturn, but Bly probably means *saturnine*, which means gloomy or reserved
vitality: life, spirit, vigor
yang: in Chinese philosophy, the active masculine principle of the universe, as opposed to *yin,* the female principle

Study the words you circled and those in this glossary. Add to your personal vocabulary list any words you want to add to your vocabulary. Then take a few minutes to review these and the other words on your list. You might even work with a partner to test yourself on some of these new words.

REACTING CRITICALLY

1. Do you agree with Bly's thesis that the American male needs to discover a deeper masculinity? Explain why you agree or disagree. What are the strengths of Bly's argument? What are the weaknesses? How successful is Bly in supporting his thesis and achieving his purpose?

2. In this story "Finding Iron John," what aspect of manhood do you think Iron John represents? Why does the young man have to "bucket out" the pond to find him? Why is Iron John covered with hair that looks like rusty iron? Why does the king imprison him? Why does the king then give the key to the queen and not keep it himself or give it to someone else?

3. How do you think the story of Iron John might end?

Responding in Writing—

Write an essay about manhood or womanhood. To give yourself a clearer purpose and direction, choose one of the specific assignments below:

1. Write an essay about manhood or womanhood. You may develop your essay with a "story"—a personal experience, an observation, or even a fictional story. You might base this story on the three-part-quest structure used by Davidson and Bly, in which the "hero" encounters a problem or a challenge, goes on a journey to solve the problem or meet the challenge, and returns with the resolution to the problem. Whatever structure you use, however, be sure your essay states or clearly implies something important about the nature of men or women.

2. Write an essay answering the question "What do women (or men) want more than anything?" Use the essay structure described in Chapter 5 to structure your essay. That is, include a clear thesis statement in your introduction, and then develop your thesis with several body paragraphs. You may support your thesis with different reasons and examples, or you may support your thesis with one extended example or anecdote—a story—as does Davidson.

3. Write an essay discussing the ideal man (or woman) of the 1990s. Is he/she soft and sensitive? Firm and decisive? Both? In tune with nature? With self? Structure your essay as suggested in Chapter 5, with your thesis clearly stated or implied in your first paragraph. You may support your thesis with several reasons and examples or with one extended example, anecdote, or story.

After you have selected one of these specific writing suggestions, decide on a specific audience. Are you writing to young men or older men? To young women or older women? To both men and women? And what is your exact purpose? Do you want to entertain while making a point? Do you want to inform your audience? Or do you want to persuade your audience to conform to your "ideal" for womanhood or manhood?

Revising Your Writing—

When you finish your essay, read it aloud to a classmate. Then work together to answer the following questions about your essay.

1. Does your essay follow the structure discussed in Chapter 5? In other words, is your thesis stated or clearly implied in your introduction or conclusion? Do you include reasons and support? Do you include several examples or one extended example, anecdote, or story? (Remember that the number of body paragraphs may vary.)

2. If your essay is developed with a story, is the story clearly structured? Do you include specific details and examples to make your story clear and interesting? If not, what details do you need to add? Does your introduction or conclusion state (or clearly imply) your main idea? What is this main idea?

3. How have you organized your essay? Have you used clear transitions? What changes, if any, do you need to make?

4. Are you satisfied with your conclusion? Why or why not? What revisions can you make to improve your conclusion?

5. What is the primary purpose of the essay? Who is the audience? Does the essay succeed in achieving its purpose and communicating to its audience? Why or why not?

After you have revised your essay, edit it for problems in sentence structure, punctuation, spelling, and word choice. Then proofread for unintentional errors and omissions. Remember that when you are editing and proofreading, you must slow your reading process down so that you don't "read in" what you meant and overlook what you actually wrote.

PART TWO
The Sentence

Each year in school you have studied the sentence—its structure, its elements, even its definition. But you may suspect that, in spite of your extensive knowledge of sentences, you still need to know more about them. You may have realized that speaking and listening to sentences are not the same as reading and writing sentences. At times, as you read and write, you need to be able to *analyze* a certain sentence—to take it apart, understand how it works, and put it back together again. The ability to analyze sentences enables you to be a better reader and writer. It also enables you to distinguish between "correct" and "incorrect" sentences—a skill that is less important than other reading and writing skills but one that is ultimately important to you and to those with whom you communicate.

A knowledge of sentence structure, then, is valuable because it enables you to be a good editor. We have discussed the importance of revising what you write so that the content and organization accurately reflect your ideas and communicate clearly to your readers. But experienced writers also *edit* their work to make it more readable and to eliminate distracting errors. The chapters that follow, therefore, will emphasize not only reading and writing sentences but also editing sentences—making them more readable, more interesting, more graceful, and, ultimately, more correct.

In this part of the book you will learn how sentences work, how to increase your comprehension of sentences, how to make choices about sentences, and how to edit sentences. You will be asked to read and write sentences and to work with them in exercises that increase your knowledge of sentence structure and reinforce your understanding of paragraphs and essays.

CHAPTER NINE
The Simple Sentence

Although we usually speak in sentences, at times we use phrases or even single words to communicate. For example, the following conversation would be perfectly clear to the two people involved:

"Going?"
"Yeah."
"Where?"
"Home."
"Okay, see you."

However, reading and writing differ from speaking and listening in that our audience is not usually present. When we communicate in writing, therefore, we usually use complete sentences—groups of words that make a statement or ask a question. Thus, in order to read and write effectively, we need to understand how sentences are constructed.

ESSENTIAL ELEMENTS OF THE SENTENCE

One can generate an almost endless variety of sentences. But every complete sentence, regardless of how it varies from other sentences, has two essential parts: a *subject* and a *verb.* The subject of a sentence is what you are writing about, and the verb makes a statement or asks a question about the subject. Although a sentence may have other elements, it must have a subject and verb. The sentence below has only these two essential elements.

    S   **V**
Maria smiled.

Most sentences, however, are longer and more detailed. Notice in the sentence pairs on p. 204 that the essential elements (subject and verb) remain the same even though more details have been added. (The subject has been underlined once and the verb twice.)

EXAMPLES

Car rolled.
The battered old car rolled down the hill.

Several stood.
Several of the construction workers stood with their backs to us.

Wind blew.
The hot, dry wind constantly blew the fine sand into our faces.

The preceding sentences are all examples of *simple sentences.* That is, they all have a single subject/verb relationship: The verb of each sentence makes a statement about the subject of the sentence. Even in a sentence in which the subject or verb is compounded (composed of two or more parts), the sentence is still considered a simple sentence if both the verbs are making the same statement about both of the subjects.

EXAMPLES

Maria smiled and nodded. (compound verb)
Maria and John smiled. (compound subject)
Maria and John smiled and nodded. (compound subject and compound verb)

All three examples are still simple sentences because they have only one subject/verb relationship. But if we change the sentence so that it expresses two subject/verb relationships (*Maria smiled,* and *John nodded*), the sentence is no longer a simple sentence.

Note: See Chapter 11 for a more extensive discussion of compound elements.

■■ EXERCISE 9.1

Sentences will vary.

Write five *simple* sentences, including at least one with a compound subject or verb. Underline the subject once and the verb twice.

1. **The nurse recorded the patient's temperature.**

2. **The snow began to fall at dusk.**

3. **Several students arrived late.**

4. **The questions and answers were printed clearly.**

5. **The little boy fell to the ground and cried.**

Subjects

Since your subject is what you are talking about, it is often a word that names someone or something. We call such words *nouns.* Look at the following list of nouns:

1. arrangement
2. warning
3. receptionist
4. politicians
5. monkey
6. actress
7. Carlos
8. pride
9. writers
10. lab technician

■ EXERCISE 9.2

Sentences will vary.

Each of the nouns listed above can function as the subject of a sentence. Write ten simple sentences using each of these nouns as a subject.

1. **The arrangement was satisfactory.**

2. **Her warning came too late.**

3. **The doctor's receptionist answered my call.**

4. **Most politicians like publicity.**

5. **The monkey made a funny face.**

6. **The actress won an award.**

7. **Carlos wrote a complete report.**

8. **Her pride was obvious.**

9. **Writers often procrastinate.**

10. **The lab technician explained the problem.**

Pronouns are words that refer to nouns. Like a noun, a pronoun can function as the subject of a sentence. For example, the following pronouns could refer to the nouns listed above.

1. arrangement—it
2. warning—it
3. receptionist—he
4. politicians—they
5. monkey—it

6. actress—she
7. Carlos—he
8. pride—it
9. writers—they
10. lab technician—she

EXERCISE 9.3

Sentences will vary.

Rewrite five of the sentences you wrote in the previous exercise, using an appropriate pronoun as the subject of each sentence.

1. **She won an award.**

2. **They often procrastinate.**

3. **It came too late.**

4. **He made a funny face.**

5. **They like publicity.**

EXERCISE 9.4

Answers will vary.

Many of the subject nouns and pronouns have been deleted from the following passage. Replace the blanks with appropriate nouns or pronouns so that each sentence has a subject that makes sense. Any word that makes sense in the context is acceptable. You should therefore study the context carefully, and then fill in the blanks with words that make sense. Do not worry about right answers or wrong answers. If the word you choose is appropriate for the context, it is "right."

He was raised by this aunt and uncle, who was his father's brother.

_____**He**_____ had been staying with them when his parents died, and he
        (1)

simply stayed on. _____**He**_____ slept in a narrow bed in a small and dingy
            (2)

room. They lived in a sunless ground-floor apartment in an old five-story red-brick

building where his uncle collected the rents for the _____**owner**_____ no one
                                                        (3)

ever saw. The _____**house**_____ was the talk of their Brooklyn neighborhood.
            (4)

There was something wrong with it; _____**something**_____ had gone awry from the
                                        (5)

very beginning. The furnace was whimsical and tended to die when it was most

needed; valves stuck, _____**pipes**_____ leaked, faucets gushed unevenly when
                        (6)

turned on, or gave off explosions of air; electrical _____**wiring**_____ shorted
                                                        (7)

mysteriously; _____**pieces**_____ of brick worked loose and tumbled to the side-
            (8)

walk; the tar covering of the roof, no matter how recently replaced, became warped, then buckled and cracked. But the rents were low, the

__**apartments**__ were always filled, and his uncle, who earned an erratic liveli-
   (9)

hood from the badly organized and decrepit Hebrew bookstore he operated in

the neighborhood, was kept very busy. Often his _____**uncle**_____ himself fired
                                                      (10)

up the furnace, on those early winter mornings when the janitor was in a drunken

stupor from which he could not be roused. _____**Janitors**_____ came and went.
                                                (11)

His uncle's _____**job**_____ was not an easy one.
              (12)

Adapted from Chaim Potok, The Book of Lights

Verbs

In addition to a subject, each complete sentence must have a verb—a word or phrase that makes a statement or asks a question about the subject. The verb of a sentence may be a single word (such as *drink*) or a verb phrase (such as *will be drinking*). Each verb has many different forms. The form of a verb changes most often to indicate tense—the time at which the stated action or being takes place. Look at the following examples of the different tenses of the verb *dance:*

> I *dance* each day to keep in shape. (present)
> I *danced* for several hours last night. (past)
> I *will dance* with you later. (future)
> I *have danced* with her before. (present perfect)
> I *had danced* for hours. (past perfect)
> I *will have danced* every dance. (future perfect)
> I *am dancing* too much. (present progressive)
> I *was dancing* energetically. (past progressive)
> I *will be dancing* in the chorus. (future progressive)
> I *have been dancing* with him. (present perfect progressive)
> I *had been dancing* for many years. (past perfect progressive)
> I *will have been dancing* for twenty years next month. (future perfect progressive)

Most speakers of English do not have to think consciously about using the appropriate tense—the one that communicates the intended relationship between the time of the action expressed in the sentence and the actual time at which the sentence is written or spoken. However, choosing the appropriate verb form is part of a writer's responsibility. Within the range of what is considered correct are many choices, but each different choice conveys a different meaning.

EXAMPLES

> I *danced* all night. (past tense, occurring in the past at a specified time)
> I *have danced* to that song before. (present perfect, occurring at some time in the past)

I *am dancing* too much. (present progressive, occurring at the present time)

Writers also use auxiliaries (such as *should, would, could, might, may, can, must,* and *do* or *did*) to make other distinctions about verbs. Readers use these auxiliaries as clues to interpret a writer's meaning.

EXAMPLES

I may dance. ⎫
I might dance. ⎬ possibility

I must dance. ⎫
I should dance. ⎬ obligation

I can dance. ⎫
I could dance. ⎬ ability

I would dance. —— condition

I do dance. ⎫
I did dance. ⎬ emphasis

■ EXERCISE 9.5

Answers will vary.

Below are four sentences that have no main verb. Using the clues that are provided in each sentence, fill in as many appropriate forms of the verb *speak* as you can:

1. Every day as he walks to work, Michael ___**should speak**___ to her.

   ___**speaks**___

   ___**can speak**___

   ___**must speak**___

   ___**has spoken**___

2. Yesterday, as he walked to work, Michael ___**did speak**___ to her.

   ___**spoke**___

   ___**had spoken**___

   ___**could have spoken**___

   ___**must have spoken**___

3. Tomorrow, as he walks to work, Michael ___**can speak**___ to her.

   ___**will speak**___

   ___**may speak**___

   ___**should speak**___

   ___**must speak**___

4. By then, Michael _____ **will have spoken** _____ to her.

_____ **will be speaking** _____

_____ **may have spoken** _____

■ EXERCISE 9.6

Answers will vary.

The main verbs have been deleted from each of the sentences in the following passage. Supply a verb for each sentence. Be sure you choose a verb that reflects the appropriate tense and that the resulting paragraph makes sense.

In March there ____**was**____ a death on the island. Like most deaths on
                    (1)

Yamacraw, it ____**came**____ with unforeshadowed swiftness; there was no
                  (2)

lingering or gradual wasting away or bedside farewells. A heart attack

____**felled**____ Blossom Smith on a Saturday, an islander raced to Ted Stone's
       (3)

house, and Stone immediately ____**radioed**____ for a rescue helicopter from Sa-
                                    (4)

vannah. Blossom was ____**carried**____ to an open field near the nightclub,
                          (5)

where half the island gathered around her wailing and praying. The helicopter

appeared, ____**landed**____ rapidly and efficiently, received the motionless
              (6)

Blossom into the dark angel with the rotating wings, ____**lifted**____ into the
                                                            (7)

sky in a maelstrom of debris and air, and then __**disappeared**__ over the top of
                                                      (8)

trees. It ____**was**____ all very quick, very impressive, and very futile. Blossom
            (9)

____**died**____ that night in Savannah surrounded by strangers and the am-
      (10)

monia smells of a death ward.

Pat Conroy, *The Water Is Wide*

■ EXERCISE 9.7

Below are two lists of verbs. One consists of five present-tense verbs, and the other consists of the same verbs in the past tense. Use each of the verbs in a sentence that provides the appropriate context for the tense:

PRESENT-TENSE VERBS	PAST-TENSE VERBS
walks	walked
is singing	was singing
eat	ate
can study	could study
does believe	did believe

EXAMPLE

He *reads* his lesson everyday.

He *read* that novel last weekend.

BASIC PATTERNS OF THE SIMPLE SENTENCE

All English sentences are derived from three basic patterns. A knowledge of these three patterns will enable you to analyze the structure of any sentence you read or write.

Pattern One: Subject-Verb (S-V)
Pattern Two: Subject-Verb-Object (S-V-O)
Pattern Three: Subject–Linking Verb–Complement (S-LV-C)

Pattern One: Subject-Verb (S-V)

This pattern has only the two essential elements of a sentence: a *subject* and a *verb*. However, it may also have modifying words and phrases that describe and/or limit either the subject or the verb. Remember also that the verb of a sentence may be a verb phrase.

EXAMPLES

Students study. (S-V)
Students will be studying. (S-V phrase)
Many students in Dr. Goff's chemistry class study together in the
    evening. (S-V plus modifying words and phrases)

Although the subject and verb in this pattern usually occur in the order shown above (subject preceding verb), the order may be inverted without affecting the pattern.

EXAMPLES

In the stacks, on the top floor of the library, study the most indus-trious, dedicated students. (The subject of this sentence is *students*, and the verb is *study*. Even though the word order has been inverted, the pattern is still S-V.)

Did the biology students study for their test? (Because this sentence is a question, the word order is inverted: the subject *students* comes between the auxiliary verb *did* and the main verb *study*.)

Sentences with inverted word order offer writers additional options for subtle differences in meaning. "The moon we could not see" is not the same as "We could not see the moon." As a writer, you need to be aware of the options that inversion of word order offers. As a reader, you need to be aware of the problems such sentences present, for they are more difficult to read than sentences in which the elements follow normal word order. A knowledge of basic sentence patterns will help you analyze and understand such sentences.

■ EXERCISE 9.8

Sentences will vary.

Write five sentences that follow the subject-verb pattern. Include at least one sentence that has inverted word order.

1. **The truck rolled into the street.**

2. **The whistle blew loudly.**

3. **Out of the darkness came a faint cry.**

4. **The attempt failed.**

5. **We barely survived.**

Pattern Two: Subject-Verb-Object (S-V-O)

This pattern has a third major element—an *object* (often called a *direct object*)—in addition to the essential subject and verb. An object completes and receives the action expressed by the verb. Like a subject, an object is a noun or a noun substitute.

EXAMPLES

Her husband washed the dishes. (S-V-O)
Her husband was washing the dishes. (S–V phrase–O)
Silently but efficiently, her husband washed the dirty dishes.
   (S-V-O plus modifiers)

The elements in this pattern, like those in the S-V pattern, usually occur in normal order (S-V-O); however, the word order can also be inverted.

EXAMPLES

        o   s   v
That book he had not read.

        o   s   v
This solution she had not considered.

Pronouns as Objects

The object form of a personal pronoun should be used when the pronoun is functioning as the object of a verb. Compare the contrasting examples of subject and object forms given below:

EXAMPLES

He caught the frisbee. (personal pronoun as subject)
The frisbee hit *him.* (personal pronoun as object)

I met Shawn at the party. (personal pronoun as subject)
Shawn met *me* at the party. (personal pronoun as object)

She sent her accountant an invitation. (personal pronoun as subject)
Her accountant sent *her* to the bank. (personal pronoun as object)

They visited their friends. (personal pronoun as subject)
Their friends visited *them.* (personal pronoun as object)

In the first example, the subject form of the pronoun (*he*) is used because the pronoun is functioning as the subject of the sentence. But in the second example, the object form (*him*) is used because the pronoun is functioning as the object of the sentence. The following chart lists both the subject and object forms of the personal pronouns.

	SUBJECT FORM	OBJECT FORM
First-person singular	I	me
Second-person singular	you	you
Third-person singular	he, she, it	him, her, it
First-person plural	we	us
Second-person plural	you	you
Third-person plural	they	them

Be sure to use the subject form of the pronoun if you are using it as a subject and the object form if you are using it as an object.

Note: Some sentences also include an indirect object (the one to or for whom the direct object is intended.)

EXAMPLE

I sent *him* a letter.

Him is the indirect object—the one to whom the letter is sent. Pronouns that function as indirect objects are in the objective case.

▓ **EXERCISE 9.9**   Write five sentences that follow the S-V-O pattern. Use a pronoun as the object of two of your sentences.

Sentences will vary.

1. **We started a fire.**

2. **She supervised him closely.**

3. **The book gave them the answer.**

4. **The guard stopped her at the gate.**

5. **Their anger surprised him.**

Pattern Three: Subject–Linking Verb–Complement (S-LV-C)

Like the S-V-O pattern, this one also has three elements: *subject, linking verb,* and *complement.* A complement, like an object, completes the meaning of the verb. However, in this pattern the verb is a linking verb, and the complement refers to the subject. In fact, the complement is often called a *subject complement.* It can be either a noun or pronoun that renames the subject or an adjective that describes the subject.

EXAMPLES

Marcus is my friend. (S-LV-C)
       (noun)

Marcus is friendly. (S-LV-C)
       (adjective)

Both of the sentences above follow the S-LV-C pattern, but the first has a noun complement (*friend* renames *Marcus,* telling who he is), and the second has an adjective complement (*friendly* describes *Marcus,* telling something about him). Both complements refer to the subject *Marcus* even though they are part of the verb. A complement, in fact, is necessary to complete the meaning of the linking verb.

Linking Verbs

A linking verb connects the subject to the noun or adjective complement. The verb *to be* (*am, is, are, was,* and *were*) is the most frequently used linking verb. (Because it is a highly irregular verb, we have listed its main forms on page 217.)

The following verbs may also function as linking verbs. Notice that each of these verbs could be replaced by some form of the verb *to be.*

VERB	EXAMPLE OF VERB IN SENTENCE
act	The dog *acts* sick. (is sick)
appear	The plants *appear* healthy. (are healthy)
become	They *became* unhappy. (were unhappy)
fall	The gorilla *fell* ill. (is ill)
feel	I *feel* great. (am great)
get	My aunt is *getting* old. (is old)
go	The dog *went* crazy. (was crazy)
grow	The child *grew* sleepy. (was sleepy)
keep	My mother *keeps* healthy. (is healthy)
look	The winner *looked* happy. (was happy)
prove	That decision *will prove* a mistake. (will be a mistake)
remain	The mockingbird *remained* quiet. (was quiet)
run	That river *runs* deep. (is deep)
seem	You *seem* sad. (are sad)
smell	That onion *smells* terrible. (is terrible)

sound	That piano *sounds* off-key. (is off-key)
stay	The door *stays* open. (is open)
taste	The apple *tastes* sour. (is sour)
turn	The leaves *were turning* brown. (were brown)

Although each of these verbs could be replaced by a form of the verb *to be,* they are essential to good writing because they are more specific, concrete ways of expressing the overused verb *to be.*

Pronouns as Complements

Personal pronouns as well as nouns can function as complements. When a personal pronoun is used as a complement, it takes the subject form rather than the object form.

EXAMPLES

She has become an experienced musician. (personal pronoun as subject)

The committee rewarded *her.* (personal pronoun as object)

In fact, the winner of the annual music contest was *she.* (personal pronoun as complement)

EXERCISE 9.10

Sentences will vary.

Write five sentences that follow the S-LV-C pattern. Be sure to include linking verbs other than the verb *to be* in some of your sentences and to use at least one personal pronoun as a complement.

1. **She became my closest friend.**

2. **The sky turned dark.**

3. **My choice was she.**

4. **Their vacation was a disaster.**

5. **The screen remained dark.**

EXERCISE 9.11

Answers will vary.

All of the objects and complements in the following passage have been deleted. Replace each blank with an appropriate noun, pronoun, or adjective that could function as the object or complement of the verb in the sentence. Be sure to use the appropriate form of any personal pronouns you insert.

He was not interested in the snow. When he got off the freight, one

early evening during the depression, Sargeant never even noticed the

_____ **snow** _____ . But he must have felt _____ **it** _____ seeping down his neck,
(1)   (2)

cold, wet, sopping in his shoes. But if you had asked _____ **him** _____ ,
(3)

he wouldn't have known it was snowing. Sergeant didn't see the

_____ **snow** _____ , not even under the bright lights of the main street, fall-
(4)

ing white and flaky against the night. He was too _____ **hungry** _____ , too
(5)

_____ **sleepy** _____ , and too _____ **tired** _____ .
(6)   (7)

The Reverend Mr. Dorset, however, saw the _____ **snow** _____ when he
(8)

switched on his porch _____ **light** _____ , opened the front _____ **door** _____ of
(9)   (10)

his parsonage, and found standing there before him a big black

_____ **man** _____ with snow on his face, a human piece of night with snow on his
(11)

face—obviously unemployed.

Langston Hughes, *Something in Common*

EDITING THE SIMPLE SENTENCE

The terms *revising, editing,* and *proofreading* are often used interchange-ably and inaccurately. Yet each refers to a distinct part of the rewriting process. We talked in earlier chapters about the need to revise, to see what you have written from your reader's point of view and, if necessary, to make significant changes in the content and organization of what you have written. Revising often means adding new material, getting rid of unnecessary material, substituting, changing, and even starting over. As part of writing as well as rewriting, revision occurs throughout the composing process. You may think of an idea and discard it before you even begin to write. This, too, is revision.

In contrast, editing involves correcting, making more readable, and polishing what you have written. Good editors are concerned with their readers. They want to eliminate distracting errors, awkward construc-tions, and unclear, difficult-to-read passages—generally to refine and improve what they have written so that the reader can read it with un-derstanding and even pleasure. Whereas revising is concerned with the essay or paragraph as a whole, editing is concerned with sentences and words.

Proofreading is the final step of the rewriting process. Only after a writer has revised and edited a paper should he or she be concerned with proofreading, which is essentially manuscript preparation. Proofreading is that final reading in which you try to alter your normal reading process so that you look at each word and mark of punctuation. It is an essential step in the composing process, for it eliminates small errors that can be distracting to a reader, but it should not be confused with revising and editing and should not occur until both have taken place.

Our concern in this section is primarily with editing. To be a good editor, a writer must understand sentences and how they are constructed well enough to identify errors in sentence structure, usage, and punctuation. In the pages that follow, we will discuss briefly some of the most common errors. You may not need to do all of the exercises in this editing section, but you will probably need to review the errors so that you can recognize them should they occur in your own writing.

Subject-Verb Agreement

The subject and verb of a sentence must agree in number. That is, if the subject is singular, the verb must be singular; if the subject is plural, the verb must be plural.

He is an actor. (singular subject *he* and singular verb *is*)
They are pals. (plural subject *they* and plural verb *are*)

This grammatical rule sounds simple enough to follow, and in most instances it is. In fact, with the exception of the verb *to be*, verbs do not change their forms to indicate number except in the present tense. In the past tense, for example, a verb has the same form in the singular and the plural.

He walked home. (singular subject and verb)
They walked home. (plural subject and verb)

Therefore, to master subject-verb agreement, you need primarily to study the present tense. Begin by looking carefully at the chart below, which gives you the different present-tense forms of a typical regular verb.

PRESENT TENSE OF *TO WALK*

SINGULAR	PLURAL
First person: I walk	First person: we walk
Second person: you walk	Second person: you walk
Third person: he, she, it walks	Third person, they walk

Notice that an *s* is added to the third-person singular form.

Note: Adding an *s* or *es* to a noun makes the noun plural. However, an *s* ending on a verb indicates that the verb is singular.

The boy walks to school each day. (singular verb)
The three boys walk to school each day. (plural verb)

EXERCISE 9.12 Supply the correct third-person singular, present-tense form of the verbs indicated in the sentences below. Be sure that all of your verbs end in an *s*.

1. In the end he always ___**reaches**___ his goals.
   (to reach)

2. He ___**works**___ at the library on weekends.
   (to work)

3. Here he ___**comes**___ now, early as usual.
   (to come)

4. He ___**plans**___ to be an accountant when he graduates.
   (to plan)

5. He ___**believes**___ that hard work is always rewarded.
   (to believe)

Now examine carefully the present-tense forms of the three irregular verbs given below. Note especially the third-person singular, present-tense form of each of the verbs.

PRESENT TENSE OF *TO BE*

SINGULAR	PLURAL
First person: I am	First person: we are
Second person: you are	Second person: you are
Third person: he, she, it is	Third person: they are

PRESENT TENSE OF *TO HAVE*

SINGULAR	PLURAL
First person: I have	First person: we have
Second person: you have	Second person: you have
Third person: he, she, it has	Third person: they have

PRESENT TENSE OF *TO DO*

SINGULAR	PLURAL
First person: I do	First person: we do
Second person: you do	Second person: you do
Third person: he, she, it does	Third person: they do

Notice that of these examples (*to be, to have, to do*) the verb *to be* is the most irregular. The other two verbs change their forms only in the third-person singular. Notice also that these irregular verbs also end in *s* in the third-person singular. In fact, the only exceptions to this pattern are the auxiliaries *can, shall, may, will, ought,* and *must.* All other verbs end in *s* in the third-person singular present tense.

■ **EXERCISE 9.13**   Supply the correct present-tense form of the irregular verbs indicated in the sentences below. Refer to the charts given above if you are in doubt.

1. You _____**are**_____ in a difficult situation.
   (to be)

2. _____**Does**_____ she commute?
   (To do)

3. They _____**have**_____ several reasons for voting as they did.
   (to have)

4. She _____**is**_____ a friend of mine.
   (to be)

5. In the morning, we _____**have**_____ an appointment with the dean.
   (to have)

6. It _____**does**_____ not matter where you park your car.
   (to do)

7. They _____**are**_____ remaining on campus during vacation.
   (to be)

8. _____**Has**_____ he been absent before?
   (To have)

9. She _____**does**_____ more studying than he does.
   (to do)

10. _____**Are**_____ they in the same class?
    (To be)

Thus far, you have been given sentences with pronouns as subjects. Look now at the following sentences, which all have noun subjects.

Sabrina has a tough schedule this semester.
Jogging is a popular form of exercise.
Children play in the park around the corner.

Now fill in the blanks in the sentences below, substituting the appropriate pronoun subjects for the deleted noun subjects.

_____**She**_____ has a tough schedule this semester.

_____**It**_____ is a popular form of exercise.

_____**They**_____ play in the park around the corner.

The pronoun *she* can replace the noun *Sabrina* in the first sentence; the pronoun *it* can be substituted for the noun *jogging* in the second sentence; and the pronoun *they* can be used instead of the noun *children* as the subject of the third sentence. All of these pronouns are third-person singular or plural.

If your noun subject is third-person singular, your verb must also be singular. And if you are using a present-tense verb, be sure that the verb has an *s* ending. When you are in doubt about subject-verb agreement, substitute a pronoun for the noun subject; you are more likely to recognize errors in subject-verb agreement if the subject is a pronoun.

EXERCISE 9.14   In the following sentences, some of the subjects are nouns and some are pronouns. Supply the correct *present-tense* form of the verbs indicated. If you are in doubt about the correct verb form, change the noun subject to a pronoun.

1. Many students _____**enroll**_____ in computer courses each semester.
    (to enroll)

2. He _____**looks**_____ as though he is bored.
    (to look)

3. Smoking _____**is**_____ not allowed in this building.
    (to be)

4. The men _____**enter**_____ after the women leave.
    (to enter)

5. There _____**are**_____ three new students in our class.
    (to be)

6. The desk _____**has**_____ three drawers.
    (to have)

7. My room _____**looks**_____ as though a storm hit it.
    (to look)

8. A different lecturer _____**visits**_____ our class each Friday.
    (to visit)

9. Julia, Sam, and Tyrone _____**have**_____ the same schedule.
    (to have)

10. My teacher _____**arrives**_____ promptly at eight o'clock.
    (to arrive)

EXERCISE 9.15   The following sentences have plural subjects and plural verbs. In the space provided under each sentence, rewrite the sentence, changing the subject and verb so that both are singular.

EXAMPLE

The *reports evaluate* the situation.
The *report evaluates* the situation.

1. They have a major problem to solve at the office.

   He (or she) has a major problem to solve at the office.

   _____

2. The computers badly need repairing.

   The computer badly needs repairing.

   _____

3. The account books have many errors.

   The account book has many errors.

   _____

4. The salesmen are frequently late.

   The salesman is frequently late.

   _____

5. The phones ring almost constantly.

   The phone rings almost constantly.

   _____

6. The secretaries take several breaks each morning.

   The secretary takes several breaks each morning.

   _____

7. The office supervisors do not arrive promptly.

   The office supervisor does not arrive promptly.

   _____

8. The statements are not prepared on time.

   The statement is not prepared on time.

   _____

9. They seldom volunteer to work late.

    He (or she) seldom volunteers to work late.

    _____

10. Machines always break down at awkward moments.

    A machine always breaks down at awkward moments.

    _____

■ EXERCISE 9.16   Errors in subject-verb agreement are more difficult to identify when they occur in the context of a paragraph. Read the following paragraph carefully. In it are ten subject-verb agreement errors. Edit the paragraph by underlining the ten verbs that do not agree with their subjects in number. Then correct the errors you identified.

       Colleges and universities were once attended mainly by young, middle-class students who had just graduated from high school. Today campuses across the United States are populated with a variety of different types of students, many of whom are not young, middle-class, or even American. Some of these new students come from lower socioeconomic backgrounds. Government loans <u>enables</u> them to attend college when once they would have been forced to get a job. In addition to students from lower economic backgrounds, U.S. colleges are also accepting increasing numbers of foreign students. A student <u>do</u> not have to be an American citizen to attend a college or a university in this country. One class may have students from several different foreign countries. Students today <u>is</u> also not necessarily young. If an older person <u>decide</u> to start college, he may discover that many of his classmates are also middle-aged or even older. Some of these students have been out of high school for ten to twenty years. Others never completed high school. Yet they <u>seems</u> capable of competing successfully with the young students. In fact, an older student often <u>have</u> an advantage over the young people in his classes because he <u>have</u> more experience and often <u>are</u> more highly motivated. These new students who are poorer, older, or not Americans by birth add variety and interest to our campuses. Although the new student

enable

does

are

decides

seem

has

has, is

has, brings   <u>have</u> not replaced the traditional young high school graduate, he <u>bring</u> a new

dimension to higher education in this country.

Special Problems with Subject-Verb Agreement

A subject and a verb must always agree in number, but in some cases the rule is difficult to apply. Some specific problems with subject-verb agreement are discussed below.

Indefinite Pronoun Subjects

Some indefinite pronouns take a singular verb even though they appear to be plural in meaning. Below is a list of indefinite pronouns that are singular.

anybody	everything	either
anyone	nobody	neither
anything	none	someone
each	nothing	somebody
everybody	one	something
everyone	another	much

The following sentences have singular indefinite pronouns as subjects. Notice that in each of the sentences the verb is singular to agree with the singular subject.

EXAMPLES

Everyone *studies* before a test.
Nobody *likes* to study.
Neither of them *is* going to the library.
Much of the information *comes* from the textbook.
None of the students *listens* to the teacher.

Other indefinite pronouns, such as *few, many, both,* and *several,* are plural and, therefore, take plural verbs.

EXAMPLES

All of them *are* in the class.
Several *attend* the special study sessions.
Many *need* additional help.

A few of the indefinite pronouns can be either singular or plural, depending on their meaning. For example, *all* and *some* are usually considered plural, but if they refer to a mass instead of individual units, they are singular.

All of the class *has* that assignment. (singular)
All of the students *are* motivated. (plural)
Some of the material *is* boring. (singular)
Some of the students *are* bored. (plural)

In addition, the indefinite pronoun *none* is frequently considered plural even though it means *no one.* Usage appears to be changing regarding this pronoun, and many educated speakers and writers now use *none* as a plural as well as a singular pronoun.

None of the tests *are* difficult.

EXERCISE 9.17   The following sentences have subjects that are indefinite pronouns. Provide the appropriate present-tense verbs.

1. Each of us _____**wants**_____ the same teacher.
   (to want)

2. Few really _____**like**_____ chicken gizzards.
   (to like)

3. Some of the new Chinese restaurants_____**serve**_____ hot, spicy food.
   (to serve)

4. Nothing _____**upsets**_____ my boss more than my being late.
   (to upset)

5. Somebody _____**locks**_____ the building at six o'clock each night.
   (to lock)

Intervening Phrases

If a subject and a verb are separated by a phrase, the agreement between them is often difficult to determine.

One *of the boys* dates a computer science major.

The subject of this sentence is *one;* therefore, the verb *dates* is singular. In this type of sentence, it is important to distinguish between the subject of the main verb and any nouns or pronouns that may be part of the phrase that occurs between the subject and verb.

EXERCISE 9.18   Supply the correct present-tense verb in the following sentences.

1. Toni, rejecting the offers of both Kim and LaKeitha, _____**rides**_____ to class with Dalton.
   (to ride)

2. Another of my friends _____**has**_____ a new car.
   (to have)

3. That student, in spite of his teacher's warnings, _____**is**_____ absent again.
   (to be)

4. One of our new neighbors _____**comes**_____ from Micronesia.
   (to come)

5. The noise of the parties _____**causes**_____ the dorm residents much concern.
   (to cause)

Compound Subjects

A compound subject is one in which two or more nouns or pronouns are joined by coordinating conjunctions (*and, or, nor*). Subjects joined by *and* are usually plural.

The book and tape *are* both available.

Subjects joined by *nor* and *or* are usually singular.

The coach or the trainer *is* with the injured player.
Neither Mary nor Sue *plans* to graduate this semester.

However, if both the subjects joined by *or* or *nor* are plural, then a plural verb should be used.

> Tapes or books *are* available.

If *or* or *nor* joins one singular subject and one plural subject, the verb agrees with the nearer subject.

> The teacher or the students *are* always unhappy.
> The students or the teacher *is* always unhappy.

■ **EXERCISE 9.19**   Choose the correct present-tense form of the verb indicated in the sentences below.

1. Both my uncle and my aunt _____**plan**_____ to come to the wedding.
   (to plan)

2. The choir members and their director _____**travel**_____ to Russia each summer.
   (to travel)

3. The mare and colt _____**seem**_____ healthy.
   (to seem)

4. Neither my fears nor my anger _____**is**_____ justified.
   (to be)

5. The veterinarian or his assistants _____**check**_____ on the animals each evening.
   (to check)

Inverted Sentence Order

Sentences in which the subject does *not* come before the verb also present special problems with subject-verb agreement.

EXAMPLES

Where are the vegetables you cooked? (vegetables *are*)
Where is the shirt you ironed? (shirt *is*)

In the door flies a bright yellow canary. (canary *flies*)
In the door fly several small birds. (birds *fly*)

There are three reasons I can't go. (reasons *are*)
There is a good reason for his not coming. (reason *is*)

■ **EXERCISE 9.20**   In each of the following sentences, locate the subject and underline it. Then choose the correct present-tense form of the verb indicated.

1. There _____**are**_____ several reasons why the plan failed.
   (to be)

2. Under the bed _____**sleeps**_____ an enormous cat.
   (to sleep)

3. _____**Have**_____ the computers been installed?
   (To have)

4. _____**Does**_____ the captain always obey his orders?
   (To do)

5. Here _____**comes**_____ the bus.
   (to come)

■ **EXERCISE 9.21**   The following paragraph contains ten errors in subject-verb agreement. Edit the paragraph by underlining the incorrect verb forms and then replacing them with the correct verb forms.

provide

make

considers

is

were

portray

are

has

become

holds

Science fiction shows on television <u>provides</u> a look into the future. These programs take a writer's dreams about the future and <u>makes</u> them seem real to the television viewers. The remarkable thing about these shows is that what the television audience considered science fiction twenty or thirty years ago is science reality today. In the fifties and sixties, for example, robots and computers began to appear on television. Now everyone <u>consider</u> these marvels of technology rather commonplace. Industry, as well as our homes, <u>are</u> increasingly dependent upon computers. And even robots are fairly commonplace in our complex society. They may not look like the ones on the early science fiction shows, but they can do basically the same things. Early television also showed man in space years before he actually accomplished this remarkable feat. Neither television nor its viewers <u>was</u> aware that within a few years our astronauts would actually be able to orbit the earth in space ships. Today movies on television often <u>portrays</u> man moving across the galaxies, visiting various planets. There <u>is</u> several reasons to expect that this fantasy too will come true in the near future. It will not be long before our technology, together with our talented scientists, <u>have</u> us to the point that we are ready to undertake these types of space voyages. Not all the science fiction shows on television <u>becomes</u> a reality, but many of them seem to be a reliable prediction of what the future <u>hold</u>.

Bill McRee, student

Pronoun Reference and Agreement

A pronoun is a noun substitute; it stands for a noun or another pronoun. The noun or pronoun to which a pronoun refers is called the antecedent. Thus, in the following sentence, *it* and *its* refer to *cat,* so *cat* is the antecedent.

The *cat* arched *its* back, and then *it* hissed loudly.

A pronoun should agree with its antecedent in number, gender, and person. Agreement in number means that if the antecedent is plural, the pronoun that refers to it must also be plural. And, if the antecedent is singular, the pronoun should be singular.

EXAMPLES

The *computer* was down again, so I called the service department
  to have *it* repaired. (singular)
The *computers* were down again, so I called the service department
  to have *them* repaired. (plural)

For a pronoun to agree in gender with its antecedent, the pronoun
should be masculine if the antecedent is masculine and feminine if the
antecedent is feminine.

EXAMPLES

The *ballerina* poised gracefully on *her* toes. (feminine)
Mr. Chiang delivered *his* lecture and left before we could speak
  with *him.* (masculine)

For a pronoun to agree in person with its antecedent, it should be
first person (*I, me, my, mine, we, us, our, ours*) if the antecedent is first
person, second person (*you, your, yours*) if the antecedent is second
person, and third person (*he, him, his, she, her, hers, it, its, they, them,
their, theirs*) if the antecedent is third person.

EXAMPLES

We lost *our* way in the dense fog. (first person)
You lost *your* way in the dense fog. (second person)
They lost *their* way in the dense fog. (third person)

These agreement rules are usually easy to follow. In fact, you usually
follow most of them without really thinking about the rules at all. But
occasionally these rules are more difficult to understand and apply. The
following section on indefinite pronouns explains one type of pronoun
that sometimes causes agreement problems.

Indefinite Pronouns

Indefinite pronouns are always third person and have only one form, but
problems sometimes arise in using these pronouns if the writer does not
know which are singular and which are plural.

SINGULAR INDEFINITE PRONOUNS

everybody	neither	somebody
everyone	none	nobody
each	one	everything
anyone	someone	nothing
anybody		

PLURAL INDEFINITE PRONOUNS

all	any
some	both
few	none
several	

If an indefinite pronoun functions as the antecedent of another pronoun, that pronoun must agree with it in number.

Everyone left *his* shoes outside the door. (singular pronouns)
All of them left *their* shoes outside the door. (plural pronouns)

■ EXERCISE 9.22   In the following sentences, correct the pronoun agreement errors.

Answers will vary.

1. Both must apply for his own parking ticket.

   Each must apply for his or her own parking ticket.

   _____

2. Does anybody know their Spanish well enough to translate this joke?

   Does anyone know his or her Spanish well enough to translate this joke?

   _____

3. Each of the routes has their advantages.

   Each of the routes has its advantages.

   _____

4. How can anyone enjoy themselves in this miserable place?

   How can anyone enjoy himself or herself in this miserable place?

   _____

5. The teacher wants everybody to furnish their own paper and pencil.

   The teacher wants everybody to furnish his or her own pencil and paper.

   _____

Relative and Demonstrative Pronouns

The problem in using demonstrative (*this, that, these,* and *those*) and relative pronouns (*who, whom, which, what,* and *that*) is that a writer sometimes fails to have a clear antecedent for these pronouns.

I had to wait two hours *which* made me angry.

Two hours is not the antecedent of the pronoun *which;* rather the "waiting" made the writer angry. But because the pronoun does not have a clear antecedent, the sentence is unclear and awkward. The sentence can be rewritten to express the same idea more clearly by eliminating the unclear pronoun *which.*

Because I had to wait two hours, I was angry.

Note: In using relative pronouns, it is also important to remember that *who* refers only to people, *which* refers only to animals and inanimate objects, whereas *that* can refer to people, animals, or objects.

■ EXERCISE 9.23   Correct the pronoun reference errors in the following sentences.

Answers will vary.

1. We found the gun in his car which suggests he is guilty.

    The fact that we found the gun in his car suggests he is guilty.

    _____

2. The person which called failed to give his name.

    The person who called failed to give his name.

    _____

3. Jim told Tom a lie. This caused a lot of trouble.

    Jim's telling Tom a lie caused a lot of trouble.

    _____

4. I frequently called home long distance, which annoyed my father.

    My father was annoyed that I frequently called home long distance.

    _____

5. My friend often works in her garden, which is obvious.

    It is obvious that my friend often works in her garden.

    _____

Using Nonsexist Pronouns

Since pronouns frequently indicate gender, a writer is often faced with a decision about which gender to choose if the sex of the antecedent is not apparent. Traditionally, masculine pronouns were used when the sex of the antecedent was not stated.

A *teacher* should motivate *his* students.

However, this solution is increasingly considered unacceptable. A fairer practice is to alternate masculine and feminine pronouns.

A *teacher* should motivate *her* students.

Or you can use both the masculine and feminine pronouns.

A *teacher* should motivate *his* or *her* students.

Using both pronouns is perhaps fairer, but the result is somewhat awkward and wordy. Another way to solve this problem is to use the plural form of the noun and thus avoid the dilemma completely.

Teachers should motivate *their* students.

■ EXERCISE 9.24   Revise the following sentences to eliminate sexist pronouns.

Sentences will vary.

1. A judge usually delivers his decision at the end of a trial.

    Judges usually deliver their decisions at the end of a trial.

2. Anyone who arrives late must take his place in line.

    Those who arrive late must take their place in line.

3. A secretary should take her notepad with her to meetings.

    A secretary should take his or her notepad to meetings.

4. The politician asked everyone to give his best for the campaign.

    The politician asked everyone to give his or her best for

    the campaign.

5. A great writer, like a great actor, must practice his craft.

    Great writers, like great actors, must practice their craft.

Consistency in Point of View

The most frequently used pronouns are personal pronouns, which have various forms to indicate number, gender, and person.

	SINGULAR	PLURAL
First person	I (me, my)	we (us, our)
Second person	you (your)	you (your)
Third person	he, she, it (him, his, her, its)	they (them)

First-person pronouns (*I* and *we*) always refer to the person who is speaking or writing. The second person (*you*), which is the same in the singular and plural, refers to the person spoken to or addressed (the audience). The third-person pronouns (*he, she, it,* and *they*) refer to a person or thing spoken or written about.

EXAMPLES

I need to exercise each day because I feel better when I am active.
    (first-person point of view)

> You need to exercise each day because you feel better when you
> are active. (second-person point of view)
> People need to exercise each day because they feel better when
> they are active. (third-person point of view)

When you are writing, it is important to be consistent in your point of view. If you choose to write from the first-person point of view (*I* or *we*), you must use this point of view throughout your paper. Avoid shifting casually from one point of view to another unless there is a good reason for doing so. In some types of formal writing, first- and second-person points of view are not often used. In fact, it is usually best to avoid using a second-person point of view (*you*) unless you are giving directions or explaining a process.

EXERCISE 9.25

Answers will vary.

Revise the following sentences to eliminate unnecessary shifts in point of view.

1. I like math because it is easy for me, and you can grasp it on your own.

    I like math because it is easy for me, and I can grasp it on my own.

2. When we had received our sheets and blankets, we were shown how to make one's bed according to army regulations.

    When we had received our sheets and blankets, we were shown

    how to make our beds according to army regulations.

3. I need to improve my writing skills. To be able to express yourself in writing is of great importance.

    I need to improve my writing skills. To be able to express myself in

    writing is of great importance.

4. To me, graduation marks the beginning of a new life, a demanding life, from which a person can expect to receive only as much as you give.

    To me, graduation marks the beginning of a new life, a demanding

    life, from which I can expect to receive only as much as I give.

5. I want to learn all the rules you need to know in order to stay out of
trouble with the authorities.

I want to learn all the rules I need to know in order to stay out of

trouble with the authorities.

EXERCISE 9.26

Answers will vary.

Correct the following paragraph using the third-person-plural point of
view consistently.

~~Every~~ teacher needs a broad liberal arts education as well as training in a

special area of study. ~~You~~ [They] must be prepared to face a variety of challenges in a

classroom for which a narrow, specialized education is inadequate. For example,

if ~~you~~ [they] are a teacher of social studies, ~~you~~ [they] also need to know something about

literature, art, and music. ~~I think that I~~ [They] will use the courses [they] have had in ~~my~~ [their] general

studies program as much as ~~I~~ [they] will those that ~~I~~ [they] have taken in ~~my~~ [their] major. ~~A~~ teacher

cannot be too well prepared. The students whom they teach will depend on ~~you~~ [them] to

answer a variety of questions and to be knowledgeable about the world in general.

EXERCISE 9.27

Correct the pronoun errors in the following sentences.

1. A person will have to learn a lot if you expect to graduate from college.

A person will have to learn a lot if he or she expects to graduate from

college. (Or, a *person* can be changed to *you*.)

2. A good student learns to ignore stress and just enjoy themselves.

Good students learn to ignore stress and just enjoy themselves. (Or,

***themselves* can be changed to *himself* or *herself*.)**

3. Most people have met someone who is at their low when they are free
of pressure.

Most people have met someone who is at his (or her) low when he (or

she) is free of pressure.

4. Homesickness, a worry that affects everyone at some time or another in their lives, is especially prevalent among college students.

   Homesickness, a worry that affects everyone at some time or another in his or her life, is especially prevalent among college students. (Or *everyone* can be changed to *all people*.)

5. The student is away from the security of friends at home and has to make it socially on their own.

   The student is away from the security of friends at home and has to make it socially on his or her own. (Or, *student is* can be changed to *students are,* and *has* to *have*.)

Consistency in Tense

When you are writing, you should be consistent in your use of tense (i.e., the time at which the stated action or being takes place). If you start a paragraph or essay in the present tense, you should keep it in the present; if you start in the past tense, you should keep it in the past. Generally, you should avoid a shift in tense unless a shift is supported by the context of your material. Unnecessary and awkward shifts in tense, such as those in the following example, can confuse your reader:

> The plumber installs the new faucets, will repair the drain, and connected the disposal.

This sentence is confusing because the writer shifts needlessly from the present tense (*installs*) to the future tense (*will repair*) to the past tense (*connected*). Since these actions occurred at approximately the same time, the tense of all three verbs should be the same, as illustrated in the edited sentences below.

> The plumber installs the new faucets, repairs the drain, and connects the disposal. (present tense)
> The plumber installed the new faucets, repaired the drain, and connected the disposal. (past tense)
> The plumber will install the new faucet, repair the drain, and connect the disposal. (future tense)

However, as the following example shows, changing tenses is permissible if the context indicates that the events or actions occurred at different times.

> The plumber installed the new faucets yesterday, is repairing the drain today, and will connect the disposal tomorrow. (past, present, and future tenses)

Do not confuse your readers by changing tenses unless a shift is clearly justified.

▓ EXERCISE 9.28

Answers will vary.

Underline any needless shifts in tense that you find in the following sentences. Rewrite the sentences correctly.

1. The war <u>was</u> horrible, and anyone who <u>goes</u> through it <u>had</u> to endure great hardships.

   The war was horrible, and anyone who went through it had to

   endure great hardships.

2. The plane <u>passes</u> over the highway and barely <u>missed</u> the tower.

   The plane passed over the highway and barely missed the

   tower. (Or _missed_ can be changed to _misses_.)

3. The concert <u>started</u> at eight o'clock, <u>will last</u> two hours, and <u>ends</u> at ten o'clock.

   The concert started at eight o'clock, lasted two hours, and ended

   at ten o'clock. (Or _started_ can be changed to _will start_ and

   ends to _will end_.)

4. Out of the jungle <u>creeps</u> a large spotted leopard, which <u>turned</u> suddenly when he <u>sees</u> the hunters on the other side of the river.

   Out of the jungle creeps a large spotted leopard, which turns

   suddenly when he sees the hunters on the other side of the

   river. (Or _creeps_ can be changed to _crept_ and _sees_ to _saw_.)

5. The planning committee <u>met</u> every Wednesday for three weeks and <u>decides</u> on the projected goals for the next year.

   The planning committee met every Wednesday for three

   weeks and decided on the projected goals for next year.

▓ EXERCISE 9.29

began, ran, lined

grew

The following paragraph is in the present tense. Correct it by changing it to the past tense. Underline the verbs you are changing, and be sure your use of tense is consistent.

The game <u>begins</u> promptly at eight o'clock as the teams <u>run</u> out and <u>line</u> up at opposite ends of the field. As the crowd of cheering fans <u>grows</u> quiet, the

gave, began	official gives the signal, and the two lines of uniformed players begin to run
was kicked, arched	toward each other. The ball is kicked by one player so that it arches high above
	the field before dropping with a decisive thud into the waiting hands of the player
had, began	who has been waiting for it. At this point, the receiver begins to fight his way down
ran, was	the field. As he runs, he is the target of every player on the opposing team. At the
attempted, was	same time, his own teammates attempt to protect him. After a long run, he is
was, tangled	tackled by a large player, and there is a pile-up as players from both teams tangle
let	in a mass of colorfully uniformed arms and legs. The crowd lets out screams of
got	delight and anguish as another football game gets underway.

READING AND WRITING ABOUT—

Gender Issues

Preparing: Freewriting—

Gender issues are those that pertain to men and women and their interactions. One of the most controversial of these issues is discrimination against women, who historically in America have had less power and less freedom than men. Although sexual discrimination is still a very real issue, the last thirty years have brought greater freedom and equality to women in both their personal and professional lives. Most men and women welcome these changes, but this new climate is not without tension and even conflict. In fact, greater freedom and equality for women may have brought such conflicts into the open.

Gender issues are the basis not only of personal conflicts between men and women but also of serious social problems, such as gender stereotyping, sexual harassment, and even date rape. Select one of these gender-related problems and freewrite about it for about five minutes. What are its causes? What are some possible solutions? In the following selections, you will read more about some of these concerns.

GENDER ROLES, INTERACTION, AND SOCIALIZATION
Ian Robertson

Before you read, think about traditional gender roles in America today. Traditionally, what kinds of jobs do men hold? What kinds of jobs do women hold? How are men and women portrayed in advertising? What "roles" are young children taught? In the following selection from his textbook *Sociology*, Ian Robertson explores and questions traditional gender roles in America today.

As you read, notice that Robertson uses the standard textbook style of separate headings for the two chapter sections. He also tries to increase student comprehension by providing a clear main idea statement near the beginning of each of these sections. Underline these main idea statements.

See text annotations.

1   American gender roles are in a state of flux, with some people adhering to much more traditional patterns . . . and others exploring new and sometimes radical alternatives. There are also important subcultural variations. Generally speaking, the lower a person's social class, the more likely he or she is to conform to traditional stereotypes. The reason is probably that lower-status people have less freedom and effective choice in their lives, and so are slower to change established patterns. . . .

MALE-FEMALE INTERACTION

2   Many routine interactions between men and women carry symbolic meanings that may not be immediately obvious. For example, the "door ceremony," in which men open doors for women, symbolically reinforces the idea of female dependency and delicacy, while asserting men's paternalism and control. Although on the surface it seems no more than a courtesy, the ceremony helps underscore existing patterns of inequality—which is one reason why a woman who opened doors for men would draw reactions of discomfort rather than gratitude. As feminists point out, just as interesting as the question of *why* men open doors for women is the question of *which* doors they open for women: certainly not the symbolic doors that lead to positions of power, wealth, and influence (Sapiro, 1986).

3   Many other aspects of daily interaction reveal and reinforce the inequality of the sexes. Most obvious, perhaps, are the names by which people are known and the titles by which they address each other. A married woman replaces her last name with that of her husband, rather than the other way around; you can see the symbolic implications more clearly if you imagine the reverse situation, the groom taking the bride's name. Married or not, a man is known only as Mr., but until recently a woman had to be known as either Miss or Mrs.—a public indication of whether or not she was already a man's property. However, as women have gained more equality with men, the title Ms. has become established as the female equivalent of Mr., particularly among younger professionals.

4   The physical interaction of the sexes also reflects and reinforces their relationships. It is generally true that higher-status people take up more space than lower-status people. This is very much the case with the sexes: men typically require more personal space than women, and spread their arms or their legs sideways and outward much more than women do. Higher-status people are also permitted more liberty in touching lower-status people: the boss, for example, can pat a subordinate on the back, but the employee cannot do the same to the boss. Similarly, men touch women much more than women touch men, even when they are not on intimate terms. And if a pair is cuddling in public, the man assumes a controlling position by putting his arms around the woman; he will

rarely allow a woman to hold him the same way if others are watching, for fear of appearing dependent (Henley, 1977).

5   Conversation between men and women is also a revealing form of social interaction. Any polite conversation follows the principle that only one person should speak at a time, but that both participants should have an equal chance to contribute. During the conversation, a speaker should watch for cues that the other party wishes to say something, and a listener should anticipate when a sentence will come to an end, so that an opportunity is created for the roles of speaker and listener to be swapped. Ideally, this transition should occur smoothly, without overlapping or interruption. Several studies have shown, however, that conversations involving a man and woman routinely violate this implicit understanding.

6   Despite the stereotype that women talk too much—that men "can't get a word in edgewise"—the fact is that when men and women are talking, men dominate the conversation. They not only speak for a disproportionate amount of time; they are also responsible, on average, for more than 95 percent of the interruptions that occur. Women, on the other hand, rarely try to interrupt; instead, they tend to treat men's contributions as more worthwhile than their own, and frequently abandon a subject that interests them in favor of whatever men wish to talk about. Women also smile more frequently while listening, and they ask between two and three times as many questions as men—tactics that support the conversation by encouraging men to continue talking. When women do manage to make a lengthy statement, they are apt to be greeted by a series of "uh huh" sounds, rather than questions or other positive invitations to keep talking. These routine forms of social interaction between men and women reflect and enhance the inequality that is built into gender roles (Zimmerman and West, 1975; Fishman, 1978, 1980; Kramarae, 1980; Kollock, Blumstein, and Schwartz, 1985).

GENDER SOCIALIZATION

7   The basic gender characteristics expected of the sexes are learned in the family environment very early in life, and are then reinforced in the schools, in peer groups, in the mass media, and in many other specific agencies, ranging from sports teams to workplaces (Stockard and Johnson, 1980).

8   From the time that children are born, their parents treat them differently on the basis of their sex. Little boys are dressed in blue, little girls in pink. Girls are treated protectively, boys are given more freedom. Girls are valued for their docile and pleasing behavior and are not required to be achieving or competitive; charm and attractiveness are apt to receive more approval than intelligence. Boys, on the other hand, are given much more rigorous gender-role training. The little girl may be allowed some tomboyish behavior, but the little boy cannot be allowed to be a sissy. Parents usually view any "effeminate" behavior or interests with great alarm, and if these tendencies persist, they may be seen as a sign of psychological disturbance. The boy is repeatedly expected to prove his masculinity, particularly by performing well at sports. He is taught to "act like a man"—in other words, to suppress his emotions and particularly his tears. The requirement that the boy avoid anything "sissy" can breed a hostility toward femininity that may later develop into an unconscious contempt for the opposite sex.

9   As a result of this training, children learn their gender roles quickly and effectively. In fact, they are certain of the existence of two sexes and of their own

identification with one of them long before they are aware of the biological basis for these distinctions. By the age of three, nearly all children know whether they are male or female, and by the age of four, they have very definite, even exaggerated, ideas of what masculinity and femininity should involve.

10   The psychological process by which children learn their gender roles is a complex one, but it contains three main elements. The first is *conditioning* through rewards and punishments, usually in the form of parental approval or disapproval. The child who behaves in the "right" way is encouraged, but the boy who plays with dolls or the girl who plays with mud is strongly discouraged. Sometimes parents deliberately arrange conditioning experiences for their children—for example, by giving them gender-related toys. But much conditioning is unconscious; as Virginia Sapiro (1986) points out, "If mommy and daddy are equally capable of driving, but mommy never drives if daddy is in the car, children nevertheless learn who is 'supposed' to drive the car." The second element in the learning process is *imitation*. Young children tend to imitate older children and adults, and are particularly inclined to imitate those whom they regard as most like themselves. Young children thus use other people of the same sex as models for their own behavior. The third and perhaps the most important element is *self-definition*. Through social interaction with others, children learn to categorize the people around them into two sexes and to label themselves as belonging to one sex rather than the other. They then use this self-definition to select their future interests and to construct their personalities and social roles (Kohlberg, 1966). (This is why children who have been assigned to the wrong sex at birth have such difficulty in identifying with the correct sex after the age of about three or four. The boy who has been raised as a girl "knows" that he is not a boy and naturally resists attempts to make him into one.)

11   The basic gender roles that children learn in the home are later reinforced, in various ways, by the school. Studies of school textbooks show that males and "masculine" activities are emphasized more than females and "feminine" activities—in readers, for example, male characters have long outnumbered female characters and have played much more diverse and significant social roles (Weitzman, 1979; Best, 1983). Additionally, many curricular and extracurricular activities—academic courses, hobbies, sports, and so on—tend to be segregated by sex. Girls are channeled into the cooking class, boys into the mechanics class; girls play softball, boys play hardball. Indeed, there is strong evidence that some girls refrain from studying mathematics and other subjects they consider "masculine," because they lack confidence in their abilities in such fields—or even because they think boys will not like girls who do well in math (Sherman, 1980; Tobias and Weisbrod, 1980). But boys, too, are under strong social pressure to conform. Today, a girl might gain entry to the printing workshop without too much difficulty, but the boy who wants to take sewing classes faces the likelihood of discouragement from his teachers and ridicule from his peers. The girl who aspires to "masculine" pursuits is behaving in a way that is at least understandable to others, for she is seeking a status that is acknowledged to be superior, if inappropriate. But the boy who has "effeminate" interests is likely to be seen as behaving incomprehensibly, for he is deliberately seeking an inferior status.

12   Beyond the home and the school, social life is saturated with messages about which sex is dominant and about how men and women ought to behave. In particular, all forms of the mass media, from television soap operas to the lyrics of popular songs, tend to emphasize fairly traditional gender stereotypes.

13   Perhaps the most insidious of these media presentations is the one com-

monly offered in advertising. Women are typically portrayed either as sex objects, in an attempt to market various products to men, or as domesticated house-wives, in order to market home-maintenance products to women. Market research has shown that one of the most effective ways for advertisers to reach a male audience is to associate a product, however remotely, with a seductive or smiling female. The sexuality of women is thus exploited by having glamorous models stroking new automobiles, cradling bottles of whiskey, or being sent into raptures by the odor of a particular after-shave. Advertising directed at women, on the other hand, shows females delighted beyond measure at the discovery of a new instant soup, or thrilled into ecstasy by the blinding whiteness of their wash. In fact, the vast majority of television advertisements that use women models are for kitchen or bathroom products (Tuchman, 1978).

14   Erving Goffman (1976) points out that when men and women appear together in advertisements, the men are always shown as taller than the women. The women never hold the advertised product in a firm grasp, and are rarely seen giving the men instructions. The eyes of the men in advertisements focus on the product or on important people, but the eyes of the women focus on men, whom they gaze at or cling to in apparent admiration. In fact, what is remarkable about advertising is how little its gender stereotypes have changed over the past quarter century. Men are the voice of authority on 80 percent of television commercials, including those directed at women. A barrage of advertisements still portray females as simple-minded creatures, bickering endlessly over which toothpaste or fabric softener is better (Klemesrud, 1981). (To fully appreciate the implications of these stereotypes, try mentally substituting men for the women on the screen the next time you watch TV advertisements, and note how utterly demeaning the portrayals would be.)

REVIEWING THE READING   Answers will vary.

See paragraphs 2–6.   1. Robertson discusses several social customs or practices of male-female interaction that reinforce "the idea of female dependency" and "men's paternalism and control." What are two of these customs or practices?

See paragraphs 8–11.   2. In our society, children are usually trained to assume traditional gender roles. What is one example of the gender training usually given to boys? What is an example of gender training for girls?

See paragraph 10.   3. Robertson points out that the "psychological process by which children learn their gender roles is a complex one." According to Robertson, what three elements does this process include?

See paragraph 11.   4. How do schools reinforce traditional gender roles?

See paragraphs 13–14.   5. How do advertisements reinforce gender stereotypes?

UNDERSTANDING VOCABULARY

Because the underlined words in the following sentences from the reading may be unfamiliar to you, we have inserted brief definitions in brackets [ ] following the words. Study these words and their definitions, and add to your personal vocabulary list those that you would like to remember.

1. "For example, the 'door ceremony' . . . symbolically reinforces the idea of female dependency and delicacy, while asserting men's paternalism [fatherly attitude] and control" (paragraph 2).

2. "However, as women have gained more equality with men, the title Ms. has become established as the female equivalent [equal] of Mr., particularly among younger professionals" (paragraph 3).

3. "Several studies have shown, however, that conversations involving a man and woman routinely violate this implicit [implied, understood] understanding" (paragraph 5).

4. "Girls are valued for their docile [obedient, submissive] and pleasing behavior and are not required to be achieving or competitive; charms and attractiveness are apt to receive more approval than intelligence" (paragraph 8).

5. "Perhaps the most insidious [deceitful, scheming, treacherous] of these media presentations is the one commonly offered in advertising" (paragraph 13).

6. "The sexuality of women is thus exploited [misused, abused] by having glamorous models stroking new automobiles, cradling bottles of whiskey, or being sent into rapture by the odor of a particular aftershave" (paragraph 13).

7. "A barrage [flood, great number] of advertisements still portray females as simple-minded creatures, bickering [quarreling] endlessly over which toothpaste or fabric softener is better" (paragraph 14).

REACTING CRITICALLY

1. According to Robertson, the " 'door ceremony' . . . symbolically reinforces the idea of female dependency and delicacy, while asserting men's paternalism and control." Do you agree or disagree? Explain why you agree or disagree with this statement. If you are a man, do you open doors for a woman? Do you open them for other men? If you are a woman, do you like to have a man open doors for you? Do you ever open a door for a man? Explain the contrast that Robertson makes between opening physical doors and symbolic doors. Is this a valid contrast? Why or why not?

2. What do the traditional gender roles discussed in this selection suggest about the distribution of power between men and women? Do you think the implications about gender and power in this selection are accurate. Why or why not? Is power in our society related to gender itself or to expected gender roles? Support your positions with specific examples from your experience and observation.

OFFICE CRIMES
Nancy Gibbs

Before you read, think about the issue of sexual harassment. Did you see the U.S. Senate hearings investigating the charge of sexual harassment that Anita Hill made against Clarence Thomas during his confirmation hearings for the U.S. Supreme Court? What did you learn about sexual harassment? Is it a major problem today in the workplace and on college campuses? Have you ever experienced or observed sexual harassment? Nancy Gibbs explores the issue of sexual harassment in the following article, which was published on 10/2/91, at the time of the Thomas-Hill hearings.

Annotations will vary.

As you read, try to define the term *sexual harassment.* Underline specific passages that help you to define this term.

1   Last week America set about smashing china and moving furniture around in the household of its public morality, with the knowledge that before it was all over no one would know where to find anything anymore. Conversation became suddenly careful; the pinups were peeled off the wall. The issue of sexual harassment—what it is, why it happens, who's to blame—was a fascinating topic to obsess upon as a nation, wonder about in private, argue about in public. It was also a long, bruising week of bumping into issues that many of us didn't know were there.

2   In America's workplaces, men and women reintroduced themselves with a suspicion that their relationships had changed forever. Men who have worked closely with women for years asked them flat out, ''Have you ever felt threatened or insulted or offended by anything I've said or done?'' Many women privately shared their experiences and their anger, for the first time taking seriously behavior they had long taken for granted. Some of them, wary of being cast as victims, wondered whether in the end all the sudden attention to the issue would do them more harm than good.

3   The issue of sexual harassment ricochets off other crucial debates this country has yet to resolve about the boundaries of morality and law. The boss who kept his employees' menstrual cycles marked on a wall calendar was, by any measure, a lout. Was he a criminal? How useful is it to establish <u>a category of behavior that runs the gamut from rudeness to rape?</u> Should it be embedded in the law that men and women react differently to the same comments and behavior?

4   The questions and conversations were all the more pointed because, despite the clarity of the legal language, <u>sexual harassment is a complex issue, its incidence difficult to measure. It is uniformly cast as a gender issue, since the overwhelming majority of cases involve female workers being harassed by male colleagues and supervisors.</u> But when pollsters ask women whether they have ever been targets of harassment, the answers depend on how the question is phrased, which helps explain why some surveys find that 90 percent of women view themselves as victims and others find less than half that number.

5   As last week's crash course made clear, most women and men, especially most Senators, had only the barest understanding of the power of the law. <u>Under Equal Employment Opportunity Commission guidelines</u> issued in 1980 and unanimously affirmed by the Supreme Court in 1986, <u>sexual harassment includes not just physical but also verbal and ''environmental'' abuse.</u> Under the law, <u>there are two broadly recognized forms. The first involves a ''quid pro quo'' in which a worker is compelled to trade sex for professional survival.</u> In 1986 an Ohio woman won a $3.1 million verdict against an employer who invited her to perform oral sex or lose her job.

6   The other part of the law refers to a ''<u>hostile working environment</u>,'' and it is here that the debates get most heated. The phrase covers <u>any unwelcome sexual behavior that makes it hard for a worker to do her job or that creates a hostile or offensive environment.</u> Charles Looney, regional director of the EEOC New England office in Boston, says the courts are <u>more concerned with the woman's reaction than the man's intent.</u> ''If I run a stop sign, I have broken the law even if I did not intend to,'' he says. ''People can create hostile environments without knowing that it would be considered sexual harassment, but they are still liable.''

7   The courts may have worked it all out, but most Americans have not. As people wrestled last week with the ambiguous definitions of sexual harassment, many were left with a conviction that, as with pornography, they know it when they see it. The ugly realities of many American workplaces give the legal language its vividness. There is, for instance, the case of Edith Magee, who worked a shovel and drove a dump truck for the St. Paul, Minn., sewage department. ''There was always this implied threat that if they didn't like you, they would use their authority to get you in trouble,'' she says of her supervisors. Her employer settled her case for $75,000 but denied any wrongdoing. ''I knew when I walked into the lunchroom and my boss was reading *Hustler,* it was going to be bad,'' she says. ''He'd show me pictures of dildoes and say, 'Is your husband's this big?' There was no way you could push him away. He would just go and go and never stop. The idea was, if you were a female and did something as low-class as shovel, then you deserved what you got.''

8   Such stories, echoed a thousand, a hundred thousand times last week, helped lawyers explain that sexual harassment is not about civility. It is not about a man making an unwelcome pass, telling a dirty joke or commenting on someone's appearance. Rather it is an abuse of power in which a worker who depends for her livelihood and professional survival on the goodwill of a superior is made to feel vulnerable. ''This is not automatically a male-female issue,'' says Wendy Reid Crisp, the director of the National Association for Female Executives, the largest women's professional association in the country. ''We define this issue as economic intimidation.''

9   Edith Magee is typical in that the most common targets of harassment in blue-collar jobs tend to be women who are breaking into fields once dominated by men. In white-collar professions, most victims are ''women in lowly positions,'' says Susan Rubenstein, an attorney in San Francisco who specializes in sexual-harassment cases. ''A secretary will get harassed before a lawyer, a paralegal will get harassed before an associate.'' Particularly in male bastions, women find that feminism becomes, ironically, a weapon in the attack.

10   ''It's not just some guy grabbing you and pushing you in a closet and saying, 'If you don't let me fondle you, I'm going to fire you,' '' explains Susan Faludi, author of a new book, *Backlash: The Undeclared War Against American Women.* ''It's more the subtler form of making women uncomfortable by turning the workplace into a locker room and then telling them, 'What's the matter, you can't handle it? You wanted equality; I'm going to give it to you with a vengeance.' ''

11   Faludi cites the case of Diane Joyce, who fought for seventeen years to become the first female skilled crafts worker in the history of Santa Clara, Calif. The real fight began after she finally started the job. When the roadmen trained Joyce to drive the bobtail trucks, says Faludi, they kept changing instructions; one gave her driving tips that nearly blew up the engine. She had to file a formal grievance just to get the pair of coveralls that she said were withheld from her. In the yard the men kept the ladies' room locked, and on the road they wouldn't stop to let her use a bathroom. ''You wanted a man's job, you learn to pee like a man,'' she recalls a superior telling her. ''She is not talking about being attacked in the office,'' says Faludi. ''It's a slow, relentless accumulation of slights and insults that add up to the same thing—the message that we don't want you here and we are going to make your hours here uncomfortable.''

12   In the years since women were integrated into the armed forces, that once all-male preserve has struggled to counter the macho image that long prevailed. SEXUAL HARASSMENT IS NOT FROWNED ON HERE; IT'S GRADED was one sign,

now removed, in the Pentagon. By and large, the military has succeeded in impressing officers with the importance of the issue, though enlisted men are not always as enlightened. But there is one big exception, according to Linda Grant De Pauw, president of the Minerva Center, an educational facility dealing with women in the armed services. "The absolute military ban on homosexuals creates an opening for sexual harassment," she says. "Military women live in mortal fear of being called a dyke. When the man says, 'Sleep with me or I'll say you're a lesbian,' it is terrifically effective where women know they may be kicked out if the charge is made."

13   Defining unwelcome or offensive advances sounds like a subjective judgment; many people last week were worried that sexual harassment is anything an accuser says it is. But in a landmark ruling, the Ninth U.S. Circuit Court in California ruled that the law covers any remark or behavior that a "reasonable woman" would find to be a problem—and acknowledged that a woman's perception might differ from a man's. Judge Robert Beezer wrote that "conduct that many men consider unobjectionable may offend many women." He noted that because women are much more likely to be victims of rape and sexual assault, they have a "stronger incentive to be concerned with sexual behavior." Men, in addition, are more likely to view sexual conduct as harmless.

14   Underneath that reasoning is the notion that there is a continuum running from the innocent gesture to the brutal assault. It is an interpretation fused to an ideology that places all behavior in the context of male power. In the view of Boston University psychology professor Frances Grossman, "From the guys who wink on the street to the biology professor who tells a sexist joke in class, to the guy who says, 'Hey, baby, let's go out,' to the guy who rapes—all are of a piece in their role of disempowering women. Men say these are not related behaviors. Flirting and jokes are fine, and rape is bad, they say. But increasingly, sociologists say they all send the same disempowering message to women."

15   That line of argument brings shouts of anger not only from men who feel maligned but also from women who feel belittled. They argue that women do themselves and their careers no favor when they play victim or perpetuate an unhealthy culture of self-pity by asking to be coddled and protected from rudeness and boorish behavior. Sexual harassment is not about sex; it is about power, the reasoning goes, and if women act powerless at work, they will almost certainly be taken advantage of.

16   Here is a rare intersection between the opinions of some ardent feminists and some profound antifeminists. "If a girl can survive high school, she ought to be able to deal with the office," says Phyllis Schlafly, a longtime crusader against feminist causes. For Schlafly, the sexual-harassment argument is a perfect example of how "feminists are asking to have it both ways." Says she: "They have spent twenty years preaching that there isn't any difference between men and women, and now they want to turn around and claim sexual harassment if somebody says something that they don't like." The very issue is patronizing, says Schlafly, because it implies that women cannot handle uncomfortable situations without the help of government.

17   This is not just the view of an extremist. Scholars such as Ellen Frankel Paul, deputy director of the Social Philosophy and Policy Center at Bowling Green State University in Ohio, argue that the courts are a dangerous mechanism for policing behavior. "Do we really want legislators and judges delving into our most intimate private lives," she asks, "deciding when a look is a leer and when a leer is a civil rights offense? Should people have a legally enforceable right not to be

offended by others? At some point, the price for such protection is the loss of both liberty and privacy rights.''

18   From this perspective, women have a lot to lose if they press the issue of sexual harassment too far. Particularly in white-collar settings, younger workers rely on mentors to help them learn the ropes and advance their careers. If a boss is afraid that his interest in a protégé's success will be misconstrued, the safer path is to avoid mentor relationships. ''While it is perfectly fine—and normal—for a mentor to say to a man, 'Let's have a drink, or play golf, and talk about that promotion,' it's harder for a mentor to do that with a woman outside strict business hours without incurring some legal risk,'' notes Terry Morehead Dworkin, a business-law professor at Indiana University. One solution, of course, is for more women to be in the position to promote younger women, but in many corporations that day is still far off.

REVIEWING THE READING   Answers will vary.

See paragraphs 5 and 6.

1. What are the two broadly recognized forms of sexual harassment? Which is the more controversial form?

See paragraphs 5, 7, 11, and 12.

2. What are two specific examples of sexual harassment given by Gibbs?

3. According to sociologists, what does a rude joke have in common with rape?

See paragraph 14.

See paragraph 18.

4. According to Gibbs, what do women have to lose if they press the issue of sexual harassment too far? What do men have to lose?

UNDERSTANDING VOCABULARY

Define the term *sexual harassment*. Before you begin, review the passages that you underlined in the reading. Then write your own brief definition.

REACTING CRITICALLY

1. Do you think sexual harassment is related to power? Support your opinion with specific reasons and examples.

2. Gibbs writes that sexual harassment "is uniformly cast as a gender issue, since the overwhelming majority of cases involve female workers being harassed by male colleagues and supervisors." Can a man be a victim of sexual harassment? Why or why not? Support your answer with specific details and arguments.

Responding in Writing—

Use one of the following specific assignments to write an essay about a gender-related issue.

1. Write an essay for parents or teachers discussing the development of gender roles. How are children and young people traditionally taught specific gender roles? What advantages or disadvantages do you see in such "gender training"? Include in your essay specific suggestions for how parents or teachers should or should not cultivate gender roles in girls and/or boys.

2. Write an essay about gender stereotyping by the media. You may focus on movies, television programs, or advertisements. You may

focus on both males and females or on only one sex. But be sure to use specific examples to achieve a specific purpose and to communicate to a specific audience—perhaps to convince producers to change their media presentations.

3. Write an essay supporting or criticizing a particular gender-related social custom or practice. For example, you could write about the "door ceremony" or about the practice of a woman's assuming her husband's last name.

4. In the Understanding Vocabulary section accompanying Gibbs's article, you wrote a brief definition of the term "sexual harassment." In an essay, write an extended definition of sexual harassment. You might consider its causes, its effects, some specific examples, and/or some possible solutions.

5. A major crime that is also an extreme form of sexual harassment is rape, and an increasingly frequent type of rape is date rape. Write an essay about the problem of date rape on college campuses. Decide on a specific focus (causes, effects, solutions, and so on) and on a specific purpose (to inform or persuade your audience). Support your point with specific examples, and direct your essay to a specific audience. For example, you might write specifically to college men or to college women, or you might write to the dean or director of campus housing suggesting a program for preventing date rape.

Revising Your Writing—

Use the following guidelines to help you revise your own paper. When you complete an independent revision, ask a classmate to read your paper and evaluate how well it accomplishes its purpose and communicates to its audience.

1. What is the primary purpose of your essay? That is, is it intended to be informative or persuasive?

2. Who is your intended audience?

3. What is the thesis, or main idea, of your essay? Have you clearly stated or implied your thesis? Where?

4. Does your essay include a description of the problem or suggestions for solutions? If your development focuses on the problem, what methods have you used to describe the problem (examples, causes, effects)? If your development consists of possible solutions, what are these solutions? Have you presented two or three solutions or one extended solution? Have you developed each solution with specific details?

5. How is your support arranged (time order, space order, order of importance)? Remember that an effective arrangement is to move from the least important point to the most important.

6. If your essay is persuasive, have you appealed to your readers' emotions as well as to their logic? How?

7. What transitions have you provided to move your reader from one idea to another? How could you improve transition?

8. Have you used simple sentences effectively for variety, transition, and emphasis? What strong, vivid verbs have you used?

9. What is your conclusion? Does it restate your main point or emphasize your purpose? How does your conclusion reinforce your main point or purpose?

10. Does your essay achieve its purpose? Does it communicate clearly to its audience?

After you have revised your essay and received a response to it from at least one classmate, make any revisions necessary to communicate your purpose to a real audience. Then use the following questions to edit your essay:

1. Is each sentence a complete sentence, with a subject and a verb?

2. Do you have any errors in subject-verb agreement?

3. Do you have any errors in pronoun reference or agreement?

4. Have you used any sexist pronouns?

5. What tense have you used? Is your use of tense consistent?

6. What point of view have you used (first person, second person, third person)? Is your point of view consistent?

7. Are any words misspelled?

8. Do you have any errors in capitalization, punctuation, or usage?

Remember to reread your essay several times, focusing on only one error at a time. For example, if you often have trouble with subject-verb agreement, you may want to underline the subject and verb in each clause or sentence and then check to make sure the subjects and verbs agree.

After you have edited your essay, write your final draft and proofread it carefully.

CHAPTER TEN

Modification: Expanding the Simple Sentence

One of the most important ways we expand the basic elements of a simple sentence is by using modifiers—words and phrases that describe, limit, point out, identify, and make more specific the words they modify. Although modifiers are not an essential part of a sentence, they add information to the basic elements of the sentence. Without modifiers we could communicate only general ideas.

EXAMPLES

Armadillos dig. (basic elements unmodified)
Two large armadillos dig ruthlessly in my yard every night. (basic elements modified)

Adding modifiers to the basic elements in the second example makes the sentence much more specific and vivid. We now know *how many* armadillos, the *size* of the armadillos, and *how, where,* and *when* they dig.

ADJECTIVES

Adjectives are modifiers of nouns or noun substitutes and can be divided into several types.

1. *Indefinite adjectives* limit the nouns they modify, usually by restricting the amount or number. Look at the following list of frequently used indefinite adjectives:

some	every	much
many	each	most
other	all	another
few	any	several

Notice in the following sentences on p. 246 how the indefinite adjectives limit in some way the nouns they modify.

EXAMPLES

Some restaurants stay open *all* night.
Several photographers and a *few* reporters were seen at *each* meeting.
Few, if *any,* policemen were at the *other* riot.

Notice also that an indefinite adjective always comes before the noun it modifies.

2. **Demonstrative adjectives** identify or point out. There are only four demonstrative adjectives—*this, that, these,* and *those*—and they, too, occur before the noun they modify.

EXAMPLES

This movie is as boring as *that* one.
These sandwiches are stale and soggy.
He selected *those* players for his team.

3. **Descriptive adjectives,** as their name implies, describe the nouns they modify. They usually occur before the noun but may occur in a variety of positions.

EXAMPLES

The *loud, pulsating* music filled the room.
Loud and *pulsating,* the music filled the room.
The music, *loud* and *pulsating,* filled the room.

As a writer, you should be aware of the options you have in placing descriptive adjectives. Try to vary your basic sentence patterns by placing descriptive adjectives in different positions. Notice, as in the examples above, that the meaning, rhythm, and emphasis of each sentence are altered slightly by the changes in the placement of the adjectives.

4. **Participles** are verb forms used as adjectives. For example, the verb *shake* has a present participle form, *shaking,* and a past participle form, *shaken.* Both of the participle forms can be used as part of a verb phrase that functions as the main verb of a sentence.

EXAMPLES

The old man *is shaking* his fist at us.
The medicine *was shaken* thoroughly.

As shown below, participles can also be used as adjectives.

EXAMPLES

The *shaking* child ran to her mother's waiting arms.
The child, *shaking,* ran to her mother.
Shaking and crying, the child ran to her mother.
The old man, pale and *shaken,* sat down carefully.
Shaken by the accident, the woman began to cry.

Notice in these examples the different positions that a participle may take in relation to the word it modifies. In your own writing, try to vary the position of the participles you use.

In the following example and in Exercise 10.1, you are given a series of short simple sentences. Using the first sentence as your base sentence, reduce the sentences that follow to modifiers that can be used to expand the base sentence.

EXAMPLES

The wall stretched for miles.
The wall was granite.
The granite was gray.
The wall was thick.
The miles were endless.
Combinations: The thick, gray granite wall stretched for endless miles.
Thick and gray, the granite wall stretched for endless miles.
The granite wall, thick and gray, stretched for endless miles.

Notice that several combinations are possible. There is no single correct combination. Try to think of as many different combinations as you can and then choose the one you like best. You may want to say some of the combinations aloud before deciding on your choice. Try to vary the positions of your adjectives so they do not all come before the nouns they modify.

Punctuation Note: Adjectives that do not come before the nouns they modify are set off by commas.

The quilt, *torn* and *ragged,* lay on the bed.

Coordinate (equal) adjectives in a series are separated by commas.

The *torn, ragged* quilt lay on the bed.

However, if adjectives in a series are not coordinate, they are not separated by commas.

The *careless young* man failed to signal as he turned.

To determine if adjectives are coordinate, insert the word *and* between them. If the resulting construction makes sense, the adjectives are coordinate.

The *torn* and *ragged* quilt lay on the bed.
The *careless* and *young* man failed to signal as he turned.

In the first sentence, the insertion of *and* makes sense, so the adjectives are coordinate and should be separated by a comma.

The torn, ragged quilt lay on the bed.

In the second sentence, the insertion of *and* does not make sense, so the adjectives are not coordinate and should thus not be separated by a comma.

The *careless young* man failed to signal as he turned.

■ EXERCISE 10.1   Combine the following sentences; discuss punctuation possibilities with your instructor or classmates.

Answers will vary.

1. The girl slept in the doorway.
   The girl was young.
   The girl was pretty.
   The doorway was cold.
   The doorway was dirty.

   The pretty young girl slept in the cold, dirty doorway.

   _____

   _____

2. The groundhog peeked out of its hole.
   The groundhog was shy.
   The groundhog was shaggy.
   The hole was private.

   The shy, shaggy groundhog peeked out of its private hole.

   _____

   _____

3. The dancers kept time to the music.
   The dancers were moving energetically.
   The music was loud.
   The music was pulsating.

   Moving energetically, the dancers kept time to the loud,

   pulsating music.

   _____

4. The candle went out.
   The candle was sputtering.
   The candle was hissing.

   Sputtering and hissing, the candle went out.

   _____

   _____

5. The woman was visiting her aunt.
   The aunt was her favorite.
   The woman was middle-aged.
   The woman was dutiful.

   The dutiful, middle-aged woman was visiting her favorite aunt.

_____

_____

6. He finished the book.
   The book was long.
   The book was fascinating.

   He finished the long, fascinating book. _____

   _____

   _____

7. My laundry is piling up again.
   My laundry is dirty.
   My laundry is stinking.
   My laundry is messy.

   Stinking and messy, my dirty laundry is piling up again. _____

   _____

   _____

8. The child looked into the box.
   The child was curious.
   The box was tiny.
   The box was carved.
   The box was wooden.

   The curious child looked into the tiny carved wooden box. _____

   _____

   _____

9. The bull rider shot out of the chute.
   The rider was shouting.
   The rider was waving his hat.
   The chute was open.

   Shouting and waving his hat, the bull rider shot out of the _____

   open chute. _____

   _____

10. The nurse checked his watch.
    The nurse was sniffing.
    The nurse was clucking.
    The nurse was starched.
    The nurse was efficient.

The watch was large.
The watch was waterproof.

Sniffing and clucking, starched and efficient, the nurse checked

his large waterproof watch.

EXERCISE 10.2

Answers will vary.

Adjectives have been deleted from the following passage. Replace the blanks with appropriate adjectives.

It was a beautiful college. The buildings were _____**old**_____ and covered
(1)

with vines and the roads gracefully winding, lined with hedges and wild roses that

dazzled the eyes in the _____**summer**_____ sun. Honeysuckle and _____**purple**_____
(2)   (3)

wisteria hung heavy from the trees and _____**white**_____ magnolias mixed with
(4)

their scents in the _**bee-humming**_ air. I've recalled it often, here in my hole:
(5)

How the grass turned _____**green**_____ in the springtime and how the mocking-
(6)

birds fluttered their tails and sang, how the moon shone down on the buildings,

how the bell in the chapel tower rang out the precious short-lived hours; how

the girls in _____**bright**_____ summer dresses promenaded the _____**grassy**_____
(7)   (8)

lawn. Many times, here at night, I've closed my eyes and walked along the

_____**forbidden**_____ road that winds past the girls' dormitories, past the hall with
(9)

the clock in the tower, its windows warmly _____**aglow**_____, on down past the
(10)

_____**small**_____ white Home Economics practice cottage, whiter still in the
(11)

moonlight, and on down the road with its sloping and turning, paralleling the

_____**black**_____ powerhouse with its engines droning earth-shaking rhythms in
(12)

the dark, its windows _____**red**_____ from the glow of the furnace, on to where
(13)

the road became a bridge over a _____**dry**_____ riverbed, tangled with brush
(14)

and _____**clinging**_____ vines; the bridge of rustic logs, made for trysting, but
(15)

virginal and untested by lovers; on up the road, past the buildings, with the

_____**southern**_____ verandas half-a-city-block long, to the sudden forking, barren of
(16)

buildings, birds, or grass, where the road turned off to the insane asylum.

Ralph Ellison, *Invisible Man*

ADVERBS

Another way of expanding basic sentence patterns is by using adverbs to modify the verb of the sentence. Although adverbs can also modify other modifiers or even entire sentences, they usually give additional information about the verb of a sentence. Adverbs that modify verbs tell *how* (in what manner), *when,* or *where.*

> The student entered the classroom *late.* (when)
> They went *home* after the party. (where)
> The judge stood up *slowly* and *majestically.* (how)

Adverbs do not necessarily occur either immediately before or after the verbs they modify, although they may occur in these positions. Notice that in the third example, the adverbs *slowly* and *majestically* occur after the verb *rose.* However, these adverbs could be shifted to the beginning of the sentence.

> *Slowly* and *majestically,* the judge stood up.

Adverbs, especially those that end in *-ly,* can be shifted from one position in the sentence to another. However, when adverbs are placed at the beginning of the sentence rather than in their normal position after the verb, they are usually followed by a comma.

EXERCISE 10.3

Answers will vary.

Following is a series of short simple sentences. Using the first sentence as your base sentence, reduce the other sentences to adverbs and use them to expand the basic sentence. Remember to vary the placement of your adverbs. If you are adding *ly* to a word that ends in *y,* change the *y* to *i* before adding the *ly* suffix.

1. The walrus waddled.
   The waddling was comical (ly).
   The waddling was clumsy (ly).
   The waddling was backward.

   Comically and clumsily, the walrus waddled backward.

   _____

   _____

2. The guitarist played.
   The playing was soft (ly).
   The playing was steady (ly).
   The playing was all evening.

   All evening the guitarist played softly and steadily.

   _____

   _____

3. The plant grew.
   The growing was unexpected (ly).
   The growing was sudden (ly).

   Suddenly and unexpectedly, the plant grew. _____

   _____

   _____

4. The president spoke to the press.
   The press was eager.
   The speaking was serious (ly).
   The speaking was unpretentious (ly).

   The president spoke seriously and unpretentiously to the eager press.

   _____

   _____

5. Alice rode the motorcycle.
   The riding was fearless (ly).
   The riding was natural (ly).
   The riding was along the trail.

   Fearlessly and naturally, Alice rode the motorcycle along the trail.

   _____

   _____

6. The wind blew.
   The blowing was constant (ly).
   The blowing was relentless (ly).
   The blowing was day and night.

   Day and night, the wind blew constantly and relentlessly. _____

   _____

   _____

7. Professor Scott peered at his class.
   The peering was uneasy (ly).
   The peering was this morning.

   This morning Professor Scott peered uneasily at his class. _____

   _____

   _____

8. The referee explained the rules.
   The explaining was clear (ly).

The explaining was emphatic (ly).

The referee explained the rules clearly and emphatically.

_____

_____

9. The bank teller whispered to the guard.
    The whispering was urgent (ly).
    The guard was at the door.

    The bank teller whispered urgently to the guard at the door.

    _____

    _____

10. We will start for home.
    The starting will be this morning.
    The starting will be later.

    Later this morning, we will start for home.

    _____

    _____

EXERCISE 10.4

Answers will vary.

The adverbs have been deleted from the following passage. Replace each blank with an appropriate adverb.

The stem of the vessel shot by, dropping, as it did so, into a hollow between the waves; and I caught a glimpse of a man standing at the wheel, and of another man who seemed to be doing little else than smoke a cigar. I saw the smoke issuing from his lips as he _____**slowly**_____ turned his head and glanced
(1)

_____**out**_____ over the water in my direction. It was a careless, unpremeditated
(2)

glance, one of those haphazard things men do when they have no immediate call to do anything in particular, but act because they are alive and must do something.

But life and death were in that glance. I could see the vessel being swallowed

_____**up**_____ in the fog; I saw the back of the man at the wheel, and the
(3)

head of the other man turning, _____**slowly**_____ turning, as his gaze struck the
(4)

water and _____**casually**_____ lifted along it toward me. His face wore an absent
(5)

expression, as of deep thought, and I became afraid that if his eyes did light upon me he would nevertheless not see me. But his eyes did light upon me,

and looked ___**squarely**___ into mine; and he did see me, for he sprang to the
(6)

wheel, thrusting the other man ___**aside**___ , and whirled it round and
(7)

___**round**___ , hand over hand, at the same time shouting orders of some
(8)

sort. The vessel seemed to go ___**off**___ at a tangent to its former
(9)

course and leapt almost ___**instantly**___ from view into the fog.
(10)

I felt myself slipping into unconsciousness, and tried with all the power of my

will to fight above the suffocating blankness and darkness that was rising around

me. A little ___**later**___ I heard the stroke of oars, growing nearer and
(11)

___**nearer**___ , and the calls of a man. When he was ___**very**___ near I
(12)   (13)

heard him crying, in vexed fashion, ''Why in hell don't you sing out?'' This meant

me, I thought, and ___**then**___ the blankness and darkness rose over me.
(14)

Jack London, *The Sea Wolf*

PREPOSITIONAL PHRASES

Prepositional phrases provide a third way to expand basic sentences.
Prepositional phrases consist of a preposition and its object (a noun or
noun substitute). The prepositional phrase itself may be expanded by
the addition of adjectives that modify the object of the preposition.

EXAMPLES

The nurse smiled *at the child.*
The nurse smiled *at the small, timid child.*

The fighter *in the corner* looked mean.
The fighter *in the far corner* looked mean.

We caught the bus *at the station.*
We caught the bus *at the central station.*

The following words are commonly used as prepositions:

aboard	behind	from	throughout
about	below	in	to
above	beneath	into	toward
across	beside	like	under
after	between	near	underneath
against	beyond	of	until
along	but (except)	off	unto
amid	by	on	up
among	down	over	upon
around	during	past	with
at	except (but)	since	within
before	for	through	without

Examples of compound prepositions follow:

according to	due to	instead of
along with	in addition to	on account of
because of	in place of	out of
contrary to	in spite of	

Function

Prepositional phrases function in a sentence as either adjectives or adverbs, depending on whether they modify a noun or a verb. Those that function as adverbs give information (*where, how, when,* or *why*) about a verb.

EXAMPLES

The party was held *at the beach.* (where)
The stunned man wandered about *in a daze.* (how)
They arrived early *in the morning.* (when)
They came *for the homecoming party.* (why)

Prepositional phrases that function as adjectives modify a noun by telling *which one* (s).

EXAMPLES

The girl *in the red dress* raised her hand.
That book *of mine* caused a lot of trouble.
The room *on the second floor* is vacant.

In the examples above, the prepositional phrases function as adjectives because they modify nouns; they tell us which girl, which book, and which room; in other words, they identify as well as describe the nouns they modify.

Placement

Most prepositional phrases that function as adverbs can be moved about freely.

EXAMPLES

During the morning, the rain fell steadily.
The rain fell steadily *during the morning.*

Notice the slight difference in emphasis and style that results from the shift in the position of the prepositional phrase. The placement of adverbial prepositional phrases is another option that a writer has. However, prepositional phrases that function as adjectives are placed *immediately after* the noun or pronoun they modify.

EXERCISE 10.5

Answers will vary.

In the following sentence-combining exercise, use the first sentence as your base sentence and reduce the others to prepositional phrases that modify a noun or verb in the main sentence. Remember to vary the placement of your adverb phrases but be sure that each adjective phrase follows immediately the word that it modifies.

1. The wilting fern sat.
   The sitting was in a dusty corner.
   The corner was of the waiting room.

   In a dusty corner of the waiting room sat a wilting fern.

   _____

   _____

2. Jeff swept the dirt.
   The sweeping was in a hurry.
   The sweeping was under his bed.

   In a hurry, Jeff swept the dirt under his bed.

   _____

   _____

3. The picture hung.
   The picture was of the church.
   The church was on the hill.
   The hanging was in the office.

   The picture of the church on the hill hung in the office.

   _____

   _____

4. The banker parked her car.
   The parking was in a no-parking zone.
   The no-parking zone was near a fire hydrant.

   The banker parked her car in a no-parking zone near a fire hydrant.

   _____

   _____

5. The father placed the small child.
   The placing was in her crib.
   The crib was beside the big bed.
   The placing was at night.

   At night the father placed the small child in her crib beside the big bed.

   _____

   _____

6. The senator spoke to the crowd.
   The senator was from Pennsylvania.

The crowd was of retired citizens.
The speaking was with great enthusiasm.

With great enthusiasm, the senator from Pennsylvania spoke to the

crowd of retired citizens.

7. Georgia rode.
   The riding was in a canoe.
   The canoe was of light aluminum.
   The riding was over the rapids.
   The rapids were of the White River.

   Georgia rode over the rapids of the White River in a canoe of light

   aluminum.

8. The window faced a brick wall.
   The window was in his bedroom.
   The brick wall was across the alley.
   The alley was narrow.

   The window in his bedroom faced a brick wall across the narrow alley.

9. The baby laughed.
   The baby was in the swing.
   The laughing was with joy.
   The laughing was sudden.

   Suddenly, the baby in the swing laughed with joy.

10. The director announced the name.
    The name was of the winner.
    The announcement was to the crowd.
    The announcement was loud.
    The announcement was clear.

    Loudly and clearly, the director announced the name of the winner

    to the crowd.

■ EXERCISE 10.6

Answers will vary.

Prepositions have been deleted from the following passages. Write appropriate prepositions in the blanks.

PASSAGE A

The distance ___**from**___ the earth ___**to**___ the moon changes
         (1)   (2)

every day, even ___**from**___ minute ___**to**___ minute, because both
             (3)   (4)

the earth and the moon travel ___**in**___ oval orbits. Since the moon's orbit
                           (5)

is not circular, but oval-shaped, the moon is closer ___**to**___ the earth
                                              (6)

___**at**___ some times and farther away ___**at**___ other times.
   (7)   (8)

___**At**___ the nearest approach to the earth, the moon is 360,000 km
   (9)

away. ___**At**___ its farthest point, the moon is 404,800 km away. . . .
      (10)

The moon does not actually change shape. It is the pattern ___**of**___
                                                        (11)

reflected light that changes. The moon does not give off light

___**of**___ its own. It receives light ___**from**___ the sun, just as
   (12)   (13)

the earth and other planets do. The moon's barren surface reflects much

___**of**___ the light into space and some ___**of**___ that light
   (14)   (15)

reaches the earth. One half of the moon is always lighted ___**by**___ the
                                                        (16)

sun and one half is always dark, just as the earth is. But the same

half ___**of**___ the moon is not lighted all ___**of**___ the time be-
     (17)   (18)

cause the moon is traveling ___**in**___ an orbit ___**around**___ the
                         (19)   (20)

earth while the earth travels around the sun.

William H. Matthews, III, et al., *Investigating the Earth*

PASSAGE B

Democratic people applauded Castro's overthrow ___**of**___
                                             (1)

Batista's dictatorship. Some in the United States gave guarded approval

___**to**___ the first steps Castro was taking to improve conditions
   (2)

___**for**___ poor Cubans. As 1960 wore on, however, the United States
   (3)

grew alarmed ___**at**___ Castro's growing ties ___**with**___ the
             (4)   (5)

Soviet Union. ___**In**___ January 1961, the United States broke dip-
              (6)

lomatic relations ___**with**___ Cuba, and ___**at**___ the end
                   (7)   (8)

_____**of**_____ that year Castro made his position clear. "I am a Marxist,"
     (9)

he proclaimed.

Marvin Perry, *Unfinished Journey: A World History*

APPOSITIVES

A final way that basic sentence patterns can be expanded is by use of appositives. An appositive is a noun or noun phrase (noun plus modifiers) that gives additional information about another noun. Unlike adjectives—which describe, limit, or identify nouns—an appositive explains or defines a noun.

EXAMPLES

The picture, *a pastel watercolor*, was for sale.
They served my favorite dessert, *raspberry sherbet*.
An energetic person, Nora Smith is always up before dawn.

In the first two examples, the appositives follow the nouns they explain. This is by far the most common position for an appositive. In the third sentence, however, the appositive comes before the noun it explains. In either case, whether the appositive comes before or after the noun it explains, it must be immediately adjacent to it. Appositives cannot be shifted about in the sentence pattern as freely as can adjectives and adverbs.

Punctuation

An appositive is usually set off by commas. In instances in which the appositive is essential to identify the noun it explains (e.g., *my friend Dale*), commas may be omitted. But most of the time—in fact, any time the appositive could be omitted from the sentence without changing the meaning of the sentence—it is set off by commas.

EXERCISE 10.7

Sentences will vary.

Combine each sentence pair into one sentence by making one of the sentences an appositive that explains a noun in the other sentence.

EXAMPLES

The swing hung from a tree.
The tree was an old live oak with low, gnarled branches.
Combination: The swing hung from a tree, an old live oak with
                   low, gnarled branches.

1. Dr. Martinez performed the delicate operation.
    Dr. Martinez is a renowned heart surgeon.

    Dr. Martinez, a renowned heart surgeon, performed the delicate

    operation.

2. The plants were set in large clay pots around the patio.
   The plants were geraniums and periwinkles.

   The plants, geraniums and periwinkles, were set in large clay pots

   around the patio.

   _____

3. They liked the other car.
   The other car was a small foreign model.

   They liked the other car, a small foreign model.

   _____

   _____

4. An aardvark was the main attraction at the zoo.
   An aardvark is one of the strangest looking animals in existence.

   One of the strangest looking animals in existence, the aardvark, was

   the main attraction at the zoo.

   _____

5. I chose a new color for my bedroom walls.
   The new color was a pale, cheerful yellow.

   I chose a new color, a pale, cheerful yellow, for my bedroom walls.

   _____

   _____

6. Amy Johnson will be the party's nominee.
   Amy Johnson is a former college president.

   Amy Johnson, a former college president, will be the party's nominee.

   _____

   _____

7. The movie was a disappointment.
   The movie was an adaptation of a novel.

   The movie, an adaptation of a novel, was a disappointment.

   _____

   _____

8. He sent his aunt a description of his new home.

His aunt is an interior decorator.

He sent his aunt, an interior decorator, a description of his new home.

_____

_____

9. The school was closed for repairs.
    The school was an old red-brick structure.

    The school, an old red-brick structure, was closed for repairs. _____

    _____

    _____

10. He introduced her to his friends.
    His friends were Eddie, Chris, and Bob.

    He introduced her to his friends, Eddie, Chris, and Bob. _____

    _____

    _____

▓ EXERCISE 10.8   This sentence-combining exercise contains a series of sentence groups that can be combined in various ways. Using the first sentence as your base sentence, reduce the sentences that follow to modifiers (adjectives, adverbs, or prepositional phrases) or appositives that can be used to expand the base sentence. Try to vary the position of the modifiers. If you are unsure of the correct punctuation, discuss the sentence with

Sentences will vary.   your instructor or classmates.

1. The cat stretched.
    The cat was fat.
    The cat was sleek.
    The cat was a Burmese.
    The stretching was lazy (ly).

    Fat and sleek, the Burmese cat stretched lazily. _____

    _____

    _____

2. The car rolled.
    The car was a Mercedes.
    The car was expensive.
    The rolling was slow (ly).
    The rolling was arrogant (ly).
    The rolling was to a stop.

    The car, an expensive Mercedes, rolled slowly and arrogantly to a stop.

_____

_____

3. I read the book.
    The reading was reluctant.
    The book was silly.
    The book was repetitious.
    The reading was to my son.

    Reluctantly, I read the silly, repetitious book to my son.

_____

_____

4. The dancer twirled.
    The dancer was holding his arms up.
    The dancer was lifting his head high.
    The twirling was rapid (ly).
    The twirling was for several moments.

    Holding his arms up and lifting his head high, the dancer twirled

    rapidly for several moments.

_____

5. The salesperson took the money.
    The salesperson was a young girl.
    The young girl was shy.
    The money was the customer's.
    The customer was complaining.

    The salesperson, a shy young girl, took the complaining customer's

    money.

_____

6. The hotel sat.
    The hotel was brick.
    The brick was whitewashed.
    The sitting was on a hill.
    The hill was overlooking a cliff.
    The sitting was precarious (ly).

    The whitewashed brick hotel sat precariously on a hill overlooking a

    cliff.

_____

7. The man wore a hat.
    The man was dignified.

The man was otherwise well dressed.
The hat was ridiculous.
The hat was a derby.
The derby was old.
The derby was black.
The wearing was unexpected (ly).

Otherwise well dressed, the dignified man unexpectedly wore a

ridiculous old black derby.

___

___

8. The child cried.
   The child was small.
   The child was hiding.
   The hiding was under the sheets.
   The sheets were on his bed.
   The crying was uncontrollable (ly).

   Hiding under the sheets on his bed, the small child cried

   uncontrollably.

   ___

9. Albert Norris voted.
   Norris was the senator from Wyoming.
   The voting was for the bill.
   The bill was controversial.
   The bill was about water conservation.

   Albert Norris, the senator from Wyoming, voted for the

   controversial water conservation bill.

   ___

10. The dishes were stacked.
    The dishes were dirty.
    The stacking was high.
    The height was dangerous (ly).
    The stacking was in the sink.
    The sink was enamel.
    The enamel was chipped.

    The dirty dishes were stacked dangerously high in the chipped

    enamel sink.

    ___

    ___

■ EXERCISE 10.9   Combine the following sentences. Then rewrite the sentences in paragraph form.

Answers will vary.

1. Santa Fe is a town.
   The town has a past.

   Santa Fe is a town with a past. _____

   _____

   _____

2. It seems to belong.
   The belonging is to another time.
   The belonging is to another place.
   It is located in the hills.
   The hills are at the foot.
   The foot is of the mountains.

   Located in the hills at the foot of the mountains, it seems

   to belong to another time and place. _____

   _____

3. One immediately notices.
   What one notices is the age.
   The age is of the town.
   The age is obvious.
   One leaves the highway.
   The highway is modern.
   The highway is four-lane.
   The four-lane is wide.
   The highway leads to Santa Fe.

   Leaving the modern, wide four-lane highway that leads to Santa Fe, one

   immediately notices the obvious age of the town. _____

   _____

4. Some buildings date.
   The dating is back.
   The dating is to the 1600s.

   Some buildings date back to the 1600s. _____

   _____

   _____

5. Even the buildings are designed.
   The buildings are new.
   The designing is to look old.

Even the new buildings are designed to look old.

_____

_____

6. Everything is built.
    The everything is new.
    The everything is old.
    The building is adobe.
    The adobe is pink.

    Everything, new and old, is built of pink adobe.

    _____

    _____

7. Streets are narrow.
    Streets are unpaved.
    The unpaving is frequent (ly).

    The narrow streets are frequently unpaved.

    _____

    _____

8. Dogs wander.
    The wandering is free (ly).
    The wandering is about the plaza.
    The plaza is central.
    The dogs ignore the traffic.
    The dogs ignore the tourists.

    Ignoring the traffic and tourists, dogs wander freely about the central

    plaza.

    _____

9. Women peddle their wares.
    The women are Native American.
    The women are wrapped.
    The wrapping is in shawls.
    The shawls are hand-woven.
    The peddling is along the sidewalks.
    The sidewalks encircle the plaza.

    Native American women, wrapped in hand-woven shawls, peddle their

    wares along the sidewalks encircling the plaza.

    _____

10. They too ignore the traffic.
     They too ignore the tourists.

     They too ignore the traffic and tourists.

     _____

     _____

11. People are dressed.
     The people are few.
     The dressing is in styles.
     The styles are current.

     Few people are dressed in current styles.

     _____

     _____

12. The Native Americans cling.
     The clinging is to their clothing.
     The clothing is traditional.

     The Native Americans cling to their traditional clothing.

     _____

     _____

13. The artists continue to wear clothes.
     The students continue to wear clothes.
     The artists and students are local.
     The clothes are unconventional.
     The clothes are comfortable.
     The clothes are of the 1960s.

     The local artists and students continue to wear the comfortable,

     unconventional clothes of the 1960s.

     _____

14. Even the tourists have sense.
     The sense is enough.
     The sense is to leave their shirts.
     The sense is to leave their bags.
     The shirts are Polo.
     The bags are Gucci.
     The leaving is in their hotel rooms.

     Even the tourists have enough sense to leave their Polo shirts and

Gucci bags in their hotel rooms.

15. The town disdains anything.
     The anything is new.
     The town reveres anything.
     The anything is old.
     The anything is with a past.

     The town disdains anything new and reveres anything old, anything

     with a past.

16. And it wears its past.
     The past is its own.
     The wearing is with pride.
     The wearing is with dignity.
     The dignity is crumbling.

     And it wears its own past with pride and crumbling dignity.

EDITING THE EXPANDED SENTENCE

Adjective or Adverb?

Adjectives modify nouns, and adverbs modify verbs or other modifiers (adjectives and adverbs). This rule usually presents few problems. It's easy to remember that you shouldn't use an adverb to modify a noun. You are not likely to say or write a sentence such as the following:

He is an *unhappily* person.

But it's more difficult to remember not to use an adjective to modify a verb, as in the following sentence:

The patient is breathing *normal* again. (should be *normally*)

It is also sometimes difficult to decide whether to use an adjective or adverb following the verb *to be.* The verb *to be* should always be followed by an adjective, since it modifies, not the verb, but the subject.

The new teacher was *nervous.* (not *nervously*)

The same rule applies when the verb is a "sense" verb (a verb such as *feel, taste, smell, sound,* and *look*) that is followed by a modifier describing the subject.

> The pizza tastes *awful.* (not *awfully*)
> He feels *bad.* (not *badly*)

The following adjectives and adverbs are especially tricky:

bad/badly	You feel *bad.* (adjective)
	You slept *badly.* (adverb)
good/well	You feel *good.* (adjective)
	You slept *well.* (adverb)
sure/surely	You are *sure.* (adjective)
	You are *surely* ready. (adverb)
real/really	You sound *real.* (adjective)
	You sound *really* angry. (adverb)

EXERCISE 10.10   Underline the adjective or adverb that is correct in each sentence below.

1. The steak was burned (bad, <u>badly</u>).
2. I slept (real, <u>really</u>) (good, <u>well</u>) last night.
3. She walked very (graceful, <u>gracefully</u>) into the room.
4. Her walk was (<u>graceful</u>, gracefully).
5. Are you (<u>sure</u>, surely) that she is (real, <u>really</u>) angry?
6. The infection made her feel (<u>bad</u>, badly).

EXERCISE 10.11   The following paragraph contains six errors in adjective/adverb usage. Identify and correct each of these errors.

quickly   The campaign started <u>quick</u>. One day there were no candidates; the next day

really, badly   six people were vying for the nomination. Each candidate wanted to win <u>real bad</u>.

well   Some of them didn't do <u>good</u> initially but became more popular as the campaign

progressed. Voters became weary of the television ads and inevitable polls as

the candidates struggled to become well known. Most of the voters only wanted

normally, definitely   to live <u>normal</u> again. In the end, everyone was <u>definite</u> relieved that it was all over

for another four years.

Misplaced and Dangling Modifiers

Although a writer has options in placing modifiers in a sentence, sometimes a misplaced or dangling modifier can confuse a reader.

Misplaced Modifiers

Most modifiers need to be as near as possible to the word they modify. Otherwise, the meaning of the sentence may not be clear.

> The clown entertained the children wearing baggy pants and an old top hat.

In the example on p. 268, it is not clear who is wearing the baggy pants and old top hat. If it is the clown who is dressed in this way, then that phrase should be placed immediately before or after the word *clown*.

> Wearing baggy pants and an old top hat, the clown entertained the children.
>
> The clown, wearing baggy pants and an old top hat, entertained the children.

■ EXERCISE 10.12

Sentences will vary.

Rewrite the following sentences so that the misplaced modifiers are appropriately placed. The misplaced modifiers are italicized.

1. The men watched the hockey match *eating sandwiches.*

   Eating sandwiches, the men watched the hockey match.

2. As we continued to tease him, the child was ready to *almost* cry.

   As we continued to tease him, the child was almost ready to cry.

3. She found a scorpion *on the floor doing exercises.*

   On the floor doing exercises, she found a scorpion.

4. Because of increasing inflation, she asked to have her salary adjusted *yearly.*

   Because of increasing inflation, she asked to have her yearly salary

   adjusted.

5. I cautioned the movers *carefully* to carry the dishes.

   I cautioned the movers to carry the dishes carefully.

6. The teacher advised the students *regularly* to go to the Writing Center.

   The teacher regularly advised the students to go to the Writing

Center. (The teacher advised the students to go to the Writing Center

regularly.)

7. The governess told the children *properly* to eat their dinner.

    The governess told the children to eat their dinner properly.

Dangling Modifiers

Sometimes modifiers are not just misplaced but occur in a sentence in which there is no word for them to modify. We call such modifiers *dangling modifiers.*

> *Sweeping the porch with a straw broom,* the dust filled the air.

In the example above, the modifying phrase *sweeping the porch with a straw broom* is dangling because there is no word in the sentence that it modifies. We need to know *who* is doing the sweeping.

> *Sweeping the porch with a straw broom,* the old woman filled the air with dust.

In the corrected example above, the modifying phrase describes the old woman.

Participles

Most dangling modifiers are participial phrases that occur at the beginning of a sentence. Since participles are modifiers that derive from verbs (*sweeping* is the present participle of the verb *to sweep*), they must modify a word that is capable of performing the action implied by the verb. Usually the subject of the sentence is the word modified by the participial phrase. The subject must, therefore, be the person or thing that is performing the action implied.

EXERCISE 10.13

Sentences will vary.

Rewrite the following sentences, correcting the dangling modifier in each one.

1. Using brainwashing techniques, the captives began to weaken in their resolve.

    As a result of the brainwashing techniques, the captives began

    to weaken in their resolve.

2. Rowing frantically, the boat began to sink.

    Even though they were rowing frantically, the boat began to sink.

3. Arriving by ship, Los Angeles looked like an enormous city.

   To the immigrants arriving by ship, Los Angeles looked like an

   enormous city.

4. By reading late that night, the examination was passed.

   By reading late that night, he passed the examination.

5. Hanging on a hook in the hall closet, my sister found her lost umbrella.

   My sister found her lost umbrella hanging on a hook in the

   hall closet.

■ EXERCISE 10.14

Paragraphs will vary.

The following paragraph contains eight misplaced or dangling modifiers. Identify the eight errors and rewrite the paragraph, correcting these errors.

She remembered the stream from her childhood. It was not very big even then, just a small stream that wound its way in and out of the trees in the wooded area behind her home. Looking at the stream now, it had changed drastically. Her parents had taught her always never to throw anything into the stream. Now it was littered with all kinds of debris obviously. Her parents had cautioned her about contaminating the water repeatedly. Now it was contaminated clearly because dead fish floated on its surface. Flowing sluggishly among the trees, she looked at the stream with tears in her eyes, ready to almost cry. The stream no longer burbled and murmured as it once had. It was silent, sluggish, and stinking. Other people had not been taught to respect and preserve nature evidently as she had. The stream was now dead.

Fragments

A fragment is a separated sentence part that does not express a complete thought. To decide whether a group of words is a sentence, ask yourself these two questions: (1) Does it have a verb *and* a subject? (2) Does it express a complete thought? If the answer to either question is "no," the group of words is not a sentence but a part of a sentence—a fragment.

Three of the sentence elements that are commonly mistaken for complete sentences are (1) participial phrases, (2) appositive phrases, and (3) prepositional phrases.

Participial-Phrase Sentence Fragments

A participle is a word formed from a verb but used as an adjective. As illustrated in the example below, present participles (*-ing* form of verbs) are frequently mistaken for main verbs, and the phrases in which they appear are frequently mistaken for complete sentences.

> Reading comic books all the time.

Although the participle *reading* is a verb form, it is not a verb since it cannot be used with a subject (I reading, you reading, he reading, and so on). Only when accompanied by a form of the verb *to be* (*am, is, are, was, were, been, being*) can a participle be used as a main verb (I am reading, you are reading).

A participial phrase most frequently functions as an adjective, modifying the subject of the main verb in the independent clause to which it is attached.

> Reading comic books all the time, Jim lived in a world of fantasy.
> Jim, reading comic books all the time, lived in a world of fantasy.
> Jim lived in a world of fantasy, reading comic books all the time.

Notice that in the preceding examples the participial phrase is separated from the independent clause by a comma or commas.

EXERCISE 10.15

Sentences will vary.

Below are six participial phrases incorrectly written as sentences. Write six complete sentences by adding an independent clause to each of the phrases. Be sure the phrase modifies the subject of your independent clause.

1. Waiting alone.

   Waiting alone, she began to feel frightened.

   _____

2. Seeing the exit sign ahead.

   Seeing the exit sign ahead, she signaled a left turn.

   _____

3. Expecting guests soon.

   Expecting guests soon, he cleaned his apartment.

4. Sitting on a bus all day.

   Sitting on a bus all day, the travelers looked rumpled and weary.

5. Working on the project for weeks.

   Working on the project for weeks, they began to know each other well.

6. Seeing no way out.

   Seeing no way out, she gave up gracefully.

Appositive-Phrase Sentence Fragments

An appositive phrase explains the noun or pronoun it follows. As shown below, neither an appositive nor an appositive phrase can stand alone as a sentence.

The eighteen sailors rowed 3,618 miles to Timor. An island near Java.

An island near Java is an appositive phrase explaining *Timor* and should be joined to the preceding sentence.

The eighteen sailors rowed 3,618 miles to Timor, an island near Java.

Notice that the appositive phrase is set off from the rest of the sentence by a comma or, as in the sentence below, two commas.

Alvin, one of my best friends, has left for college.

EXERCISE 10.16

Sentences will vary.

Combine the following sentences and appositive phrases, attaching the appositive phrases to the nouns from which they have been incorrectly separated. Change punctuation and capitalization whenever necessary.

1. We enjoy playing Parcheesi. A game from India.

   We enjoy playing Parcheesi, a game from India.

2. The entrance to the Mediterranean is guarded by a rocky peninsula. Gibraltar.

   The entrance to the Mediterranean is guarded by Gibraltar, a rocky

peninsula. _____

_____

3. Astronomers have recently photographed Saturn. The planet encircled by rings.

   Astronomers have recently photographed Saturn, the planet encircled

   by rings. _____

   _____

4. Thursday was named for Thor. The Norse god of thunder.

   Thursday was named for Thor, the Norse god of thunder. _____

   _____

5. We went to a double feature. A mystery and a western.

   We went to a double feature, a mystery and a western. _____

   _____

6. _The Twilight Zone_ was made into a movie. A successful television series.

   The Twilight Zone, a successful television series, was made into a

   movie. _____

   _____

7. The Battle of Marathon was won by the Greeks. One of the famous battles in the history of the world.

   The Battle of Marathon, one of the famous battles in the history of

   the world, was won by the Greeks. _____

   _____

8. The telephone can be both a blessing and a curse. An invention that has changed our lives.

   An invention that has changed our lives, the telephone can be both a

   blessing and a curse. _____

   _____

9. The water in Cypress Gardens near Charleston, South Carolina, is black because it contains tannic acid. A secretion of the cypress trees.

    The water in Cypress Gardens near Charleston, South Carolina, is black

    because it contains tannic acid, a secretion of the cypress trees.

10. Confucius said, "Learning without thought is labor lost." A famous Chinese philosopher of the fifth century B.C.

    Confucius, a famous Chinese philosopher of the fifth century B.C., said,

    "Learning without thought is labor lost."

Prepositional-Phrase Sentence Fragments

Less frequently, but occasionally, a very long prepositional phrase or series of prepositional phrases will be mistaken for a sentence. Sometimes such phrases are attached to an element that could be part of a complete sentence.

The following example is a fragment because even though it has a word that could function as its subject (*dancer*), there is no verb—only a series of prepositional phrases.

> The dancer in the short, pink skirt with the orange ribbon in her hair and purple scarf in her hand.

The next example also is a fragment because it begins with a word (*day*) that could either be a subject or an adverb but is followed only by a long series of prepositional phrases.

> The other day on the plane to Miami with my new luggage from Bloomingdale's on the seat beside me.

The following example has only prepositional phrases: *in the summer, around the old swimming pool, in the field*, and *behind our house*. There is no subject or verb.

> In the summer around the old swimming pool in the field behind our house.

We could correct this fragment by supplying a subject and verb so that a statement is made.

> In the summer *we meet* around the old swimming pool in the field behind our house.

■ EXERCISE 10.17

Sentences will vary.

Supply the fragments below with the essential elements they need in order to be complete sentences.

1. Without looking in the direction of the traffic on the street.

    Without looking in the direction of the traffic on the street, the

jogger dashed to the other side.

2. My broker at the respected firm of Jones, Jones, and Jones.

   My broker at the respected firm of Jones, Jones, and Jones

   called me today.

3. Out of the bushes to the right of the large oak tree.

   Out of the bushes to the right of the large oak tree came a

   large buck.

4. Occasionally in the morning after a night out with my friends.

   Occasionally in the morning after a night out with my friends, I

   try to sleep late.

5. The fly in my cup of lukewarm coffee on the table before me.

   I stared at the fly in my cup of lukewarm coffee on the table

   before me.

▨ **EXERCISE 10.18**   The following paragraphs contain six fragments. Rewrite the paragraphs, joining the fragments to independent clauses so that they become part of complete sentences.

Answers will vary.

   The American frontier, if we are to believe the tales that have been handed down, was populated with some amazing personalities. The men about whom we hear were always at least six feet tall and often reached the height of giants. Not only were these men large; they were also strong and clever. Eating enormous amounts of food, performing astounding feats of strength and courage, inventing miraculous methods of accomplishing difficult tasks, and doing an amazing amount of work. These heroes could out-run, out-jump, out-brag, out-drink, out-shoot, and out-fight anyone foolish enough to challenge them. These giants among men were our folk heroes. Super humans created to populate and tame the rugged, often dangerous frontier.

   These folk heroes tell us something about the people who created them. Faced with countless dangers and constant weariness. The frontiersmen created mythical men who were capable of facing dangers and doing work in unusual and often humorous ways. Many of these supermen, such as Paul Bunyan and Pecos Bill, were entirely the products of the frontiersmen's imagination. However, sometimes the early Americans glorified actual men. For example, Davy Crockett and John Henry. In an effort to transform them into larger-than-life heroes. Whether based on fact or fancy, these heroes were projections of the men who created them. Ordinary mortals needing to be superhuman in order to tame the frontier.

READING AND WRITING ABOUT—

Social Issues

Preparing: Cubing and Freewriting—

Human beings are social creatures. That is, they interact with one another in their homes, in their neighborhoods, in class or at work, and in leisure activities. This interaction—complicated by psychological needs, personal prejudices, and economic problems—creates specific issues of great importance to society as a whole. Often, we are not aware of a particular social issue (a matter of public concern that affects the well-being of society) until it erupts into a crisis situation.

Three important social issues and specific problems that have arisen in relation to these issues are listed below. Read and think about these social issues and problems. In your opinion, which issue is most important? Which problem is most critical?

SOCIAL ISSUES	SOCIAL PROBLEMS
Providing shelter for members of society	The homeless
Protecting the health and safety of society	a. Alcohol abuse among young people b. Unprotected sex that leads to AIDS and other diseases
Protecting human rights and dignity	Racial prejudice and discrimination

Select one of these social issues or problems and explore it from each of the six viewpoints given below. As in your earlier cubing exercise in Chapter 7 (pp. 158–160), spend a certain amount of time (about three minutes) responding to each side, or viewpoint.

1. *Describe* the problem. How serious is it? Where is the problem the worst? When does it get started? (For example, how can you describe the situation of the homeless in America?)

2. *Compare* the problem to another social problem. What are the similarities? What are the differences?

3. *Associate* the problem with the human beings involved. Who are its victims? What happens to these people?

4. *Analyze* the problem. What are its causes? What are its effects?

5. *Apply* a possible remedy. What can society as a whole do to solve the problem? What can you do as an individual?

6. *Argue for or against* a particular response to the problem. (For example, you might argue for or against the distribution of condoms in schools to reduce the instances of unprotected sex.)

When you finish your cubing, reread it. Select one side of the cube, or one idea, that interests you more than the others and freewrite about this idea for an additional five minutes.

▧ "WE'RE NOT BUMS"
Peter Swet

Before you read, think about the plight of the homeless in America today. Have you seen a homeless person on a city street or an interstate highway? Did you really look at this person, or did you look the other way? What did you *see*? How often are homeless people able to re-enter mainstream society? In the following article,* Peter Swet gets to know one person who was able to escape the trap of homelessness.

As you read, pay particular attention to Swet's descriptive characterization of his subject, Gerald Winterlin. Underline the words and phrases that Swet uses in the first three paragraphs to describe Winterlin.

Annotations will vary.

1   For more than three years, Gerald Winterlin, now in his 40s, was one of the estimated 3 million homeless Americans. Forced by joblessness to live in his car or abandoned buildings, he had to cope with a sense of hopelessness and despair that could, and occasionally did, destroy others like himself.

2   Now he lives in a warm, modest apartment near the University of Iowa, where he's a scholarship student working on his degree in accounting and maintaining a 3.9 average. I traveled to Iowa to speak with him, hoping to understand how this bright, well-spoken, typical-seeming American could ever have hit such a deep low in his life. Just as important, I wanted to know how he fought his way back.

3   On the first of two long nights we would spend talking together, the burly Winterlin sat at his kitchen table and recalled an incident that still haunts him.

4   "I was on the cashier's line at a supermarket," he began, "behind this young, healthy-looking black woman. When her groceries were rung up, she pulled out a bunch of food stamps. I said, 'Hey, get a job. I'm tired of having money taken from my paycheck for people like you!' I expected a sharp answer, but instead she looked embarrassed and said, 'There's nothing I'd like better than a job, but nobody will give me one.' 'Bull,' I shot back, then turned away. Twenty years later, I'd love to find that lady and tell her I'm sorry. Little did I realize that what happened to her could happen to anyone. It happened to me."

5   Winterlin was born in an area known as the Quad Cities, encompassing Davenport and Bettendorf on the Iowa side of the Mississippi River, with Rock Island and Moline on the Illinois side. One of four children of a tool-and-die man,

---

* Reprinted with permission from *Parade,* copyright © 1990, and the author.

he graduated from Bettendorf High and eventually began work at the International Harvester plant. ''I worked there about eight years,'' he said, ''till '82, after the farm recession hit. Quad Cities is a world center for manufacturing farm equipment, and over 18,000 people, including me, were laid off.''

6   ''At first we figured the government would help,'' he said, adjusting his large framed glasses. ''Hell, they bailed out Chrysler, right? But, instead, weeks turned into months with no work. With only two or three weeks of unemployment left, my demands dropped real fast, from $15 an hour to begging to sweep floors—anything. One day I just picked up the phone book and started with the A's. I made a list of every company I applied to. The final number was 380, and I remember realizing that what few jobs there were went to younger people. Still, I'd go out all day looking.''

7   Winterlin heaved a deep sigh and glanced out the window at the cold Iowa night: ''I kept thinking there'd be a tomorrow. Late one night, I finally said, 'Well, Gerry, this is it. No tomorrow.' I packed what I hadn't already sold or pawned and walked out. I never planned on living in my car for long,'' he added, ''but then, no one *plans* to be homeless.''

8   What about his family—couldn't they help? ''They'd have probably taken me in,'' he said, ''but people who ask that don't understand how impossible it is to say, 'Hey, folks, here I am in my late 30s, such a pathetic loser I can't even take care of myself.' Besides, my old man had lost his own job after 25 years, just six months shy of a full pension.''

9   I asked about welfare, and Winterlin laughed. ''Don't get me started on that,'' he said. ''Welfare is the fast route to nowhere. They give you everything except what you need—a job. Some people have no option, like women with kids, but guys like me who want just enough to get started again would rather freeze than fall into a system that gives you a roof but robs you of hope. You trade your individualism and spirit for survival, and for some of us that's not a fair trade. Homeless people are proud people too.''

10   For months, Winterlin lived in his '60 Mercury with rags stuck in the rust holes. Finally, the car died, and he was forced to find shelter wherever he could. ''Somehow I made it from day to day,'' he said. ''I tried to look as good as I could, to keep clean. Sometimes I did odd jobs, but never enough to put a roof over my head. I kept trying, but before I knew it, three years of my life were gone.''

11   ''Unless you've been there, you can't understand the loneliness, the misery, the humiliation, the self-disgust at what you've been reduced to,'' Winterlin continued. ''I knew guys who just couldn't take it anymore and did themselves in. We're talking big, proud men, not junkies or drunks. They killed themselves, but I say they died of broken hearts because they couldn't handle the way people look at you, the loss of self-respect.''

12   We both fell silent for a moment, then I asked how he had managed to persevere. ''When times got darkest,'' Winterlin answered, ''when thoughts of death and feelings of hatred began to overwhelm me, I thought of the people in my life who have known how to give, not just take. One of them was Linda, the girl I should have married. I wish I could name all the others, but the good people know who they are. It's for them that I wanted to succeed.''

13   ''Anyway,'' he added, ''I read about something called the Dislocated Workers Program, which was designed to help people from old, dying industries become trained in new technologies. They put me into Scott Community College in the Quad Cities. I got straight A's. Everything looked great, then the program was cut back after six months. I almost fell apart, but because my grades were so good

a woman named Mary Teague took the time to care, to help me piece together enough funding to keep going.''

14   I noted the framed scholarship certificates displayed proudly on the wall, and Winterlin smiled, putting a hand up to conceal the spaces where he'd once been forced to pull his own teeth. ''No big secret to that,'' he laughed. ''Just plain hard work.'' He studies 50 hours a week, besides attending classes and working 20 hours at a part-time job. He has no friends, he admitted, and spends weekends alone. ''I know it wasn't my fault, but when you're homeless you lose so much self-respect, you stay away from people.'' I asked if he felt his fellow Americans understood the homeless problem.

15   ''The thing most people *don't* understand,'' he replied, ''is that most of the folks you see huddled in doorways in Eastern cities or living in parks in Santa Monica or begging for a roof right here in America's Heartland aren't there by *choice.* I didn't ask to lose my job. None of us did. We're not bums,'' he said pointedly, his voice rising. ''We're good, hardworking Americans who happened to fall between the cracks.''

16   How does he see his future? He hopes that, after receiving his degree, ''at least one person out there will say, 'Hey, I hire a person by what he's got, not by his age or where he has been.' '' He added, ''I've got to prove I can be part of society again, that Gerald Winterlin and the millions of other homeless out there really do count. There are just five words I'm determined to leave behind me— words that no one can ever, ever take away from me. The words are 'Gerald Winterlin, summa cum laude.' ''

REVIEWING THE READING   Answers will vary.

See paragraphs 1–3.   1. What words does Swet use to describe Winterlin? How do these words help to characterize Winterlin?

See paragraph 4.   2. What incident from his past still haunts Winterlin? Why is this incident so disturbing to him?

See paragraphs 5 and 8.   3. Why did Winterlin lose his job? Why could he not go to his family for help?

See paragraphs 10–12.   4. Describe Winterlin's life and feelings when he was homeless.

See paragraphs 13 and 14.   5. How did Winterlin get another chance? How did he react to that chance?

See paragraph 16.   6. What are Winterlin's future goals? Are these realistic goals?

UNDERSTANDING VOCABULARY

According to Swet, Winterlin's goal was to graduate "summa cum laude." The Latin words *magna cum laude* and *summa cum laude* are used to describe two levels of honor graduates. *Magna cum laude* means "with high honors." What does *summa cum laude* mean?

REACTING CRITICALLY

Reread paragraph 15, in which Winterlin declares, "We're not bums." Do you agree or disagree with Winterlin's claim about the homeless? Support your answer.

▓ DRINK UNTIL YOU FINALLY DROP

John Elson

Before you read, think about the problem of alcohol abuse by teenagers in your home town. How many teenagers drink? How much do they drink? Where do they drink? Why do they drink? If the problem of teenage drinking exists in your home town, what is the reaction of parents? In the following article from the December 16, 1991 issue of *Time,* John Elson attempts to answer these and other questions about teenage drinking.

See text annotation.

As you read, underline the thesis of the article. Notice also the kind of support that Elson uses to back up his thesis.

1   Live, from anywhere, it's Friday night: time for the youth of America to "rage." Time also to get broasted, buzzed, catatonic, messed up, ripped, screwed, trashed, wasted, zoned out. Time, to put it in language older folks can understand, to get totally, hopelessly drunk. Not at bars, of course: everywhere in America you have to be 21 to drink there—legally, that is—and anyway it's not the hip thing to do. These days teenagers buy into keg parties at homes where parents have left town for the weekend, where dangerous chugalug games are played to get booze and beer flowing into their system faster. Or they hang out at impromptu, one-night-only underground clubs that youthful entrepreneurs have set up in abandoned factories or warehouses, with the same goal in mind.

2   Despite the fact that the nation's per capita alcohol consumption has been on a decline for years, drinking among minors, in the words of Surgeon General Antonia Novello, "is out of control." More specifically, "unsupervised parties where kids drink are out of control. And the perception among parents that drinking is O.K. is out of control. We're going to lose a whole generation if we don't pay attention."

3   A study issued by Novello's office last June showed that 8 million of the nation's 20.7 million youths in grades 7 through 12 drink alcoholic beverages every week. Of those kids, 454,000 admit to weekly "binges"—meaning they consume five or more drinks in a single brief sitting. Another study, by the University of Michigan, reports that almost one-third of high school seniors drink to excess at least once every two weeks. And according to a survey prepared for *USA Today,* 46 percent of student leaders say drinking is their high school's biggest problem, followed by apathy. "Serious drinking is a fact of life," says Phuong Nguyen, senior-class president at Bethesda–Chevy Chase High School in a Washington suburb.

4   The problem isn't new, nor is the concern to control it. During the 1980s, states that had set 18 as the legal drinking age gradually adopted what is now the national standard: you must be 21 to purchase alcoholic beverages. But there are loopholes in the various regulations. Curiously, the binge-drinking epidemic among teens comes at a time when drug abuse in this age group has been declining. The University of Michigan survey, taken in 1990, found that only 27 percent of the seniors had smoked marijuana in the past year, compared with 49 percent of seniors who took part in a 1980 poll. Andrew McGuire, head of the Trauma Foundation at San Francisco General Hospital, says "alcohol abuse is the No. 1 health problem of young people in America."

5   More than that, it appears to be the leading cause of death among teenagers. For many of these deaths, predictably, the police verdict is driving while intoxicated. In New York City last month, six youths were killed when the car in

which they were riding went out of control while it was speeding late at night on a deserted street in the Bronx. The 18-year-old driver, who had only a learner's permit, had consumed more than twice the amount of alcohol required to qualify as legally drunk. In 1989, according to the National Traffic Safety Administration, (S) 3,539 deaths in the 15-to-20 age group resulted from traffic accidents in which alcohol played a part.

6   Government officials are only now beginning to focus on what they believe is the vastly underreported number of alcohol-related incidents among those in their teens and early 20s: suicide, murder, date rape, family violence. Alcohol (S) abuse was a major factor in 41 percent of all academic problems and 28 percent of college dropouts, according to a 1991 study by Virginia's George Mason University and West Chester University of Pennsylvania.

7   If kids start drinking in their teens, they usually keep on doing it in college, (S) unless some trauma intervenes. The federal Office of Substance Abuse Prevention reports that undergraduates currently spend $4.2 billion a year on booze— far more than they spend on textbooks. Nearly three-fourths of all college students drink at least once a month, says the Department of Health and Human (S) Services, and 41 percent of them indulge in heavy drinking—that is, four or five drinks in a row—at least once every two weeks. Many of those students are still underage. Academic officials say booze is almost invariably present when stu- (Q) dents get into trouble. ''Alcohol continues to be the No. 1 drug of choice on campus and everywhere else,'' says Mary Rouse, dean of students at the Uni- (Q) versity of Wisconsin at Madison. ''The correlation between sexual assault and drinking, vandalism and drinking, racism and drinking, is predictable. The trouble never starts until drinking begins.''

8   Where it often begins is at home—without adult monitoring. Large unsuper-vised parties where kids drink to get drunk as fast as possible are regular weekend happenings for many American teenagers. And parents who grew up in the drug culture of the late '60s and early '70s often look the other way. ''I know they are drinking in the basement, but I never go down there,'' admits a mother of Washington teenagers. ''If anything happens, my excuse is that I don't know what they are doing.''

(Ex) 9   What they are doing can be fatal. Last August 15-year-old Brian Ball of Trenton, Texas, died after downing 26 shots of vodka in 90 minutes at an all-you-can-drink party. Guests paid $3 to attend, but once they were in the door, liquor cost just 50¢ a shot. At many such booze fests, the kids play drinking games like ''Three Man Up,'' to speed up consumption. In this game players roll dice, and every time someone rolls a multiple of three, the player who has been designated the ''Three Man'' must take a drink. If the Three Man rolls a multiple, his title passes to another player.

(Ex) 10   If you can't find a house with look-the-other-way parents, there's always an illegal club. In Los Angeles a smart young promoter type will locate a vacant building that can be broken into for a one-night stand, hire a pal with a good sound system to put together dance tracks and serve as deejay, and then hand out flyers urging kids to call a certain number if they want to party at a ''major rager.'' An hour before show time, the organizer tapes an answering-machine message telling customers the location. Of course the club promoters play it safe. When teenagers drive to the touted locale, someone will be there—with a map showing where the party really is. Cost of the map: $20. Don't expect refunds if you get lost—cash collectors are changed every 15 minutes, just in case the police show up.

11   Why are so many kids drinking themselves into a stupor? Boredom, peer pressure, escape from psychological pain and wanting to feel good are the usual answers. Since most of their parents drink, teenagers tend to think of alcohol as a less threatening drug than cocaine or marijuana. Says White House drug czar Bob Martinez: "Adults often send a message to their kids that this is acceptable behavior. With marijuana, cocaine and heroin, there is no mixed message. With alcohol, there is." To David Anderson, a research professor at George Mason University's Center for Health Promotion, teenagers who indulge in binge drinking "delude themselves into thinking they can find their identity with alcohol. These kids are in search of community. And they have a quest for intimacy—who can I be at one with?"

12   Belatedly, America's elders are beginning to treat teenage drinking with the seriousness it deserves. The White House office coordinating the Administration's drug-control policy has recently broadened its mandate to include alcohol abuse, and is scheduled to give President Bush a strategy for combatting the problem by January. Surgeon General Novello is among those who are trying to eliminate loopholes in states' minimum-age laws that make it easy for minors to buy and drink booze. For example, 35 states allow minors to possess alcohol under certain circumstances—with parental consent, for instance, or in private residences. And 19 states have no laws that would punish teens for using false IDs to purchase alcohol.

13   Slowly, the legal picture is changing. Nine states have passed "social host" laws that allow adults to be sued if minors drink in their home no matter whether the adults are aware of the drinking. High schools have added courses on alcoholism, and many colleges feature alcohol-awareness weeks, during which students pledge themselves to abstain from booze. But there is a paradox here that symbolizes the depth of the problem. All too often these instant Lents end with alcohol-fueled "I survived the week" blasts in frats and dorms. The party animal is a tough beast to tame.

WHAT CAN BE DONE

■ **Talk openly with minors about your own use of alcohol and set a good example.**
"The biggest problem we have is the complacency of parents," says Surgeon General Antonia Novello.

■ **Develop strong alcohol-abuse programs that tell teens how drinking affects the body.**
According to Surgeon General's office surveys, 2.6 million teens do not know that an overdose of alcohol—20 shots of 86-proof alcohol within 90 minutes, for example—can be fatal.

■ **Demand that state legislators close loopholes that make it relatively easy for minors to buy booze.**
Novello strongly favors laws that make householders liable for accidents caused by anyone who drinks in their home.

■ **Enforce 21-minimum-age laws by requiring minors to carry distinctive IDs.**
Good example: In New Jersey, teen driving permits have a profile rather than a full-face photo.

■ **Stop youth-oriented alcohol advertising.**
Says Elaine M. Johnson, director of the Federal Government's Office of Substance Abuse Prevention: "Glamorous and misleading alcohol promotion should be eliminated."

REVIEWING THE READING   Answers will vary.

See paragraph 2.   1.   What is the thesis of the article? Where is it stated?

See text annotations.   2.   Elson supports this thesis with several kinds of evidence—quotations from experts, statistics, and examples. Find instances of each of these types of evidence and use the margins of your book to label them according to type (Q, S, EX).

(a) See paragraph 6.
(b) See paragraphs 5 and 6.

3. What statistics does Elson provide to establish a connection (a) between drinking and academic problems of teenagers, and (b) between drinking and teenage deaths?

(a) See paragraph 8.
(b) See paragraph 11.

4. According to the article, (a) how and where does teenage drinking often begin? (b) What often causes teenagers to drink?

5. This chapter focuses on the use of modifiers in sentences. What modifiers can you find in paragraph 5?

UNDERSTANDING VOCABULARY

The first paragraph lists several slang synonyms for *drunk*. What are five of these synonyms? Do you know other slang terms for "getting drunk"? Why do young people use these terms?

REACTING CRITICALLY

Study the table that accompanies this article. Evaluate each of the five suggestions of "What Can Be Done" to reduce or eliminate the problem of teenage drinking. Which suggestions are the most practical? Which are the most effective?

▧ SAFER SEX

Newsweek Staff Writers

Before you read, think about what you know about AIDS. Where did you get your information about AIDS and other sexually transmitted diseases? Do you think your information is accurate? What can you do to protect yourself from AIDS or other social diseases? Although AIDS can be transmitted in other ways, it is most often transmitted through sexual contact. In the following article from the December 9, 1991, issue of *Newsweek,* reporters consider the social issue of "safer sex."

As you read, notice how the article captures your attention at the very first. Also, circle any unfamiliar words that you encounter.

Annotations will vary.

1   This is a story about the power of love, as it is understood by a certain 17-year-old San Francisco high-school student. Carmen had sex for the first time when she was 13, with a teenage boy from the neighborhood. She had symptoms of venereal disease—possibly chlamydia—at 14 and was finally treated for it a year after that, when she saw a gynecologist for the first time. Now, when she has sexual relations with her teenage boyfriend, she doesn't use a condom because she thinks she has something better. "Even if he was screwing around nothing would happen because he says he'll never do anything that would mess me up, and I believe him," she explains, changing buses on her way home from her Roman Catholic school. "We don't need no condom because he says he loves me."

2   Love: next to the mosquito, probably the greatest disseminator of deadly microbes ever devised by the cruel hand of fate. Not only does it draw people into intimate contact, it addles their brains in the process. For the things a condom

is intended to prevent, it doesn't matter whether Carmen's boyfriend loves her or not; what counts is whether he has been infected by one of the seven major diseases known to be transmitted through sexual contact. There are 12 million cases of sexually transmitted disease [STD] each year, according to the Centers for Disease Control [CDC]. . . . Even as the overall rate of new HIV (AIDS) infections appears to be leveling off, the disease is becoming endemic in disadvantaged communities, where syphilis and gonorrhea are also on the increase. Middle-class whites are coming down with herpes, genital warts (which can lead to cancer of the cervix) and chlamydia (which can make women infertile). Three million teenagers contracted one of these diseases last year. How many of them got it from someone who loves them?

3   And yet STDs are among the easiest of diseases to prevent. Anyone who has mastered washing his hands after using the toilet has the intellectual capacity to avoid most venereal infections. Their prevalence represents an apparent failure of the quintessential liberal solution to social problems, education. For nearly a decade society has been throwing education at AIDS. *Newsweek* has run 11 cover stories on the subject. Lectures on safe sex now start in the fourth grade in some schools. . . . Homemade safe-sex programs have sprung up in all sorts of unlikely places, like the Columbia, S.C., salon of beautician DiAna DiAna, who recorded her own instructional videos on her home camcorder. Almost no one is ignorant of AIDS in this country. ''You have to sample Mars to find someone who doesn't know the basic facts,'' says Jeffrey Kelly, a professor of psychiatry at the Medical College of Wisconsin.

4   Much of this effort has been directed at getting people to use condoms, which are more widely available than ever. Sample packages, along with graphic guidance on their use, are thrust into the hands of passersby on San Francisco streets and New York City subway stations; sober matrons on their way home to Sausalito or Pelham stuff them into their purses as if they were sailors heading for the fleshpots of Bangkok. Last week New York began handing them out to high-school students, no parental approval required. In Chicago, anyone embarrassed to ask a drugstore clerk for condoms can go to a month-old store named Condomplation, where they never give you Tums by mistake instead.

5   If education alone could affect people's behavior, STDs would be a thing of the past—but then, so would drugs. The one group that has unquestionably changed its behavior is middle-class homosexual men, who had the most incentive, and the example of countless friends who died of AIDS. It would be almost inconceivable now for a man to lead the kind of life described by songwriter and author Michael Callen, who estimates he had more than 3,000 different sexual partners between 1973 and 1982—contracting in the process ''hepatitis A, hepatitis B, hepatitis non-A/non-B, herpes, syphilis, gonorrhea, chlamydia, cytomegalovirus . . .'' and eventually AIDS. . . . The changes in [heterosexual] lifestyles have been less pronounced. More typical is someone like Sharon Taylor, 34, a Denver lawyer who hit a rocky patch with her husband last spring when she questioned his fidelity. ''We decided to work on our relationship and see a counselor,'' she says, ''but when I insisted we start using a condom he balked. I think I surprised myself by sticking to my guns. He kept saying 'don't you trust me?' and I kept saying, 'no'.'' They separated for a while, reconciled, and recently have begun sleeping with each other again. Now that she's not so mad at him anymore, she has relented on the question of condoms. ''I figure I'm taking a risk no matter what I do,'' she says. ''Safe sex is an option, but at some point you have to draw the line and leave it in the hands of providence.''

6   *College Students*   If a mature, educated woman like Taylor considers safe sex optional, what can one expect from college students, much less younger teenagers? There were a million teenage pregnancies last year, representing uncounted millions of acts of unprotected copulation. This is not just a problem of minority high-school dropouts. Janice Baldwin and John Baldwin, sociologists at the University of California, Santa Barbara, have done large-scale surveys of California college students, the great majority of them white. In one they found that "less than 20 percent of the currently sexually active women and men reported using condoms 75 percent of the time or more." This was not due to lack of information. They knew enough to be worried about AIDS, especially those who were most sexually active, with three or more sexual partners in three months. It just didn't make them any likelier to use condoms. On the contrary, the Baldwins found, "the people most at risk are taking the least precautions."

7   And even when students take precautions, they often take the wrong ones. Jeffrey D. Fisher, a psychologist at the University of Connecticut, has found that undergraduates have taken to heart the advice of the surgeon general to "know your partner." But they know the wrong things about them. Rather than directly ascertain whether their partners have AIDS or another disease, they inquire about their hometowns, families and academic majors and on those irrelevant and useless facts draw a conclusion about how safe it is to sleep with them. Fisher calls this "implicit personality theory," but it's essentially a form of superstition, not unlike Carmen's conviction that her boyfriend won't give her AIDS because he loves her. Of course, it isn't always easy to get real information about sexual histories. This is partly a definitional problem. To teenagers, says Leslie Kantor of Columbia's student health service, "monogamy means you're sleeping with one person at a time." It is also partly an ethical one. Yet another study of southern California college students found that nearly half the men and two fifths of the women said they would lie about how many other people they had slept with. One man in five said he would lie about having been tested for the AIDS virus. Says one of the authors: "A partner telling you he hasn't done anything doesn't tell you anything."

8   But outright duplicity between lovers may be a lesser problem than anxiety, embarrassment and simple misunderstanding. "I wouldn't know where to start," says a 19-year-old Berkeley student who gave only the name Patricia. "What if he said no? What if he got mad? I just wouldn't be able to ask that." Some people worry that if they insist on using a condom, their partners will suspect they already have a venereal disease. Or, conversely, their partners will be offended by the implication that *they* might have a disease. Fisher has found that students don't use condoms because they're afraid of being thought of as unhip, repressed and neurotic. Contrariwise, Alicia Carmona, a 20-year-old "peer sex educator" at Columbia, knows many women who don't like to think or talk about condoms because they are "fundamentally afraid to acknowledge they're being sexual." Kenneth Traum, a junior at Berkeley, doesn't use condoms with his girlfriend because "they're uncomfortable and they take away from the whole experience. Sometimes they can really take away from what making love is." His girlfriend presumably concurs, although she assumes they have a monogamous relationship; Traum admits they don't. Still, Traum knows what he *should* be doing. He has to; he wants to be a "peer counselor" too. . . .

9   Obviously, education has some frontiers to conquer. We need . . . a video for the woman who showed up at Houston's Thomas Street Clinic testing positive for the AIDS virus but insisted she couldn't possibly infect any men because she'd

had a hysterectomy. Let's bring Magic Johnson around to talk to the prostitutes, studied by sociologist Kirk Elifson at Georgia State, who now scrupulously insist on condoms when they are working but not when they're having off-duty sex with their boyfriends. Education is sure to be a major theme [for] Surgeon General Antonia Novello . . . [whose message is] that "we have to alert the public that the epidemic is changing: more heterosexual spread, more women, children, young people."

10   *Strong Sanctions*   But at the same time we are coming up against the limits of mere knowledge to change behavior; the studies of college students show that. To a cultural conservative like Camille Paglia, author of *Sexual Personae,* this is no surprise. The "dark, turbulent drama of sexual desire" resists rational criticism, however well-intentioned, she asserts. Historically only the strong sanctions of religion and family have succeeded in reining in this primal force. People have risked marriages, jobs, inheritances and death by stoning to go to bed with someone they liked—can we really expect to conquer passion with the threat of *genital warts?* Backed up with a *subway poster?*

11   The logic of Paglia's position leads to a call not for more information but for moral absolutes. Officially, the administration endorses sexual abstinence, outside of a monogamous relationship, as the best preventive for AIDS. But when asked exactly who might be a candidate for this measure, Fred Kroger, head of CDC's AIDS education unit, mentions "the very young, [people] past 90 and others when abstinence is forced on them—with two broken legs, for instance." Chastity as a policy has been so neglected that Vice President Dan Quayle made headlines last month with a few casual words in its defense. Still, some unexpected voices are now being heard on the subject, like that of Harvard child psychiatrist Robert Coles. Coles regrets that "liberals won't talk about abstinence; it's been left to Catholic bishops and the political right. As psychoanalysts, we know that kids need self-control and discipline. But I don't hear anyone speaking out. . . . Magic Johnson has been turned into a hero, this man who slept with unnumbered women and now has AIDS. Is that what black kids need?"

12   Perhaps not. But neither will most young Americans today be moved by the threat of everlasting damnation, much less the disapproval of the vice president. What will work is a change in attitudes, in the perceived social norm. . . . Already there is anecdotal evidence that high-school students in some cities are getting the message that sex is no fun at all when you're dead; when they get to college this attitude may start showing up in the surveys. It took nearly three decades for social attitudes to harden against smoking, but when they did, millions of people who could never quit gave it up rather than be pariahs. A similar shift is occurring with respect to heavy drinking, and even drugs. And it will happen with sex; it has to happen. People want to live.

REVIEWING THE READING   Answers will vary.

1. This article is both informative and persuasive. What is its primary purpose—to inform or to persuade? Support your answer.

See paragraph 1.   2. This article begins with an anecdote about a seventeen-year-old girl's experience with sex. Does the anecdote capture your attention? Is it an effective introduction to the article? That is, does it help the writers achieve their purpose?

3. The main idea, or thesis, of this article is stated in the third para-

graph. Underline phrases and sentences that suggest this main idea; then state the main idea in your own words.

4. From the information in this article, how safe do you think most college students are from sexually transmitted diseases? What support from the article can you give to support your opinion?

5. According to the article, has education been effective in reducing sexually transmitted diseases? Explain your answer.

See paragraph 12.

6. What solution do the authors of the article give for the problem of sexually transmitted diseases?

7. What point about social attitudes do the authors make in their final paragraph? With what other social issues do they compare the issue of sex?

8. In this chapter, you have been studying how to use modifiers in sentences. But as you learned in Chapter 9, a simple sentence without modifiers can have great stylistic effects. When contrasted with longer compound or complex sentences, for example, a simple sentence can add emphasis to an important point. The most emphatic simple sentence in this article occurs in the final paragraph. Underline it.

UNDERSTANDING VOCABULARY

1. This article identifies several sexually transmitted diseases. Are you familiar with all of them? Working with a group of your classmates, obtain information from your college infirmary, library or counselor's office about the following diseases. How is each contracted? What are the symptoms? Can the disease be treated? If so, how can it be treated?
   a. AIDS (HIV virus)
   b. chlamydia
   c. cytomegalovirus
   d. genital warts
   e. gonorrhea
   f. hepatitis A and B
   g. herpes
   h. syphilis

2. How many unfamiliar words did you circle as you were reading this selection? Discuss these words with a group of your classmates, looking up definitions that the group cannot define. Then add these to your vocabulary list.

REACTING CRITICALLY

Write a one-paragraph summary of this article, beginning with its main idea. Remember to include only main ideas, omitting specific examples and statistics. Then write a one-paragraph reaction to the article. What are the strengths and weaknesses of the article? Do you agree with its thesis? Why do you agree or disagree? How would you evaluate the article as a whole?

CROSSING A BOUNDARY

Athlone G. Clarke

Before you read, think about the title of this essay. What could it mean? What kinds of boundaries exist in our society? In this essay, which was first published in a *Newsweek* "My Turn" column, Athlone G. Clarke describes his experience with one social boundary. A free-lance writer living in Atlanta, Clarke is currently working on his first novel.

As you read, underline words and phrases that directly relate to the title—to the idea of "crossing a boundary."

Annotations will vary.

1   There was a big sign that warned of a NEIGHBORHOOD WATCH IN PROGRESS and then there were the less obvious ones. Placed strategically at the entrances of mile-long driveways bordering multi-acre lawns were smaller signs emblazoned with the names of some of America's finest security companies. Something told me I had strayed from the beaten path.

2   Being a creature of habit, I have always jogged a path that takes me under a certain bridge into a recreational park for a breathtaking three-mile run. I've stuck to this path like a bus route. This particular evening, I accepted the challenge of trying a new route. Brad, a white middle-aged jogging acquaintance with the stamina and speed of a Derby winner, thought it would break the monotony. As usual, 10 minutes into the run he chose to quicken his pace, while I chose to continue living. It wasn't long before he disappeared. I remembered his directions and instead of going under the bridge, I crossed over it and made a few extra turns. Twilight Zone it must have been because within minutes, I was in unfamiliar territory where homes boasted titles like "chateau," "estate" and "villa." The vegetation was orderly and even the light breeze seemed to cooperate. There were signs with pictures of dogs baring their fangs and words like "patrol and protection."

3   The way I figured it, the warnings were meant for those harboring criminal motives or acting suspiciously. Being a clean-shaven black male in broad daylight, wearing no bulky attire to hide weapons, no suspicious bag, no dark glasses (and not being in South Africa where they have the Group Areas Act), I had nothing to worry about. Wrong! I started to get an eerie feeling. A lot of expensive cars were suddenly slowing down, almost as if there were a visibility problem. I assumed I was it. A silver-haired older lady, who oozed power from every pore, abruptly halted her Jaguar and sweetly inquired whether I worked for the McArthurs. On hearing "No," she sped off in apparent concern. Still, I reassured myself that this was America. I would not retreat, even while drowning in sweat and adrenaline.

4   I thought back to the media depiction of a white middle-class suburbanite who gets lost in the heart of a tough inner-city neighborhood and takes leave of his nerves. At that moment if I could have had my choice, I would have chosen the inner city. It wasn't long before a police car cruised by and I noticed the driver adjusting his rear-view mirror. As he didn't stop I knew trouble was stalking me.

5   I saw a few other blacks in the neighborhood but they wore the working clothes of gardeners, nannies and utility technicians. I wore a spandex running outfit, headphones and an ingratiating smile. The teeth of the black man have been known to get him out of some tight spots, and my father did not raise a fool. There were a few fellow joggers and some walkers who moved with im-

pressive alacrity as they crossed the street and responded to my nervous nod with furtive glances. It was not hard to imagine that to come face to face with a stranger the same color as Willie Horton must have been, for them, a terrifying experience.

6   I tried to quicken my pace, hoping that through some miracle I could catch up with Brad or at least keep him in sight. Experience has taught me that a little ethnic buffering serves the politics of acceptance and at the very least lessens the shock factor. However, it seemed decreed that I would do this journey alone. I kept reminding myself that this was not Bensonhurst and there was little chance of a mob-induced fracas. These people obviously had class and believed in maintaining secure borders.

7   I sensed I was being followed and looked around. My fears were confirmed. Driving about 150 yards behind me at funeral-procession speed was a lone police car. As it pulled alongside my flank, a portly white police officer in the trademark sunglasses ordered me to pull over. "Do you live around here, sir?" he asked. "May I see some kind of ID?" As I never go jogging with my driver's license, or my wallet for that matter, I knew this would make "Bull Connor" a little upset. I explained my predicament. He then said something I was not ready to hear. "That's OK sir," he said, "I've been watching you for the last 15 minutes and you do seem like a runner going about his business. The problem I'm having, and I hope you'll try to understand, is that some of these people think their snot can make cole slaw; fact is, I still have to do my job." He went on to explain that the police had gotten a flood of phone calls about a suspicious black man roaming the area.

8   We spoke for another two minutes. I went on to point out that in my own neighborhood, I had witnessed a few white strangers running by in the name of exercise and wondered if maybe I ought to start calling the police. As he got back into his car he removed his glasses. His weary eyes appeared to plead for some kind of tacit understanding: in the future, he would be counting on me not to make his life more difficult by running through this forbidden stretch. I sensed a conspiracy to cooperate with the forces of bigotry.

9   Later I recounted my journey to Brad and wasn't surprised when he said the only problem he'd had was his hamstring acting up again. He also thought I was being a little sensitive. On reflection, I think I can see Brad's point. Yet where would we be today if Rosa Parks's "sensitivity" hadn't gotten her into all that mess in Montgomery 35 years ago?

REVIEWING THE READING   Answers will vary.

1. Clarke's thesis is not stated but is clearly implied. Write this thesis in your own words.

2. As a student writer, you usually want to avoid fragments. But fragments can sometimes be used effectively. For example, in his third paragraph, Clarke uses a fragment to answer an implied question and emphasize a point related to his thesis. What is this fragment? What effect does the fragment create?

3. In paragraph 2, to explain how it felt to be running through such unfamiliar territory, Clarke uses the metaphor (comparison) of the "Twilight Zone." What is the "Twilight Zone"? Why is this metaphor appropriate?

4. In this chapter, you have been studying the use of modifiers in sentences. Clarke makes especially effective use of participles (-*ing* and -*ed* verb forms used as modifiers) in this essay. For example, he describes the "mile-long driveways *bordering* multi-acre lawns" and "signs *emblazoned* with the names of some of America's finest security companies." Both *bordering* and *emblazoned* follow the words they modify (*driveways, signs*), but note that -*ing* and -*ed* modifiers can occur before or after the words they modify. Read the following sentences from Clarke's second paragraph and underline the -*ing* and -*ed* modifiers in each:

a. <u>Being</u> a creature of habit, I have always jogged a path that takes me under a certain bridge into a recreational park for a <u>breathtaking</u> three-mile run.

b. Brad, a white middle-aged <u>jogging</u> acquaintance with the stamina and speed of a Derby winner, thought it would break the monotony.

c. There were signs with pictures of dogs <u>baring</u> their fangs and words like "patrol and protection."

See paragraphs 3 and 4.

5. What are two examples of prejudice and suspicion that Clarke encounters in his run?

See paragraph 7.

6. How did Clarke expect the policeman to react? How did the policeman handle the situation? Were you surprised, pleased, or disappointed? Explain your reaction.

7. To what audience is Clarke speaking? Is his purpose primarily to inform or to persuade? Do you think he accomplishes his purpose? Support your opinion.

UNDERSTANDING VOCABULARY

1. When you think of word definitions, you usually think of *denotations,* or dictionary meanings. However, the *connotation* of a word is often as important as the denotation. Connotations are the attitudes, feelings, and associations we connect with words. For example, many different words mean "house." You probably have few associations with the neutral word *house,* but *home* brings to mind family warmth and love, and the word *shack* makes you think of poverty. In paragraph 2 Clarke uses several other words that mean "house." What connotations do *chateau, estate,* and *villa* have for you? What do these words suggest about the people who live in these houses?

2. If you found in this essay other words that you do not know, look them up in a dictionary and add the words and their definitions to your personal vocabulary list.

REACTING CRITICALLY

Clarke alludes, or refers, to three people whom you may not recognize. Rosa Parks was a black woman whose courageous refusal in 1955 to give up her seat to a white on a bus in Montgomery, Alabama, prompted Martin Luther King to organize a protest that eventually led to the desegregation of buses. Bull Connor was the white sheriff in Birmingham during the late 1950s when racial riots were occurring there. He has become a symbol of prejudice and bigotry. And Willie Horton was the subject of a Republican political advertisement during the 1988 presidential election. Playing on stereotypical fears that some whites have of blacks, the advertisement focused on the release of Horton—a black prisoner who was convicted of a major crime after his release. How do these allusions help Clarke to make his point?

Responding in Writing—

Select one of the following specific assignments as the basis for an essay about a particular social issue.

1. What social problems did you discuss in your prewriting exercise? Use this prewriting to help you select a specific focus for your essay. For example, you might *describe* the social problem that you chose, *compare* it with another social problem, *associate* it with its victims, *analyze* the causes or effects of the problem, or *argue* for a possible solution.

2. Write an essay discussing one cause and/or effect of homelessness in America. Why are so many people homeless today? What effect does homelessness have on an individual? On a family? On society?

3. Write a persuasive essay about alcohol abuse and its effects, based on a specific instance you have experienced or observed. Include specific details to make the experience real and to appeal to the emotions as well as to the intellect of your readers.

4. Write an essay in which you argue for one or more ways to reduce the spread of sexually transmitted diseases. Use specific reasons, examples, and/or statistics to persuade your audience that your solution will be effective.

5. Write an essay about the effect(s) that one form of prejudice or discrimination has had on you. For example, have you ever experienced discrimination because of your sex? Your race? Your age? Your religion? Your marital status? Your size? Your economic status? Where you live? Or even your smoking habits?

Revising Your Writing—

Use the following questions to help you revise your essay. You may work independently or with a group of your classmates.

1. What is the purpose of your essay?
2. Who is your audience?
3. What is the thesis, or main idea, of your essay? Is it clearly stated or implied? Where is it stated or implied? Does it need to be revised? How might you revise it to make it more effective?
4. What primary method of development did you use in the essay? What other methods of development did you use?
5. What specific support (details, reasons, examples, statistics) for the main idea have you included? What additional support, if any, should you include?

6. How are your supporting points arranged (time order, space order, order of importance)? How might you rearrange these supporting points to make your essay more effective?

7. What transitions have you included? What additional transitions do you need? Where are they needed?

8. Are your sentences effectively varied? Is your word choice clear and appropriate? Have you used any unnecessary or repetitious words? What revisions should you make in sentence style and word choice?

9. What kind of conclusion does the essay have? How can it be improved?

10. Does your essay achieve your purpose and communicate to your audience? If not, what revisions should you make?

After you have made the major revisions needed in your draft, edit it carefully. As you edit, consider the following questions:

1. Is each sentence a complete sentence, with a subject and a verb?

2. Do you have any errors in subject-verb agreement?

3. Do you have any errors in pronoun reference or agreement?

4. Have you used any sexist language?

5. What tense have you used? Is your use of tense consistent?

6. What point of view have you used (first person, second person, third person)? Is your point of view consistent?

7. Do you have any errors in modification? That is, have you used an adjective when you should have used an adverb, or vice versa?

8. Do you have any dangling or misplaced modifiers?

9. Do you have any misspelled words?

10. Do you have any errors in capitalization, punctuation, or usage?

After you have finished editing, write your final draft and proofread it carefully.

CHAPTER ELEVEN
Coordination: The Compound Sentence

Coordination is a concept that we discussed earlier in connection with reading and writing paragraphs. Elements that are coordinate are equal. For example, if a paragraph has three equally important major supporting points, we say that those points are coordinate. Similarly, if a subject is composed of two or more nouns or a complement of two or more adjectives, we say that these elements are coordinate. We can also describe these coordinate elements as *compound.*

Each of the following sentences has a compound element composed of two or more coordinate words or phrases:

1. *Compound subject:*
   A cup of coffee and *the morning paper* entice me out of bed each morning.
2. *Compound verb:*
   She *ran* to the edge of the cliff and *looked* at the trail far below.
3. *Compound direct object:*
   The secretary typed *the long report* and *several letters.*
4. *Compound subject complement (adjective):*
   The gymnast was *small* but *strong.*
5. *Compound modifier (adverb):*
   The mayor ended her speech *quickly* but *gracefully.*
6. *Compound modifier (prepositional phrase):*
   Maya reached *into the drawer* and *under the papers.*

All of these compound, coordinate elements are connected by *coordinating conjunctions.* The chart on p. 296 lists the coordinating conjunctions that are used to connect compound, coordinate elements.

ADDITION	CONTRAST	CAUSE AND EFFECT
and	but	for
both . . . and	or	so
	nor	
	yet	
	either . . . or	
	neither . . . nor	

EXERCISE 11.1   Using the coordinate conjunctions from the chart above, combine the following pairs of sentences so that the resulting sentence has a compound element.

1. Compound subject:
   The *truck* ran the stop sign.
   The *bus* ran the stop sign.

   The truck and the bus ran the stop sign.

2. Compound verb:
   She *opened* the door.
   She *helped* him from the car.

   She opened the door and helped him from the car.

3. Compound modifier (adverb):
   I called him *loudly.*
   I called him *urgently.*

   I called him loudly and urgently.

4. Compound subject complement (adjective):
   The hot dog was *messy.*
   The hot dog was *good.*

   The hot dog was messy but good.

5. Compound modifier (prepositional phrase):
   She drove *over the steep hill.*
   She drove *across the broken-down bridge.*

   She drove over the steep hill and across the broken-down bridge.

6. Compound object:
The painting had *vivid colors.*
The painting had a *sense of movement.*

The painting had vivid colors and a sense of movement.

7. Compound subject complement (noun):
I could become an *acrobat.*
I could become an *accountant.*

I could become an acrobat or an accountant.

8. Compound verb (with modifiers):
The desk was *cluttered with papers.*
The desk was *stacked high with books.*

The desk was cluttered with papers and stacked high with books.

9. Compound object:
My uncle makes delicious *cakes.*
My uncle makes delicious *pies.*

My uncle makes delicious cakes and pies.

10. Compound modifier (participial phrase):
Dodging traffic, he called to the driver of the car.
Waving frantically, he called to the driver of the car.

Dodging traffic and waving frantically, he called to the driver of the car.

COMPOUND SENTENCES

In Chapter 9 you learned that a simple sentence consists of one subject/
verb relationship and makes a single statement or asks a single question. But we do not always speak and write in simple sentences. Often we
combine two or more related thoughts in the same sentence. Entire sentences can, therefore, be compound.

EXAMPLES

The taxi driver honked his horn. (simple sentence)
The pedestrian yelled back. (simple sentence)
The taxi driver honked his horn, and the pedestrian yelled back.
    (compound sentence)

Simple sentences are called independent clauses when they become part of a compound sentence. Therefore, a compound sentence can be described as a combination of two or more independent clauses—groups of words that have a subject and verb and can function as a simple sentence.

Notice that the two independent clauses (simple sentences) in the example above are coordinate. That is, they are equal; each could function as a sentence on its own, each has a subject and verb, and each contributes equally to the meaning of the sentence.

A compound sentence can be diagrammed as shown in Figure 26 on p. 299. In reading and writing compound sentences, you need to understand the relationship that exists between independent clauses. Like other compound elements, independent clauses are often connected by coordinating conjunctions. These coordinating conjunctions indicate the relationship between the elements they connect. For example, the meaning of each of the sentences that follows is completely altered when the coordinating conjunction is changed.

> He was defeated, *but* he kept trying.
> He was defeated, *or* he kept trying.
> He was defeated, *yet* he kept trying.
> He was defeated, *and* he kept trying.
> He was defeated, *so* he kept trying.

In the compound sentences above, a different relationship is indicated by each coordinating conjunction used. As a reader, you must be alert to these words that signal the relationship between the two thoughts, and as a writer, you must be careful to choose the connecting word that indicates the appropriate relationship.

In addition to being connected by coordinating conjunctions (*and, or, nor, for, but, yet, so*), the independent clauses in a compound sentence can be connected by *conjunctive adverbs.* These connecting words, like coordinating conjunctions, indicate relationships between the independent clauses. The chart below lists some of the most common conjunctive adverbs and indicates the relationships they express.

ADDITION, EMPHASIS, COMPARISON	CONTRAST	CAUSE/EFFECT, CONCLUSION	EXAMPLE	TIME
moreover	however	therefore	for example	then
also	nevertheless	accordingly	for instance	later
too	instead	as a result	to illustrate	next
besides	on the contrary	consequently	that is	first, second,
plus	on the other	hence		third, etc.
furthermore	hand	thus		meanwhile
in addition	otherwise	in conclusion		afterward
indeed	in contrast	in summary		finally
in fact		in other words		
likewise		of course		
similarly		then		
certainly				
again				
another				
at the same time				

FIGURE 26

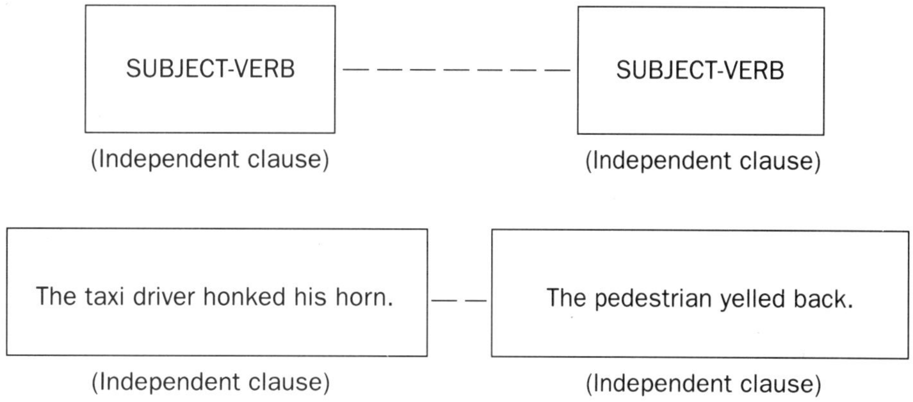

PUNCTUATING COMPOUND SENTENCES

There are three ways to connect independent clauses and to punctuate correctly the resulting compound sentence.

1. *Use a coordinating conjunction and place a comma before the conjunction.*

   Some students want an education, but others simply want a degree.

2. *Use a conjunctive adverb and place a semicolon before the conjunction and a comma after it.*

   Some students want an education; however, others simply want a degree.

   Note: Conjunctive adverbs may appear in a sentence in which they do not introduce an independent clause.

   Some students, however, simply want a degree.

   When used in this way, the conjunctive adverb is set off by commas but requires no semicolon because it is not introducing a second independent clause.

3. *Use no conjunction and place a semicolon between the two independent clauses.*

   Some students want an education; others simply want a degree.

   Notice that the independent clauses in a compound sentence are closely and logically related in thought. If the relationship between them is not apparent, the resulting sentence will be ridiculous.

   Some students want an education; teachers should receive higher salaries.

If independent clauses are connected with just a semicolon and no connecting word or phrase that indicates their relationship, the two clauses must be clearly related in meaning. If a coordinating conjunction or a conjunctive adverb is used, the relationship can be less obvious but should, nevertheless, be clearly expressed by the connecting word.

Joan studied hard; _____ she failed the test.

A good choice for the connecting word in the example above would be *however* because the relationship here is one of contrast. If a conjunctive adverb such as *moreover,* indicating addition, or *therefore,* indicating result or conclusion, were used, the sentence would not make sense because the relationship between the two clauses would not be logical.

▓ **EXERCISE 11.2**   In this exercise, all of the coordinating conjunctions and conjunctive adverbs that connect the independent clauses have been omitted. Write in each blank an appropriate connecting word. In making your choice, consider (1) the relationship between the two clauses and (2) the existing punctuation. Remember that a comma is placed before a coordinating conjunction that connects two independent clauses and a semicolon is placed before a conjunctive adverb that connects two independent clauses.

Answers will vary.

Many of today's young students have an attention span that has been conditioned by years of watching television. They focus their attention on an issue for a very few minutes, approximately the length of a television commercial; _____**then**_____ , they expect something different, _____**and**_____ they grow
    (1)   (2)
bored. As a result, teachers must constantly arrange for a variety of learning activities, _____**or**_____ they lose the attention of their students. Teachers,
         (3)
in effect, assume the role of entertainers; ___**in contrast**___ , students assume
                                                (4)
the role of audience. One of the problems that arises from this situation is that students who perceive themselves as an audience tend to be passive. Learning requires active participation rather than passivity; ___**therefore**___ , these pas-
                                                          (5)
sive students are often nonlearners.

▓ **EXERCISE 11.3**   In this exercise, you are given one independent clause and a connecting word, either a coordinating conjunction or a conjunctive adverb. Supply a second independent clause that is related appropriately to the first.

Sentences will vary.

1. The sentimental good-bys were over, and **the lovers parted.**

   _____

2. The sentimental good-bys were over; however, **the lovers**

   refused to part.

3. The sentimental good-bys were over; therefore, **the lovers went**

   their separate ways.

4. The airplane must land quickly, or **it will crash.** _____

_____

5. The airplane must land quickly, for **it is low on fuel.** _____

_____

6. The airplane must land quickly; consequently, **the pilot must** _____

lower the landing gear. _____

_____

7. The airplane must land quickly; otherwise, **it will run into bad** _____

weather. _____

8. Children often disobey, and **their parents react with frustration.** _____

_____

9. Children often disobey; then **they are punished.** _____

_____

10. Children often disobey, yet **they are not really rebellious.** _____

_____

11. Children often disobey; for example, **they fail to clean their** _____

rooms. _____

12. Large cars tend to use more fuel, so **they cost more to operate.** _____

_____

13. Large cars tend to use more fuel; in contrast, **small cars consume** _____

very little gas. _____

_____

14. Large cars tend to use more fuel; in addition, **they are expensive** _____

to repair. _____

_____

15. Large cars tend to use more fuel; of course, **they are also more** _____

comfortable. _____

_____

Punctuation Review

Coordinate Conjunction and Comma

Independent clause	, coordinate conjunction	independent clause

Carlos took sixteen hours last semester	, and (addition)	he worked twenty hours each week.
Rachel liked most music	, but (contrast)	she didn't like rock and roll.

Conjunctive Adverb and Semicolon

Independent clause	; conjunctive adverb,	independent clause

Carlos took sixteen hours last semester	; moreover, (addition)	he worked twenty hours each week.
Rachel liked most music	; however, (contrast)	she didn't like rock and roll.

Semicolon

Remember also that if two independent clauses are closely and obviously related, you may connect them by using just a semicolon.

Independent clause	; independent clause
Carlos took sixteen hours last semester	; he worked twenty hours each week.
Rachel liked most music	; she didn't like rock and roll.

EXERCISE 11.4

Answers will vary.

Read each of the following pairs of independent clauses carefully to determine the relationship between them. Then, noting the punctuation that is given, write in each blank an appropriate connecting word.

1. The price of oil declined; ____**therefore**____, the economy of the oil-producing states suffered.

2. The politician spoke longer than she was supposed to; ____**however**____, her speech was interesting.

3. The money was missing from the cash drawer, ____**and**____ the valuables had been taken from the safe.

4. The children behaved badly; ____**for example**____, one refused to eat.

5. You may want the pecan pie for dessert, _____**or**_____ you may prefer the cheesecake.

6. His handwriting was barely legible; _____**however**_____, we could make out the words.

7. First, he opened the door carefully; _____**then**_____ he peered inside the dimly lit room.

8. The weather was hot and humid; _____**as a result**_____, everyone was terribly uncomfortable.

9. The wine tasted sweet and fruity; _____**therefore**_____, it went well with the bread and cheese.

10. Somehow they managed to move the huge chest, _____**but**_____ they were not able to get it through the door.

11. Her suit looked soiled and wrinkled; _____**moreover**_____, her shoes were scuffed and unshined.

12. The book lay unopened on her desk for years, _____**for**_____ she rarely disturbed anything that had belonged to her mother.

13. The grass remained green late into the summer, _____**for**_____ the rains had been plentiful and timely.

14. The theater was almost completely dark, _____**yet**_____ the usher was able to direct them to their seats.

15. Her face became pale and lifeless; _____**nevertheless**_____, her voice remained strong.

EXERCISE 11.5

Sentences will vary.

Combine the following pairs of independent clauses into compound sentences. Punctuate each sentence appropriately.

1. The yellow Camaro swerved dangerously.
   The driver remained in control of the car.

   The yellow Camaro swerved dangerously, yet the driver remained in

   control of the car.

2. The young widow lived alone.
   She was occasionally lonely.

   The young widow lived alone, and she was occasionally lonely.

3. The rain fell steadily all day.
    By evening the water had risen dangerously.

    The rain fell steadily; therefore, by evening the water had risen

    dangerously.

    _____

4. The Yomiko sisters resemble each other.
    They are not twins.

    The Yomiko sisters resemble each other, but they are not twins.

    _____

    _____

5. Hunting is not permitted in these parks.
    Many animals are killed.

    Hunting is not permitted in these parks, yet many animals are killed.

    _____

    _____

6. The television commercial lasted only a few moments.
    It seemed to last forever.

    The television commercial lasted only a few moments, but it seemed to

    last forever.

    _____

7. He must pay in cash.
    He will lose the merchandise.

    He must pay in cash, or he will lose the merchandise.

    _____

    _____

8. This is not the first time.
    It will be the last.

    This is not the first time; however, it will be the last.

    _____

    _____

9. Rainfall is scarce.
   Water is precious.

   Rainfall is scarce, so water is precious.

   _____

   _____

10. The clouds were thick.
    The eclipse was not visible.

    The clouds were thick; consequently, the eclipse was not visible.

    _____

    _____

11. She looked into the lighted mirror for a long time.
    She sighed and turned away.

    She looked into the lighted mirror for a long time; then she sighed

    and turned away.

    _____

12. Jim fell asleep almost at once.
    He was exhausted.

    Jim fell asleep almost at once, for he was exhausted.

    _____

    _____

13. The house is built to be energy efficient.
    The windows all have double-paned glass.

    The house is built to be energy efficient; for instance, the windows all

    have double-paned glass.

    _____

14. I want that job.
    I intend to have it.

    I want that job; moreover, I intend to have it.

    _____

    _____

15. The leading man could sing.
    He couldn't act.

    The leading man could sing, but he couldn't act.

■ EXERCISE 11.6   Write the following types of compound sentences, punctuating each appropriately.

Sentences will vary.

1. Three compound sentences in which the two independent clauses are connected by a coordinating conjunction:

   a. **Her suggestion was ridiculous, but his was worse.**

   b. **The lights were on, and the door was opened.**

   c. **The young politician worked very hard, for he was determined**

      to win.

2. Three compound sentences in which the two independent clauses are connected by a conjunctive adverb:

   a. **The artist refused to paint what people wanted to see; therefore,**

      he was starving.

   b. **The movie was excellent; however, it was very violent.**

   c. **The soldier learned several useful skills; for example, he learned to**

      use a computer.

3. Three compound sentences in which no connecting word is used:

   a. **The television blared; the music filled the room.**

   b. **He took one car; she took the other.**

   c. **The social worker took the case; the administrator filed the report.**

EDITING COMPOUND SENTENCES

Although the compound sentence is an effective way of combining two or more thoughts in the same sentence, a writer must be careful to choose an appropriate method of combining the two independent clauses. A compound sentence that is not punctuated correctly can be awkward and confusing for your reader. The following compound sentences are all incorrectly punctuated:

> I like the Nelsons but I'm not inviting them to my party.
> Then it dawned on us we were here to work.
> The man threw his hat on the floor, then he stomped on it.

In the first example, a coordinating conjunction connects the two independent clauses, but no comma has been placed before the conjunction. (I like the Nelsons/but I'm not inviting them to my party.) The second example is a run-on sentence because there is no punctuation between the two independent clauses. (Then it dawned on us/we were here to work.) The final example is also a run-on sentence because a comma has been incorrectly used to separate two independent clauses connected by the conjunctive adverb *then*. (The man threw his hat on the floor/then he stomped on it.)

These sentences could be corrected in the following ways.

1. Write the two independent clauses as two separate simple sentences.

   EXAMPLE

   I like the Nelsons. But I'm not inviting them to my party.

   Then it dawned on us. We were here to work.

   The man threw his hat on the floor. Then he stomped on it.

2. Punctuate the two independent clauses correctly as a compound sentence.

   EXAMPLE

   I like the Nelsons, but I'm not inviting them to my party.

   Then it dawned on us; we were here to work.

   The man threw his hat on the floor; then he stomped on it.

Note: Remember that *then* is a conjunctive adverb, not a coordinating conjunction. Therefore, if you use *then* to connect two independent clauses, you should place a semicolon before it, but you do not need to place a comma after it.

EXERCISE 11.7   Edit the following sentences carefully by supplying punctuation where it is needed. Some of the sentences are correct.

1. My cousin plays the flute and clarinet_and my aunt plays the harp.

2. Every Thanksgiving my grandmother bakes a pumpkin pie_and mother cooks the turkey.

3. It was a long, dull, boring lecture, and the student at the back went to sleep.

4. He trimmed the shrubbery very carefully, for he hoped to keep the hedge alive for the entire summer.

5. Rain is needed now, or the plants will die.

6. Today was a holiday; he was determined to have a good time.

7. Night falls quickly in the mountains, yet the cabin is comfortable and warm.

8. This is the most beautiful part of the river, but boats should avoid its treacherous currents.

9. The nets were full of fish, but we were too exhausted to haul them in.

(correct)   10. You must buy that house today; tomorrow will be too late.

11. He did not play football in college; he played soccer and tennis.

(correct)   12. The snow continued to fall, so I remained at the hotel.

13. We ran into heavy snow by the river; consequently, we arrived late for the meeting.

14. The little girl held my hand, but her brother walked on ahead.

15. There was no moon; we could not see.

16. He had lost his key; nevertheless, he got into the house by the side door.

(correct)   17. Shut the door, but do not bang it.

18. The car broke down; therefore, he had to walk all the way to the service station.

19. Several answers appeared likely; none was absolutely correct.

20. Don't worry; you are not late.

21. My grandmother was a talented gardener; she raised a number of exotic plants.

22. They pulled into the driveway; then they turned off the motor and the headlights.

23. I can't eat any more candy; it is too fattening.

24. In her lab the chemist tested the product; in her office she typed her report.

25. You can come; however, you can't bring your horse.

■ **EXERCISE 11.8**

Answers may vary.

The following paragraph has ten compound sentences that are incorrectly punctuated. Identify the errors and punctuate the sentences correctly.

Yesterday morning I looked up from my hot tea and bagel and noticed an aardvark nibbling on the okra in my back yard. I had no idea where the aardvark had come from, and I certainly did not know where it was going. I sat for a moment, munching on my bagel, thinking about what I should do. I could run into the back yard and chase the animal away, or I could take it inside and housebreak it. Somehow I must stop it from eating all of my okra, for I loved okra. Walking to the back door, I considered other plans. I was leaning toward the idea of buying a muzzle for the aardvark; however, I wasn't sure that the usual sizes would fit this particular animal. Before stepping into the back yard, I stood watching the aardvark. He, or perhaps she (I couldn't really be sure), finished eating one large okra plant; then he went on to a smaller one in the next row. I hesitated to disturb him; he seemed so content. But I had my okra to think of, so I walked toward him briskly, making friendly noises and trying to look disapproving but gracious. I suggested to him in a helpful way that eating too much okra could be dangerous for his health. He looked up at me and nodded in agreement, or perhaps he was just chewing the last bite of the small okra plant. Then an idea hit me; I would call the Society for the Prevention of Cruelty to Aardvarks. The aardvark would be taken off my hands; furthermore, my okra would be saved. It was the perfect solution.

READING AND WRITING ABOUT—

Educational Issues

Preparing: Answering Questions and Writing a Journal—

Education comes from life experience as well as from formal instruction. However, when most people think of "education," they think of the experiences they have had in school and college. To help you prepare for the readings on education, think about your education. To give your thinking focus, write a journal entry answering the following questions.

1. *What* is education? Define it. What do you hope to obtain from a college education?
2. *When* did you decide to attend college? Are you a recent high school graduate, or have you been out of school for a while?
3. *Where* did you get your best education? Your worst? Explain.
4. *Who* has contributed the most to your education? How did that person contribute to your education?
5. *Why* did you decide to pursue a college education?
6. *How* can you best succeed in your education?

▓ LILIA

Mike Rose

Before you read, think about the concept of remedial, or developmental, education. Are the tests that are often used to place students in remedial classes fair and accurate? Do such classes help students who are having problems to succeed? Why do such classes help (or not help)? In the following selection, Mike Rose describes the journey that one remedial student made to success. Rose is himself a respected authority on remedial education. In fact, his book *Lives on the Boundary,* from which this reading is taken, and two articles that he has co-authored have been given major awards by the Conference on College Composition and Communication.

As you read, try to identify the experience that led to Lilia's success—to her "crossing the boundary" from remedial classes to honors classes. In addition, circle any unfamiliar words that you encounter as you read.

Annotations will vary.

1   I sit with Lilia, the tape recorder going. "We came from Mexico when I was four years old. When I went into school, I flunked the first grade. The first grade! I had to repeat it, and they put me in classes for slow learners. I stayed in those classes for five years. I guess there was a pattern where they put me in those really basic classes and then decided I would go through my elementary school years in those classes. I didn't learn to read or write. My parents got my cousins—they came here prior to us, so they knew English really well—and they had

me read for them. I couldn't. They told my parents I didn't know anything. That's when my parents decided they would move. They moved to Tulare County. My aunt was there and told them that the schools were good and that there was work in agriculture. I picked grapes and cotton and oranges—everything—for six straight summers. I kinda liked it, out there with all the adults, but I knew it wasn't what I wanted for the future. The schools *were* good. The teachers really liked me, and I did very well. . . . Between the eighth and ninth grades I came to UCLA for six weeks in the summer. It was called the MENTE program—Migrants Engaged in New Themes of Education—I came here and loved the campus. It was like dreamland for me. And I made it my goal to come here.''

2   The school that designated Lilia a slow learner is two miles from my old neighborhood on South Vermont. She arrived as a child about eight years after I left as an adult. The next generation. We make our acquaintance in an office of the University of California at Los Angeles. Lilia is participating in an unusual educational experiment, one developed by some coworkers of mine at UCLA Writing Programs. Lilia and fifteen other freshmen—all of whom started UCLA in remedial writing courses themselves—are tutoring low-achieving students in Los Angeles area schools. The tutoring is connected to a special composition class, and Lilia and her partners write papers on their tutorial work and on issues of schooling. Lilia is writing a paper on the academic, social, and psychological effects of being placed in the remedial track. Her teacher suggested she come to see me. I can't stop asking her questions about growing up in South L.A.

3   Desire gets confused on South Vermont. There were times when I wanted so much to be other than what I was, to walk through the magical gate of a television cottage. But, strange blessing, we can never really free ourselves from the mood of early neighborhoods, from our first stories, from the original tales of hope and despair. There are basic truths there about the vulnerability and power of coming to know, about the way the world invites and denies language. This is what lies at the base of education—to be tapped or sealed over or distorted, by others, by us. Lilia says the tutoring makes her feel good. ''Sometimes I feel that because I know their language, I can communicate. I see these kids and I see myself like I was in elementary school.'' Lilia stops. She asks me what it was like in South L.A. when *I* was there, when I was going to school. Not much different then, I say. Not as tough probably. She asks me if I've ever gone back. I tell her I did, just recently. . . .

4   The place was desolate. The power plant was still standing, smaller than I remembered it, surrounded now by barbed wire. All the storefront businesses were covered with iron grating; about half of them, maybe more, were shut down. The ones that were open had the grating pulled back the width of the door, no further. The hair and nails shop was closed. The Stranger's Rest Baptist Church was closed. Teddy's Rough Riders—an American Legion post—was battered and closed. The Huston Mortuary looked closed. My house had been stuccoed over, a dark dirty tan with holes in the walls. 9116 South Vermont. My old neighborhood was a blighted island in the slum. Poverty had gutted it, and sealed the merchants' doors. ''It's worse now,'' I tell Lilia, ''much worse. No one comes. No one goes.'' At Ninety-sixth Street two men were sitting on the curb outside a minimart. East on Ninety-first a girl sat in the shadows of steps tucked back from the pavement. At Eighty-ninth Street, a woman walked diagonally in front of me, moving unsteadily in a tight dress, working the floured paper off an X-L-NT burrito. As I drove back by my house, I saw a little boy playing with two cans in the dirt. Imagination's delivery. Fantasy in cylinders and tin.

5   Lilia is telling me about one of her fellow classmates who had also been designated a slow learner. "She said it was awful. She had no friends because everyone called her dumb, and no one wanted to be seen with a dumb person. . . . Because they were calling her dumb, she started to believe she was really dumb. And with myself and my brother, it was the same thing. When we were in those courses we thought very low of ourselves. We sort of created a little world of our own where only we existed. We became really shy."

6   What we define as intelligence, what we set out to measure and identify with a number, is both in us and out of us. We have been socialized to think of intelligence as internal, fixed, genetically coded. There is, of course, a neurophysiology to intelligence, but there's a feeling to it as well, and a culture. In moving from one school to another—another setting, another set of social definitions—Lilia was transformed from dumb to normal. And then, with six powerful weeks as a child on a university campus—"opening new horizons for me, scary, but showing me what was out there"—she began to see herself in a different way, tentatively, cautiously. Lilia began the transition to smart, to high school honors classes, to UCLA. She could go back, then, to the schools, to the place where, as she says, she "knows the language."

7   The promise of community and equality is at the center of our most prized national document, yet we're shaped by harsh forces to see difference and to base judgment on it. The language Lilia can speak to the students in the schools is the language of intersection, of crossed boundaries. It is a rich language, filled with uncertainty. Having crossed boundaries, you sometimes can't articulate what you know, or what you know seems strange. What is required, then, is for Lilia and her students to lean back against their desks, grip the firm wood, and talk about what they hear and see, looking straight ahead, looking skyward. What are the gaps and discordances in the terrain? What mix of sounds—eerie and compelling—issues from the hillside? Sitting with Lilia, our lives playing off each other, I realize that, finally, this is why the current perception of educational need is so limited: It substitutes terror for awe. But it is not terror that fosters learning, it is hope, everyday heroics, the power of the common play of the human mind.

REVIEWING THE READING   Answers will vary.

1. Rose's thesis is implied rather than stated. What is it?

See paragraphs 1 and 5.

2. What effect did failure and remediation have on Lilia? Support your answer.

See paragraphs 3, 4, and 6.

3. Rose implies that there is a relationship between environment and learning. What does he suggest about this relationship?

See paragraphs 1 and 6.

4. What experience changed the direction of Lilia's education? Why did this experience have such an important effect?

5. Study the following sentences and their punctuation. Which are compound sentences? Which contain compound elements? Be prepared to explain the punctuation in each sentence.

Compound nouns

a. "I picked grapes and cotton and oranges—everything—for six straight summers" (paragraph 1).

Compound sentence, nouns, and phrases

b. "The tutoring is connected to a special composition class, and Lilia and her partners write papers on their tutorial work and on issues of schooling" (paragraph 2).

Compound sentence

c. "All the storefront businesses were covered with iron grating; about half of them, maybe more, were shut down" (paragraph 4).

Compound adjectives

d. "What mix of sounds—eerie and compelling—issues from the hill-side?" (paragraph 7).

Compound sentence, nouns, and phrases

e. "The promise of community and equality is at the center of our most prized national document, yet we're shaped by harsh forces to see difference and to base judgment on it" (paragraph 7).

Compound nouns

f. "What are the gaps and discordances in the terrain?" (paragraph 7).

UNDERSTANDING VOCABULARY

Whereas a prefix changes the meaning of a word, a suffix changes its function, or part of speech. Study the following suffixes and their functions:

-able	adjective (capable of)
-ance	noun (action, quality, condition)
-ate	adjective (have qualities of)
-ed	verb (past tense)
-ity	noun (state or quality)
-ive	adjective (having tendency to)
-ly	adverb (characteristic of, in a specified manner)

Now, use your knowledge of suffixes, the parenthetical information that is given, and—if necessary—a dictionary to define the underlined words in the following sentences:

1. "There are basic truths there [at home on South Vermont] about the vulnerability [from Latin *vulner-*, "to wound"] and power of coming to know, about the way the world invites and denies language" (paragraph 3).

2. "This is what lies at the base of education—to be tapped or sealed over or distorted [from prefix *dis-*, meaning "apart" and *tort*, or "twist"], by others, by us" (paragraph 3).

3. "The place was desolate . . . [from prefix *de-*, meaning "completely," and *solus*, or "alone"]. My old neighborhood was a blighted island in the slum. Poverty had gutted it, and sealed the merchants' doors" (paragraph 4).

4. "And then, with six powerful weeks as a child on a university campus . . . she began to see herself in a different way, tentatively [from *tentare*, "to try, to tempt"], cautiously" (paragraph 6).

5. "What are the gaps and discordances [from prefix *dis-*, meaning "apart" and *cor*, or "heart"] in the terrain? What mix of sounds—eerie and compelling—issues from the hillside?" (paragraph 7).

Add to your personal vocabulary list any of these words and other new words that you circled in the reading.

REACTING CRITICALLY

From your observations or experiences, what positive or negative effects do remedial classes have on students? Are remedial classes the best way to help students who are academically underprepared? Discuss these

questions with a small group of your classmates, supporting your opinion with evidence, examples, and/or personal experiences. What alternatives for remedial classes can you suggest?

■ OVERCOMING AN INVISIBLE HANDICAP

Thomas J. Cottle

Before you read, think about the many older students who are attending
college—perhaps for the first time. What advantages do these "returning
students" have? What disadvantages must they often overcome? In the
following essay,* Cottle describes the rewarding experiences of one such
returning student.

Cottle, a respected sociologist and psychologist who observes and
listens to his subjects personally, has lectured at Harvard Medical School
and has been a visiting distinguished professor at Amherst College.

See text annotations.

As you read, identify and underline Lucille Elmore's "invisible handicap." How is she overcoming it?

1   On her 30th birthday, Lucille Elmore informed her husband that she was going
through a crisis. "I was 30 years old, active, in good health—and I was illiterate,"
she recalls. "I didn't know books, I didn't know history, I didn't know science. I
had the barest understanding of the arts. Like a physical condition, my knowledge limped, my intelligence limped."

2   She was not only the mother of two young children but also was working full
time as an administrative assistant in a business-consulting firm. Nevertheless,
at age 30, with her husband's agreement, Lucille Elmore enrolled in college. "I
thought getting in would be difficult," she says. "It was easy. I thought I couldn't
discipline myself, but that came. Half the people in the library the first day
thought I was the librarian, but that didn't deter me."

3   For Lucille, the awareness of her invisible limp came only gradually. As a
young woman, she had finished high school, but she had chosen not to go on with
her education. Her parents, who had never completed high school themselves,
urged her to go to college but she refused. At the time, she was perhaps a bit
timid and lacked a certain confidence in her own intellectual or academic abilities. Besides, a steady job was far more important at that point to Lucille than
schooling: she felt she could read on her own to make up for any lack of education.

4   At 20, working full time, she married Ted Elmore, a salesman for a foodstore
chain, a man on his way to becoming more than modestly successful. There was
no need for her to work, but she did so until her first child was born; she was then
22. A second child was born two years later, and three years after that, she went
back to work. With her youngest in a day-care program, she felt no reservations
about working, but her lack of education began to nag at her as she approached
the age of 30. She thus gave up her job, entered a continuing-education program
at a nearby university, and began what she likens to a love affair.

5   "I'm carrying on an open affair with books, but like a genuinely good lover,
I'm being guided. Reading lists, suggested reading, recommended readings—I

* Reprinted with permission from *Psychology Today* magazine. Copyright © 1980 (Sussex Publishers,
Inc.)

want them all. I must know what happened in the 12th, 13th, 18th centuries. I want to know how the world's major religions evolved. Papal history, I know nothing of papal history and succession, or the politics involved. I read the Bible, but I never studied it. It's like music: I listened, but it wasn't an informed listening. Now all of this is changing.

6   "I must tell you, I despise students when they talk about 'the real world,' as if college were a dream world. They simply don't understand what the accumulation of knowledge and information means. Maybe you have to be 30 at least, and going through a personal crisis, to fully appreciate what historical connections are.

7   "A line of Shakespeare challenges me more than half the jobs I'll be equipped for when I'm finished. I'm having an affair with him, too, only it's called Elizabethan Literature 606. I think many people prefer the real world of everyday work because it's less frightening than the larger-than-life world of college.

8   "There's a much more important difference between the rest of the students and me. We don't agree at all on what it means to be a success. They think in terms of money, material things. I suppose that's normal. They don't understand that with a nice home, and decent job prospects, and two beautiful children, I know I am a failure. I'm a failure because I am ignorant. I'm a failure until I have knowledge, until I can work with it, be excited by and play with ideas.

9   "I don't go to school for the rewards down the line. I want to reach the point at which I don't measure knowledge by anything but itself. An idea has value or it doesn't. This is how I now determine success and failure."

10   " 'How can I use it?' That's what students ask. 'What good will this do me?' they don't think about what the question says about them, even without an answer attached to it. Questions like that only build up competition. But competition is the bottom line for so many students, I guess, getting ahead, getting a bit of a step up on the other guy. I know, it's my husband's life.

11   "I'll tell you what I think I like most about my work: the library. I can think of no place so exclusive and still so open and public. Millions of books there for the taking. A chair to sit in, a row of books, and you don't need a penny. For me, the library is a religious center, a shrine.

12   "Students talk about the real world out there. What about the free world in here? Here, no one arrests you for what you're thinking. In the library, you can't talk, so you have to think. I never knew what it meant to think about something, to really think it through. I certainly never understood what you had to know to even begin to think. I always thought it was normal to limp."

REVIEWING THE READING   Answers will vary.

See paragraph 1.

1. When she decided to start college, how did Lucille feel about herself? What was her "invisible handicap"?

See paragraphs 2, 3.

2. Why didn't Lucille attend college before she was thirty?

See paragraph 5.

3. What attitude does Lucille have toward books and learning?

4. How did Lucille's self-concept change after attending college?

See paragraph 9.

5. How does Lucille define knowledge? How does she define success and failure?

See paragraph 11.

6. What place on campus does Lucille like most? Why does she like that place so much?

UNDERSTANDING VOCABULARY

As defined in the *American Heritage Dictionary,* the word *illiterate* has each of the following definitions. Read these definitions and select the one that best describes the word as Lucille uses it.

1. Unable to read and write. **2.a.** Marked by inferiority to an expected standard of familiarity with language and literature. **b.** Violating prescribed standards of speech or writing. **3.** Ignorant of the fundamentals of a given art or branch of knowledge.

REACTING CRITICALLY

1. An *analogy* is a comparison in which a familiar object, experience, or idea is used to explain a less familiar one. Explain the analogy that Lucille Elmore makes between her college experience and a love affair. In your opinion, is the analogy appropriate? Explain your answer.

2. As a returning student, Lucille has apparently been quite successful. What advantages do returning students have over traditional students who have just graduated from high school? What disadvantages do returning students have?

CHEATING: ALIVE AND FLOURISHING
Claudia H. Deutsch

Before you read, think about the educational and ethical issue of academic cheating. Have you observed students cheating in high school or college? Have you ever cheated yourself? What kinds of cheating are most common? Why do students cheat? What is the result? In the following essay from the *New York Times,* Claudia H. Deutsch considers the problem of academic cheating and reports on a proposed solution.

Annotations may vary.

As you read, look for the strategies that some schools and colleges are using to prevent cheating. Underline these strategies.

1   Trying to get a handle on scholastic cheating is as frustrating as surveying American eating patterns. Everyone says he is watching his weight—yet the streets are full of overweight folk, and the snack-food industry reports record sales.

2   Talk to students, and you get the same kind of dichotomy. Most say that, yes, they cheated when they were younger, but no, they would not dream of cheating now, and no, cheating is not a big problem at their schools.

3   But talk to their teachers, and a very different picture emerges, one that shatters many of the comfortable middle-class myths about who cheats and why. It is a picture of cheating among top students at top schools; of habits that take root in elementary school, bud in high school and flower in college; of parents who care more about their children's success than about their moral development, and of a problem that is more likely to get worse than to get better.

4   National statistics are hard to find, but every now and then a school, a district or a research organization does its own survey. The results are discouraging, to say the least. For example:

• The College Board, whose Scholastic Aptitude Tests help determine whether students get into their first-choice colleges, is detecting more cases of "questionable validity of test scores." Robert H. Parker, director of test security, says the increase may well be traceable to better detection methods—but he cannot be sure.

- The Cooperative Institutional Research Program at the University of California at Los Angeles recently asked some 290,000 college freshmen whether they had ever cheated on a test in their last year of high school. Some 30.4 percent said that they had. That sounds like a low percentage—except that in 1966, the last time the research group asked the question, only 20.6 percent said they had cheated.

- A survey of students in California in 1985 showed that three-quarters of *all* of the state's high school students, starting as freshmen, cheated on exams.

- A similar survey last year of students in Amherst, N.Y., an affluent suburb near Buffalo, showed that more than 80 percent had cheated at least once in 1987.

5   Several schools are trying to cut down on the opportunity to cheat by giving more open-book exams. Others are holding seminars for their teachers to discuss the cheating phenomenon—often with students invited to attend. But psychologists say that the roots of the problem must be dealt with in the home. It is there, they say, that children must be imbued with enough self-esteem to make occasional failure an unthreatening prospect, and with enough of a sense of right and wrong to overcome the urge to cheat.

6   Unfortunately, teachers say, too many parents are abdicating that responsibility. "Kids just aren't brought up to see cheating as dishonest," said Patrick L. Daly, who taught high school in the Detroit area for 30 years before retiring last year. "To them, shoplifting is dishonest; writing a couple of math formulas on their hand is not."

7   "A child cheats on an exam and his parents get outraged," said Young Jay Mulkey, president of the American Institute for Character Education, a San Antonio-based foundation that helps teachers develop students' self-esteem. "Yet he keeps hearing his folks talk about cheating on expense accounts or income taxes. The inconsistency drives children crazy."

8   Perhaps most troubling, teachers and psychologists say that it is often the most gifted students, the ones who presumably could get good grades without cheating, who are the worst offenders. They are the ones who believe that getting into a top college—or later, a top graduate school—is the most important goal, and will do anything they must to attain it. At first, the pressure is from their parents; eventually, those values become their own.

9   Indeed, it was students at New York City's prestigious Stuyvesant High School and Bronx High School of Science who were caught using stolen tests and answers to Regents exams in 1980. And this past November, it was students at the Brunswick School, in Greenwich, Conn., who broke into another private school, the Greenwich Academy, and opened sealed copies of the S.A.T. the day before the test was to be administered.

10   A case can be made, and often is, that such incidents get publicity precisely because it is so unusual for top schools to be involved. But teachers in schools with less lofty reputations make an equally convincing case for themselves. They note that not many students in schools with poor national standings and high dropout rates care enough about their grades to cheat, while students in vocational schools care more about the subject matter than they do about test scores.

11   "Many of our kids are poor, and they really want to learn these skills because

it's the only way they can better their economic situation," said Mary Spilotro, an English teacher at the High School of Graphic Communication Arts (formerly the New York School of Printing). "I saw a lot more cheating when I taught in academic high schools."

12   She would also see a lot more cheating, it seems, if she taught at the college level. Poll after poll shows that college students, not just high schoolers, are making cheating a way of life. Campus newspapers abound with articles dealing with the subject. Last fall Dartmouth College, for one, devoted almost an entire issue of *Common Sense*, its new student paper, to the growing problem of cheating on campus. Universities are holding special seminars at which professors and students discuss the problem. At least one school, the University of Illinois, issues a pamphlet for its faculty that describes some of the more ingenious methods students may use to cheat (written crib sheets attached to cap visors, oral ones playing on a Sony Walkman) and ways to thwart them. Several others are tightening their computer security, after having discovered that computer hackers were breaking into electronic college files in order to alter their grades.

13   Yet despite the precautions, students still offer papers churned out by term-paper companies—or by other students—as their own. And they still seem to find peeking at each other's tests to be irresistible. . . .

14   Most agree that by high school, cheating should be dealt with more seriously. But usually it is not. Some teachers, under tremendous pressure from local school districts to bring their students' performance above national norms, are loath to interfere with a process that yields higher grades. Others, students say, just do not seem to care.

15   "I got through my sophomore year in high school by cheating," said Sherry L. Brendel, a 19-year-old sales assistant at Oppenheimer & Company. "I would have hesitated if I thought the teachers cared, but they didn't even look. They'd walk out of the room during an exam."

16   Ms. Brendel is now going for a degree at Fordham University at night, and she says she no longer cheats at all. "The college teachers seem to care whether their students learn," she says.

17   "They stay in the room, they answer questions, they spend more time explaining things."

18   But do they crack down on cheaters? At worst, most schools make students caught cheating retake the entire course; more often, they simply make them retake the exam or redo the paper.

19   The leniency is a source of frustration to those academicians who find cheating abhorrent. "When I catch students cheating, I want to nail them for it," said Mr. Berkowitz of Marquette. "But I once caught a doctoral student plagiarizing and took him to his dean. It became the dean's decision, and the dean let him stay at the university."

20   Students, too, say that official policies are more honored in the breach. Mr. Socas at the University of Virginia concedes that professors often do not report cheating to the honor committee because they are not comfortable with the idea that convicted cheaters will be expelled. Ms. Sokolik, the Nebraska senior, also says that the few cheaters at her school are not dealt with severely enough. "Rarely is the punishment worse than a reprimand," she said. "The official policy is that cheaters fail the class, but teachers don't follow it."

21   If psychologists and a small but growing number of college officials have their way, enforcement policies will become a non-issue. They are focusing on pre-

22   venting cheating, both through the quick-fix method of making tests cheatproof and the longer-term method of rekindling in students a desire to learn.

22   Increasingly, professors are turning to open-book exams that test students more on how well they have learned to apply concepts than on how well they have memorized arcane facts or formulas. The approach serves a dual purpose: it fosters conceptual thinking and makes crib sheets and peeking obsolete.

23   "I give open-book problems with unique solutions," said Stanley R. Liberty, dean of the engineering school at the University of Nebraska. "Students know there's an unbelievably low probability of two people coming up with the same approach."

24   Cornell University, meanwhile, has set up a faculty subcommittee to create a campus-wide dialogue on the "pedagogical" goals of exams. "Talking about cheating would be divisive," says Larry Walker, vice president of academic programs. "I want professors and students to discuss ways that exams can be used as a learning device, not an evaluation tool."

25   For the most part, academicians seem optimistic that changes in teaching methods and in exams will cut down on academic dishonesty. But teachers and child psychologists say that the only way to stop kids from cheating in college is to keep them from developing the habit in high school. They are worried whether, in a society where two-income families and high-pressure jobs are prevalent, that is an ever more elusive goal.

26   Said Beverly Betz, who teaches at New York City's High School for the Humanities, "Parents have got to make their kids feel that if they don't do well on a test it's not the end of the world, but just an indication that more work needs to be done."

REVIEWING THE READING   Answers will vary.

1. Deutsch implies rather than states her thesis. Write it in your own words.

See paragraph 4.

2. Deutsch includes several national statistics to support her thesis. What statistic impressed you the most?

See paragraphs 5, 21, 22, and 24.

3. How are some schools trying to reduce the opportunity for students to cheat?

4. According to Deutsch, what are some reasons for academic cheating?

See paragraphs 8 and 12.

5. Which students are most likely to cheat? Why might those students be more tempted than others to cheat?

See paragraphs 14–15 and 18–20.

6. How do most schools react to academic cheating? What penalties, if any, are usually given to those who are guilty of academic cheating?

UNDERSTANDING VOCABULARY

Notice that the context or the structure of the following underlined words gives you some clues to their meaning. Study the definitions that are provided for you. Then add to your personal vocabulary list the four or five words that you think you are most likely to encounter in your reading or to use in your own writing.

1. "Talk to students, and you get the same kind of dichotomy. Most say that, yes, they cheated when they were younger, but no, they would not dream of cheating now" (paragraph 2). As suggested by the orig-

inal meaning of *dicho* (Greek, "two") and the contrast between what students say and do, *dichotomy* means "divided into two contradictory elements."

2. "Unfortunately, teachers say, too many parents are abdicating that responsibility" (paragraph 6). As suggested by the context, *abdicate* means "to disclaim, to abandon or give up responsibility."

3. "Indeed, it was students in New York City's prestigious Stuyvesant High School and Bronx High School of Science who were caught using stolen tests and answers to Regents exams in 1980" (paragraph 9). A *prestigious* school is one that has gained respect and prominence because of its success or wealth.

4. "At least one school, the University of Illinois, issues a pamphlet for its faculty that describes some of the more ingenious methods students may use to cheat (written crib sheets attached to cap visors, oral ones playing on a Sony Walkman) and ways to thwart them" (paragraph 12). As suggested by these examples, an *ingenious* method or person is "inventive, cunning, imaginative."

5. "Some teachers, under tremendous pressure from local school districts to bring their students' performance above national norms, are loath to interfere with a process that yields higher grades" (paragraph 14). As suggested by its context, the word *loath* means "unwilling, reluctant."

6. "Students, too, say that official policies are more honored in the breach" (paragraph 20). A *breach* is "a violation, as of a law or a rule, or a gap."

7. "Increasingly, professors are turning to open-book exams that test students more on how well they have learned to apply concepts than on how well they have memorized arcane facts or formulas" (paragraph 22). Something that is *arcane* is "known only by a few."

8. "The approach serves a dual purpose: it fosters conceptual thinking and makes crib sheets and peeking obsolete" (paragraph 22). Something that is *obsolete* is "no longer in use, no longer fashionable."

REACTING CRITICALLY

As explained in the Cottle reading earlier in this chapter, an *analogy* is a comparison in which a familiar object or idea is used to explain a less familiar or more abstract idea. In her first two paragraphs, Deutsch compares academic cheating to familiar eating patterns. Explain the specific elements of this analogy. Is the analogy effective? That is, does it work? Why does it work (or not work)?

Responding in Writing—

Use one of the following assignments to write an essay about education.

1. Select one of the questions from your prewriting for the focus of your paper. For example, you could write an essay telling *what* education is (defining it) or what your goals are for a college education, about *where* you got your best or worst education, about *who* has contributed the most to your education, about *why* you decided to go to

college, or about *how* you can best succeed in college. Remember to begin with a clear introduction that states your thesis and to develop your essay with specific reasons, details, or examples.

2. Write an essay about the practice of remediation. Do remedial classes help students to learn? What is good about such classes? What is bad about them? How fair and effective are systems that place students in remedial classes? You may want to direct your essay to the administrators of your college or university.

3. Write an essay about returning students. What advantages do older students have over recent high school graduates? What disadvantages do older students have? What advice would you give on succeeding in college to those older returning students?

4. Deutsch reports that Cornell University has set up a faculty subcommittee to consider the "pedagogical," or educational, goals of examinations. Write an essay in which you discuss and evaluate the effectiveness of examinations in promoting an education.

5. If a committee were established at your college to study cheating on campus, what suggestions would you give the committee to help eliminate the problem of cheating? Write an essay presenting and arguing for your solutions.

Revising Your Writing—

Use the following questions to help revise your essay. You may work independently or with a group of your classmates.

1. What is the purpose of your essay?

2. Who is your audience?

3. What is your thesis, or main idea? Is it clearly stated or implied? Where is it stated or implied? Does it need to be revised? How could you revise it?

4. What primary method of development did you use in the essay? What other methods of development did you use?

5. What specific support (details, reasons, examples, statistics) for the main idea have you included? What additional support, if any, should you include?

6. How are your supporting points arranged (time order, space order, order of importance)? How might you rearrange these supporting points to make your essay clearer and more effective?

7. What transitions have you included? What additional transitions do you need? Where are they needed?

8. Are your sentences effectively varied? Is your word choice clear and appropriate? Have you used any unnecessary or repetitious words? What revisions should you make in sentence style and word choice?

9. What kind of conclusion does your essay have? How can it be improved?

10. Does your essay achieve your purpose and communicate to your audience? If not, what revisions should you make?

After you have made the major revisions needed in your draft, edit it carefully. As you edit, consider the following questions:

1. Is each sentence a complete sentence, with a subject and a verb?
2. Do you have any errors in subject-verb agreement?
3. Do you have any errors in pronoun reference or agreement?
4. Have you used any sexist language?
5. What tense have you used? Is your use of tense consistent?
6. What point of view have you used (first person, second person, third person)? Is your point of view consistent?
7. Are all of your compound sentences punctuated correctly?
    a. Have you inserted a comma before coordinate conjunctions (*and, or, nor, for, but, yet,* and *so*) connecting independent clauses?
    b. Have you inserted a semicolon before conjunctive adverbs (*then, moreover, however, furthermore,* and so on) connecting independent clauses?
    c. Have you inserted a semicolon between independent clauses not connected by a transition word?
8. Do you have any run-on sentences?
9. Do you have any misspelled words?
10. Do you have any errors in capitalization, punctuation, or usage?

After you have finished editing, write your final draft and proofread it carefully.

CHAPTER TWELVE
Subordination: The Complex Sentence

Like coordination, subordination is a concept that is essential to reading and writing. We must understand subordination in order to understand relationships among ideas in essays, paragraphs, and sentences. Whereas coordinate elements are equal, a subordinate element is dependent on another element. In an essay, the topic sentences are subordinate to the thesis statement; in a paragraph, major details are subordinate to the topic sentence, and minor details are subordinate to major details; and in sentences, some ideas, clauses, or details are subordinate to others.

In a simple sentence or a compound sentence, modifiers are subordinate to the main idea expressed by the subject and verb. Subordination within sentences most clearly occurs, however, in the complex sentence. A complex sentence consists of an independent clause that contains within it a subordinate, or dependent, clause. Unlike the compound sentence, which consists of two equal (coordinate) independent clauses, the complex sentence is made up of two different types of clauses: an independent clause and a subordinate clause. The independent clause expresses the main idea of the sentence, and the subordinate clause expresses a supporting idea or detail. As shown in Figure 27 on p. 324, the subordinate clause functions as *part of* the independent clause.

FIGURE 27

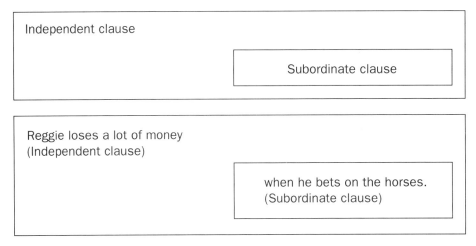

To understand subordinate clauses, you must first understand phrases and independent clauses because a subordinate clause has characteristics of both. The chart in Figure 28 below summarizes the characteristics of both phrases and clauses.

FIGURE 28

PHRASE (to the theater)	Does not have a subject and verb	Functions as a unit in a sentence	Cannot stand alone as a sentence
SUBORDINATE CLAUSE (when he went to the theater)	Has a subject and verb	Functions as a unit in a sentence	Cannot stand alone as a sentence
INDEPENDENT CLAUSE (he went to the theater)	Has a subject and verb	Does not function as a unit in a sentence	Can stand alone as a sentence

As the chart indicates, a subordinate clause, unlike an independent clause, cannot function as a sentence even though it has a subject and a verb. A subordinate clause is like a phrase in that it is part of an independent clause and functions as an adverb, an adjective, or a noun within the independent clause. Thus, the two clauses of a complex sentence are not equal (coordinate) as are the clauses of a compound sentence. In a complex sentence, the subordinate clause is dependent on—or subordinate to—the independent clause.

EXAMPLES

Although the forests are old, much undergrowth is recent. (adverb clause)

The actress *who appeared in the second act* had a shrill voice. (adjective clause)

The jury concluded *that he was guilty of the murder.* (noun clause)

ADVERB CLAUSES

An adverb clause is a subordinate clause that functions as an adverb within the independent clause in which it appears. Adverb clauses usually modify the verb of the independent clause. Listed below are some of the signal words, or subordinate conjunctions, that are commonly used to introduce adverb clauses.

after	as if	although	even if
before	as soon as	though	even though
when	if	since	where
whenever	unless	because	wherever
while	whether	until	
as	whereas	so that	

The following complex sentences contain adverb clauses. Observe how the placement and punctuation of the adverb clause differ in the two sentences.

Adverb clause at the beginning of a sentence:
Unless you save carefully, you will not have enough money for your tuition next semester.

Adverb clause at the end of a sentence:
You will not have enough money for your tuition next semester *unless you save carefully.*

Notice that in the first sentence the adverb clause comes at the beginning of the sentence and is followed by a comma. In the second sentence, the adverb clause comes after the independent clause and is not separated from it by a comma. An introductory adverb clause is always followed by a comma; adverb clauses that occur at the end of a sentence, however, require *no* punctuation.

■ **EXERCISE 12.1**

Sentences will vary.

Combine each of the following pairs of sentences into a complex sentence with an adverb clause. Vary the position of your adverb clauses and punctuate appropriately. You may wish to refer to the list of signal words for adverb clauses provided above.

1. The desert is hot and dry.
   Many flowers grow there.

   Although the desert is hot and dry, many flowers grow there.
   _____

   _____

2. Several states are passing stricter driving-while-intoxicated laws. The number of traffic deaths connected with drinking may be reduced.

   Because several states are passing stricter driving-while-intoxicated

laws, the number of traffic deaths connected with drinking may be

reduced.

3. In recent years several airlines have suffered record losses.
    The days of low airline rates may be over.

    Since in recent years several airlines have suffered record losses,

    the days of low airline rates may be over.

4. In extremely hot weather elderly people can die from heat stroke.
    They stay in an air-conditioned environment.

    In extremely hot weather elderly people can die from heat stroke

    unless they stay in an air-conditioned environment.

5. I put my arm out the window of the car.
    I came to a stop at the busy intersection.

    I put my arm out the window of the car after I came to a stop at the

    busy intersection.

6. The Jacksons escaped from their burning house.
    Their three-year-old son was awakened by the heat.

    The Jacksons escaped from their burning house because their

    three-year-old son was awakened by the heat.

7. Last evening I was reading the paper.
    I noticed a peculiar odor coming from the kitchen.

    Last evening I was reading the paper when I noticed a peculiar odor

    coming from the kitchen.

8. I broke my leg.
    I went skiing in Colorado.

    When I went skiing in Colorado, I broke my leg.

_____

_____

9. The room was uncomfortably hot.
   The speaker opened a window.

   Because the room was uncomfortably hot, the speaker opened a

   window.

_____

10. Fifteen spectators were injured in the accident at the racetrack.
    No one was killed.

    Even though no one was killed, fifteen spectators were injured in the

    accident at the racetrack.

_____

■ EXERCISE 12.2

Sentences will vary.

In the spaces below write five complex sentences with adverb clauses. Be sure to vary the position of the adverb clauses you use. Punctuate your sentences appropriately.

1. **The spaniel sat obediently when his master gave the command.**

_____

_____

2. **As the traffic increased, the motorists grew more irritable.**

_____

_____

3. **After the baby was delivered, she was placed beside her mother.**

_____

_____

4. **The minister left early because she had a meeting.**

_____

_____

5. **Unless we hurry, we will be late.**

_____

_____

ADJECTIVE CLAUSES

An adjective clause modifies a noun or a noun substitute within the independent clause in which it appears. Signal words used to introduce adjective clauses are listed below:

who	which
whom	where
whose	when
that	why

Adjective clauses that are needed to identify the words they modify are called *restrictive* clauses and require no punctuation. Nonrestrictive adjective clauses must be set off by commas. Both of the following sentences contain adjective clauses. As you read the sentences, notice the difference between them.

Restrictive:

The woman *who married Hitler* committed suicide to prevent capture by the Allies.

Nonrestrictive:

Eva Braun, *who married Hitler,* committed suicide to prevent capture by the Allies.

In the first sentence the word *woman* is identified by the adjective clause *who married Hitler.* In the second sentence the adjective clause is not needed to identify Eva Braun; the clause is therefore nonessential, or *nonrestrictive.*

Note: *That* usually introduces restrictive clauses; *which* usually introduces nonrestrictive clauses.

■ EXERCISE 12.3

Sentences may vary.

Combine each of the following pairs of sentences into a complex sentence with an adjective clause. Be sure to punctuate each sentence correctly. You may wish to refer to the signal words for adjective clauses provided above.

1. The city council supports a rapid-transit plan.
    The plan will reduce freeway traffic.

    The city council supports a rapid-transit plan, which will reduce

    freeway traffic.

    _____

    _____

2. The junkyard dealer has been robbed several times.
    He now uses a seven-foot ostrich as a night guard.

    The junkyard dealer, who has been robbed several times, now uses a

    seven-foot ostrich as a night guard.

3. The citizens of Buffalo rallied to the defense of the man.
   The man was accused of stabbing his daughter's rapist.

   The citizens of Buffalo rallied to the defense of the man who was

   accused of stabbing his daughter's rapist.

4. The blue lake mirrored the snow-capped mountains.
   The lake was crescent-shaped.

   The blue lake, which was crescent-shaped, mirrored the snow-capped

   mountains.

5. I shopped at the new mall with my sister Myra.
   Myra lives in Anaheim.

   I shopped at the new mall with my sister Myra, who lives in Anaheim.

6. Charles Lindbergh was received in New York with wild enthusiasm.
   He had accomplished a remarkable feat.

   Charles Lindbergh, who had accomplished a remarkable feat, was

   received in New York with wild enthusiasm.

7. On a trip to the Rockies last summer I met an interesting old man.
   He claimed to be ninety-nine years old.

   On a trip to the Rockies last summer I met an interesting old man,

   who claimed to be ninety-nine years old.

_____

_____

8. The student looked surprised but happy.
   The student's paper had received the *A*.

   The student whose paper had received the *A* looked surprised but

   happy.

   _____

   _____

9. We went to the ballet.
   It was performed by the Royal Canadian Ballet Company.

   We went to the ballet, which was performed by the Royal Canadian

   Ballet Company.

   _____

   _____

10. John Kennedy was elected president of the United States in 1959.
    He was a Roman Catholic.

    John Kennedy, who was a Roman Catholic, was elected president

    of the United States in 1959.

    _____

    _____

■ EXERCISE 12.4

Sentences will vary.

In the spaces below write five complex sentences with adjective clauses. Be sure to include at least one sentence with a restrictive clause and one with a nonrestrictive clause. Punctuate your sentences appropriately.

1. **The patient, who was very ill, was admitted to the hospital.**

   _____

2. **She chose the plant that had the most blooms.**

   _____

3. **The restaurant, which had just opened, was very popular.**

4. **The student, whose schedule was busy, decided to quit his job.**

5. **She pointed to the house where he was hiding.**

NOUN CLAUSES

A noun clause functions as the subject, object, subject complement, or object of a preposition within the independent clause of a complex sentence. Signal words used to introduce noun clauses are listed below.

who	that	whichever	wherever
whom	whoever	whatever	when
which	whomever	where	whenever
what			

Below are four sentences that illustrate the different kinds of noun clauses. Following each sentence is a second sentence in which a simple noun or pronoun has been substituted for the noun clause. By comparing these sentence pairs, you will be able to see more clearly how the noun clause functions within a complex sentence.

1. *Noun clause as subject: Whoever arrives early* can set up the tables and chairs. (*They* can set up the tables and chairs.)
2. *Noun clause as direct object:* He knew *what she wanted to do.* (He knew her *plan.*)
3. *Noun clause as subject complement:* The problem was *that we were already late.* (The problem was our *lateness.*)
4. *Noun clause as object of a preposition:* I will go to the play with *whoever asks me first.* (I will go to the play with *Fran.*)

Note: Since noun clauses function as an essential element within a sentence, they require *no* added punctuation. If you are not sure whether a clause is a noun clause, substitute a noun or pronoun for the clause. If the substitution makes sense, the clause is functioning as a noun.

■ EXERCISE 12.5

Sentences may vary.

Combine each of the following sentence pairs into a complex sentence with a noun clause. You may wish to use the signal words suggested in parentheses.

1. The patient knew something. (that)
   The operation might be fatal.

The patient knew that the operation might be fatal.

2. Please select something. (whichever)
   The dessert is your favorite.

   Please select whichever dessert is your favorite.

3. The disposal of waste was the problem. (for which)
   They were seeking a solution.

   The disposal of waste was the problem for which they were seeking

   a solution.

4. The candidate is someone. (whoever)
   Someone wins the primary.

   The candidate is whoever wins the primary.

5. Please give the package to someone. (whoever)
   Someone answers the door.

   Please give the package to whoever answers the door.

6. (that) Imelda had not read her assignment.
   Something was apparent to her psychology professor.

   That Imelda had not read her assignment was apparent to her

   psychology professor.

■ EXERCISE 12.6   In the spaces below write five complex sentences with noun clauses.

Sentences will vary.   1. **He knew what she meant.**

_____

_____

2. **They will do whatever they must do.** _____

_____

_____

3. **That the water was rising was obvious.** _____

_____

_____

4. **The pilot spoke to whoever came aboard.** _____

_____

_____

5. **You may answer whichever question you choose.** _____

_____

_____

■ EXERCISE 12.7

Sentences will vary.

The following groups of sentences can be combined into complex sentences. Combine the sentence groups, being sure to punctuate each new sentence appropriately. Remember to put main ideas in independent clauses and supporting ideas in subordinate clauses. Then rewrite the sentences in paragraph form.

1. Tennessee Williams reveals something.
   The revelation is in *The Glass Menagerie.*
   The something is that dreams are fragile.

   In *The Glass Menagerie,* Tennessee Williams reveals that dreams

   are fragile.

   _____

   _____

2. Laura Wingfield is extremely shy.
   Laura is physically handicapped.
   Laura has retreated from the real world.
   Laura has retreated into a world of Victrola music.
   Laura has retreated into a world of little glass animals.

   Laura Wingfield, who is extremely shy and physically handicapped,

   has retreated from the real world into a world of Victrola music and

little glass animals.

_____

_____

3. Her mother is Amanda Wingfield.
    Amanda lives in the past.
    The living is with her girlhood memories.
    The memories are of "gentleman callers."

    Her mother is Amanda Wingfield, who lives in the past with her

    girlhood memories of "gentleman callers."

    _____

    _____

4. Laura's brother Tom escapes.
    Tom works at a job.
    The job is drab.
    The job is at a warehouse.
    The warehouse is for shoes.
    He escapes by going to the movies.
    He escapes by writing poetry.

    Laura's brother Tom, who works at a drab job at a shoe warehouse,

    escapes by going to the movies and writing poetry.

    _____

    _____

5. Tom's dilemma is something.
    The something is he feels responsible.
    The responsibility is for his family.
    He needs freedom.
    The freedom is for himself.

    Tom's dilemma is that he feels responsible for his family but needs

    freedom for himself.

    _____

    _____

6. The situation is brought to a climax.
    The situation is tense.
    The situation is in the Wingfield household.
    Tom brings home a "gentleman caller."
    The "gentleman caller" is named Jim O'Connor.
    The "gentleman caller" is to meet Laura.

    The tense situation in the Wingfield household is brought to a

climax when Tom brings home a "gentleman caller" named

Jim O'Connor to meet Laura.

_____

7. Jim comes home with Tom.
    Jim is kind.
    The kindness is to Laura.

    When Jim comes home with Tom, he is kind to Laura.

    _____

    _____

8. Laura comes out of her world.
    The world is of dreams.
    The coming out is only for a while.
    Laura thinks something.
    The something is that she has found someone.
    The someone is to love her.

    Laura comes out of her world of dreams for a while because she

    thinks that she has found someone to love her.

    _____

    _____

9. However, Jim breaks something.
    The breaking is accidental.
    The something is a unicorn.
    The unicorn is little.
    The unicorn is glass.
    The unicorn is Laura's ornament.
    The ornament is her favorite.
    Jim shatters her hopes.
    Jim tells her something.
    The something is that he is already engaged.

    However, Jim accidentally breaks a little glass unicorn, which is

    Laura's favorite ornament, and shatters her hopes when he tells her

    that he is already engaged.

    _____

10. Jim leaves.
    Laura is left with her dreams.
    Laura is left with her animals.

The animals are little.
The animals are glass.
The dreams comfort her.
The animals comfort her.

When Jim leaves, Laura is left with her dreams and her little glass

animals to comfort her.

11. Amanda discovers something.
The something is that Jim is engaged.
The something is that Laura has no hope.
The hope is of marrying Jim.
Amanda accepts reality.
Amanda admits something to herself.
The admission is that Laura is handicapped.

When Amanda discovers that Jim is engaged and that Laura has no

hope of marrying him, she accepts reality and admits to herself that

Laura is handicapped.

12. The play ends.
Tom has joined the merchant marines.
Tom is looking back at his memories.
The memory is of his mother.
The memory is of his sister.

As the play ends, Tom has joined the merchant marines and is

looking back at his memories of his mother and sister.

SIGNALING RELATIONSHIPS IN COMPLEX SENTENCES

Good readers and writers are able to determine main ideas and supporting ideas within sentences and to understand the relationships between those ideas. One of the best ways to identify supporting ideas in subordinate clauses is to look for the signal words that introduce them. The signal words also indicate the relationship that exists in a complex sentence between the subordinate clause and the independent clause of which it is a part.

In previous exercises you have used signal words to connect independent and subordinate clauses. The following chart should be helpful to you because it not only lists the most common signal words used to introduce subordinate clauses but also indicates the relationships shown by the signal words. Study the words carefully so that you can use them appropriately to connect independent and subordinate clauses.

PLACE	CONTRAST	EXAMPLE
where	although	such as
wherever	though	as
	even though	
MANNER,	even if	AGENT
CONDITION	whereas	who
if	than	whom
unless	except	whose
as, as if	except that	which
lest		that
provided	TIME	whichever
provided that	after	whoever
in case	before	whomever
just as	when	whosoever
whether	while	whatever
how	until	wherever
	whenever	
CAUSE / EFFECT,	as long as	
CONCLUSION	as soon as	
so that	as often as	
in order that		
because		
since		

EXERCISE 12.8

Answers will vary.

Read each sentence carefully and then insert in the blank a signal word that shows the proper relationship between the main idea expressed in the independent clause and the supporting idea expressed in the subordinate clause.

EXAMPLE

The concert was canceled ___*because*___ rain was forecast.

(The relationship here is one of cause and effect, so either *because* or *since* would be a good choice.)

1. _____**If**_____ a left-handed child is forced to write with his or her right hand, the child may become confused.

2. The nurse ran into the patient's room ____**so that**____ he could assist the doctor.

3. Most college students call their parents ____**when**____ they run out of money.

4. I wasn't sure _____**who**_____ had given me the flowers until I read the card.

5. I don't know _____**whether**_____ the test is being given on Tuesday or Thursday.

6. _____**Although**_____ he is no longer a child, a teenager is not an adult.

7. The baby didn't know _____**that**_____ the stove was hot.

8. _____**After**_____ the car stopped, I crossed the street.

9. Cats can never be owned; they live with _____**whoever**_____ takes care of them.

10. I hope _____**that**_____ I have time to eat lunch _____**before**_____ I have to go to my next class.

11. _____**Since**_____ Althea has been jogging, her health is much better.

12. _____**Even though**_____ the dog seemed friendly, I was afraid of him.

13. My brother was as happy _____**as**_____ he could be with his new job.

14. _____**Because**_____ the rain has stopped, we can play golf.

15. Mario tries to take his classes during the mornings _____**when**_____ his children are in school.

EXERCISE 12.9

Answers will vary.

In the following paragraph signal words used to introduce subordinate clauses have been omitted. Read the paragraph carefully and write in the blanks appropriate signal words.

Young people _____**who**_____ choose to teach today are a special breed. They are not primarily interested in money or prestige, for teaching affords neither. _____**If**_____ they wanted wealth, they would choose law or medicine or business as a career. These aspiring young teachers know _____**that**_____ teachers work long hours and receive little recognition and less pay. But they choose teaching _____**because**_____ they want to serve society, or _____**because**_____ they enjoy children, or _____**because**_____ they love knowledge. _____**When**_____ they make the decision to become teachers,

they realize _____**that**_____ they are giving up some important things, but

they also know _____**that**_____ they will realize important dreams and goals

as teachers. Once upon a time young females became teachers

_____**because**_____ they had few other professional choices. Today teaching

gives both males and females _____**what**_____ they value most —a sense

of satisfaction.

■ EXERCISE 12.10

Sentences will vary.

In this exercise, you are given an independent clause and a connecting word. Supply a dependent clause that fits the relationship indicated by the signal word and punctuate each sentence correctly.

1. They left the house before **we returned.** _____

   _____

2. They left the house so that **it could be cleaned.** _____

   _____

3. They left the house although **it was raining.** _____

   _____

4. They left the house because **it was too hot.** _____

   _____

5. We believe that **he will win the election.** _____

   _____

6. We believe what **she told us.** _____

   _____

7. We believe whoever **tells us the best story.** _____

   _____

8. We believe whatever **we hear.** _____

   _____

9. Because **he is not afraid,** _____

   the child sleeps peacefully.

10. After **the music stops,** _____

the child sleeps peacefully.

11. Whereas **his mother lies awake until morning,** _____

the child sleeps peacefully.

12. If **his mother is near,** _____

the child sleeps peacefully.

13. The man who **can repair the copier** _____

is here.

14. The letter, which **they mailed yesterday,** _____

is here.

15. The man whose **name I forgot** _____

is here.

16. The package that **you ordered** _____

is here.

17. Hazel Johnson, who **came to lunch often,** _____

ate heartily.

18. The black cat, which **we found in the alley,** _____

ate heartily.

19. Ian Stokes, whose **appetite is enormous,** _____

ate heartily.

20. The Wongs' baby, who **is only nine months old,** _____

ate heartily.

EDITING COMPLEX SENTENCES

Subordination is a necessary tool for indicating relationships between ideas. Each time you use a subordinate clause in your writing, however, you should be sure (1) that it is punctuated correctly and (2) that it is connected to an independent clause and is therefore not a subordinate clause fragment.

Punctuation of Subordinate Clauses

As you have seen earlier in this chapter, different types of subordinate clauses require different punctuation. Review the following punctuation guide:

1. ***An introductory adverb clause is set off by a comma:*** *Because the rain was coming down in torrents,* the game was delayed.
2. ***An adverb clause at the end of a sentence is not set off by a comma:*** The game was delayed *because the rain was coming down in torrents.*
3. ***A nonrestrictive adjective clause is set off by commas:*** Jim, *who is president of my fraternity,* is my best friend.
4. ***A restrictive adjective clause is not set off by commas:*** The man *who is president of my fraternity* is my best friend.
5. ***A noun clause is not set off by commas:*** Did you know *that I was here?*

■ EXERCISE 12.11   Edit the following complex sentences carefully by supplying punctuation where it is needed. Some sentences are correct.

1. When the party is over, we'll have our meeting.

2. We took a vacation on Padre Island, where there is a good beach.

3. I'll take you to Venice, where you can ride in gondolas.

(correct)   4. You have some very important decisions to make when you graduate.

5. Paul Farrell, to whom my sister is engaged, graduated from Yale.

(correct)   6. The cook that the boss hired is very efficient.

(correct)   7. Mrs. Thomas fired the secretary that Mr. Thomas liked so well.

8. Mr. Crockett, who used to be a football player, is enormous.

9. When I push this button, the motor begins to run.

10. Because it was hot, he opened the window.

(correct)   11. This ball club never won a game until Jack was named manager.

12. When I married Sara, she weighed only ninety pounds.

(correct)   13. His car skidded around the corner because the tires were slick.

14. When I came home late, I entered quietly.

(correct)   15. I bought him a card because it was his birthday.

(correct)   16. That I lost my library card caused me many problems.

(correct)   17. I discovered that I was overdrawn when I balanced my checkbook.

18. Although my sister loves to cook, she hates to do the dishes.

(correct) 19. The horse that broke through the fence did not hurt itself.

(correct) 20. Your roommate wanted to know what time you got home.

21. Since I am a mountain man, I like high places.

(correct) 22. He visits his parents when he can.

(correct) 23. The flight attendant who spilled my drink apologized profusely.

24. Their club president, who was elected by only one vote, resigned yesterday.

25. Although missing one class may not be serious, missing a week of classes can hurt your grades.

Subordinate Clause Fragments

A subordinate clause has a subject and a verb but does not express a complete thought. It cannot stand by itself as a sentence but must always be attached to an independent clause. The diagrams in Figures 29 and 30 illustrate a subordinate clause that is used correctly as part of an independent clause and incorrectly as a fragment unattached to an independent clause.

FIGURE 29 SUBORDINATE CLAUSE AS PART OF AN INDEPENDENT CLAUSE (CORRECT):

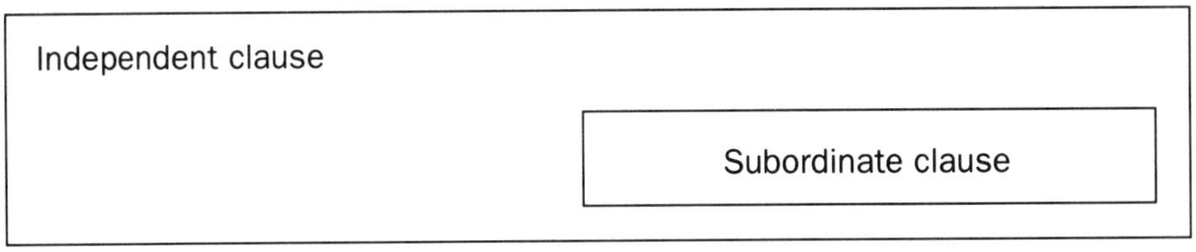

```
┌─────────────────────────────────────────────────────────┐
│ Independent clause                                        │
│                                                           │
│                          ┌──────────────────────────────┐ │
│                          │  Subordinate clause           │ │
│                          └──────────────────────────────┘ │
└─────────────────────────────────────────────────────────┘
```

She knew with certainty

that he was the prowler.

FIGURE 30 SUBORDINATE CLAUSE AS A FRAGMENT (INCORRECT):

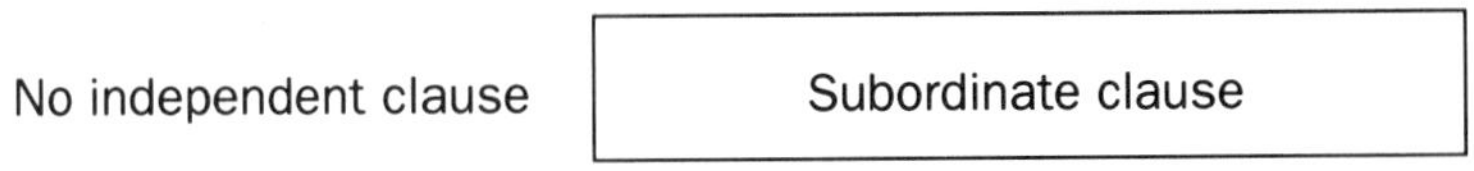

```
                          ┌──────────────────────────────┐
No independent clause     │  Subordinate clause           │
                          └──────────────────────────────┘
```

That he was the prowler.

■ **EXERCISE 12.12**

Sentences will vary.

Change each of the following fragments into a complete sentence by adding an independent clause to the subordinate clause that is given.

EXAMPLE

Because I missed the bus by seconds. (A subordinate clause—a fragment)

I was twenty minutes late to school because I missed the bus by seconds. (An independent clause modified by a subordinate clause—a complete sentence)

1. Who broke her glasses.

   The woman who broke her glasses called her optometrist

   immediately.

   _____

2. Because the lights on the stage went out during the performance.

   The play could not continue because the lights on the stage went

   out during the performance.

   _____

3. While the motor was running.

   The taxi driver couldn't leave his cab while the motor was running.

   _____

   _____

4. After the burglar ran away.

   After the burglar ran away, we called the police.

   _____

   _____

5. Who is president of the student senate.

   Jackson, who is president of the student senate, asked me to serve

   as secretary.

   _____

6. That we had made a mistake.

   It was obvious that we had made a mistake.

   _____

   _____

7. If you want to buy a computer.

   You should examine several models if you want to buy a computer.

_____

_____

8. Which raced across the lake.

   His boat, which raced across the lake, came in first.

_____

_____

9. Because the library closes at ten o'clock.

   Because the library closes at ten o'clock, you should get there by

   eight o'clock.

_____

_____

10. Whom I met at your party.

    The man whom I met at your party called me yesterday.

_____

_____

_____

■ EXERCISE 12.13

Answers will vary.

The following passage contains twelve fragments, each of which is a subordinate clause incorrectly written as a sentence. Rewrite the passage on a separate sheet of paper, connecting each fragment to a related independent clause.

Almost every book on art includes a reproduction of the "Mona Lisa." Which is one of the most famous paintings in the world. The "Mona Lisa" was painted by Leonardo da Vinci. Who worked on it for four years (1503–1506). The painting was never quite finished. After he had worked for several hours. Leonardo would sit down in front of the "Mona Lisa" to quiet his nerves. Some people say. That Leonardo did not finish the painting. Because he wanted an excuse to keep it with him.

On the face of the woman in the painting there is a mysterious smile. Which has intrigued people for centuries. Although no one knows the true explanation of the smile. Several different legends have grown up about it. One story says that the woman was smiling sadly. When she sat for the portrait. Because her child had died. Another story, however, goes on to say that Leonardo hired musicians, flutists and violinists, to play during the sittings. So that he could capture the young woman's rapt expression.

When Leonardo left Italy and moved to France. He took the painting with him. The French king persuaded him to sell the painting. Which now hangs in the Louvre, an art museum in Paris.

READING AND WRITING ABOUT—

Ethical Issues

Preparing: Mapping and Freewriting—

People of all times and all places have been concerned with ethical issues—with questions about "What is right?" and "What is wrong?" Ethical questions concern moral choices that individuals make in their relationships with other people. Thus, the study of ethics encompasses a wide range of subjects: marriage, family, government, politics, religion, business, economics, society, race relations, education, medicine, and so forth.

Explore the ethical issues found in *one* of these areas by mapping the subject, branching down from it with several levels of details and examples. For example, if you selected "ethical issues in business," you might branch down with such subdivisions as "personal business," "the banking business," "corporate business," and so forth. To develop your map further, be sure to consider areas and specific instances in which ethical choices must be made. For example, your map of the subtopic personal business might include such matters as "reporting income for taxes" and "receiving too much change." At this stage, however, don't worry too much about making your categories parallel. Just try to get your thoughts and ideas on paper. After you complete your mapping, freewrite for five minutes about the ethical issue that you have mapped.

MONEY FOR MORALITY
Mary Arguelles

Before you read, think about what you would do if you found a bank envelope with $600 in it. Would you try to find the owner? Would you return the envelope to the bank whose name is printed on it? What would most people do? Would you expect a reward? Would most people? Why or why not? In the following "My Turn" column from *Newsweek,* Mary Arguelles explains how an eight-year-old boy responded to this situation and how others reacted to his action.

As you read, determine Arguelles's thesis. Also identify and underline Arguelles's suggestion for making honesty and integrity more attractive to young people.

See text annotation.

1   I recently read a newspaper article about an 8-year-old boy who found an envelope containing more than $600 and returned it to the bank whose name appeared on the envelope. The bank traced the money to its rightful owner and returned it to him. God's in his heaven, all's right with the world. Right? Wrong.

2   As a reward, this man who lost the money gave the boy $3. Not a lot, but a token of his appreciation nonetheless and not mandatory. After all, returning

money should not be considered extraordinary. A simple "thank you" is adequate. But some of the teachers at the boy's school felt a reward was not only appropriate, but required. Outraged at the apparent stinginess of the person who lost the cash, these teachers took up a collection for the boy. About a week or so later, they presented the good Samaritan with a $150 savings bond, explaining they felt his honesty should be recognized. Evidently the virtues of honesty and kindness have become commodities that, like everything else, have succumbed to inflation. I can't help but wonder what dollar amount these teachers would have deemed a sufficient reward. Certainly they didn't expect the individual who lost the money to give the child $150. Would $25 have been respectable? How about $10? Suppose that lost money had to cover mortgage, utilities and food for the week. In light of that, perhaps $3 was generous. A reward is a gift; any gift should at least be met with the presumption of genuine gratitude on the part of the giver.

3   What does this episode say about our society? It seems the role models our children look up to these days—in this case, teachers—are more confused and misguided about values than their young charges. A young boy, obviously well guided by his parents, finds money that does not belong to him and he returns it. He did the right thing. Yet doing the right thing seems to be insufficient motivation for action in our materialistic world. The legacy of the '80s has left us with the ubiquitous question: what's in it for me? The promise of the golden rule—that someone might do a good turn for you—has become worthless collateral for the social interactions of the mercenary and fast-paced '90s. It is in fact this fast pace that is, in part, a source of the problem. Modern communication has catapulted us into an instant world. Television makes history of events before any of us has even had a chance to absorb them in the first place. An ad for major-league baseball entices viewers with the reassurance that "the memories are waiting"; an event that has yet to occur has already been packaged as the past. With the world racing by us, we have no patience for a rain check on good deeds.

4   Misplaced virtues are running rampant through our culture. I don't know how many times my 13-year-old son has told me about classmates who received $10 for each *A* they receive on their report cards—hinting that I should do the same for him should he ever receive an *A* (or maybe he was working on $5 for a *B*). Whenever he approaches me on this subject, I give him the same reply: "Doing well is its own reward. The *A* just confirms that." In other words, forget it! This is not to say that I would never praise my son for doing well in school. But my praise is not meant to reward or elicit future achievements, but rather to express my genuine delight in the satisfaction he feels at having done his best. Throwing $10 at that sends out the message that the feeling alone isn't good enough.

5   *Kowtowing to Ice Cream*   As a society, we seem to be losing a grip on our internal control—the ethical thermostat that guides our actions and feelings toward ourselves, others, and the world around us. Instead, we rely on external "stuff" as a measure of our worth. We pass this message to our children. We offer them money for honesty and good grades. Pizza is given as a reward for reading. In fact, in one national reading program, a pizza party awaits the entire class if each child reads a certain amount of books within a four-month period. We call these things incentives, telling ourselves that if we can just reel them in and get them hooked, then the built-in rewards will follow. I recently saw a television program where unmarried, teenaged mothers were featured as the participants in a parenting program that offers a $10 a week "incentive" if these

young women don't get pregnant again. Isn't the daily struggle of being a single, teenaged mother enough of a deterrent? No, it isn't, because we as a society won't allow it to be. Nothing is permitted to succeed or fail on its own merits anymore.

6   I remember when I was pregnant with my son I read countless child-care books that offered the same advice: don't bribe your child with ice cream to get him to eat spinach; it makes the spinach look bad. While some may say spinach doesn't need any help looking bad, I submit it's from years of kowtowing to ice cream. Similarly, our moral taste buds have been dulled by an endless onslaught of artificial sweeteners. A steady diet of candy bars and banana splits makes an ordinary apple or orange seem sour. So too does an endless parade of incentives make us incapable of feeling a genuine sense of inner peace (or inner turmoil).

7   The simple virtues of honesty, kindness and integrity suffer from an image problem and are in desperate need of a makeover. One way to do this is by example. If my son sees me feeling happy after I've helped out a friend, then he may do likewise. If my daughter sees me spending a rainy afternoon curled up with a book instead of spending money at the mall, she may get the message that there are some simple pleasures that don't require a purchase. I fear that in our so-called upwardly mobile world we are on a downward spiral toward moral bankruptcy. Like pre-World War II Germany, where the basket holding the money was more valuable than the money itself, we too may render ourselves internally worthless while desperately clinging to a shell of appearances.

REVIEWING THE READING   Answers will vary.

See paragraphs 2, 7.

1. State Arguelles's thesis in your own words.

See paragraphs 1 and 2.

2. Is Arguelles's introduction effective? How does it capture your interest?

See paragraphs 5 and 6.

3. Arguelles gives several examples of "bribing" young people to succeed. What are these examples? Does Arguelles agree or disagree with giving such bribes? Do you agree or disagree with the practice? Why or why not?

See paragraph 7.

4. Underline Arguelles's suggestion for making the "simple virtues of honesty, kindness and integrity" more attractive to young people. In her last paragraph, Arguelles provides two examples of this suggestion. Identify these examples and number them in the margins.

5. Who is Arguelles's audience? (Remember that this article was published in *Newsweek*'s "My Turn" column.) What is her purpose? Is her purpose primarily informative or persuasive?

UNDERSTANDING VOCABULARY

1. A particularly interesting word that occurs in this reading is *kowtow*. Originally, a *kowtow* was a Chinese salutation in which a person touched his or her forehead to the ground as an expression of submission or respect. Although this meaning is still in use, the word is more generally used today as a verb meaning "to show great submission or compliance" or a noun meaning "an extremely submissive or servile act."

2. Use the context and parenthetical information provided to help you define the underlined words in the following sentences.

a. "As a reward, the man who lost the money gave the boy $3. Not a lot, but a token of his appreciation nonetheless and not <u>mandatory</u> [from Latin *mandere,* "to command"]. After all, returning money should not be considered extraordinary" (paragraph 2).

b. "The legacy of the '80s has left us with the <u>ubiquitous</u> [from Latin *ubique,* "everywhere"] question: what's in it for me?" (paragraph 3)

c. "Modern communication has <u>catapulted</u> [from Greek *kata,* "down" and *pallein,* "to throw"] us into an instant world. Television makes history of events before any of us has even had a chance to absorb them in the first place" (paragraph 3).

Add these and any other unfamiliar words that you encountered in the reading to your personal vocabulary list.

REACTING CRITICALLY

What does Arguelles mean by the advice "don't bribe your child with ice cream to get him to eat spinach; it makes the spinach look bad." Do you agree or disagree with her advice? What other examples of "kowtowing to ice cream" can you think of?

■ THE LIES THAT BIND
Paul Thaler

Before you read, think about the question of truth and falsehood. Is it always bad to tell a lie? Is it always good to tell the truth? In the following "About Men" column from the June 9, 1991, issue of the *New York Times Magazine,* Paul Thaler states his position on this question. Thaler is Director of Journalism at Mercy College in Dobbs Ferry, New York.

Annotations may vary.   *As you read,* underline Thaler's thesis. Why does he believe as he does? Also, circle any unfamiliar words that you encounter as you read.

1   The other day I lied to Amy. It wasn't a big lie, but it was big enough to assuage her doubts. Asked how I had spent the previous evening, I explained that work at the college had kept me late into the night. At another time, with perhaps a different person, another answer—a more truthful one—would have been offered. But not for Amy. Knowing that the evening was shared with a former girlfriend—albeit eating an innocent dinner· at a very public restaurant—would have opened an old wound that has never fully healed. It all seems like a contradiction: our ties are forged by a strong symbiosis, and yet I realize I have continually lied to keep it so. <u>The "truth," as I have discovered, often hurts and is less a prerequisite for a meaningful relationship than we may think.</u>

2   This realization, a recent one, has come as quite a surprise for me. I once thought that love meant abandoning the lies of your life, those fences built to quarantine your real self from the everyday world. Falling in love meant the building of trust, honesty and openness, the coming together of two hearts, two minds. Love letters espoused such thoughts; marriage vows codified them. Certainly this was a delightful myth, sustained by advertisers, Dr. Ruth, pulp novels, *Cosmopolitan* magazine and B movies. Love, explained Erich Segal in his novel *Love Story,* meant never having to say you're sorry. The translation was clear:

love meant complete acceptance of wrongdoings, disappointments, hurts, character flaws and selfishness. And, for the most part, we have bought the script.

3   But the romantic language of love never included the vocabulary of the lie. Unspoken was the thought that love could also be tied to concealing the painful truths that trample sensitivities and whittle away at self-esteem.

4   In our attempt to idealize the notion of romance, we have lost a sense of our own vulnerability. And vulnerable we are, coping with a rapidly changing and confusing culture. In trying to understand our roles as men and women, a connection lost in the sweep of societal gender chaos, we are in danger of being overloaded. A lie can help keep the circuits intact.

5   Of course, lovers lie all the time, although they may fervently deny it. A close friend insists that honesty is paramount in his relationship with his wife—well, except for those small "white lies." Indeed, his are small lies about matters having to do with personal habits and predilections. The lies protect the vulnerable shell of his relationship and forestall confrontations. The lie has given him a retreat for doubts and indecisions.

6   Another friend wags a finger at me, complaining that I should have told Amy about my date with the former girlfriend. Even if it was hard to swallow, she said, Amy was entitled to a knowledge of "the real world."

7   Would my friend consider telling her husband about an old affair that had gone sour?

8   "Of course not," she replied. "It would destroy him and our marriage."

9   And that, of course, is the point. Some truths chip away at relationships, others chop them down whole. It is a matter of drawing lines, and we all draw different ones when it comes to the truth.

10   Most lies that I spin are inconsequential, simply intent on maintaining the day-to-day stability of my relationship. I have applauded Amy for her cooking, her new dress, her latest diet. Neither the cooking (overdone chicken with a peculiar white sauce), her dress (an obtuse floral pattern) or her weight loss (which effectively cut the appealing lines of her body) elicited much excitement. Or the truth. In each case, a lie served as a salve, not a sword.

11   There are also bigger lies about more important things. Amy has asked me on more than one occasion, "Do you love me?" If ranked, this inquiry would probably top the universal list. If I were always truthful, and sometimes I am not, I would confide to Amy the fluctuating tide of my emotions, a response that might stab into the heart of our relationship. But at those times I search for a more positive answer. And why not? When we talk about love, what do we say and what does it mean? Language is often too neutered to express complex feelings.

12   And yet, once such hard "truths" are out in the air, it's impossible to push them aside. Misspent words continue to haunt long after that particular emotion has changed into something else. So when Amy asks whether I love her, I always do, even if, at times, I don't. The lie is a support system that is part of the ritual of intimacy. It may not be truthful, but it is confirming. It is a paradox, indeed, that in writing this article, I have revealed my lies.

13   I should note that Amy herself is not a great believer of the lie. Amy is especially quick to point out when I try to lie to myself. She fails to understand that at times self-deception also plays a vital role in a healthy relationship.

14   I usually dabbled in self-deception each time the subject of marriage was broached. Ever since we met six years ago, Amy had wanted to marry; I opted for the status quo. As a single person, I had long valued the independence and freedom that a marriage might limit. But Amy astutely noted that if bachelorhood

were a guiding principle, why then had I chosen a rather conventional, monogamous relationship with her during these years? She was right, of course, and the contradiction between my words and life style was evident. But this longstanding lie gave me time to wear the skin of our relationship to see how it fit and felt. Had I been forced to confront my ''true'' feelings before, our relationship might not have survived, much less flourished. Finally I did reach a decision. Just recently, Amy and I were married, and our lives have never been more secure.

15   As intimacy deepens, the need for lying deepens also. The more that's exposed, the more there's a need to guard those unflattering secrets. A reflexive action to confide in people outside a relationship—a friend or professional counselor—comes from our emotional wellsprings, our need to protect and not harm the people we love. So we exchange confidences with friends that we could not share with a lover. We find the need to estrange ourselves from an intimate relationship in order to discover the problems that may exist within it. The reason is apparent: often a partner is least capable to help, caught herself (or himself) in the entanglements of intimacy and unable to provide perspective or detachment. In my case, I talk to my brother. I tell him of my fears, insecurities and doubts; the problems with commitment, monogamy and sex, the confusion that stems from loving too little or too much.

16   Within the confines of intimacy, however, such truths can hurt, and often needlessly. The problem of being truthful often centers on what in fact is truth. I have found that it is an entity in constant flux. Yesterday's truth may be less than truthful tomorrow. So perhaps a lie gives us the chance to be introspective about love in a way that truth can't. Perhaps, in a real way, it is a truer reflection of love. The lie allows us to question silently, letting us withhold judgment, at least for the time being. It may not necessarily make intimacy more valuable or answer deep-seeded problems. But perhaps it does.

REVIEWING THE READING   Answers will vary.

See paragraphs 1, 16.   1. What is Thaler's thesis? Where does it occur?

See paragraphs 1 and 10–12.   2. Give two examples of lies that Thaler told his wife to keep from hurting her.

See paragraph 15.   3. In Thaler's opinion, does the need for lying increase or decrease with greater intimacy? What reasons does he give for the increase or decrease?

4. Thaler uses complex sentences sparingly but effectively. Identify the relationship between the independent and dependent clauses in the following sentences by filling in an appropriate subordinate conjunction:

See paragraph 11.   a. "_____ I were always truthful, . . . I would confide to Amy

the fluctuating tide of my emotions."

See paragraph 12.   b. "Misspent words continue to haunt long _____ that par

ticular emotion has changed into something else."

See paragraph 12.   c. "So _____ Amy asks whether I love her, I always do,

even _____ , at times, I don't."

See paragraph 15.   d. " _____ intimacy deepens, the need for lying deepens also."

UNDERSTANDING VOCABULARY

Use the context and parenthetical information provided to help you define the following underlined words.

1. "It all seems like a contradiction: our ties are forged by a strong symbiosis [from *syn-*, "together," and *bios*, "life"], and yet I realize I have continually lied to keep it so" (paragraph 1).

2. "In our attempt to idealize the notion of romance, we have lost a sense of our own vulnerability [from *vulnere*, "wound"]" (paragraph 4).

3. "If I were always truthful, . . . I would confide to Amy the fluctuating [from *fluctus*, "a flowing"] tide of my emotions" (paragraph 11).

4. "It is a paradox [from *para*, "beyond" and *doxa*, "opinion"], indeed, that in writing this article, I have revealed my lies" (paragraph 12).

5. "But Amy astutely noted that if bachelorhood were a guiding principle, why then had I chosen a rather conventional, monogamous [from *mono-*, "one," and *gamy*, "marriage"] relationship with her during these years?" (paragraph 14).

Add to your personal vocabulary list the meanings of these words and of other words that you circled while you were reading Thaler's essay.

REACTING CRITICALLY

Do you agree or disagree with Thaler that lies are sometimes necessary to avoid hurting those we love? Support your answer.

◼ AIDS AND THE RIGHT TO DIE
Andrew H. Malcolm

Before you read, think about the kind of medical treatment you would want for yourself or for a close family member in the case of a painful terminal illness. Would you want medical professionals to keep you or your family member alive in all circumstances? Who has the right to make such a decision—a doctor, a family member, a patient? In the following article from the October 4, 1987, issue of the *New York Times,* Andrew H. Malcolm considers a patient's right to die. Author of *Unknown America* (1974) and winner of the George Polk Memorial Award for National Reporting, Malcolm has been affiliated with the *New York Times* for much of his career.

As you read, try to imagine that you are the judge who heard Thomas Wirth's case. What would have been your decision?

1   It seemed the stuff of a nightmare from fiction: a fatal disease ravaging the man's body from within, his decision to forgo heroic, life-prolonging steps and the doctors' decision to ignore those wishes and perform their medical magic on the comatose body.

2   But the nightmare came true in recent weeks for Thomas Wirth, a New Yorker

who became a victim not only of AIDS but also of the ethical and moral fog that surrounds many of modern medicine's confrontations with the end of life. Should doctors ignore a patient's wishes and treat pneumonia or other serious infections because they can, knowing that they are "saving" the patient only so he can die later from something much worse? When and how can a terminally ill patient say, "Enough!" without exposing doctors and hospitals to legal and moral culpability in allowing a death?

3   Last week New York State took a first step toward giving competent patients the ironclad right to authorize in advance a proxy to make such life-and-death decisions if the patient becomes incompetent. The legislative proposal by the Governor's Task Force on Life and the Law could be introduced as soon as January.

4   Who can make such decisions is hardly a new question. But it is one certain to be faced increasingly with the inevitable spread of the inevitably fatal AIDS, which destroys the body's defenses against many otherwise treatable infections.

5   *"You Know the Outcome"* "It's different from other diseases because you—and every patient—know the outcome from the start," said one New York physician who treats many AIDS patients and who asked to remain anonymous. "You both know he'll be dead within two years, weighing perhaps 65 pounds, incontinent, in severe pain, with 80 percent experiencing mental changes."

6   "AIDS telescopes what we all will go through. Most of us will not have the luxury of living until 80 and then being hit by a truck. Most of us will die of a chronic, progressive disease that will be painful to experience, painful to watch, expensive, and ultimately fatal."

7   Mr. Wirth, 47 years old, had watched friends die slow, painful deaths from acquired immune deficiency syndrome. To avoid that, Mr. Wirth signed a living will with notarized instructions saying he wished to be allowed to die with dignity and without "extraordinary measures." He even designated a friend to make medical decisions in the event that he became incapacitated.

8   Mr. Wirth did become ill. He fell into a coma in Bellevue Hospital. His friend sought to halt aggressive medical treatment. Doctors refused, saying that while the AIDS would certainly prove fatal over time, the immediate medical problem, a brain infection, was treatable. In July, a state court judge agreed. Treatment was continued. Mr. Wirth died the next month.

9   "That case should never have happened," said Giles Scofield, a staff attorney for Concern for Dying, a right-to-die group. "But I'm afraid there will be many others that shouldn't happen, either."

10   Mr. Wirth's designation of a proxy to make decisions, an arrangement authorized by last week's legislative proposals, is not now recognized under New York law. But part of the problem stemmed from the wording of Mr. Wirth's will. He spoke of ill-defined "extraordinary measures" at a time when today's amazing technology can become tomorrow's ordinary treatment. Better, Mr. Scofield said, to specify "a reasonable hope of recovery," which is easier for doctors to agree on.

11   Competent patients have the legal right to refuse life-support systems, in theory. But emergency medical crews may not know an accident victim's wishes. And, as the Wirth case demonstrated, once begun, such treatment may prove impossible to stop.

12   Methods of decision-making are developing anyway. Court decisions, hospital ethics committees and medical associations provide guidelines, which in-

creasingly stress the patient's rights. California's bar association has approved a resolution that would allow doctors to give terminally ill patients lethal drugs under some circumstances, as is done in the Netherlands.

13   The Hastings Center, a private research group specializing in ethics issues, recently published guidelines on terminating treatment, favoring the patient's choices. "I think the AIDS crisis is provoking a lot of thought on advance planning," said Susan M. Wolf, who directed the project. "The worst place to make these decisions is in the emergency room or the hallway when the doctor needs to know what to do immediately."

14   *A Matter of Negotiation*   Not every state recognizes living wills, and only Nevada, California and Rhode Island specifically recognize the delegation of medical authority. With 80 percent of the average day's 5,750 deaths in this country occurring in institutions, many are quietly negotiated between doctor, patient and family, and are becoming more open discussions and less open secrets.

15   The New York doctor, for instance, tells every AIDS patient, "I will do as much as you want, but any time you want to call it quits, you'll get no argument from me." He said he has had more than 400 such patients. After long, painful periods of treatment and heavy medication, only four have opted out.

16   The doctor recalled: "They say, 'would 20 of these pills kill me?' And I say, 'No, 30 would.' Too many doctors have reserved to themselves the right to give up medical treatment, but they don't give that right to the patient himself. I do."

REVIEWING THE READING   Answers will vary.

1. Malcolm implies his thesis rather than stating it. What is his thesis?

2. How does Malcolm capture your interest in his first paragraph?

See paragraph 2.   3. What is the primary ethical question that arises in the treatment of AIDS?

See paragraph 5.   4. Why is the treatment of AIDS different from the treatment of other diseases?

See paragraphs 7 and 8.   5. How did Thomas Wirth attempt to determine his own medical treatment? Was his attempt successful? Why did it succeed or fail?

See paragraphs 15 and 16.   6. What does the New York doctor in the essay tell his AIDS patients?

UNDERSTANDING VOCABULARY

In the sentences below, we have provided a synonym for each of the underlined words from the reading selection. Study these words, and then add to your personal vocabulary list any that are new to you.

1. "It seemed the stuff of nightmare from fiction: a fatal disease ravaging [destroying] the man's body from within, his decision to forgo heroic, life-prolonging steps and the doctors' decision to ignore those wishes and perform their medical magic on the comatose [unconscious] body" (paragraph 1).

2. "Last week New York State took a first step toward giving competent patients the ironclad right to authorize in advance a proxy [representative, replacement] to make such life-and-death decisions if the patient becomes incompetent" (paragraph 3).

3. " 'You both know he'll [the AIDS patient will] be dead within two years, weighing perhaps 65 pounds, <u>incontinent</u> [uncontrolled—usually referring to body functions], in severe pain, with 80 percent experiencing mental changes' " (paragraph 5).

4. "He even designated a friend to make medical decisions in the event that he became <u>incapacitated</u> [disabled]" (paragraph 7).

5. "California's bar association has approved a resolution that would allow doctors to give <u>terminally</u> [finally, mortally] ill patients <u>lethal</u> [deadly, fatal] drugs under some circumstances" (paragraph 12).

6. "The Hastings Center . . . recently published guidelines on <u>terminating</u> [ending, stopping] treatment, favoring the patient's choices" (paragraph 13).

REACTING CRITICALLY

In your opinion, who should determine the kind of treatment—and how much treatment—a patient should receive? Support your opinion.

Responding in Writing—

Write an essay based on one of the specific assignments below.

1. Look back over the mapping and freewriting that you did at the beginning of this Reading and Writing About assignment. Use these materials as the basis for an essay about a particular ethical issue. Remember to narrow your focus as much as possible, to include a clearly stated or implied thesis, and to support your thesis with specific details and examples.

2. Write an essay about personal financial ethics or business ethics. For example, do people return money they find, correct favorable mistakes in bills, report all income on taxes, and so forth? Do most businesses operate on the principle of what is legal or what is ethical? Include specific examples to support your thesis.

3. Write an essay discussing the motivation people have for doing the "right" things. Are people primarily motivated by doing what is right for the sake of doing what is right or for the possibility of a reward? Give reasons and examples to support your opinion.

4. Write an essay about the ethical issue of telling the truth. Should a person always tell "the complete truth and nothing but the truth"? Why or why not? Do different situations call for different responses? State your thesis clearly in your introduction, and support it with specific reasons and examples.

5. Write a persuasive essay about a patient's right to die. Try to convince your audience—perhaps legislators considering a bill on the issue—to agree with your position.

Revising Your Writing—

Use the following questions to help revise your essay. You may work independently or with a group of your classmates.

1. What is the purpose of your essay?

2. Who is your audience?

3. What is your thesis? Is it stated or clearly implied? How can you make it clearer to your readers?

4. What primary method of development did you use in the essay? What other methods of development did you use?

5. What specific support (details, reasons, examples, statistics) for the main idea have you included? What, if any, additional support should you include?

6. How are your supporting points arranged (time order, space order, order of importance)? How might you rearrange these supporting points to make your essay clearer and more effective?

7. What transitions have you included? What additional transitions do you need? Where are transitions needed?

8. Are your sentences effectively varied? Is your word choice clear and appropriate? Have you used any unnecessary or repetitious words? What revisions should you make in sentence style and word choice?

9. How do you conclude your essay? How can this conclusion be improved?

10. Does your essay achieve your purpose and communicate to your audience? If not, what revisions should you make?

After you have made the major revisions needed in your essay, edit it carefully. As you edit, consider the following questions:

1. Is each sentence a complete sentence, with a subject and a verb?

2. Do you have any errors in subject-verb agreement?

3. Do you have any errors in pronoun reference or agreement?

4. Have you used any sexist language?

5. What tense have you used? Is your use of tense consistent?

6. What point of view have you used (first person, second person, third person)? Is your point of view consistent?

7. Are all of your compound sentences punctuated correctly? Do you have any run-on sentences?

8. Are all of your complex sentences punctuated correctly?

    a. Have you inserted commas after adverb clauses at the beginning of sentences?

    b. Have you set off nonrestrictive adjective clauses with commas?

    c. Have you incorrectly separated a noun clause from the rest of a sentence with a comma?

9. Do you have any misspelled words?

10. Do you have any errors in capitalization, punctuation, or usage?

After you have finished editing, write your final draft and proofread it carefully.

APPENDIX A
Capitalization

The following rules illustrate many situations in which capital letters are needed:

1. Capitalize the first word of every sentence. Also capitalize the first word of direct quotations.

   The repairman took the television set with him.
   I said, "We'll leave for the game from my house."

2. Capitalize proper nouns. A proper noun is the name of a specific person, place, or thing: Ernest Hemingway, Florida, Greenville, the Washington Monument, Honda Accord, *New York Times.*

   The Mississippi River is the longest river in the United States.

3. Capitalize adjectives and nouns that are derived from proper nouns.

   The former Soviet Union was dominated by Stalinism during the 1940s.
   She was an expert in Marxist philosophy.

4. Capitalize titles of persons when they precede proper names. When used in place of proper names, titles of officers of high rank should be capitalized. Other titles should not.

   Senator Smith, Admiral Lacy, and the Attorney General came to the party for Professor Andrews.
   The postmaster of our town appealed to the Postmaster General for help.
   Ms. Murray called Dr. Brinkman for an appointment.

5. Capitalize names of family members only when used in place of proper names.

Today Mother called to tell me about my father's trip.
My mother gave Dad a new fishing rod for his birthday.

6. Capitalize names referring to the people or language of a nation, religion, or race.

Most of the French and the Spanish who settled Louisiana were Catholic.
Mary took German and Russian courses to satisfy her foreign language requirements.

7. Capitalize cities, states, and countries and adjectives derived from them.

On vacation we flew to Paris, France, and then to London, England.
The bus broke down in Denver, Colorado, on its way to Amarillo, Texas.
We hope to take a cruise to Alaska next summer.

8. Capitalize organizations such as clubs, churches, corporations, governmental bodies and departments, and political parties.

The members of the Senate passed a resolution praising the American Cancer Society.
The J. P. Stone Insurance Company made large contributions to both the Democratic and Republican parties.

9. Capitalize geographical areas. Do not capitalize directions.

Mark Twain writes about his boyhood adventures in the South.
Go north when you get to Lee Street.

10. Capitalize brand and commercial names.

I bought a can of Right Guard deodorant spray at Walmart's.
The Safeway store received new shipments of aspirin, including Bayer and St. Joseph's.

11. Capitalize days of the week and months.

My birthday, June 9, will fall on a Tuesday this year.
The annual company Christmas party will be held on Friday, December 23.

Notice that seasons are *not* capitalized.

The first Monday in January was the coldest day of winter.
Last Thursday marked the end of summer and the beginning of autumn.

12. Capitalize abbreviations when the words they stand for would be capitalized.

My brother transferred to UCLA (University of California, Los Angeles).
The USMC (United States Marine Corps) has a long, proud tradition.

13. Capitalize only the official title of a particular course unless the course refers to a nationality or language.

My history class for next semester will be History 122.
I hate math and science, but I enjoy my French class.

14. Capitalize the first word and all nouns, verbs, adjectives, and adverbs in the titles of books, plays, articles, movies, songs, and other literary or artistic works. Do not capitalize words such as articles (*a*, *an*, and *the*), conjunctions, and prepositions.

To Kill a Mockingbird is a famous novel by Harper Lee.
The professor wrote an article entitled "Too Far from the Shore" about Hemingway's *The Old Man and the Sea.*

15. Capitalize the first word in the greeting and complimentary close of a letter.

Dear Madam, Dear President Carter, Dear Sir
Sincerely yours, Yours very truly

16. Capitalize the pronoun "I."

I passed my examination.
Although I worked until two o'clock in the morning, I didn't finish my paper.

■ **EXERCISE A.1**   Correct the following sentences, adding capital letters wherever needed and deleting capitals if necessary.

1. The _I_ international _S_ students _O_ organization is planning a pancake sale to raise funds for _E_ ethiopian refugees.

2. The cities of _N_ new _Y_ york, _L_ london, and _M_ madrid are all popular vacation sites.

3. Some people prefer _S_ schlitz or _B_ budweiser, but my favorite beers are _C_ coors and _P_ pabst.

4. Mother cried out, "_S_ shut that door, and be quick about it!"

5. If you begin in _S_ san _D_ diego, go north to _L_ los _A_ angeles, head east to _S_ st. _L_ louis, and then go down to _B_ baton _R_ rouge, you will be in the _S_ south.

6. When I finally got my children to bed, I settled down to read _L_ larry _M_ mc _M_ murtry's book _L_ lonesome _D_ dove.

7. I live in _B_ berry _H_ hall, but I spend most of my time in the _H_ hall of _L_ languages, which is where the _E_ english, _S_ spanish, and _F_ french classes are held.

8. The ~~b~~^Battle of ~~g~~^Gettysburg was an important battle for both the ~~n~~^North and the ~~s~~^South.

9. As we studied in my ~~h~~^History 121 class, the ~~m~~^Mexican ~~w~~^War was very important to ~~a~~^American ~~H~~^history, but it is one of the least studied events in history today.

10. My interest in going to ~~C~~^college at the ~~u~~^University of Oklahoma is to major in business and computer science.

EXERCISE A.2   Correct the following sentences, adding capital letters wherever needed and deleting capitals if necessary.

1. The ~~u~~^University of Wisconsin played a football game against the ~~n~~^Nebraska ~~c~~^Cornhuskers last fall on ~~s~~^Saturday, ~~o~~^October 27, at ~~m~~^Memorial ~~s~~^Stadium in ~~l~~^Lincoln, ~~n~~^Nebraska.

2. Bill doesn't like his ~~f~~^French class or his history class, but he enjoys ~~s~~^Sociology 121.

3. Members of the U.S. ~~h~~^House of ~~r~~^Representatives will fly south on a fact-finding mission to ~~b~~^Brasilia, ~~b~~^Brazil, and then east to ~~v~~^Volgograd, ~~r~~^Russia.

4. When my grandfather was a young man, he and ~~g~~^Grandma traveled throughout the ~~w~~^West selling bottles of homemade medicine called "~~f~~^Fountain of ~~y~~^Youth ~~s~~^Serum and ~~c~~^Colic ~~c~~^Chaser."

5. Roberta wasn't sure if she should begin her letter to the ~~w~~^White ~~h~~^House in ~~w~~^Washington with "Dear ~~s~~^Sir," "~~m~~^My honorable dear sir," or "Dear ~~m~~^Mr. ~~p~~^President."

6. My ~~M~~^mother's article about her vacation, which she entitled "Around the ~~w~~^World in ~~e~~^Eight ~~d~~^Days," was printed in *Reader's ~~d~~^Digest.*

7. "The picnic will be held tomorrow," said ~~m~~^Mrs. ~~w~~^Wilson, "unless it rains."

8. "Come over and watch the game," Sam said. "~~t~~^The Dallas ~~c~~^Cowboys are playing football."

9. The winter *PTA* p.t.a. meeting will be held at *J*jefferson *H*high *S*school on *W*wednesday, *J*january 5, at eight o'clock.

10. My father made A's in *E*english and in math as a freshman in college, and *M*mom got A's in chemistry and *E*european *H*history 251.

■ EXERCISE A.3 Correct the following paragraph. Add and delete capitals wherever necessary.

People in the southern part of *T*texas can visit *O*old *M*mexico and stay as long as they wish, but citizens of *M*mexico often find it difficult to visit *T*texas. Because many *M*mexican citizens like to come to *S*south *T*texas not only to visit but also to work, Texas border patrols check visiting permits very carefully—particularly in the summer months of June, *J*july, and *A*august. *W*why do you suppose this is so? One reason is that during these months many *M*mexican citizens try to stay in Texas illegally in order to work for the *f*farmers during this busy season. *T*through its recent amnesty program and its border patrols, the *U.S.*u.s. *G*government discourages such illegal labor because many *A*american citizens believe that these migrant workers deprive them of jobs. Also, although many farmers treat all workers fairly, *m*Migrant *w*Workers are often the objects of discrimination and cruelty. Such cruelty is described by *J*john *S*steinbeck in his novel *T*the Grapes *o*Of *W*wrath.

APPENDIX B
Spelling

IMPROVING SPELLING SKILLS

Many excellent writers have poor spelling skills but have learned to correct their spelling errors because they know that misspelled words are distracting to a reader. If you have difficulty with spelling, you need to learn how to minimize your spelling errors so that your reader is not unduly distracted by them. Although there is no certain or simple way to become a good speller, there are several approaches that will help you become a *better* speller.

1. *Concentrate on your own particular spelling problems.* You need to keep a careful record of each word you misspell on your writing assignments and to study these words *regularly* until you master them.

2. *Learn the little words.* Almost everyone misspells a word occasionally, especially difficult words. However, educated people do not misspell common words. Some of these words are difficult in that they frequently look or sound like other words with which they can easily be confused; a glossary of these words is included in this appendix for you to study.

3. *Use the rules that work.* Most spelling rules are so complicated or have so many exceptions that they are not worth learning. However, a few of them work most of the time. These rules are really patterns because they do not always apply but are a general indication of how words are put together in English. Included in this appendix are four of the most useful spelling patterns plus the rules for forming possessives and plurals.

4. *Improve your vocabulary.* Spelling and vocabulary skills are closely related. Each time you learn a new word, be sure that you master its spelling as well as its meaning.

5. ***Depend on your dictionary.*** Accept the fact that you will always need to check on the spelling of many words. However, as you improve your spelling, the number of words you will need to look up should decrease markedly.

PROBLEM WORDS THAT LOOK AND SOUND ALIKE

a	article used before a consonant sound (*a* book, *a* lamp)
an	article used before a vowel sound (*an* onion, *an* hour)
accept	to receive (I *accept* your apology.)
except	not included (Everyone *except* the teacher laughed.)
advice (noun)	an opinion as to what should or should not be done
advise (verb)	to recommend or suggest; to inform or notify (Please *advise* your employer that his *advice* was appreciated.)
affect (verb)	to have an influence on (The illness *affected* his mind.)
effect (noun)	a result or consequence (What *effect* will the new law have?)
a lot	a large amount, many (two words; not spelled *alot*)
already	previously or by this time; one word (Summer is *already* here.)
all ready	completely prepared; two words (I am *all ready* to go.)
are	present tense form of *to be*; used with *you, we,* and *they* and plural nouns (You and they *are* free to go, but we *are* required to stay.)
our	possessive pronoun (We lost *our* way.)
or	coordinate conjunction (Joe *or* I will stay with you.)
capital (noun)	a city; a sum of money (Legislators in Austin, the *capital* of Texas, control the flow of *capital* in the state.)
capital (adjective)	chief or excellent (What a *capital* suggestion!)
capitol	a building where legislative sessions are held (The state *capitol* has a large dome.)
conscience	knowledge of right and wrong (Your *conscience* should hurt you.)
conscious	aware or alert (Was he *conscious* after the accident?)
complement	to make complete (Her blond hair *complemented* her tan.)
compliment (verb)	to praise (He *complimented* her tan.)
compliment (noun)	an expression of praise (She gave him a *compliment.*)
council	an assembly of persons called together for consultation or deliberation (The student *council* met with the faculty.)
counsel	advice or guidance, especially from a knowledgeable person (She sought the *counsel* of her minister and school counselor.)
coarse	low or common, of inferior quality or lacking in refinement; not fine in texture (That cake has a *coarse* texture.)
course	route or path taken; regular development or orderly succession; a prescribed unit of study (In the *course* of a year, twelve new buildings were built.)
of course	naturally, without doubt (*Of course,* I will.)
dessert	what is eaten at the end of a meal (*I like ice cream for dessert.*)

desert (verb)	to leave; to abandon (The father *deserted* his son.)
desert (noun)	land area characterized by sand and lack of water (The camel is used for transportation in the *desert*.)
fill	to make full (Please *fill* the dog's water dish.)
feel	to experience; to touch (I didn't *feel* very happy.)
fourth	to be number four in a sequence (We are *fourth* in line.)
forth	onward; in view; forward in place or time (Please step *forth*.)
idea (noun)	a thought; mental image or conception (My *idea* would be helpful.)
ideal (adjective)	perfect; without flaw (The gulf is an *ideal* place to fish.)
ideal (noun)	standard or model of perfection (Her teacher was her *ideal*.)
imply	to suggest; to express indirectly
infer	to conclude, as on the basis of suggestion or implication (A writer *implies*; a reader *infers* from what has been written.)
its	possessive pronoun meaning "belonging to it" (Virtue is *its* own reward.)
it's	contraction meaning "it is" or "it has" (*It's* a shame you are sick.)
knew	past tense of *to know* (He *knew* the name of the song.)
new	not old (She was *new* in town.)
know	to be mentally aware of (Do you *know* the answer?)
no	opposite of yes; not any (That is *no* way to treat a lady.)
lie	to recline (The book *lies* unopened on the table.)
lay	to place (Please *lay* the book on the table.) **Note:** The past tense of *lie* is *lay*; the past tense of *lay* is *laid*.
loose (adjective)	not tight; unfastened (The car has a *loose* wheel.)
lose (verb)	to allow to get away; to misplace (Did you *lose* your umbrella?)
mine (pronoun)	possessive pronoun meaning "belonging to me" (That book is *mine*.)
mind (noun)	mental capacity (Your *mind* can play tricks on you.)
mind (verb)	to obey (You should *mind* your mother.)
passed (verb)	past tense of *to pass* (The train *passed* through the town.)
past (noun)	former times or belonging to former times (It is easy to forget the *past*.)
past (preposition)	beyond in time or position (The burglar slipped *past* the guard.)
peace	opposite of war; tranquillity (The U.N. was determined to keep the *peace*.)
piece	part of (May I have that *piece* of cake?)
personal (adjective)	of or pertaining to a particular person; private (Is this a *personal* call?)
personnel (noun)	those employed by an organization or business (He was referred to the *personnel* department.)
principal (noun)	a governing officer of a school (The *principal* of our high school is Mr. Drake.)
	sum of money on which interest is calculated (I was able to pay the interest on my loan but not the *principal*.)
principal (adjective)	first in importance (The *principal* actor in the play was ill.)
principle	a fundamental truth, law, or doctrine; a rule of conduct (Mr. Adams is a man of *principle*.)
quiet	not noisy (The library was unusually *quiet*.)
quite	somewhat or rather (The girl was *quite* shocked by the remark.)

rise	to ascend; to move upward (The sun *rises* in the east.)
raise	to lift or cause something to move upward (He wants to *raise* his grades in French class.)
sight	a spectacle; view; scene (The *sight* of the mountains awed him.)
site	a location (They chose a new *site* for the building.)
cite	to quote or use as evidence (He *cited* me as an authority.)
sit	to assume a seated position (Please *sit* in that chair.)
set	to place something (Please *set* the chair by the window.)
than	used in a comparison (Ray is faster *than* George.)
then	at that time (Can you leave *then*?)
there	an adverb of place (*There* is our room.)
their	possessive pronoun meaning "belonging to them" (Where is *their* living room?)
they're	contraction of "they are" (*They're* in that room.)
threw	past tense of *to throw* (They *threw* the frisbee across the room.)
through	in one side and out the other; by way of (It went *through* the rear window.)
though	despite; commonly used with *as* or *even* (He looked as *though* he were exhausted.)
to	used as a preposition (*to* the stars) or with a verb as an infinitive (*to* go)
too	also; to an excessive degree (The car was *too* crowded for him to go, *too*.)
two	the number *2* (The child was *two* years old.)
weather	pertains to the climate (The *weather* is expected to turn cold.)
whether	if it is the case that; in case (I'm not sure *whether* he is going.)
who's	a contraction meaning "who is" or "who has" (*Who's* there?)
whose	a possessive pronoun meaning "belonging to whom" (*Whose* car are we taking?)
your	possessive pronoun meaning "belonging to you" (I like *your* idea.)
you're	contraction meaning "you are" (*You're* wrong about that!)

■ **EXERCISE B.1**   Underline the correct words in the exercise below.

1. Your (conscious, <u>conscience</u>) should hurt you for defending the robber.

   The motorists were still (<u>conscious</u>, conscience) after the accident.

2. There's (a, <u>an</u>) antelope in my yard.

   I was expecting (<u>a</u>, an) moose.

   The antelope has eaten (alot, <u>a lot</u>) of grass.

3. The (capitol, <u>capital</u>) of Montana is Helena.

   The state (<u>capitol</u>, capital) in Austin is built of pink granite.

4. The letter (<u>implied</u>, inferred) that he had not paid his phone bill.

   I (implied, <u>inferred</u>) from that remark that he wouldn't be able to balance the budget.

5. My pet elephant (<u>rises</u>, raises) slowly in the mornings.

She has (risen, <u>raised</u>) two baby elephants.

6. A rabbit is (lose, <u>loose</u>) in my garden.

I would hate to (<u>lose</u>, loose) all that lettuce.

7. He asked a (<u>personal</u>, personnel) question about my love life.

He asked if I ever dated any of the (personal, <u>personnel</u>) at the office.

8. If (your, <u>you're</u>) not careful, she'll make you a member of her committee.

Why didn't you answer (<u>your</u>, you're) phone when he called?

9. (Who's, <u>Whose</u>) elephant is this?

(<u>Who's</u>, Whose) going to feed it and housebreak it?

10. My favorite (desert, <u>dessert</u>) is strawberry shortcake.

Camels are found in the (<u>desert</u>, dessert), but aardvarks are not.

The soldier (<u>deserted</u>, desserted) his platoon.

11. (Its, <u>It's</u>) difficult to make up for lost time.

Can a zebra change (<u>its</u>, it's) stripes?

12. I will eat any vegetable (accept, <u>except</u>) okra.

Will you (<u>accept</u>, except) a collect call from your son?

13. I have (<u>already</u>, all ready) talked to my daughter.

The committee members are (already, <u>all ready</u>) for the meeting.

14. I (<u>advise</u>, advice) you to eat more okra.

That is silly (advise, <u>advice</u>).

15. An organization of home owners is seeking (<u>counsel</u>, council) from a lawyer.

The (counsel, <u>council</u>) passed an ordinance to muzzle dogs within the city limits.

■ EXERCISE B.2   Underline the correct words in the exercise below.

1. After eating the okra, she didn't (fill, <u>feel</u>) well.

Did you (<u>fill</u>, feel) your tank with gas?

2. Either John (are, our, <u>or</u>) I will slice the tomatoes.

They (<u>are</u>, our, or) exceptional people.

Will they honor (are, <u>our</u>, or) request?

3. She always pays her bills on the (<u>fourth</u>, forth) day of the month.

The soldier stepped (fourth, <u>forth</u>) eagerly.

4. That (knew, <u>new</u>) song is simply atrocious.

The student (<u>knew</u>, new) all the answers.

5. Be sure to (site, sight, <u>cite</u>) the source of your quotation.

The sunset was a beautiful (site, <u>sight</u>, cite).

The architect will meet us at the building (<u>site</u>, sight, cite).

6. I ate a large (peace, <u>piece</u>) of chocolate pie.

Every president should work for world (<u>peace</u>, piece).

7. The wine was the perfect (<u>complement</u>, compliment) to our dinner.

I went to the kitchen to (complement, <u>compliment</u>) the chef.

The chef received many (complements, <u>compliments</u>) on his cake.

8. (Through, Threw, <u>Though</u>) the boy (through, <u>threw</u>, though) the ball with force, it did not go (<u>through</u>, threw, though) the window.

9. The actress gave (quiet, <u>quite</u>) a performance.

The audience was (<u>quiet</u>, quite) throughout the play.

10. Do you (<u>know</u>, no) where they went?

(Know, <u>No</u>) one really likes okra.

■ **EXERCISE B.3**   Underline the correct words in the exercise below.

1. Some people believe that eggplant is the (idea, <u>ideal</u>) vegetable.

That's a stupid (<u>idea</u>, ideal).

2. The zoo had more monkeys (<u>than</u>, then) it knew what to do with.

First he took out his harmonica; (than, <u>then</u>) he began to play.

3. He had never been taught the (principal, <u>principle</u>) of right and wrong.

The (<u>principal</u>, principle) fired the geometry teacher.

How much interest do you owe on the (<u>principal</u>, principle) of your loan?

4. (There, <u>They're</u>, Their) fun-loving people.

The fishermen mended (there, they're, <u>their</u>) nets every night.

(<u>There</u>, They're, Their) is the spot where I had my wreck.

5. Burlap is a (course, <u>coarse</u>, of course) fabric often used to bag onions.

While I was in college, I took a (<u>course</u>, coarse, of course) in oceanography.

(Course, Coarse, <u>Of course</u>), no one in the class understood the lesson.

6. My grandmother lives in the (passed, <u>past</u>).

The bus (<u>passed</u>, past) the corner where I wanted to get off.

7. I went (too, two, <u>to</u>) the store (too, two, <u>to</u>) buy some candy for Uncle Monroe.

Uncle Monroe eats (<u>too</u>, two, to) much candy; Aunt Sophie does (<u>too</u>, two, to).

The (too, <u>two</u>, to) of them really love candy.

8. I will (lie, <u>lay</u>) my books on the sofa.

Then I will (<u>lie</u>, lay) down and rest for a while.

9. My pet monkey was (<u>sitting</u>, setting) in my favorite chair.

He was watching me (sit, <u>set</u>) the table for dinner.

10. The (<u>weather</u>, whether) has been bad all week.

They couldn't decide (weather, <u>whether</u>) it was a wolf or a coyote.

■ EXERCISE B.4   Underline the correct words in the letter below.

May 14, 1979

Dear Mr. Jones:

We regretfully (<u>accept</u>, except) (you're, <u>your</u>) resignation, which you plan to submit to our (personal, <u>personnel</u>) office next month. (You're, <u>Your</u>) leaving will (effect, <u>affect</u>) our entire organization. I hope that your (<u>advice</u>, advise) and (council, <u>counsel</u>) will continue to be available to us after your retirement.

I realize that (<u>personal</u>, personnel) reasons force you (<u>to</u>, two, too) take this step, but I certainly do hate to (loose, <u>lose</u>) such an (idea, <u>ideal</u>) employee. Your (<u>principal</u>, principle) contribution has been your patience and (conscience, <u>conscious</u>) effort to be a good employee. Of (coarse, <u>course</u>), I will miss your (personnel, <u>personal</u>) friendship also.

Many years have (past, <u>passed</u>) since you first came to work at Smith & Smith, Inc. (Your, <u>You're</u>) going to miss our organization, and we are certainly going to miss you.

(Its, <u>It's</u>) with sincere regret that I see you leave.

Sincerely yours,

J. R. Smith

J. R. Smith
President

ADDITIONAL PROBLEM WORDS

Although, as a rule, spelling lists are practically useless in improving spelling skills, there are a few words that are so consistently misspelled by students that it might be worth your time to master them. Notice, as you look at this list of problem spelling words, that many of them are misspelled because they are often not pronounced correctly. The words are divided into syllables, with the accented syllables marked so you can check your pronunciation. Say the words aloud as you study them. If you are saying the words incorrectly, try to correct your pronunciation. Pay particular attention to the underlined letters because that is the part of the word that usually causes the spelling error.

athlete (ath′ lete)—two syllables, not three, not (ath<u>e</u>lete)
different (dif′ fer ent)—three syllables, not two
environment (en vi′ ron ment)—notice the <u>n</u>
February (Feb′ ru ar y)—notice the <u>r</u>
finally (fi′ nal ly)—three syllables, not two
government (gov′ ern ment)—notice the <u>n</u>
grammar (gram′ mar)—ends in <u>ar</u> not <u>er</u>
interest (in′ ter est)—three syllables, not two

library (li′ brar y)—notice the r
listening (lis′ ten ing)—three syllables, not two
probably (prob′ a bly)—three syllables, not two
quiet (qui′ et)—two syllables, not one; do not confuse with quite
recognize (rec′ og nize)—notice the g
separate (sep′ a rate)—middle vowel is a not e
similar (sim′ i lar)—last syllable is lar not ler or liar
sophomore (soph′ o more)—three syllables, not two; notice the o
supposed (sup posed′)—don't forget the d if you are using past
    tense (*He was supposed to call.*)
used (used)—don't forget the d if you are using past tense (*I used
    to sing.*)

■ **EXERCISE B.5**   Identify the misspelled words in the sentences below. Correct them on a separate sheet of paper or in the margin of your textbook.

(supposed)   1. Mrs. Rodriguez is suppose to speak at the city council meeting.

(athletes)   2. The coaches at our college are establishing a program to promote scholarship among our atheletes.

(grammar)   3. I detest grammer, don't you?

(library)   4. Are you going to the libary to study tonight?

(probably)   5. Yes, I probly will study for my history test in the study room.

(sophomore)   6. I will be a sophmore next semester if I pass all of my final exams.

(environmental)   7. The speaker at the symposium next week will speak on enviromental problems.

(interesting)   8. I hope he gives an intresting lecture.

(similar)   9. Wasn't last year's symposium theme similiar to this year's?

(government, separate)   10. Yes, but this year we are focusing on what the goverment and seperate individuals can do to solve these problems.

COMPOUND WORDS

Many words are formed in English by a process known as compounding. That is, a new word is made by combining two familiar words. *Truck stop,* for example, is a relatively new compound that is still written as two words. The tendency, however, is for compound words to be written (eventually) as one word, as in *hangover, handbook, babysitter,* and *typewriter.* Historically, compound words are initially written as two words, then as a hyphenated word, and finally as one word. For example, *week end* became *week-end* and then *weekend.* Recently the trend has been for compound words to change from two words to one without going through the hyphenated stage.

Most compound words are easy to spell because they are made up of two familiar words. However, it is sometimes difficult to remember whether the compound is written as one word or two. Occasionally, also, the spelling of the compound word is altered slightly when it becomes one word. Thus, the word *although* is spelled with one *l* in *all* rather than two.

The following categories of compound words will help you remember whether the compounds in them should be written as one word or two. However, you should consult your dictionary if you are in doubt.

1. Compound words spelled as two words
   a lot, all right (These two words are frequently misspelled as one word rather than two.)

2. Hyphenated compound words

   a. *mother-in-law, son-in-law*, etc.
   b. *self-concept, self-image, self-hypnosis* (all compounds beginning with *self*)
   c. *ex-husband, ex-wife, ex-president*, etc.
   d. *pro-Communist, pro-abortion*, etc.

3. Compound words spelled as one word

   a. *everybody, somebody, anything, everyone, someone, something, anybody, sometime, anyplace, someplace*, etc.
   b. *whenever, wherever, whatever, whichever*, etc.
   c. *although, altogether, always, already, almost* (Note that each of these compound words has only one *l*.)
   d. *moreover, therefore, however, nonetheless*.

■ **EXERCISE B.6**   Several compound words are misspelled in the sentences below. Identify these words and correct them on a separate sheet of paper or in the margin of your textbook.

(Everybody, Somebody, Sometime

1. Do you remember the old song "Every body Loves Some body Some time"?

(ex-husband)

2. Yes, my exhusband Robert used to sing it all of the time.

(a lot)

3. You had alot of trouble with that marriage, didn't you?

(mother-in-law)

4. Yes, I hated his singing, and he hated his mother in law.

(self-concept)

5. Well, your self concept certainly has improved since your divorce.

FORMING THE PLURAL OF NOUNS

By far the most common way to change a singular noun to a plural noun is to add the inflectional suffix *s* to the word (*car, cars; feeling, feelings; note, notes*). There are, however, several other rules for the formation of plurals you should also know.

1. To form the plural of words that end with an *s* sound (*s, x, z, ch, sh*), add *es* (*boss, bosses; fox, foxes; buzz, buzzes; ditch, ditches; dish, dishes*).

2. To form the plural of words that end in *y* preceded by a single vowel, add just an *s* (*tray, trays; key, keys; toy, toys; guy, guys*). But to form the plural of words that end in *y* preceded by a consonant, change the *y* to *i* and add *es* (*baby, babies; enemy, enemies*).

3. To form the plural of words that end in *is*, change the *is* to *es* (*basis, bases; analysis, analyses; synopsis, synopses*).

4. To form the plural of some words that end in *f* or *fe*, change the *f* to *v* and add *es* (*leaf, leaves; knife, knives; wife, wives; loaf, loaves; self, selves*).

5. To form the plural of words that end in *o*, add *s* or *es*. The plural

of many of these words can be formed either way; with some, how-ever, there is no choice. The following clues are helpful in deter-mining which ending some words require:

a. To form the plural of words that end in a vowel plus *o* (*ao, eo, io, oo, uo*), add just an *s* (*stereo, stereos; duo, duos; studio, stu-dios*).

b. To form the plural of musical terms that end in *o*, add just an *s* (*piano, pianos; solo, solos; combo, combos; cello, cellos*).

c. To form the plural of *tomato* and *potato*, add *es* (*tomato, toma-toes, potato, potatoes*).

   To determine whether other words that end in *o* require an *s* or *es*, check your dictionary.

6. Some words form the plural irregularly by changing internally rather than by the addition of an inflectional suffix (*man, men; woman, women; child, children; mouse, mice; foot, feet*).

7. Some words have the same form in both the singular and the plu-ral (*fish, moose, sheep, deer*).

■ **EXERCISE B.7**   Change the following singular nouns to plural nouns.

1. radio   radios

2. teacher   teachers

3. dish   dishes

4. beauty   beauties

5. bush   bushes

6. leaf   leaves

7. schedule   schedules

8. thesis   theses

9. monkey   monkeys

10. fox   foxes

11. contralto   contraltos

12. alley   alleys

13. opinion   opinions

14. theory   theories

15. foot   feet

16. match   matches

■ **EXERCISE B.8** Change the following singular nouns to plural nouns.

1. friend   **friends**

2. joy   **joys**

3. fact   **facts**

4. tomato   **tomatoes**

5. chair   **chairs**

6. ally   **allies**

7. industry   **industries**

8. church   **churches**

9. thief   **thieves**

10. valley   **valleys**

11. comedy   **comedies**

12. sheep   **sheep**

13. crisis   **crises**

14. dress   **dresses**

15. rule   **rules**

16. wife   **wives**

FORMING POSSESSIVES

Both nouns and pronouns have possessive forms, but the rules for forming possessive nouns and pronouns differ. Learning to form possessives correctly will enable you to eliminate another spelling problem.

Possessive Nouns

Failure to indicate correctly that a noun is possessive causes many needless spelling errors. The rules for forming the possessive are regular and easy to apply.

1. To form the possessive of singular nouns, add an apostrophe and an *s* (*'s*) to the noun.

> George's car was in the garage.
> My boss's hat is ridiculous.
> Today's mail needs to be sorted.

Notice that it does not matter what letter the noun ends in; *all singular* nouns form the possessive by the addition of an apostrophe and an *s* to the noun.

> **Note:** The rule for forming the singular possessive is presently in some dispute. Some authorities now say that if the singular noun ends in an *s*, you may add just an apostrophe after the *s*. Others say that only if the singular noun is a proper noun of one syllable may you omit the *s* and add just the apostrophe. To avoid confusion and controversy, it is better to apply the simple rule given above to all singular nouns, regardless of their final letter or whether they are common or proper.

1. To form the possessive of plural nouns that do not end in an *s*, you also add an apostrophe and an *s* ('*s*) to the noun.

   > The children's coats were unbuttoned.
   > He looked into the deer's eyes.
   > The women's club is meeting in the auditorium.

2. However, to form the possessive of plural nouns that end in *s*, you add just an apostrophe after the *s* ('*s*).

   > The cats' tails have all been cut off.
   > Dust covered the books' covers.
   > The boys' teachers were invited to the meeting.

Now review the steps in forming the possessive of a noun:

1. Determine if the noun is possessive.
2. Determine if the noun is singular or plural.
3. Apply the appropriate rule.

Possessive Pronouns

The possessive pronouns are *my, mine, your, yours, our, ours, his, her, hers, their, theirs,* and *its.*

> *My* dress is torn.
> That book is *hers.*
> The tree has shed *its* leaves.
> Do they want *their* papers returned?

Notice that possessive pronouns *do not* require apostrophes. Rather than adding an inflectional ending (such as an apostrophe and *s* or just an apostrophe) as you do in forming the possessive of nouns, you form the possessive of pronouns by changing the word itself. Thus the pronoun *I* changes to *my* or *mine; we* becomes *our* or *ours; you* becomes *your* or *yours,* and so on.

> **Note:** Three possessive pronouns (*its, your,* and *their*) are pronounced exactly the same as three contractions (*it's, you're,* and *they're*), which do require apostrophes. *It's* is a contraction of *it is; you're* is a contraction of *you are;* and *they're* is a contraction of *they are.* Be careful in your writing not to confuse the contraction with the possessive form. Remember that possessive pronouns *do not* require apostrophes.

■ EXERCISE B.9   Some nouns in the following sentences should be possessive. Rewrite correctly any noun that requires the possessive form. Write "C" if no nouns need to be changed to the possessive form.

C

1. My sisters have all gotten married.

brother's

2. My brothers wife was in a terrible accident yesterday.

brothers'

3. My brothers wives are both in school.

C

4. The realities of the situation must be faced.

father's

5. My fathers attitudes about education differ from mine.

politicians'

6. All politicians promises are worthless.

C

7. The waiters served the food skillfully.

students'

8. Several students papers had been plagiarized.

friend's

9. Is this car yours or your best friends?

Johnson's

10. Dr. Johnsons secretary took the message.

■ EXERCISE B.10

Answers will vary.

On a separate piece of paper, use each of the following nouns in three sentences. In the first sentence use the noun as a singular possessive; in the second sentence use the same noun as a plural possessive; in the third sentence make the noun plural but not possessive.

1. uncle
2. nation
3. child
4. waitress
5. newspaper

■ EXERCISE B.11   Underline the correct word in the following sentences.

1. (Its, <u>It's</u>) (<u>their</u>, they're) car that was in the accident.
2. (<u>Its</u>, It's) body was in need of repair.
3. Where are (<u>your</u>, you're) books?
4. (Their, <u>They're</u>) there on the chair.
5. (<u>They're</u>, Their) not very happy about being there.
6. This is (they're, <u>their</u>) last visit; you can be sure of that.
7. (Your, <u>You're</u>) going to have to stay up late tonight to finish (<u>your</u>, you're) paper.
8. (<u>Their</u>, They're) teacher is Mr. Jones.
9. (Their, <u>They're</u>) in big trouble about taking (<u>their</u>, they're) father's car without permission.
10. (Its, <u>It's</u>) an important meeting for the entire university.

■ EXERCISE B.12   Add apostrophes where they are needed in the following sentences. Write "C" if no apostrophes are needed.

1. The boy's hat was on the chair.

C

2. They left their doors unlocked.
3. It's not her fault.
4. Two weeks' vacation is provided by our company.

c
c

5. Many exciting things occurred on our expedition.

6. The popularity of operas has increased every year.

7. The Continental Mens Shop is having a sale on sport coats.

8. The childrens section of the library is always crowded.

9. The Policemens Ball is always a popular event in our town.

10. Viewing the Pacific Ocean with Balboas crew would have been exciting.

c

11. Your cars are parked side by side.

12. Grandmothers new house was designed by a famous architect.

13. The Filipinos system of government was based on that of the United States.

14. Was the colonists desire for equal representation the cause of the American Revolution?

15. The expansion of Napoleons army over Europe posed a threat to England in the nineteenth century.

c

16. His novels are widely read by the general reading public.

17. The company presidents office is a large spacious room.

18. Miss Flannery O'Connor is probably the Souths most important writer since William Faulkner.

19. A students study time is often reduced by the pressure of social activities.

20. Because of its depreciated value, buying a dollars worth of groceries does not mean very much.

21. Theyre late again.

c

22. The reward is ours.

c

23. The snake has shed its skin.

c

24. My books are in her locker.

25. Youre an obvious liar.

FOUR USEFUL SPELLING PATTERNS

There are no simple rules that will eliminate all spelling problems, but the following spelling patterns will help you improve your spelling.

Spelling Pattern for Dropping or Keeping Final *E*

1. To add a suffix beginning with a vowel to a word ending in a final *e*, drop the silent *e* (examples: *usage, safest, caring*).
   Exceptions:
   Words that have a *c* or *g* before the final *e* keep the *e* before the suffixes *-able* and *-ous* (examples: *noticeable, courageous, changeable, advantageous, peaceable*).

2. To add a suffix beginning with a consonant to a word ending in a final *e*, keep the silent *e* (examples: *lovely, useless, safety*).
   Exceptions:
   a. Words ending in *ue* drop the final *e* before a suffix beginning with a consonant (examples: *argument, duly, truly*).

b. awe + ful = awful
c. whole + ly = wholly

■ EXERCISE B.13   Apply the spelling pattern for dropping or keeping final *e*'s to the words listed below. Some of the words are exceptions to the pattern.

1. change + able   **changeable**

2. come + ing   **coming**

3. service + able   **serviceable**

4. shine + ing   **shining**

5. arrange + able   **arrangeable**

6. love + able   **lovable (loveable)**

7. fame + ous   **famous**

8. scarce + ly   **scarcely**

9. write + ing   **writing**

10. use + ing   **using**

11. simple + ly   **simply**

12. mere + ly   **merely**

13. resource + ful   **resourceful**

14. argue + ment   **argument**

15. use + ful   **useful**

16. care + less   **careless**

17. pursue + ing   **pursuing**

18. complete + ly   **completely**

19. love + ly   **lovely**

20. guide + ance   **guidance**

Spelling Pattern for Final *Y*

1. To add a suffix not beginning with an *i* to a word that ends in *y* preceded by a consonant, change the *y* to *i* (examples: *happiness, copier, cried*).
2. To add a suffix to a word that ends in *y* preceded by a vowel (*a, e, i, o, u*), do not change the *y* to *i* (examples: *employer, keys, enjoyment*).

3. To add a suffix beginning with an *i* to a word that ends in *y*, do not change the *y to i* (examples: *copying, fortyish, playing*).

Exceptions: *daily, gaily, paid, said, laid, shyly, shyness, slyly, slyness, dryly, dryer* (the machine), all proper nouns (Kennedy + s = Kennedys; Harry + s = Harrys)

■ EXERCISE B.14   Apply the spelling pattern for final *y* to the words listed below. Watch for exceptions.

1. survey + ed	surveyed
2. pity + ed	pitied
3. monkey + s	monkeys
4. mercy + ful	merciful
5. employ + er	employer
6. gay + ly	gaily
7. happy + ness	happiness
8. accompany + es	accompanies
9. shy + ly	shyly
10. enjoy + able	enjoyable
11. study + ing	studying
12. chimney + s	chimneys
13. hurry + ed	hurried
14. Grady + s	Gradys
15. defy + ance	defiance
16. deploy + ing	deploying
17. lay + ed	laid
18. apply + ance	appliance
19. day + ly	daily
20. beauty + ful	beautiful
21. wealthy + er	wealthier
22. relay + ing	relaying

23. twenty + ish   _____**twentyish**_____

24. clumsy + ly   _____**clumsily**_____

25. empty + ness   _____**emptiness**_____

Spelling Pattern for *EI/IE* Words

1. The *i* comes before the *e* if a *c* does not immediately precede it (examples: *believe, niece, yield*).
2. The *e* comes before the *i* if these letters are immediately preceded by a *c* (examples: *receive, deceit, ceiling*).
3. If the sound of *ei/ie* is a long *a*, the *e* comes before the *i* (examples: *vein, weight, neighbor*).

This pattern is most often stated in the form of this familiar rhyme:

Write *i* before *e*
Except after *c*
Or when sounded as *a*
As in *neighbor* and *weigh.*

Exceptions: There are a number of exceptions to this rule. Concentrate on remembering the five most common: *either, neither, seize, weird,* and *leisure.*

EXERCISE B.15   Apply the spelling pattern for *ei/ie* words to the following sentences. Again, watch for exceptions.

1. I cannot bel__**ie**__ve that she is so conc__**ei**__ted.

2. The army finally ended its long s__**ie**__ge.

3. The fr__**ei**__ght train was long and slow.

4. The freshmen were rel__**ie**__ved when the bell rang.

5. Does Santa still use r__**ei**__ndeer?

6. The president is also commander in ch__**ie**__f of our armed forces.

7. Will the parents y__**ie**__ld to the kidnappers' demands?

8. They will s__**ei**__ze him when he returns.

9. The children tried to dec__**ei**__ve the teacher.

10. How much do these apples w__**ei**__gh?

11. The pr__**ie**__st could read Latin, Greek, and Hebrew.

12. His reputation as a th__**ie**__f followed him everywhere.

13. I have no l__**ei**__sure time this semester.

14. Did you rec___**ei**___ve the letter?

15. She gave a p___**ie**___ce of candy to her little brother.

16. Always rev___**ie**___w your themes before turning them in.

17. The victims were nearly dead when rel___**ie**___f came.

18. She could not forgive his dec___**ei**___t.

19. The blood in his v___**ei**___ns ran cold at the sight.

20. The r___**ei**___gn of the queen was br___**ie**___f.

21. They ach___**ie**___ved more than___**ei**___ther had expected.

22. In the darkness, she could barely perc___**ei**___ve the wire strung across the c___**ei**___ling.

23. The for___**ei**___gn students attended the rally.

24. I can't conc___**ei**___ve of how that happened.

25. N___**ei**___ther of the students who failed the course was allowed to graduate.

Spelling Pattern for Doubling the Final Consonant

Double the final consonant when adding a suffix beginning with a vowel if the word ends in a single consonant preceded by a single vowel and meets either of the following additional criteria:

1. It consists of only one syllable (examples: *bigger, dimmer, stopper*).
2. It is accented on the last syllable (examples: *referred, occurred, beginning*).

EXERCISE B.16   Apply the rule for doubling the final consonant to the following words.

1. begin + ing   _____**beginning**_____

2. counsel + ing   _____**counseling**_____

3. drop + ed   _____**dropped**_____

4. commit + ed   _____**committed**_____

5. commit + ment   _____**commitment**_____

6. equip + ed   _____**equipped**_____

7. forgot + en   _____**forgotten**_____

8. hope + ing   **hoping**

9. hop + ed   **hopped**

10. occur + ence   **occurrence**

11. plan + ing   **planning**

12. equip + ment   **equipment**

13. compel + ed   **compelled**

14. hit + ing   **hitting**

15. benefit + ed   **benefitted**

16. stop + ed   **stopped**

17. strip + ed   **stripped**

18. stripe + ing   **striping**

19. refer + ence   **reference**

20. honor + able   **honorable**

21. omit + ing   **omitting**

22. refer + ed   **referred**

23. debar + ed   **debarred**

24. hinder + ed   **hindered**

25. red + ness   **redness**

APPENDIX C
Forms of Irregular Verbs

PRESENT TENSE		PRESENT PARTICIPLE (Use with form of *to be*)	PAST TENSE	PAST PARTICIPLE (Use with *have, has,* or *had*)
First & Second Person Singular	Third Person Singular			
1. arise	arises	arising	arose	arisen
2. awake	awakes	awaking	awoke (awaked)	awoke (awaked)
3. bear	bears	bearing	bore	borne (born)
4. beat	beats	beating	beat	beaten
5. begin	begins	beginning	began	begun
6. bend	bends	bending	bent	bent
7. bite	bites	biting	bit	bitten
8. bleed	bleeds	bleeding	bled	bled
9. blow	blows	blowing	blew	blown
10. break	breaks	breaking	broke	broken
11. build	builds	building	built	built
12. burst	bursts	bursting	burst	burst
13. catch	catches	catching	caught	caught
14. choose	chooses	choosing	chose	chosen
15. cling	clings	clinging	clung	clung
16. creep	creeps	creeping	crept	crept
17. deal	deals	dealing	dealt	dealt
18. draw	draws	drawing	drew	drawn
19. dream	dreams	dreaming	dreamed	dreamed
20. drink	drinks	drinking	drank	drunk

	PRESENT TENSE		PRESENT PARTICIPLE (Use with form of *to be*)	PAST TENSE	PAST PARTICIPLE (Use with *have, has,* or *had*)
	First & Second Person Singular	Third Person Singular			
21.	dwell	dwells	dwelling	dwelt (dwelled)	dwelt (dwelled)
22.	eat	eats	eating	ate	eaten
23.	fall	falls	falling	fell	fallen
24.	feed	feeds	feeding	fed	fed
25.	fling	flings	flinging	flung	flung
26.	fly	flies	flying	flew	flown
27.	forget	forgets	forgetting	forgot	forgotten (forgot)
28.	freeze	freezes	freezing	froze	frozen
29.	get	gets	getting	got	got (gotten)
30.	give	gives	giving	gave	given
31.	go	goes	going	went	gone
32.	grow	grows	growing	grew	grown
33.	hang	hangs	hanging	hung (hanged)	hung (hanged)
34.	have	has	having	had	had
35.	hide	hides	hiding	hid	hidden
36.	hit	hits	hitting	hit	hit
37.	keep	keeps	keeping	kept	kept
38.	know	knows	knowing	knew	known
39.	lay	lays	laying	laid	laid
40.	lead	leads	leading	led	led
41.	leave	leaves	leaving	left	left
42.	lend	lends	lending	lent	lent
43.	lie	lies	lying	lay	lain
44.	light	lights	lighting	lighted (lit)	lighted (lit)
45.	lose	loses	losing	lost	lost
46.	mean	means	meaning	meant	meant
47.	pay	pays	paying	paid	paid
48.	ride	rides	riding	rode	ridden
49.	rise	rises	rising	rose	risen
50.	see	sees	seeing	saw	seen
51.	sew	sews	sewing	sewed	sewn (sewed)
52.	shine	shines	shining	shone (shined)	shone (shined)

	PRESENT TENSE		PRESENT PARTICIPLE (Use with form of *to be*)	PAST TENSE	PAST PARTICIPLE (Use with *have*, *has*, or *had*)
	First & Second Person Singular	Third Person Singular			
53.	shrink	shrinks	shrinking	shrank (shrunk)	shrunk (shrunken)
54.	sink	sinks	sinking	sank	sunk
55.	sit	sits	sitting	sat	sat
56.	sleep	sleeps	sleeping	slept	slept
57.	slide	slides	sliding	slid	slid
58.	sling	slings	slinging	slung	slung
59.	speak	speaks	speaking	spoke	spoken
60.	spend	spends	spending	spent	spent
61.	spit	spits	spitting	spit (spat)	spit (spat)
62.	split	splits	splitting	split	split
63.	spoil	spoils	spoiling	spoiled (spoilt)	spoiled (spoilt)
64.	spread	spreads	spreading	spread	spread
65.	spring	springs	springing	sprang	sprung
66.	stand	stands	standing	stood	stood
67.	steal	steals	stealing	stole	stolen
68.	stick	sticks	sticking	stuck	stuck
69.	sting	stings	stinging	stung	stung
70.	stink	stinks	stinking	stank (stunk)	stunk
71.	string	strings	stringing	strung	strung
72.	swear	swears	swearing	swore	sworn
73.	sweat	sweats	sweating	sweat (sweated)	sweat (sweated)
74.	swell	swells	swelling	swelled	swelled (swollen)
75.	swim	swims	swimming	swam	swum
76.	swing	swings	swinging	swung	swung
77.	teach	teaches	teaching	taught	taught
78.	throw	throws	throwing	threw	thrown
79.	wake	wakes	waking	waked (woke)	waked (waken)
80.	weep	weeps	weeping	wept	wept
81.	wring	wrings	wringing	wrung	wrung
82.	write	writes	writing	wrote	written

EXERCISE C.1   Write the correct forms of the verbs in parentheses.

1. If I had (knew) _____**known**_____ the weather was going to drop

   below zero last night, I would have taken better precautions.

2. It was so cold in our apartment last night that our water pipes

   (freeze) _____**froze**_____.

3. Were they (break) _____**broken**_____ when they thawed?

4. No, but we didn't have any water to (drink) _____**drink**_____

   until this morning.

5. Last year the temperature got so cold that two of our pipes (burst)

   _____**burst**_____, and water (run) _____**ran**_____ all

   over our carpet.

6. I should have (give) _____**given**_____ you my extra electric

   heater to use.

7. I wish you had because I think our carpet has (shrink)

   _____**shrunk**_____.

8. Wasn't it just (lay) _____**laid**_____ last week?

9. Yes, and after we had (choose) _____**chosen**_____ the new car-

   pet, we (throw) _____**threw**_____ the old carpet away.

10. Well, at least this experience has (teach) _____**taught**_____ us to

    prepare for the next cold weather.

EXERCISE C.2   Write the correct forms of the verbs in parentheses.

1. Have you (forgot) _____**forgotten**_____ that we are going to

   Galveston for spring break?

2. No, that trip has (keep) _____**kept**_____ me going all through

   final examinations.

3. Yes, I have been (dream) _____**dreaming**_____ about it all week,

   too.

4. Have you ever (see) _____**seen**_____ the water as blue as it

was last year when we (go) _____**went**_____ during the summer?

5. No, and I have never (eat) _____**eaten**_____ as many fresh shrimp as I did then.

6. I can hardly wait to (lie) _____**lie**_____ on the beach and (swim) _____**swim**_____ in the water.

7. Yes, last year I (lie) _____**lay**_____ on the beach in the morning and (swim) _____**swam**_____ in the afternoons.

8. Have you already (pay) _____**paid**_____ for the hotel reservation?

9. No, I haven't even (write) _____**written**_____ to get a reservation.

10. Well, let's (choose) _____**choose**_____ a hotel and call right away so we won't miss our vacation.

APPENDIX D
Punctuation

Period

1. Use a period after a declarative sentence.

   A zebra cannot change its stripes.

2. Use a period after an abbreviation (*examples:* Mr., Ms., U.S., approx., p.m., a.m.).

Question Mark

Use a question mark after a direct question.

Does this elephant belong to you?

Semicolon

1. Use a semicolon in a compound sentence that does not include a coordinating conjunction to join the two independent clauses.

   The elephant belongs to my cousin; the giraffe is mine.

2. Use a semicolon in a compound sentence in which a conjunctive adverb joins the two independent clauses.

   The elephant is too wide; however, the giraffe is too tall.

3. Use a semicolon to separate items in a series if the items contain internal commas.

   The awards were presented to Big Foot, the elephant; Long Tusk, the walrus; and Long Neck, the giraffe.

Apostrophe

1. Use an apostrophe for a possessive noun.

   The giraffe's neck is too long.

2. Use an apostrophe for a contraction (*examples:* it's, can't, doesn't, wasn't, couldn't).

Quotation Marks

1. Use quotation marks to enclose a direct quotation.

   My cousin asked, "Can my elephant get through the door?"

2. Use quotation marks to enclose the title of a short work (story, essay, song, or poem) to which you are referring.

   I like the song "Giraffes Are a Man's Best Friend."

Note: Italicize, or underline, the titles of longer works such as books, plays, and movies.
Dances with Wolves is my favorite movie.

Comma

1. Use a comma to *separate* the following:

   a. Two independent clauses connected by a coordinating conjunction

      I took my giraffe for a walk, but my cousin stayed at home with his elephant.

   b. Items in a series

      I would like to adopt an aardvark, a walrus, and a crocodile.

   c. Coordinate adjectives that precede a noun

      A neat, courteous rhinoceros would not be a bad pet either.

   d. An introductory modifier from the main clause, especially if it is long or loosely connected to the rest of the sentence

      Wandering through the zoo last week, I saw several animals that I liked.
      However, my wife thinks that we have enough pets.
      Of all the women I have known in my lifetime, she is the most unreasonable.

   e. An introductory adverbial clause from the main clause

      Until we move to a larger house, I guess I'll have to be satisfied with my giraffe and kangaroo.

   f. Items in dates and addresses

      Until then, we'll continue to live at 4321 Animal Crackers Avenue, Beastville, Iowa.
      But by January 1, 1999, I hope to move to New York, New York, and rent a large penthouse that will accommodate as many as fifteen new animals.

2. Use commas to *enclose* the following:

    a. A nonrestrictive adjective clause

       My cousin, who also owns a buffalo, lives in a smaller house.

    b. An appositive

       The buffalo, a large male with an impressive hump on its back, stays in the back yard.

    c. A parenthetical expression or interrupter

       My cousin, of course, is not married.

    d. A noun used in direct address

       "Don't worry, Cousin George, someday you will find a woman who loves animals."

    e. Expressions designating the speaker in direct quotations

       "I'm not worried," he said, "just lonely."

Colon

1. Use a colon at the end of a sentence to direct attention to a summary or appositive.

   Eventually, George and I would like to have the following animals: a walrus, a rhinoceros, a crocodile, a sea lion, an aardvark, and a laughing hyena.

2. Use a colon after the salutation of a business letter.

   Dear Ms. Wolf:

3. Use a colon between a title and subtitle, between figures indicating the chapter and verse of a biblical reference, and between the hour and minute of a time reference.

   Adopting Animals: Theory and Practice

   Luke 2:13

   Monday at 4:30 P.M.

Dash

1. Use a dash to mark a sudden break in thought or tone.

   Most animals—notice that I said *most,* not *all*—are friendly and gentle.

2. Use a dash to set off a brief summary or an appositive that is loosely related to the sentence in which it appears.

   My giraffe—the animal I have had longest and that I love best—is named Alfred.

3. Use a dash to set off a parenthetical element or appositive that has commas within it.

   I have never met an ugly animal—an animal that I couldn't love, admire, and enjoy.

■ EXERCISE D.1   Correct the following sentences, providing appropriate punctuation where it is needed.

1. My offer, and it's my final bid, is $200.

2. Please mail the order form to Discount Records, 4206 Beverly Street, Albany, New York 60639.

3. Mr. B. W. Swanson, who was defeated for governor last year, will speak at the Boy Scout Annual Banquet.

4. Even though Mr. Brinkley, the most successful salesman, insisted on a raise in salary, the boss replied, "It's out of the question."

5. John, what is the subject of your paper?

6. Ms. Cheevers purchased a water hose, garden shears, and plant food.

7. Before setting a time for the trial, Judge Thompson's clerk checked a calendar for a day when the case load was light.

8. Most of the old books were worthless, but a first edition of *The Scarlet Letter* turned out to be quite valuable.

9. Mr. Johnson, the fire-chief of Fire Station 109, will hold a press conference on Wednesday, June 9, at 2:00 p.m.

10. The defense lawyer argued a brilliant, convincing case, but the jury found his client guilty anyway.

■ EXERCISE D.2   Rewrite the following sentences, providing appropriate punctuation where it is needed.

1. On July 20, 1987, the First National Bank of Orion, Tennessee, will have been in business for fifty years.

2. After answering the phone, Professor Reynolds' secretary stated that the report was due today.

3. Dr. L. M. Weber, who won the Lion's Club Award last year, will give the major address.

4. Please address your response to Liz Keller, 2208 Peachtree Street, Atlanta, Georgia 30309.

5. The labor organizations usually support the Democratic nominees for national, state, and local offices.

6. When Ms. Russell, the new personnel manager, asked about the afternoon mail, Hal responded, "It's already here."

7. We lost the Miller account; however, we gained two new accounts: Morton Department Store and the Security National Bank.

8. We have branch offices in the following cities: San Francisco, California; Denver, Colorado; and Houston, Texas.

9. Jason wrote his paper on Stephen Crane's short story "The Open Boat."

10. "Lakeitha, what score did you make on your last examination?"

394

Index